Kisses aren't Contracts

Enjoy Ad-Hoc Relationships and Avoid Getting Divorced

Lewis Tagliaferre

Library of Congress Catalog Card Number 97-90635

ISBN Number 0-9659584-1-8

Published in the United States of America by:
C-E-C Group[sm]
P.O. Box 1739
Springfield, VA 22151-0739
lewtag@aol.com

After A While

After a while you learn
the subtle difference between
holding a hand
and chaining a soul.
You learn
that love doesn't mean
security,
and you begin to learn
that kisses aren't contracts and
presents aren't promises.

With every goodbye
and with every experience
you learn ...

Veronica A. Shoffstall

Kisses aren't Contracts

A Special Book For A Few Special People

TABLE OF CONTENTS

ACKNOWLEDGMENTS

I am grateful for all the people who continue coming into my life when I need to learn the lessons they teach me. Credit is due all those authors listed in the bibliography who contributed to the needs of wounded single adults. They all share in the development of this book. It evolved from my personal need to consolidate their best ideas into a synthesis of golden nuggets about healthy ad hoc relationships. In that respect, I am a reporter who has reported what he has learned from these experts through their publications. In addition, they stimulated me to apply my own training, life experience, and intuitive inspiration to reframe all that disconnected information into this powerful, integrated guidebook. Although I don't know your name, I believe this book is especially for you.

I am especially grateful for members of the Widowed Persons Service of Northern Virginia who walked with me through the devastating loss of my wife, and to the 12-step meetings of the Unity Club in Falls Church, VA. Some of my relationships with recovering codependents and adult children suffering major losses demonstrated warped lives resulting from dysfunctional families, divorce, and widowhood. Others showed me that single life can be beautiful, joyous, and full of love.

In particular, I appreciate Debra Ann Witt, Janet Baker, Elizabeth Pritchard, and Gary and Margaret Hartzler, Ph.D. Debbie showed me what friendship is through 20 years of a professional and personal relationship. She just would not give me up no matter how difficult it was to stay a friend. Janet was my capable professional assistant and walked beside me during the darkest times. Margaret and Gary came into my life when I needed new friends and mentors desperately. They walked me through the deepest valley of grief imaginable, and taught me acceptance of my own and others' personalities. Also, I want to thank the one who taught me that love can leap across international borders, it can arc across generation gaps, and it can vault over language barriers.

I appreciate the encouragement and editorial suggestions provided by professional associates who reviewed the manuscript and made helpful suggestions. I wish to acknowledge the therapeutic contribution to my life and to this work provided by: Jack Baruch, MD, The Rev. Michael H. Greene, Ph.D., Stuart Maynard, Ph.D., John Riskind, Ph.D., Lawrence I. Sank, Ph.D., Carolyn Shaffer, EdD, and Elizabeth Sur, LCSW. I especially want to acknowledge the personal support of Gary L. Harbaugh, Ph.D. He encouraged me to begin this project after our collaboration on *Recovery From Loss* (Health Communications, Inc. 1990), from which this work emerged.

Introduction

DO YOU WANT HEALTHY INTIMATE RELATIONSHIPS?
Yes ☐   *No* ☐

HAVE YOU REPEATEDLY CHOSEN UNHEALTHY INTIMATE PARTNERS?
Yes ☐   *No* ☐

HAS YOUR LOVE LIFE LEFT YOU FEELING EMPTY AND FRUSTRATED?
Yes ☐   *No* ☐

DO YOU OFTEN EXPERIENCE PERSONALITY CLASHES WITH CLOSE FRIENDS?
Yes ☐   *No* ☐

WERE THE ADULTS IN YOUR CHILDHOOD FAULTY ROLE MODELS?
Yes ☐   *No* ☐

IS IT DIFFICULT TO UNDERSTAND THE OPPOSITE GENDER?
Yes ☐   *No* ☐

DO THE BURDENS OUTWEIGH THE BENEFITS IN YOUR FRIENDSHIPS?
Yes ☐   *No* ☐

DO YOU FEEL PANIC AND ABANDONED WHEN YOU ARE ALONE?
Yes ☐   *No* ☐

WAS YOUR CHILDHOOD ABUSIVE AND DAMAGING TO YOUR SELF ESTEEM?
Yes ☐   *No* ☐

DO YOU WONDER IF YOU WILL EVER FIND THE RIGHT INTIMATE PARTNER?
Yes ☐   *No* ☐

DO YOU FEAR THE PROSPECT OF INTIMACY AND COMMITMENT?
Yes ☐   *No* ☐

HAVE YOU BEEN HURT DEEPLY BY LOSING A HIGHLY VALUED LOVER?
Yes ☐   *No* ☐

HAVE YOUR RELATIONSHIP TROUBLES ACTUALLY BEEN MAKING YOU SICK?
Yes ☐   *No* ☐

If you answered YES to only a few of these questions, there is a good chance you have been stung by the pain of an ad hoc relationship. You will benefit significantly from learning the contents of this book.

- It will help you understand and accept more fully who you are and what you have to offer another person in an intimate relationship.

- It will explain the many dynamics of human interactions among intimate couples.
- It will give you power to set realistic goals, to find healthy partners, and to choose those relationships offering the highest benefits.
- It will give you insight and specific instructions to improve communication and intimacy with your partner.
- It will ease you through the inevitable conflicts and disagreements while strengthening the bond and commitment with him/her.
- It will help you to let go of unhealthy past relationships, to grieve your losses when separations are inevitable, and to enjoy the here and now.
- It will give you confidence that you can manage the suffering that is a normal part of life in a society where ad hoc relationships are becoming the norm.

Kisses aren't Contracts will be your map to holistic love, happiness, contentment, and fulfillment in temporary, ad hoc relationships. It will give you the physical, intellectual, emotional, and spiritual skills you need to be a successful partner within marriage as well. It is a reference you will want to keep in a safe place, so you can refer to it throughout your life when you encounter relationship difficulties.

More

Buddhists have a saying, "When the pupil is ready, the teacher will come." I believe you are now ready for the teachings of this book. America now is a culture of growing ad hoc relationships. Ad hoc means "for a specific purpose." People are getting together for specific objectives, and when they are achieved many leave and move on to others. In the 1990 census, the U.S. Government recognized unmarried cohabitating couples as a form of family unit for the first time. Less then one third of new borns will grow up in a family with two parents. Nationally, an estimated 2.5 million people now live together in relationships not sanctioned by marriage. However, ten major cities and the District of Columbia have passed laws assuring them the same rights as married couples, regardless of their gender. Many unmarried couples own residences jointly and are raising children. However, the census report indicated that the average time unmarried couples remain together before getting married or splitting up is three years. Consequently, some experts estimate that up to half of all children now spend a part of their lives in single-parent households.

During the 1970s every state but South Dakota adopted no-fault divorce laws. In less than a decade divorce rates nearly doubled. Now, more than half of all marriages end in divorce. The social impact of no-fault divorce is now apparent. When families fall apart children are the ones who are hurt the most. The National Center for Health Statistics found that children in single-parent families are far more likely to have behavioral problems, to be high school drop-outs, pregnant teenagers, drug abusers, and to have police records. The Council on Families in America concluded, "America's no-fault divorce revolution has failed." This book is intended to address that problem.

Many people do not know how to behave in this new ad-hoc culture. Consequently, they have painful experiences, suffering losses repeatedly as they form relationships, break them, and recycle them. Many young people cannot control their libido; fully 25% of white births are out of wedlock, 40% of Hispanic, and 70% of blacks, according to the Washington Kiplinger Letter. Many self-help books treat specific aspects of relationships, but none of them really capture the overall education in intimate relationships people need. The fragmented bits and pieces of information are all very confusing without a map to guide you through the maze. I have intended this comprehensive book to be an enlightening solution to that problem that average people can understand and apply practically to their lives.

This book grew out of my personal experience and research into modern concepts about healthy, intimate relationships. It is different because it is based on my lifetime of experience and extensive therapy, as well as the research reported by over 300 authors from many human relations disciplines. I think it is time to bring all that work together into one comprehensive volume so that others can benefit from their wisdom.

Most people just take for granted that they know how to live with another person. Few of us ever confront the possibility that we have a lot to learn when it comes to intimate human relationships. This book may shock you out of denial of your ignorance concerning what it takes to maintain a healthy intimate relationship with a significant other person. Some material discussed in this book may challenge your personal values and beliefs. It may raise questions or concerns that are not covered here. Some of this material may seem impractical or irrelevant to your needs. Some material may bring up feelings that make you uncomfortable. But, don't worry. Now, you can learn new, healthier behavior that can help you avoid repeating the learned mistakes of your adult role models. If you are open to these lessons and take responsibility for your own life, ad hoc relationships can be full of joy instead of dissension, conflict, separation, and divorce driven only by the genetic instinct to reproduce the human species. I am convinced that new, healthy relationships can be developed if you forgive and let go of the past, and learn the modern skills that are presented in this book.

A Short Summary of the Book

Here is a brief description of what this book contains. Part I is intended to help you understand and work through the unique environmental and inherited dysfunctional tendencies that drive your behavior. When you understand how you became the person you are, you will have more control over the person you want to be. We can change much of what we are, but it is easier if we are aware of the possibility of changing and the benefits that changing behavior may impart to our relationships.

We cannot remove all our baggage, but if we recognize it we may be able to avoid some of its negative impact in our relations with significant other people. We can also learn to be more accepting of others when we understand more of their makeup as well.

In Chapter 1, I explain the potential for recovery from the harmful effects of faulty adult role modeling during childhood. The chapter describes the symptoms of codependence, maybe the most common psychological malady of this generation, and offers some means of growing beyond faulty parenting to become more healthy.

Chapter 2 presents a description of dysfunctional social factors related to three generations of people who now must live together in our population: the preboomers, the boomers, and the postboomers. The chapter also describes major social changes which account for the difference in behavior and values of these groups. It presents hope for a better life ahead as these social changes are absorbed and directed into new respect and cooperation between the genders.

Chapter 3 applies a popular, but scientific, model of personality based on the Myers-Briggs Type Indicator to interpersonal relations. This model of behavior provides a powerful vocabulary for understanding and communicating the inherited preferences that make people unique. It encourages increased acceptance of our differences, and increases understanding of the contributions we can make to each other.

Part II contains the core of the book. It begins with searching for a partner and making rational choices, and moves to creating harmony and contentment through intimate commitments.

Chapter 4 explains why people seek intimate relationships, and includes descriptions of the stages through which relationships develop, according to several useful models. It includes specific guidance in making healthy choices in partners, with confidence the benefits will exceed the burdens sufficiently to sustain long term commitment.

Chapter 5 discusses the origin and range of sexual options available in our ad hoc society. It provides some guidelines to help readers make healthy, ethical decisions about your sexual behavior. And, it explains some crucial gender differences in how men and women view their sexuality.

Chapter 6 organizes various professional opinions about romantic and rational love and self esteem, from the view of their role in building and maintaining a healthy whole person within intimate relationships. It develops a new model of holistic love, which I think is the basis of all human happiness. It concludes with new patterns for building self esteem and uncovering your native self worth, which are necessary for loving others.

Chapter 7 provides instruction on healthy intimate communications. It explains how to negotiate personal boundaries of money, proximity, touch, self disclosure, and sexuality, using the latest understanding of human interactions. We can know each other only through our interpersonal communications.

Chapter 8 explores the issues involved in developing holistic intimacy and commitment. It includes criteria for a successful marriage and a healthy family now, and into the next century. It also presents detailed instructions on gaining intimacy in ad hoc relationships.

Part III deals with the conflicts that occur in all relationships. It also offers empathy for those who grieve and suggestions on how to survive the likely prospect of suffering loss of a loved one. It ends with an explanation of the benefits of modern psychotherapy that will help you get the most from this powerful, but little understood, form of stress reduction and behavior modification.

In **Chapter 9,** methods are presented for recognizing and handling the inevitable disagreements and boundary issues that occur normally in all relationships. It helps partners retain closeness and commitment, while they grow at different paces and in different directions.

Chapter 10 helps you deal with the grief that accompanies likely breakups you may experience in our ad hoc culture. It provides encouragement for gaining the spiritual strength and moral courage when alone to go on to try again, and again.

The book concludes, in **Chapter 11**, with guidelines for entering, managing, and terminating, professional therapy. This chapter will help overcome some of the social taboo against therapeutic counseling. It will also help you find the most suitable therapist and manage that relationship through to its successful completion. The chapter ends with instructions on how to form and conduct an effective support group when therapy is unavailable or has been completed.

The many references in the bibliography provide numerous sources for more in-depth study of specific issues. Dysfunctional habits may be so rigidly entrenched in your behavior that it may take hearing the same message from several different sources to get your attention. As you peel off one layer of the seemingly infinite human psyche another one is disclosed, so you may wish to acquire your own personal library from the books that interest you the most.

You might compare this book with a country quilt that has been carefully crafted by experience and lovingly stitched together from a selection of random pieces cut from larger cloths. Each piece is cut from old cloth, but the quilter combines them to make something more beautiful and comforting than all of the pieces separately could be. The result is more valuable than the sum of all of its parts because of the loving contribution of the craftsperson. In this book the pieces are golden nuggets of wisdom culled from the best of psychology published this century. Keep this book in a safe place and use it as a reference whenever your personal life turns cold and unpleasant. Its warmth and protection will keep you safe and comfortable through those winter months of loneliness and bereavement, when things are not going well with your ad hoc relationships.

Caution: Your goal in using this guidebook should be to change your behavior to ensure more happiness and joy in life than you ever imagined. I recommend that you read it only one chapter at a time. Let each chapter soak in for a while before going on to the next one. Your growth will not come overnight because you cannot cram all these golden nuggets down in short order. If you try to absorb it all at once, you may be overwhelmed and you may be tempted to avoid completing it.

After you go through it once, then refer to the study guide in the appendix and work through the chapters again one week at a time, completing the personal exercises for each chapter. This phase may be facilitated by participating jointly in a support group that meets weekly to discuss progress. Then, keep it handy for ease of reference, as you slowly but surely develop into the successful intimate partner I think you were meant to be.

If you are not ready to learn these lessons, then please pass the book along to someone you know who might be ready. Do not discard it in the trash.

One:
Outgrowing Imperfect Role Models

Before I start discussing how to create healthy ad hoc relationships, it will be helpful to review how we got to where we are and how we might become more healthy, because only healthy people can create healthy relationships and avoid getting divorced. Then, we can learn to build more healthy intimate relationships to provide the human connection we need for holistic balance. Sharing a bit of my family background with you may help to establish why I chose to begin with the material in this chapter.

Before I was a teenager, I was thrust into the role of caretaker and surrogate spouse for my mother. She was obese and chronically ill with untreated diabetes. She hated doctors and would not take insulin. My father came from Naples, Italy in 1904 when he was 14 years old. I was born when my father was 43 and my mother was 38 years old.

My father lost his job in a tire plant at the outset of World War II, and had to take night shift work on the railroad, so he was never around much when I was home. He left instructions with my mother for chores that he expected me to do after school, and I always did them as he instructed. I am thankful that I had some very understanding school teachers who encouraged me to achieve my potential and who helped me to build my self esteem.

I met my wife, Rosalene, when we were seniors in different area high schools, on a United Nations trip to New York. Our courtship was mostly by letter during my years in the Air Force and hers in college. Her parents adopted me into their family as a son, along with their own, and they became my surrogate parents.

The first few years were busy, but they were a very happy time, as we took in all the sights of Washington, D.C., the museums, and the free concerts. Rosalene saved the money for a down payment on our first house, while I went to school on the G.I. Bill. It was the middle of the 1950s and our lives settled into a comfortable, if not exciting, pattern.

We were opposites in personality type and we differed in many opinions from color preference (she was a winter and I am a summer) to politics (she was liberal and I am conservative.) People called Rosalene a free spirit, and I said she could be one because she had me to take care of the necessities of life. I found the perfect mate to help me duplicate the codependent, care taking role of my childhood in a marriage.

Rosalene contracted breast cancer at age 42 and died at age 52 from complications of leukemia. I was thrust into single life and empty nesting without any preparation. I began a serious study of what experts presently teach about healthy relationships. My search included extensive reading and lengthy therapy with social workers, psychologists, psychiatrists and pastoral counselors.

I learned that, besides inherited traits, we bring to all relationships the total of our training and experience, integrated into a pattern of perception and decision making that drives our behavior. Often, the adults we encountered during childhood provided faulty role models and imperfect care taking for healthy adult living. All of our adult role models may have done the best they could under the circumstances, but through the immature eyes of a child some of us saw them as threatening or harmful to our infant well being. We may have felt discounted, devalued, abandoned, rejected, shamed, or even emotionally and physically abused periodically. These distorted images can stay with us unconsciously for life and mar all adult relationships if they are not brought into consciousness and dispelled. The purpose of this chapter is to help you understand their influence and to outgrow their power to control your adult behavior. It explains the common behavioral impact of codependence and how it affects intimate relationships.

Dependent children have little choice about their mentors. Although we are born with the potential to become whole and complete, our development often is defective, and we grow up with many holes and false impressions in our makeup. Some anonymous observer has noted, "If a child experiences criticism, he learns to condemn. If he experiences hostility, he learns to fight. If he experiences ridicule, he learns to be shy. If he experiences shame, he learns to feel guilty. If he experiences tolerance, he learns to be patient. If he experiences encouragement, he learns confidence. If he experiences praise, he learns to appreciate. If he experiences fairness, he learns justice. If he experiences grief, he learns how to feel and to express his emotions. If he experiences security, he learns to have faith. If he experiences approval, he learns to like himself. If he experiences acceptance and friendship, he learns to find love in the world."

Usually, we do not recognize our dysfunctions until some relationship crisis brings them into conscious awareness. Often, they go completely unrecognized, and mar all our relationships. When you understand this introductory chapter, you can recognize the symptoms of codependence in your self and others. You can deal with those symptoms and begin to prevent them from driving your life in negative ways. As you heal the wounded child within, you will become a healthier partner who can create healthier ad hoc relationships and reduce the possibility of getting divorced.

From the Beginning

We must recognize our dysfunctional condition because only as we strive to become more balanced, mature people can we bring holistic health to close relationships. Although we are born with basic instincts for survival and reproduction, people need to relearn healthy social behavior for themselves in each generation. Because we don't know any better as dependent children, most of us assume that model roles displayed by members of our family, sports heroes, actors/actresses, public leaders, teachers, and other adults are valid and desirable for us to adopt in our adult lives. Children are born with instinctive drives for survival. When their care giving adults do not supply all their needs, children fabricate a "self" to make up for the deficiencies in their families. Their true self may be submerged as they perfect a false self instead. As adults, the false self drives their behavior as they choose either to emulate childhood models or to act in opposite ways from parents and other adult models. Since the behavior of all these adults usually is flawed, whether intentional or not, we learn both the good and the bad and integrate it all into our adult lives as though those models were qualified mentors. Then we continue to pass both the learned mistakes and our newly created ones along to our children. As adults, we then must dig deeply to find our true selves, and learn for ourselves what healthy intimate behavior really is.

A new generation of people is questioning the model roles handed down to them from the past. People are getting together in support groups all over the country to do for themselves what was not done for them by their families of origin, i.e., learning how to live with more joy, happiness, and abundance. I think we need a better model to follow, and I hope this book will help you construct it.

Codependence Defined

Codependence is defined by Robert Hemfelt, et al., as an addiction to unhealthy people, behaviors, or things that destroys your freedom to grow as an independent person. Codependents guess at what normal in relationships really is because their experience does not include healthy role modeling. A more descriptive phrase might be Adult Children of Dysfunctional Families. So many people are seeking professional help for it that the problem is being called an epidemic in our culture. John Bradshaw labeled it a crisis and attributed it to what he called "poisonous pedagogy," toxic rules of dysfunctional family life.

Bradshaw defined codependence as a "recognizable pattern of fixed personality traits, rooted in the internalized shame resulting from the abandonment that naturally happens to everyone in a dysfunctional family system." The results manifest in divorce, relationship difficulties, compulsive behaviors, anger beyond reason, depression, and more. These symptoms arise from unmet emotional needs, lost childhood, and the compulsion to fix dysfunctional family relationships that are beyond our ability to control. We pass these traits along to the next generation through our children. They think it is normal behavior unless they experience healthier role models in relationships outside the family of origin.

Codependence is defined by Codependence Anonymous (CODA) as an inability to maintain healthy relationships with others and ourselves. The cause lies in long standing dysfunctional patterns of living. These patterns fall into two general categories: over compliance through pleasing others, and over controlling through manipulating others. Typical symptoms defined by CODA are listed as follows:

CODEPENDENCY COMPLIANCE PATTERNS

1. I assume responsibility for others' feelings and behaviors.
2. I feel guilty about others' feelings and behaviors.
3. I have difficulty identifying what I am feeling.

4. I have difficulty expressing my feelings.
5. I am afraid of anger, yet I sometimes erupt in a rage.
6. I worry how others may respond to my feelings, opinions, and behavior.
7. I have difficulty making decisions.
8. I am afraid of being hurt and/or rejected by others.
9. I minimize, alter, or deny how I truly feel.
10. I am very sensitive to how others are feeling and I feel the same way.
11. I am afraid to express differing opinions or feelings.
12. I value others' opinions and feelings more than my own.
13. I put other peoples' needs and desires before my own.
14. I am embarrassed to receive recognition, praise, and gifts.
15. I judge everything I think, say, or do harshly, as never good enough.
16. I am a perfectionist.
17. I am extremely loyal, remaining in harmful situations and relationships too long.
18. I do not ask others to meet my needs and desires.
19. I do not perceive myself as a lovable and worthwhile person.
20. I compromise my own values and integrity to avoid rejection and anger of others.

CODEPENDENCY CONTROL PATTERNS

1. I must be needed to have a relationship with others.
2. I value others' approval of my thinking, feelings, and behaviors over my own.
3. I agree with others so they will like me.
4. I focus my attention on protecting and providing for others.
5. I believe most other people cannot take care of themselves.
6. I keep score of my good deeds and favors, and become very hurt when they are not repaid.
7. I am very skilled at guessing how other people are feeling.
8. I anticipate others' needs and desires, meeting them before they are asked to be met.
9. I become resentful when others will not let me help them.
10. I am calm and efficient in the crises of other people.
11. I feel good about myself only when I am helping others.
12. I freely offer advice and directions to others without being asked.
13. I put aside my own interests and concerns to do what others want.
14. I ask for help and nurturing only when I am ill, and then only reluctantly.
15. I cannot tolerate seeing others in pain.
16. I lavish gifts and favors on those I care about.
17. I use sex to gain approval and acceptance.
18. I attempt to convince others of how they truly think and should feel.
19. I perceive myself as completely unselfish and dedicated to the well being of others.

Since no one is trained to be a perfect parent, practically everybody is raised with some faulty parenting, leading to some behavioral or personality dysfunction. It may include alcohol, tobacco, drugs, work, chronic illness, sex, physical or emotional abuse, or other psychological disparity that goes untreated and unhealed. The members of a family are all codependent upon each other for their psychological as well as their physical well being. We learned to survive by developing a personal kind of power that resulted from sacrificing some of ourselves as children. We gave up some of our own reality as children to take care of our parents or to help meet the needs of the family system as best we could. We learned to survive, but we learned to abandon some of our true self in the process. Therefore, everybody can benefit from the inner work needed to reconstruct an inventory of healthy adult behavior.

Most codependent people have internalized shame and have strong feelings of low self worth. Many codependents try to make themselves indispensable by taking care of others. They are willing to do whatever it takes to feel loved or worthwhile. They often throw themselves into work to the point of workaholism or burnout. They sublimate their needs to meet needs of others to the point of becoming invisible victims to themselves. Codependence is emerging as the social problem of today because modern high-tech lifestyles, and changing attitudes about family life and social goals, magnify the symptoms. Adult children of dysfunctional families exhibit faulty behavior and distorted values that read like a litany of all the complaints presented to mental health professionals. Codependence is considered the underlying cause of addictive behavior. Codependents are people who have never fully developed their ego selves.

Dysfunctional parents are likely to impede the growth of their children by stifling some of their independence and emotional spontaneity. If one or the other parent is chemically or work addicted, chronically ill, self-righteously religious, or otherwise dysfunctional, the codependent opposite parent may impose some missing marital functions on the defenseless child. I now realize that is what happened to me. Some psychologists call it emotional incest.

In the systems theory of families, all the functions must be performed by somebody. Sometimes, the child is forced into a role of surrogate spouse, which either distorts or retards his development as the child. Instead of giving permission to experiment, feel, grow, learn, and leave home, both physically and psychologically, a dysfunctional parent may cling in a dependent, manipulative manner, or otherwise stifle normal development. Because young children are dependent upon their parents, they can be forced into an unhealthy alliance. If outright physical abuse is not involved, at the least this is a form of emotional abuse. The controlling-dependent relationship between parent and child can continue throughout both their lifetimes, unless some professional intervention occurs. Children internalize this faulty behavior and transfer it to others among their own families, co-workers, and friends when they become adults.

Not all dysfunctional parents are substance addicts. Some are single, divorced, widowed, ill, or unhappily married. Many are "normal" by yesterday's standards of parenting. But, what is normal is not always healthy. As children who are dependent upon our parents, we have no alternative but to play the role assigned to us by these powerful adults, often well into our own adulthood. A few such people are lucky enough to get professional help in their youth. Others must wait until the obvious, healthy progress of their peers exposes their own stagnation. Some must wait for a divorce, mid-life crisis, or the death of the parent or spouse, to trigger their search for wholeness. Many stay in denial all their lives. The longer we wait to start recovery, the more severe, impulsive, dramatic, and turbulent are the accumulated feelings that must be worked through to become free, mature adults. And, the more precious unrecoverable time we lose working through unhealthy relationships, or succumbing to compulsive addictions of many types to medicate the unconscious pain we carry from lost childhoods. Much of alcoholism, drug addiction, compulsions to gamble, overeat, and overspend, and promiscuity can be attempts to medicate the pain from unresolved issues we all carry as baggage into adult life.

Adults seem to have the primal need to recreate their familiar family-of-origin even if it was destructive and painful. Subconsciously, we seem to attract the kind of person who will help us repeat the mistakes of our parents in our relationships, repeatedly, until we learn to get it right. Some of us never do. We let our parents shape most of our choices and the way we perceive things, even after they are deceased. The pattern is now all very apparent.

Research reported in the anonymously written workbook, *"The 12 Steps, A Way Out,"* resulted in the following descriptions of behaviors commonly seen among those raised in dysfunctional families:

1. We have feelings of low self esteem as a result of being perpetually criticized. We perpetuate these messages by judging ourselves and others harshly. We try to cover up our poor opinions about ourselves by being perfectionistic, controlling, contemptuous, and gossipy.

2. We tend to isolate ourselves out of fear and to feel uneasy around other people, especially authority figures.

3. We are desperate for love and approval and will do anything to make people like us. Not wanting to hurt others, we remain loyal in situations and relationships even when evidence indicates our loyalty is undeserved.

4. We are intimidated by angry people and personal criticism. This causes us to feel inadequate and insecure.

5. We continue to attract emotionally unavailable people with addictive or dependent personalities.

6. We live life as victims, blaming others for our circumstances, and are attracted to other victims as friends and lovers. We confuse love with pity and tend to love people we can pity and rescue.

7. We are either super-responsible or super-irresponsible. We take responsibility for solving others' problems and expect others to be responsible for solving ours. This enables us to avoid being responsible for our own lives and choices.

8. We feel guilty when we stand up for ourselves or act in our own best interest. We give in to others' needs and opinions instead of taking care of ourselves.

9. We deny, minimize or repress our feelings. We are unaware of the impact our inability to identify and express our feelings has had on our adult lives.

10. We are dependent personalities who are so terrified of rejection or abandon-

ment that we tend to stay in situations or relationships that are harmful to us. Our fears and dependency stop us from ending unfulfilling relationships and prevent us from entering into fulfilling ones.

11. Denial, isolation, control, shame, and inappropriate guilt are legacies from our family of origin. Because of these symptoms, we feel hopeless and helpless, which often causes depression.
12. We have difficulty with intimacy, security, trust and commitment in our relationships. Lacking clearly defined personal limits and boundaries, we become enmeshed in our partner's needs and emotions.
13. We tend to procrastinate and have difficulty following projects through from beginning to completion.
14. We have a strong need to be in control. We overreact to change or actions of others over which we have no control.

At first reading of the above descriptions, you may say, "So, what's wrong with that? Sounds to me like a perfectly normal lifestyle among committed couples." That is just the point. So many adults in our culture teach these dysfunctional behaviors that they appear to be normal. Many wounded adult children don't know what healthy really is. They are expressed and reinforced daily in our television sitcoms, our movies and books, our popular music (especially the music), our magazines, and our newspapers. Hemfelt says if pushing codependence were illegal, most lyric writers of popular music would be in jail. So, it is easy to deny our unhealthy condition really exists. However, what is normal in society is not necessarily healthy. What is perceived as healthy in relationships is a matter of judgment for each person, based on many learned values and observing both healthy and dysfunctional models. This "common sense" is not always desirable as a mentor, when our teachers are not competent to demonstrate healthy behavior.

The codependent may not improve with time unless some intervention is made. Life may get worse as personal happiness and contentment slowly fade even further. Physical health can deteriorate, and the malfunction can lead to depression and illness. It actually can be fatal. If you need help to speed your recovery from codependence, I heartily recommend that you consider attending regular meetings of a Codependents Anonymous support group in your area. If there isn't one near you, perhaps it is time for you to organize one for your own healing, in addition to that of the adult children in your area.

You can locate the codependent support group nearest to you by contacting Codependents Anonymous at P.O. Box 33577 in Phoenix, Arizona 85067-3577, telephone (602) 277-7991. Or, ask your local telephone operator for help in locating the Codependents Anonymous (CODA) groups in your area. The CODA national office staff also can provide help in setting up a new group.

You may have gradually and unknowingly permitted yourself to become codependent in many relationships of your life. Many people never recognize this problem as a source of their social difficulties. When we become aware of the behavioral family dysfunction we are living with, many often experience despair or rage. After the realization of it breaks through denial into conscious awareness, you can begin to reconstruct the resources you were born with to manage your intimate interpersonal relationships. You can learn how to reconstruct your own intimate relationships for a more healthy lifestyle and grow toward more healthy interdependence.

Emily Marlin observed that the transition from codependence to health moves through three stages. First is the eye-opener stage, in which denial is faced and the realization of a need to change becomes conscious. Second is the pioneer stage in which a serious commitment is made to work hard at recovery, either through self-help groups, therapy groups, or private counseling. Third is the stage of developing a mutual partnership with another in which both partners enjoy the full range of human experience. In recovery, Marlin says that recovering codependents:

1. try to listen actively to their own instincts, as well as to the voice of significant others;
2. internalize many lessons from their individual recovery programs,
3. continue to change, and to grow all the time;
4. honestly and openly trust, talk, and feel;
5. take action and try to resolve conflicts;
6. take risks and make decisions;
7. freely admit mistakes and feel okay about them;
8. don't blame themselves or others;
9. establish a healthy balance between closeness and distance from other people;
10. bind to others through commitment, common goals, and communications; and
11. enjoy themselves, their relationships, and their freedom.

If codependence is part of your family history, it may be a waste of time trying to develop healthy ad hoc relationships before you clear your life of this dysfunction. There is help out there and in this book, but you must clear away denial, and make a commitment to your own recovery to take advantage of it. That recovery begins with rebuilding your self esteem.

We All Need Self Esteem

The experience of falling in love resembles taking on personal ownership of an ideal imprint or visual image that reflects your own self esteem. If the partner has been similarly stimulated or imprinted, the love affair can be very intense and durable. The more one-sided or skewed from reality this ideal imprint is, the more likely the chances are that the relationship will be pulled apart. Unfortunately, the image of self derived from thousands of experiences throughout childhood comes short of the ideal of perfection that we were born with. We may have obtained reinforcement by being weak, poorly coordinated, discontented, angry, and helpless. To survive in imperfect families, according to John Welwood, we may adopt a negative self image that speaks to us with such negative concepts as the following:

1. I don't deserve love.
2. I have to earn love.
3. I can never get what I really want so there is no sense in trying.
4. I will only be loved if I play hard to get (or easy to get).
5. If I let others see my real needy self, they will run away.

6. I can't trust love because it is a form of control.
7. I must take care of (men or women).
8. I must always be pleasing to (men or women).
9. No one will love me if I show them who I really am.
10. The pain of loneliness is less than the pain of abandonment.

Although these negative thoughts may no longer have any basis in our adult lives, their grounding in childhood can still drive our behavior, although unconsciously. Robert L. McKinley says that we must continually work on creating low self esteem because if we stopped the negative self talk we do on ourselves, we would recover inner peace automatically. If we do not have enough self worth, we can choose people unconsciously who cannot reflect holistic love and intimacy. We can fear the pain of potential self rejection so much that we choose people who cannot be close and endow them with a reflection of our own distorted fantasy. Such a dysfunctional pair-bond can be maintained romantically, typically for a maximum of two or three years, unless each partner begins to change toward the other. Each has an idealistic image of the other that neither can live up to for long. Under the pressure of disillusionment, if it follows, the pair-bond weakens.

The environment in a dysfunctional family can destroy a child's innate self esteem and replace it with unconscious guilt and shame. We may conclude that we are worthless and do not merit the acceptance of ourselves, much less that of others. When that happens, our boundaries are controlled by others and we become unable to defend against unwanted intrusions that limit the potential of our lives. We may seek self-affirmation from acceptance by significant others and may be driven into unhealthy relationships to pursue that goal. The resulting pain of frustration, as our reality does not measure up to the image of native self worth we were born with, can drive us into unhealthy ways of proving our perceived worthlessness. People in this state of mind can do harm to themselves through alcohol or drug abuse, promiscuous sex, overeating, and compulsive gambling, or other types of addictive indulgence, in their attempt to prove their perceived lack of self esteem.

The ancient Jewish law that Jesus converted to the second highest commandment states, "You shall love your neighbor as yourself." (Leviticus, 19:18) We can only give what we have, so it is important to love ourselves first. Confidence that we have value and are precious as a unique person is one of the most significant possessions anyone can have. I think such confidence is the greatest gift we can bring to another in an intimate relationship. Learning something about modern ideas regarding self esteem and self worth can help you exhibit healthy love. It can help you care for people without being victimized by their dependency, and outgrow the harmful reactions to your childhood deficit.

Here is an excellent check list by John and Linda Friel to help measure your level of healthy self esteem:"There needs to be a balance over the long run between what you give and what you receive, although at times giving more when an intimate friend is in need is OK. You will know when you are beginning to care too much for others and not enough for yourself. You will be able to avoid getting into relationships where you feel smothered, pressured, or abandoned. You can listen, support, encourage, be honest, share feelings, and trust that others will do the same. You can take care of your own hurts, emptiness, and pain before you help other people. You care by treating others as competent adults, able to look out for themselves. You do not have to hover over others, doing nice charitable things for them constantly. Your caring is balanced between being too detached and too intimate. You can acknowledge the pain of others and empathize with them, but let go of it and go about your own life without being consumed by their suffering."

When self esteem is low, we also do not know how to ask directly for what we want or to get our needs met. If we learned from our dysfunctional families that we are not worth having our needs met, we may have learned devious manipulations to control those closest to us. Although we may get some of our needs met that way, satisfaction usually comes with a great deal of resentment and anger when others sense our controlling manipulations. More healthy ways of getting what we want will be explained in Chapter 7.

Adult children who do not have a well-constructed image of self will continue to believe they must be successful or good or approved of by significant others if they are to have any sense of self worth. Infants may learn to get their needs met by displaying many negative symptoms, including discontent, suffering, and anger. If people extend these methods into adulthood, they have little sense of being intrinsically worth while inside themselves and seek it in the images reflected from acceptance by others whom they often idealize. Such people are unnaturally vulnerable to the adversity that life inevitably imposes on everyone. They lack the inner resources they might use when misfortune and loss come. Hazards that merely are challenges to others present feelings of helplessness and hopelessness to codependents. They even cause clinical depression to adult children with low self esteem. Although the deficit of self esteem may be unconscious, symptoms of it may drive us to seek self worth from meaningful social relationships in the following three ways, developed by Gary Smalley and John Trent:

1. Reconstruction of the reflected self can come from having the acceptance and reinforcement of healthy significant others in our lives. We are social creatures, and we can whither and die if we are forced into a life of isolation. The need for a sense of personal value is met by people who welcome our meaningful touch, by verbal affirmation through a spoken message of approval, by thinking of ourselves as highly valuable, by picturing a successful future, by active commitment from loved ones, and by intimate involvement with others that goes deeper than mere frivolous social encounters. If this need is not met during our first three years of life, we can be starved for it the rest of our lives. If we lacked sufficient nurturing through this form of "blessing" from our childhood, we must learn to reconstruct our lives to obtain it for ourselves, and to provide it to those meaningful others with whom we live out the rest of our days.

2. Those who can obtain self esteem from creative work may have an advantage over those whose self esteem depends more on intimate relationships. Codependent people who marry or commit to a parent-figure may not

learn self competence if the partner continues the control and manipulative dominance modeled by the parent. The loss of such a partner may aggravate belief in helplessness and depress the survivor who perceives life as uncontrollable. Loss in the present can trigger unconscious feelings of loss in the past.

3. Those people who are not part of an integrated, healthy family structure may find nurture for the child within in support groups or other social groups, as in churches or activities groups. There, they can obtain a sense of belonging and share in the sense of self worth that results from being a member of the community. Self esteem also is connected with feeling competent. Therefore, it can be improved temporarily by doing something competently that you value. The completion of it will give you a sense of accomplishment to boost your worth and self-image.

Matthew McKay developed a very comprehensive plan for improving self esteem that employs a wide combination of therapies. A brief description of his plan follows:

1. Recognize and disarm the pathological critic within, i.e., the negative parental voice we all hear that puts us down and keeps in a state of "not OK." Talk back to this inner critic, make it useless, and refute all its claims with positive counter attacks.

2. Develop a more accurate self assessment of your assets and liabilities, physical, intellectual, emotional, and spiritual. Create a personal inventory through a self description of your strengths and positive attributes.

3. Identify and counter all your negative distortions in thinking, including the errors of overgeneralizing, global labeling, filtering, black-white thinking, self-blame, taking personal responsibility, control fallacies, and emotional reasoning.

4. Develop a more compassionate view of yourself, with more understanding, acceptance, forgiveness. Learn to set reasonable expectations and achievable goals.

5. Overcome the tyranny of the irrational "shoulds" in your life. Replace unhealthy values with more healthy beliefs that can meet your basic needs for love, approval, belonging, and emotional and physical well being.

6. Reframe mistakes as necessary feedback for the learning process of life. Assume that you always make the reasonable choice given the information you had at the time. A mistake only means that your awareness at some future time has changed with new insight. Assume you always have the opportunity of choosing again.

7. Defend your self esteem against criticism from every source, including your inner critic. Recognize that reality is subjective for both participants in any disagreement. Disconnect your self esteem from the encounter and strive for understanding and mutual acceptance of imperfect behavior.

8. Ask the universe to supply your physical, intellectual, emotional, spiritual, and social needs. Recognize your rights to healthy relationships.

Express your true feelings to others as a prerequisite to their understanding of your need. Use "I" statements in making requests of your intimate others, and give them the responsibility for choosing their response.

9. In your imagination, create scenes in which your needs are being met, your realistic goals are being achieved, and your self-image is appropriate for the situation. If you think you are weak and helpless, visualize yourself as strong and resourceful. If you think you are unworthy and undeserving, visualize yourself as valuable and making an important contribution. If you think you are sickly and depressed, counter with scenes of healthy and cheerful behavior.

10. Think of self esteem as something you really have, but are only out of touch with. Develop self affirmation statements that are short, simple statements of your unqualified value and accomplishment of goals. Give yourself permission to deserve and to receive the good things of life that are your birthright.

If your self esteem is derived only from the reflected acceptance by significant others, you can be devastated when they are unavailable, leave, or die. Self esteem that is based on others is temporary. self worth that is derived from your opinion of yourself is much more durable. Therefore, it is much more healthy to develop a sense of self worth that is not derived from the acceptance of others, but is based on your native inheritance as a child of your creator.

Since you cannot gain pseudo-support from your dysfunctional family of origin any longer, now may be the time to begin reaching out to others in need of what you have to give. It may be that by providing such nurturing self esteem for others, we obtain it for ourselves. If you act as though you have it, you will. Jesus spoke of this reverse phenomenon when he said, "Give, and it will be given to you; good measure, pressed down, shaken together, running over, they will pour in your lap. For by your standard of measure it will be measured to you in return." (Luke 6:38) In terms of attitudinal healing, giving and receiving are the same. So, we may need to learn to give what we want in order to receive it for ourselves. That seems to be a universal law, just like gravity. In other words, sow what you want to reap.

You may need to reconfirm a sense of your own self worth outside of the normal, socially derived sources. True self worth may be found only in the realization that you are as worthy as everybody else (but not more so), regardless of your material possessions or profession, personal recognition, social accomplishments or their lack, in comparisons with others. You may need to relearn how to measure your self worth by your own yardstick and that of no one else. In any event, you will need to strike a balance between your need for self esteem and the burden of obtaining it in ad hoc relationships.

Matthew McKay reported how faulty, distorted thinking about our self image can depress self esteem. By becoming more conscious of the many ways we put ourselves down, we can begin to practice countering our negative thinking in ways to enhance a sense of self worth. We can become aware of automatic negative thinking and challenge the inner critic that demeans us left over from childhood criticism. Many people have found that by repeating positive affirmations about themselves, their self worth improves and they become more loving, successful, and happy. By repeating affirmations until we drive them into our subconscious minds, they cannot help but improve our self worth.

To help you through each day, one day at a time, try to memorize these affirmations from CODA or place them in a visible location and repeat them often. Alternatively, you can record them on a tape cassette using the second person "you" instead of "I" and play them back to yourself while in a relaxed and restful posture, lying down or sitting comfortably with your eyes closed. To deepen your relaxation mode, you can count slowly backward from 50 to zero as you exhale your normal breathing before and during the playback. After a few weeks of this daily practice you may be surprised at how much better you feel about yourself.

POSITIVE SELF AFFIRMATIONS

I am (you are) worthwhile just because I exist and try to survive.
I have legitimate needs and wants that are worthy of satisfaction.
Each thought and action I take is the best I am capable of at the time.
I accept my mistakes without self blame or judgment.
I make the best choices, taking myself into consideration first.
Just for today, I am respecting my own and other's boundaries.
Just for today, I am vulnerable to someone I trust.
Just for today, I am taking one compliment and holding it in my heart.
Just for today, I am acting in a way that I admire in someone else.
I am a child of God.
I am a precious person.
I am a worthwhile person.
I am a beautiful person inside and outside.
I love myself unconditionally.
I have ample time for leisure without feeling guilty.
I deserve to be loved by myself and by others.
I am loved because I deserve love.
I am a child of God and I deserve love, peace, prosperity, and serenity.
I forgive myself for hurting myself and others.
I forgive myself for letting others hurt me.
I forgive myself for accepting sex when I wanted love.
I am willing to accept love.
I am not alone, I am one with God and the Universe.
I am whole and good.
I am capable of changing.

The Opportunity to Grow

Although I have explained codependence as it begins in dysfunctional families, this is not a book about parent bashing. Undoubtedly some of them deserve that, and even more. However, although I believe it is both loathsome and abhorrent, this book is not about intentional, outright child abuse. No doubt many children suffer physical and emotional abuse from parents, adults, siblings, and even peers and friends, as was thoroughly explored by Beverly Engel. According to her, virtually everybody is subjected to some form of physical and emotional abuse by one or more of the close associates we all have in childhood that retards healthy adult development. Therapists are divided over how much impact such childhood experience has on adult behavior. The latest information indicates that genetic inheritance has more to do with the outcome than does childhood environment.

There is certainly enough blame, guilt, and shame to go around for everybody in our culture because no one can be such a perfect parent. However, it is difficult for normal parents to distinguish between healthy discipline and downright abuse, because they did not have perfect role models either. Barbara Goulter and Joan Minninger explored all the many ways a father can inadvertently and unintentionally spoil relations with a daughter. Laurence E. Hedges laid blame for female personality disorders at the feet of faulty mothering. The tendency to attribute painful adulthood to parental abuse sometimes goes beyond competent, ethical therapy.

Many therapists, who seem to be more popular on the west coast, imply that finding some childhood trauma to blame is good therapy for all the problems that beset troubled adults. Some therapists apparently cannot avoid the temptation to solicit creative memories from vulnerable clients who suffer from dysfunctional lifestyles. Stan J. Katz and Aimee E. Liu documented many cases in which the growth of their clients actually was retarded and families were needlessly poisoned by well-intentioned but untrained leaders of many 12-Step support groups.

Memories from childhood can be faulty and tainted with the suggestive implications of unethical counselors. We may allow our memories to be completely reshaped by counselors who have impressive credentials or present themselves as experts. Such unhelpful persuasion often does more harm than good.

So many parents have been accused by hurting offspring decades after the allegations allegedly occurred that the False Memory Syndrome Foundation (FMS) was formed to provide support and professional guidance to falsely accused families. The legitimate codependency of wounded adults has too often been twisted into fictitious physical and emotional abuse by misguided counselors.

Obviously, it is quite likely that teachers, siblings, parents, and peers will do or say something that is harmful to a child at some time or other. Sometimes it is easy to cross the line, and unintentional physical, emotional, and verbal abuse certainly can affect adults throughout their lives. But, I think it is irresponsible for counselors to encourage troubled adults who come to them for care to blame their parents and other caregiving adults, and even siblings and peers, for all the unpleasant feelings and mental suffering they have as adults.

Since there are no absolute truths in life, perception is everything. If you choose to believe childhood abuse is the cause of all your adult misbehavior, that is reality for you whether or not it is true. However, please note that Kenneth Levin pointed out how powerful unconscious fantasies can be in response to perceived trauma. He presented compelling case histories that illustrate how virtually the entire spectrum of problematic behaviors, discontents, and emotional conflicts can be falsely related to abusive parenting. In their inevitably frustrating pursuit of long-cherished fantasies engendered by earliest experience and focused on an imagined redress or early disappointments, such people often find counselors to support their contentions of childhood abuse. Levin showed how even seemingly contradictory behaviors, and contradictory feelings ranging from anger and resentment to self-deprecation and guilt, can be understood as meaningful expressions of one's pursuit of dominant fantasies. Fantasies are thought to be a means of obtaining some control in life over past events that we could not control.

Some children undoubtedly are intentionally abused. Many other books address that issue, and it is not to be taken lightly. *If you actually were abused, I suggest you seek a competent therapist immediately.* But, blaming well meaning and untrained parents for everything that goes wrong in your life is to deny your accountability for your own actions as an adult. You had no control over the genes you inherited, and you had very little control of how you were treated as a child. However, you do have control over how you think and behave as an adult. Engel quoted Eleanor Roosevelt as saying, "Nobody can make you feel inferior without your consent." Parents, teachers, and care givers often are blamed for everything from chemical addictions and divorce, to neurosis, to schizophrenia.

The result of all this distortion is a wounded adult with an inner child that lives unconsciously in torment, passively suffering or lashing out, and expressing himself in the only unhealthy ways he knows how, not knowing why. When we realize what we missed during our childhood that we could have had, we may feel furious at our care givers for their incompetence or abuse. To overcome our distorted childhoods, some counselors promote the need to recover our forgotten memories and bring our repressed anger toward our infantile care givers into consciousness, letting the feelings of grief and anger wash through us as a cleansing process to permit our original healthy, spontaneous self to reassert itself in a controlled manner. They claim that only after such a catharsis can we really love ourselves enough to love anyone else and forgive our faulty care givers. Such a process usually cannot be done without some form of professional therapeutic intervention.

No care giver can meet the perfect model that we needed as individual infants, much less siblings and peers. We need to grant our parents permission to be imperfect and to make mistakes. Moreover, each child responds to his/her imperfect care giving with a unique, often distorted, perception of reality sensed through immature, dependent eyes and ears, and genetic inheritance. Katz and Liu reported longitudinal research studies that indicate inherited temperaments affect how people react and adapt to their life circumstances much more than previously was thought. The results of work by Emmy Werner showed that children who were most resilient to abuse, poverty, and health and family issues during childhood who became happy, well-adjusted grown-ups despite their troubled backgrounds tended to have extremely engaging personalities. Even as infants, the resilient individuals were described by their parents as "active, affectionate, cuddly, easygoing, and even tempered."

It seems the temperaments we were born with set us up for responses to the experiences we have with other people, including our families. Katz concluded, "Some people are simply born with optimistic, easygoing natures that persist, even with abuse and misfortune in early life. If you were not lucky enough to be born with these traits, you will have to work harder at developing self esteem, strong social supports, and positive values." He recommended developing the following dimensions of life: successful professional achievement, continuing education and skills training, sports and hobbies, physical conditioning through rest, diet, and exercise, stable rituals and routines, intimate supportive nurturance, community involvement, and spirituality.

The development of healthful adult patterns also is furthered if from early on we see those around us enjoy and respect not only babies but also themselves and others; if they are self-confident and reasonably trusting, can enjoy what they are doing, can afford making mistakes and admit them, or get angry with one another without excessive guilt, shame, or anxiety; if they can afford to cry and be depressed when there is cause, and eventually emerge from grief and depression with refreshed vitality; if they can be straightforward in speaking about any feeling that needs to be talked about; if they are consistent in their attitudes and actions and live as they preach; in other words, if they can serve as models for the spontaneous patterns of response that would help us cope with (the work of maturing)."

Since no one has perfect parents, everyone carries the scars and pain of their imperfect childhood into adult relationships. However, some psychologists now believe children have all the resources they need to rise above faulty parenting.

Gertrude Blanck stated, "For much too long, psychology has put the emphasis on what the parent does. Our latest information, however, is that most of the job of development is up to the child. Human infants, if they are normally endowed, come into the world equipped to make the most of what awaits them. Parents only have to provide favorable conditions."

Parents who need to be perfect are caught up in a no-win situation as they cannot meet the child's adult needs for both autonomy and security simultaneously. Since this distorted form of perfection is not possible, there must be some more realistic and reasonable way of evaluating parenting. If we carry these habits into our adult relationships that fail it is easy, but unfair and incorrect, to blame our parents for the outcome. It is just the result of our experience as infants when the only way we could get our needs met was to display discontent.

We can choose to leave the past behind and grow into the future. Many things happen to us in life that we do not control. We can feel guilty about the actions we control that harm others or ourselves. A guilty conscience may be appropriate response to our own willful acts of sin, neglect, or irresponsibility. We need to face all the demons of the past, feel the rage, experience the grief, work through the numbness and the fear of change, peel away the layers of self-deception, and uncover all the deep dark secrets that seem to be life threatening.

Growing up is about recognizing who your care givers were, appreciating what they could give, acknowledging what they could not give, feeling the disappointment, learning who they really were, forgiving them or at least understanding them, and moving on. I think there comes a time when we should take responsibility for ourselves and stop dumping guilt onto our parents. We can begin to re-parent the child within us and take responsibility for our own adult development. We can recognize when our inner child is bored, frightened, tired, playing, overreacting, fantasizing, rejected, exposed, hungry, or lonely, and express our adult concern and acceptance toward him.

We can grieve the loss of perfect childhood, what Carl Jung called legitimate suffering, and rebuild our inner child in healthier ways if we let go of the responsibility for behavior we lay on our parents that they could not provide. It is only by letting the feelings of grief do their healing that we can become whole adults. We must get out of our heads long enough to let our emotions wash us clean. If we don't, neurosis can become the substitute for this legitimate suffering. It often is manifested as a chronic low-grade depression clinically labeled as dysthymia. This process of healing the inner damaged child is explained fully by John Bradshaw in his classic book, *Homecoming*. I recommend you complete his process to heal the wounded child within you and learn the skills of re-parenting. He divides childhood development into the stages of infant self, toddler self, preschool self, school age self, and adolescent self to develop a new model of personal wholeness.

Healing of the wounded inner child undoubtedly is very important so we can bring a healthy adult into intimate relationships. Working through the stages of shock and depression, anger, hurt and sadness, remorse, and toxic shame and loneliness is essential to healing the wounded inner child. But I think we must also develop the healthy inner adult and the inner parent as well. Then they can support the needy child within. Healing must be based on reality as it existed and not on childish fantasy or faulty, illogical thinking. The fact is that we are free to choose our behavior from a very early age. If we are given the opportunity for deep self assessment as adults, we may ultimately realize that responsibility for our situation rests primarily with ourselves. As we grow, we need to assume more responsibility for our own choices.

At some point, I think we should become adult enough to accept our parents for whom they are, even if they are pathologically ill. We can choose to forgive them for not being perfect, and move beyond the childish need for their acceptance and permission to be who we are so we can take our own place in the world. When that point comes, we may expect a quick fix and be disappointed and outraged when we realize how much energy and time it takes to get better at living a healthy, independent, adult life.

Forgiveness heals the past and frees up our energy for the present. While we secretly hate our parents we remain attached to them, whether living or not, and this provides us with a way of avoiding growing up. Through forgiveness, we can leave home internally. You can learn that it is ok as an adult to feel what you feel, want what you want, see and hear what you see and hear, have fun and play including sexuality, tell the truth, know your limits and delay gratification, accept the consequences of your choices, make mistakes as a learning experience, respect other people's feelings, needs, and wants, and have problems.

We can choose to believe the benefits of changing our learned behavior outweigh the fear and psychic cost of doing so enough to make the effort worthwhile. We can start to be and do more of what we like and reduce being and doing what we do not like. We can celebrate our strengths, accept our limitations, and change our circumstances. If we don't work on changing ourselves and our circumstances, we may attempt to change others, which is next to impossible, and drive ourselves crazy in the process.

If we accept the idea that we are born totally free and continue to be so, we can then be released of all the conflicts that are involved in every choice that we make. I think it is fear of the pain of growth that prevents us from growing. The ego inside us determines more of what we are than do events on the outside. We can accept the idea that everything we have ever done and everything we shall ever do is voluntary. We can then begin to act in good faith with all other human beings whom, we assume, also are free to make their own choices. We are freed of the responsibility for the responses we get from all other human beings. We are free at last from all judgments about our selves and others. We can experience total, unconditional love for ourselves and for all things in the universe, mineral, plant, animal, and human. We can reach that level of bliss that prompted Dr. Martin Luther King, Jr. to proclaim, "Thank God, I am free at last."

The Challenge to Change

The resources are within you, and must be brought into consciousness so they can be used. Now you must **ACT**, i.e., **Accept** reality, **Choose** to be more independent of the past, and **Take** action, as instructed by Robert and Jeannette Lauer.

Acceptance is a letting-go process. You can choose to let go of your wishes and demands that life should be different. There are no permanent victories or solutions. When you peel off one layer of self, another awaits your attention. You continue to hurt if you don't accept what is in front of you. Your mind can make this difficult task seem impossible by denying that you have a problem. However, you can *choose* to let go or not let go of the past. It is a conscious choice. Once you accept something you don't like, you can also choose not to be dependent on it. You now can become a more healthy, interdependent person, maybe for the first time in your life.

Unfortunately, you have to act when you are afraid, when you feel inadequate, when you are embarrassed, when you don't want to. Nevertheless, it is the action that makes you grow, not the choice or the acceptance. It is painful, and it requires courage and self control to extend your boundaries, but it is possible.

The self-controlled person maintains progress toward a goal even when he is not in the mood, doesn't feel like making the effort, currently would enjoy something else, or finds working toward the goal downright unpleasant. Doing what you have to do to achieve goals, like taking the initiative to make new friends, or overcoming chronic depression, are behavioral modes you can learn. What keeps the self-controlled person in motion is what he tells himself about the progress he is making. Many modern medical and psychological experts believe that behavior and feelings are controlled by the beliefs that always are flowing through your stream of inner consciousness. When Pablo Casals was asked why he still practiced the cello after age 90 he replied, "I think I am making some progress."

People always act in a way that is consistent with their beliefs, whether they are based on faulty assumptions, or truth that is founded in reality. When the truth is replaced by nonsense, we can be expected to behave in ways that prevent reaching goals.

Taking action means making decisions by responding to your personal motivation, or the voice of your intuition, Higher Power, or God as you conceive him to be. Motivation to act can arise either from fear that things will get worse or hope that they will get better. In either case, being content where you are is the surest way to lose out on your future. Therefore, overcoming contentment may be your biggest personal challenge. Complacency must be erased from your makeup if you are to make continual progress. Sure, with every choice there is the risk that things won't turn out as you expected or wanted. There is always the chance that your hopes will be scrambled into disappointment by unpredictable results. But, without the attempt to change there can be no growth, just a continuation of the troubled present.

We cannot avoid making choices because no decision actually is still a decision. We must learn how to grow by defining the underlying problems, setting realistic goals or defining wanted results, identifying the options available or that can be created, testing the options against reality, and having a contingency plan in case things don't go as planned. While managing life, you must employ the courage to take risks in the face of uncertainty, trust in your capacity to redeem a mistake, avoid limiting your capacity for change, and be willing to consider unusual (for you) options.

The following ten-point plan offered by Robert and Jeannette Lauer may be very helpful for learning to master life's unpredictable experiences. Their points are:

1. **Take responsibility for your own life.** Release the responsibility for the lives of significant others whom you do not control. Losses and bad luck come to all of us sooner or later; unfortunately, that's life. We cannot regard ourselves as victims and continue to grow. Face the pain without artificial anesthetics, work through it, choose to grow, and create a new lifestyle for yourself.

2. **Affirm your own self worth.** Self esteem is a precarious possession. In times of recovery, you can doubt your own ability, capacity, and value. It is important to settle this issue if you are to grow through the crises of life.

3. **Balance concern for yourself with concern for others.** Codependence not only attacks our self- esteem, it can hurl us into self-absorption, harming our relationships with others. A person cannot remain totally focused on self and continue to grow. It is also difficult to make and keep friends when you are very narcissistic.

4. **Find and use your available physical, intellectual, emotional, and spiritual resources.** There must be a balance in these four areas of life. Some resources are internal to ourselves and some are external. Some may have to be developed from embryonic beginnings. Assume that there always are options because there always are resources.

5. **Reframe inevitable problems and mistakes** into an adaptive, useful, learning experience.
6. **Look for the positives** in otherwise undesirable situations with silver-lining thinking. Harboring negative thinking causes a lowered sense of wellness. Positive thinking aloud can help you to cope by enhancing your sense of well-being.
7. **Persevere, but within reason.** The key is to sense when you are making progress, but to move on to other alternatives when further growth is unlikely without change.
8. **Lower your threshold of awareness.** Become more sensitive to signals from others. Pay attention to the outer, social world and your self absorption will diminish, making it easier to sense new opportunities and let go of old, obsolete beliefs. That's right, beliefs are not set in concrete and can be changed when you choose to accept new responses to current issues.
9. **Restructure your life.** Use a current crisis, and the inevitable others to come, to redirect your character into new, appropriate, changed values, beliefs, and behavior.
10. **Develop personal hardiness.** Confront life and actively engage it rather than facing it passively or trying to avoid the pain of it. Assume the degree of control that is possible over options and engage your Higher Power to influence outcomes. Accept change as the essence of life rather than as a threat.

The challenge is to move from knowledge of these principles to using them in your everyday life. For the devastated, unmanageable life of the codependent, and those whose lifestyle has been scrambled by trauma of death or divorce, this ability may come in small, tentative steps over a long period of time. Through the harmful, abusive experiences of their lives and their own faulty logic, some people learn a habitual lifestyle of helplessness and defeat. When in that state of pessimism, they have few coping resources to pull themselves out of depression toward inner control and more successful living. Professional help and medication may be required to overcome chronic pessimism and depression.

The key for those who are successful at growing through the adversities of life is the ability to visualize yourself as the person you want to be in the various roles you want to play with significant others — professionally, socially, personally, and privately. Positive visual imaging is a technique used by many therapists to help people achieve personal and professional growth. It is also being recognized, even by some in the medical community, for its power to aid in healing physical disease. Medical research is proving that many diseases and even surgical wounds are relieved quicker when patients are confident that their caregivers are providing treatment that will be successful. Faith often works, even when the medication is a placebo. Scientific evidence shows that we can control more of our biological being than we usually do, if we apply conscious effort and thought.

Whatever the interpersonal role you seek with another person is, being able to see yourself as successfully performing in that situation is important to your chance of achieving the goal. Conversely, if you cannot see yourself as successfully performing, then, guess what? Chances are the goal will be further from reality. The key is expectation, belief, or faith that what you want will happen. Do you honestly believe a healthy, intimate relationship is possible with your partner? Do you have a clear image of what a healthy ad hoc relationship is? Can you see yourself living in harmony with that person? Can you imagine meeting each other's physical, intellectual, emotional, and spiritual needs, growing, and learning together? A clear and affirmative yes to these questions helps assure you of a successful relationship. If you cannot, in all honesty, see yourself in the role you want chances are less that you will ever achieve it.

The next chapter will build more fully on this background of how we got to where we are. But, you will learn that you do not have to stay there. You can work at overcoming a dysfunctional family, develop self esteem, and grow toward the potential for joyful, complete, and abundant life the creator intended for you. No matter what our family of origin was like, we can let go of the past and learn to develop more healthy ad hoc relationships. They lead to more healthy families and happier lives.

To quote the opening comments of welcome that start off meetings of Codependents Anonymous: "No matter how traumatic your past or despairing your present may seem, there is the hope of a new day. No longer need you rely upon others as a power greater than yourself. May you instead find here a new strength to be that which God intended for you - Precious and Free."

The way in which the outer world affects and alters our makeup and adult behavior is the subject of the next chapter. In addition to some additional concepts about relations with siblings and parents, the chapter discusses the larger social influence that helps to mold the assumptions and behavior that we bring to ad hoc relationships. In particular, it focuses upon the social changes that accelerated during the baby boom generation that reshaped our national culture in the 20th century.

Two:

Overcoming Social Factors

This chapter discusses additional common family and social factors that I have learned make us what we are as adults, and points to more healthy approaches to resolution. It also discusses how several aspects of the cultural and social environment in which we grew up are changing. I am presenting this material to help you understand how you got to where you are, and its impact on all your relationships, so that you will not put all the blame on your unsuspecting parents and care givers. The chapter includes a forecast of the possibility of a better future in loving relationships. Finally, it presents some effective ways of putting the past behind us so we can develop more healthy, intimate relationships in the new ad hoc culture.

Before the feminist movement got rolling in the 1960s, complementary gender assignments prevailed. People assumed that women would be concerned about the welfare of others, more nurturing, more emotionally sensitive, more interpersonally expressive, and economically dependent. People assumed men would be more assertive and controlling, more independent, more self-sufficient and self-confident, and more rationally objective, and the head of the household. There were firmly established gender roles. Men were expected to pursue, protect, and provide for women. Women were expected to stimulate, acknowledge, and nurture men. Some experts believe these are basic genetic gender traits that we have inherited from our cave dwelling ancestors. Outside was man's work and inside was woman's work. This model of relationships was offered by Marabel Morgan in her best selling book, *The Total Woman,* published in 1973 as a backlash to the feminist movement. However, feminist movement leaders successfully held that the benefits of this model did not overcome its burdens, which were demeaning and stifling for women. Now, both genders can decide for themselves where they are and how much they wish to change. Perhaps this chapter will help you prepare your own plan for future growth in all aspects of wholeness, physically, emotionally, intellectually, and spiritually.

Normal Dysfunctional Families

Every family functions as a system. In every family, dependent children exhibit different roles to survive and carry out all the functions needed by the family system. What affects one member affects them all. Unfortunately, the roles of family members have been shifting dramatically since 1960. Since then, the feminist movement has been changing the ratio of power between men and women, husbands and wives, toward more equality. These shifts have created uncertainty about their future roles for both male and female children, so many are drifting through their youth with fuzzy role models from both genders. From dysfunctional families come dysfunctional parents.

In every family, children adopt or exhibit certain behavior to cope with their perceived circumstances. Typical family roles of children, as defined by Hemfelt, *et al,* are the **Hero,** the **Scapegoat,** the **Mascot,** and the **Lost Child.** These are not necessarily healthy patterns of behavior, but they are found in most families and are, therefore, considered normal in this present culture. A brief description of them may help you understand and recall how you developed the role that you played in your family.

The **Hero** is the trustworthy, conscientious, mature, capable, healthy kid who gets straight A's and/or excels at sports. He/she is the glue who helps by doing laundry, fixing meals, minding smaller kids (he/she usually is the oldest) and taking up the slack when the parents don't have it all together. The **Scapegoat** is the black sheep, the restless, nonconforming "bad seed" who is misunderstood even when he/she tries to be reliable. The **Mascot** is the family clown who tries to make everyone forget that life hurts sometimes and makes the tension bearable by grabbing for attention. The **Lost or Left Out Child** is just not there, but is usually off in her/his room or out in the garage playing or working alone. These roles are found in many American families. They are not healthy because they prevent the kids from finding out whom they really are. In addition, another role is added in a dysfunctional family, that of Enabler.

The **Enabler** supplies the yeast that keeps the dysfunction fueled. Enablers lie, deny, and clean up the messes the sick members are making constantly. They can change their behavior as the situation demands to support the dysfunction. At various times they assume the subroles of placater, martyr, rescuer, persecutor, and victim. Enablers also develop a distorted relationship with God, or their spiritual life. As adults, they may have a detailed intellectual grasp of religious scripture. Their idea of God is one who demands legalism, perfectionism, self-sacrifice, and self-abuse. They produce whatever behavior will prove their worthiness because they think, in their own hearts, they are worthless. This is the only way they can find to survive the dysfunctional situations in which they must live.

Elements of various religious levels exist throughout our culture, and they affect how people behave in families, among occupations, and in wider social involvement. Religious beliefs influence children during formative years of development. Each level of religious belief can be a source of both freedom and enslavement, depending on how it is practiced in society. Parents who impose their religious views (whatever they are) on their children without attention to their needs for love, acceptance, and self esteem, create spiritual holes in their offspring who emerge as immature, codependent adults.

Several common faulty parenting behaviors can warp a child's sense of self worth. They often set children up for a life of painful, unconscious attempts to overcome them. Some additional faulty parenting behaviors, described by Kevin Leman, are: **perfectionist** parents who are strong on performance, discipline, and criticism; **authoritarian** parents who are always barking orders and commands, always on the child's back; **over permissive and over submissive** parents who let the child rule the roost; **overindulgent** parents who substitute gifts for love; **abusive** parents who both physically and verbally motivate with guilt and fear; **neglectful** parents who don't share feelings and just can't be bothered with their children; **incestuous** parents who abuse their children to meet sick physical and emotional needs, and **rejecting** parents who refuse to accept their children in any way. Elements of all these faulty behaviors are part of the baggage we all carry for life, and that we try to overcome in relations with others as adults.

Birth order also may have something to say about our adult behavior in close relationships. The implications of sibling position were documented from thorough research by Dr. Walter Toman, a German psychologist, in the early 1960s. Not only is sibling position important, it is interrelated with that of the parents as well. **First borns** and only children often are perfectionistic, reliable, conscientious, list makers, well organized, critical, serious, and scholarly. They are eager to please, goal oriented, and respectful of authority. (That's me.) **Middle** children tend to be mediators, conflict avoiders, and independent, with extreme loyalty to their peer group, with many friends. **Last borns** often are manipulative, charming, able to blame others easily, good at showing off, people persons, good at persuasion, precocious, engaging.

Since the primary relationship with infantile care givers serves as a model for all others, its flaws interfere with normal adult pair bonding. However gifted, people with narcissistic wounds may cause serious problems in social structures, families, work groups, clubs, societies, etc. They may never be capable of healthy love because they were not able to give up infantile self love that is absolutely necessary in order to survive. If they become parents, they may transfer their dysfunction onto their children through their controlling attempts to recover their lost dependency. For narcissistic parents, children become extensions of themselves instead of independent and separate individuals. Healing the narcissistic wound that many people endure enables the wounded adult to give and to receive love unconditionally. Healthy relationships require an appropriate balance between self love and object love. However, unless they find a substitute for the missing primitive parental connection that provides a corrective emotional experience, the prognosis for narcissistic wounded individuals is poor.

It may be helpful for intimate partners to come from different places in birth order, because they can complement each other if they have opposite tendencies. For example, if firstborns match up with last borns, the last borns get somebody more responsible for taking care of things. The firstborns get someone more carefree to lighten up life. Middle children often make great partners because they know how to hang in there from the experience of being sandwiched between older and younger siblings with opposite tendencies. They learned how to survive while being overlooked. Potential for problems between partners are: middles and middles sometimes are too peaceful, too accommodating; babies and babies may not take care of necessary details like paying the bills; firstborns and onlys may have too little fun and compete for leadership with no one following. Understanding these birth order influences and narcissistic wounds can help you understand and accept different patterns of behavior with intimate partners.

As an adult child, the task is to live without all the answers to the mysteries of life. You can choose a lifestyle that will enable you to continue on your own path of growth and development as a whole person. You can avoid being stuck in your current stage of development for the rest of your life. While the outcome cannot be foretold, with enough determination and persistence, we can learn to enjoy the process of life in the present moment, each moment, for the rest of our lives without knowing all the answers. However, learning something about how we got to where we are as individuals in our society may make the task easier and help you to make more effective choices. I shall now turn to some social issues that have helped to shape the culture in which we grew up in this country. These issues also helped to make you what you are.

Where We Were

Besides what happened inside the structure of our family, the influence of the outer social world also helped to create who we are now. We unconsciously integrated much of this influence into our behavior as adults. By bringing these issues into consciousness, we can choose more rationally how we want them to affect our lives from now on. How we absorb the main aspects of life including social, political, religious, economic, and family events during our years between 10 and 20 tends to stay with us the rest of our lives. This concept helps explain why boomers who matured in the decade of the `60s have a different set of values from those maturing in the `50s or the `80s. Their tastes in music, religion, politics, and lifestyle are different. They will bring differing patterns of behavior to any relationship.

We can change our learned values, but it usually takes a significant emotional event to stimulate the motivation to change our basic beliefs. Loss of a primary intimate relationship through death or divorce or breakup, and the task of social reconstruction afterward, is such a watershed event. While people are in denial of their unhealthy condition, growth is impossible. When the denial is stripped away, a conscious confrontation with your codependence, narcissistic, or addictive behavior is another significant and painful emotional event. Psychotherapy also can enable a self-induced basis for changing basic beliefs, but it is too expensive for many people.

Social changes also affect who we are now. We can divide the current national population into three groups: (1) the preboomers who were born before 1945, (2) the boomers born in the baby boom between 1945 and 1965, and (3) the postboomers born to the boomers.

The pre-boomers had their youth usurped by the years of depression in the 1930s and the years of war during the 1940s. They wanted their post-war children to enjoy a life free of all forms of suffering, and they granted them privileges that would change culture dramatically. They indulged their children's whims and desires, and scarcely over disciplined them for even the most self-destructive behavior.

People who reached maturity in the boomer era after World War II created a different way of life than their parents were used to when they were single. Consequently, the boomers are a bridge generation seeking personal growth and self indulgence without self-imposed limits and tolerance for delayed gratification that their parents failed to pass on to them. Their influence has changed western society dramatically, even flaunting disregard of established legal limits without regard for the future implications of their behavior. Therefore, their children, generation X, or the post-boomers, live in a different world than their grandparents did.

Four major social developments occurred during the last half of the 1960 decade that have had a revolutionary impact on lifestyles ever since:

1. the availability of the birth control pill that removed the threat of unwanted parenthood from casual sexual encounters,
2. legal interpretation by the Supreme Court of freedom of the press to allow a more open, liberal portrayal of sex in the communications media,
3. the challenge to authority and established institutions (including traditional patriarchal families) growing out of the controversy over the Vietnam War, the assassination of President Kennedy in 1963, the Watergate scandal, and
4. the economic and social impact of the womens' equality movement, along with loss of family stability and social acceptance of the increasing rate of divorce.

Most boomer adults born between 1945 and 1965 were raised by traditional parents. However, the combination of decline in reliability of traditional national and family institutions and the shattering of family structures created a new culture of individualism that leads many people into depression, according to Martin Seligman. Many women of the boomer generation now live in a state of stressful conflict that pulls them toward individual independence, while they still are driven by the traditional values and dependent life tapes of the past. According to Doris Bernstein, many of them show up in her counseling chambers, trying to reconcile the difference between the role models presented by their homemaking mothers and their economically competitive peers. For many, pursuing a career in the competitive world of men is not an option if their families are to enjoy a decent standard of living. However, their economic need often conflicts with their feminine instinct to mate and mother children for over 20 years of their lives. Bernstein says this conflict is likely to produce guilt in boomer women, no matter which role they choose, especially among those with more rigid superegos.

Men of the boomer generation are wrestling with their femininity and the women are wrestling with their masculinity, both of which were denied before. The Department of Labor reported that 50 percent of women with children under one year of age worked at full time jobs in 1994. Children of these parents are being raised by professional day care centers, leaving much to be desired in cultural and family values among the young. Together, these mothers are a transitional generation in our culture, bridging the past to the future. Some social studies have indicated the impact of single parenting on children results in much higher teen pregnancy, more school drop outs, lower income prospects, and higher crime. Absentee parenting appears to be taking its toll on the next generation.

Those who matured after 1980 are parts of a new postboomer generation X that lives with a new set of values and behavioral skills. Older traditions of their preboomer grandparents have faded and no longer influence their lives much. The newer lifestyles now must be reconciled with the traditional roles passed down from previous generations.

Many people still thought that complementarity was the basis for a successful marriage, going into the 1960s. Each partner had certain roles to fulfill and each assumed responsibility for their differing contribution to the union. If each partner accepted his/her role, the relationship was stable. Many remained so for a lifetime, since neither partner wanted a shift in their roles. Studies showed the ideal self of men to be competitive and exploitative and that of women to be docile and dependent. Consistency in the enactment and acceptance of the socially assigned roles was necessary to avoid conflicting interactions and to maintain marital stability. With the changed perceived self image that began in the feminist movement of the late 1960s, a form of relationship based on sexual equality began to revolutionize western society.

By 1965, studies showed that many women thought the traditional form of marriage discriminated against them. The feminist leaders saw traditional male-female roles in marriage as denying the personhood of the woman. Consequently, the boomers saw the family life of their parents as outmoded and needing changes to redefine the roles of women. The feminist movement gave women permission as individuals to discover their own path to life satisfaction instead of having it defined for them by society.

Many women who matured after 1975 have adapted readily to their new freedoms and social equality with men. But many men still are restrained from changing by the traditional sexist roles of the past. I believe many boomer people of both sexes are caught in the conflict between their traditional upbringing and the new diversity in lifestyles. If you learned traditional model roles, were married, or out of the singles life for other reasons during this period of major social changes, you may find it difficult to adjust to the changed social life and uninhibited dating behavior as a single person. As you meet these changes, you may need to decide how much motivation you have for changing to catch up with the times.

Carol Becker has shown that many women find unexpected surprises in their new search for equality. Along with the career options they brought, social changes demanded by feminists also brought new responsibilities for taking care of themselves that some women underestimated. As the option to work has turned into the necessity to work, many women have felt double duty imposed upon them as homemaking still requires much of their free time after the work day is finished. While some men have become more equal partners in homemaking and childcare, others have not assumed the new complementary roles that women expected of them. While women want their men to feel comfortable if they wear pants, they still have difficulty with men who want to wear dresses. When their own biological nature betrays them, some women wonder if benefits gained by the feminist movement have been worth the burdens. Becker refers to the "necessity to struggle" to overcome their native tendencies if the feminist ideal is to be achieved. When women feel deprived of intimacy, tenderness, compassion and eroticism, they often regress to "type" and become dependent and cling to unhealthy relationships.

In spite of the changes, I think social conditioning in our culture still programs males and females differently. Men were to be active in the world, to dominate, to make things happen. Males still are taught to be macho, violent, and warlike by the public media, including magazines, movies, and television, and by some male spokesmen. Men must be tall, strong, financially powerful, logical, hairy, rugged, emotionally tough, and have a sense of humor. In short, they must play their genetic gender role of pursuing, protecting, and providing for women.

Many women still are being taught to be the opposites of men; nurturing and comforting, smooth, sexy, tender, feeling, hairless, shorter, loving, beautiful, domestic, giving, etc., in short to play their genetic gender role of stimulating, acknowledging, and nurturing men. However, they are trying to overlay their genetics with new masculine roles as career professionals in competition with men simultaneously. Unfortunately, social values are changing much more rapidly than human genetic structure can. The result is considerable social ambivalence between the sexes.

Warren Farrell cites dozens of current situations that he says illustrate the myth of male power. Some very unusual social changes are being perpetrated by this generation in the name of female equality. For example, judges in California must inform juries that they must convict a male rape suspect on the testimony of a female accuser without any corroborating evidence. And, the supreme court of New Jersey overturned six centuries of English common law when it permitted a single mother to give her surname to the child instead of that of the father.

Farrell says that males and females are driven by genetic roles that originated with our cave dwelling ancestors. The male role is to pursue, protect, and provide for females, as I noted above. The traditional female role is to stimulate bravado, acknowledge male accomplishment (read cheer at athletic contests), and nurture families. While women have been working on freeing themselves to choose new roles, many still cling to their genetic inheritance. A Louis Harris random poll in 1995 conducted for the Families and Work Institute disclosed that if money were not a consideration, 33 percent of women would like to work only part time, 31 percent would prefer to work at home caring for a family full time, 20 percent would select volunteer service, and only 15 percent would choose to work full time. When asked to define success, 48 percent mentioned either having good family relationships or having happy, well adjusted children.

Similarly, men have not moved very far from their masculine genetic roles. They still want to pursue, provide, and protect, and most women like it that way, according to a special "Frontline" report by the Public Broadcasting Service (5/16/95).

Although a few men have filed sexual harassment complaints, overtures from females are more likely to be taken as a compliment than an insult by heterosexual men. Just as it was with the cave dwellers, women still encourage and entice men to pursue them so they can have the option to choose who will carry on their genes through reproduction. Women still permit their kind to be used as sex objects in advertising and entertainment, while men still permit themselves to be used as sex objects in competitive sports and business.

While men are still compulsively fighting to protect women, feminist women are fighting only to protect themselves. In many legal ways, government has assumed the male role of protecting women, although I expect those who have found their standard of living reduced by a judge after a divorce would disagree. Although there are exceptions, women still have not achieved true equality in the workplace in both compensation and assignment. Women Navy fighter pilots not withstanding, Farrell points out that men still perform most of the life threatening jobs while women perform most of the nurturing jobs, while still pursuing equality.

Frank Pittmen divides the current generation of men into three camps: **Philanderers,** those who can only prove to themselves they are men by sleeping with as many cooperative women as possible; **Contenders,** who set up contest after contest whether on the golf course, in the board room, on the sports field, or at the local pub, to prove they are men worthy of procreation; and **Controllers,** who think that dominion of people and things was passed on from God to Adam to Dad to them. All three of these archetypes merely are the ways 21st century man tries to win mating rights with a female - not too much differently than the way male animals compete for their genetic place in reproduction. The difference is that laws on abortion and availability of contraceptives make it much easier for women to choose among their suitors without regard to any of the above. They make up their own rules intuitively that shift with time and circumstance, leaving men almost completely bewildered as was Freud so many years ago. He said that after working with women in therapy for 30 years, he still did not understand them. Gender confusion abounds, and anxiety drives many singles and couples into therapy to find the solutions.

Although the postboomer generation is trying to balance the social roles between the sexes more, some people are over correcting. Some men are denying their genetics and becoming masochistic, leaning too much on women for their security and appearing to be wimps. Some women are adopting masculine aggressiveness and hyper-sexuality, relying too much on careers for personal happiness and fulfillment. In trying to reverse their traditional gender roles arbitrarily, some couples often create uncertainty, pain, and conflict for both partners and complete confusion for their children.

Marion Solomon noted from troubled couples who come to her therapy chamber, that both genders are making impossibly conflicting demands on each other. She notes that women say they want their men to be aggressive, ambitious, financially successful, tender, strong and sensitive, supportive, friendly, and a gentle but ardent lover. She observes men want their women to be slender, attractive, well groomed, have a stimulating career, be socially sophisticated, feminine, athletic, a caring mother by day and a sexual dynamo at night. Obviously, these impossibly idealized standards are full of contradictions. Social standards of behavior that have been passed down through the generations cannot be replaced in a single generation without trauma and stress.

Equality of power also implies equality of responsibility. Thus, women who want their men to assume family obligations must also assume commensurate career obligations. Although it may be naive to assume equality in all respects, the modern opinion of many people is that if either sex has the ability and the desire to pursue a goal, be it baking, oil drilling, nursing, engineering, or flying fighter planes, they should have equal opportunity of access. However, I think people of each sex are unequal from each other in many different ways, despite gender. No two people have exactly the same set of talents and gifts. What is more ethical than attempting to be unrealistically equal may be being absolutely fair with each other. If one is more equipped to handle the finances than the other, the couple gains if the better equipped partner does the bookkeeping, despite gender. If one prefers gardening and the other cooking, the relationship and both partners gain when gender does not control how the work is divided among them. I do not think family roles should be driven strictly by gender roles anymore.

However, freedom is a two-edged sword. Freedom to be yourself also implies granting freedom to your partner to be her/him self as well. It also means being willing to lead sometimes and follow sometimes. Some people are reluctant to lead for fear of rejection, fear of failure, fear of being conspicuous, fear of the competition, fear of blame, fear of responsibility, and fear of our partner's anger. Some are reluctant to follow for fear they won't get their needs met, fear of being over controlled, fear of being embarrassed, and fear of giving up control that really is fear of losing self. By developing unshakable self esteem, we can overcome these fears and enjoy the dance of intimacy that comes with freedom of release from sexual stereotype roles.

Changing Family Values

The definition and structure of families in our country have been changing. The "National Report on Work & Family," published by Buraff Publications, reports that less than 10 percent of the United States population now lives in the "Ozzie and Harriet" two-parent family where Dad is the sole financial support and Mother is a full time homemaker. At the end of 1987, 72 percent of women with children between ages six and 17 were in the workforce, according to this report. During the 1980s, the number of working women with children under one year of age increased 70 percent. Single parents with children are so prevalent that local housing codes are being changed to permit higher density house sharing among single parents. The "DINK" (Dual Income No Kids) family has driven prices up in many urban areas, making it difficult for a single person or single-wage-earner family to buy a car or a house. It is necessary for both parents to work in many families with children, making it impossible for many mothers who want to be home with their young children to do so. It is impossible to tell which came first, the extra income of two working mates that drove up prices, or the higher costs that require two working mates.

Some men are redefining parenting roles and assuming a greater share of domestic duties, but studies show many women still feel more help from males is needed. Many working couples are confronting major relocation conflicts as both pursue independent careers, sometimes in different places. The children of many dual wage earners are being raised by surrogate parents and teachers in day care centers and schools, where professional care takers have replaced parental guidance, mentoring, and discipline. Admittedly, some of these new care givers are better trained at parenting than the blood parents are. More people in their prime are caring for elderly, often disabled, parents and relatives. What do these changes say about the dysfunctions in family relations being experienced by children who will be the adults of the 21st century? How can today's parents prepare their children for healthy, intimate relationships? What kind of model does today's family present to its children? Is it better or worse than the family structure of past generations? Only the future will tell.

Many boomer women have gained all the stress of economic competition but haven't yet gained equal pay for equal work, and they haven't been released from the traditional homemaking role either. While they want their men to be more nurturing and expressive than their fathers, they also want the economic benefits that come with financial independence. No matter how much professional success she achieves, the boomer woman may still want a man she can depend upon and look up to, like the model lifestyle her mother may have enjoyed. Some boomer men find their demands too big of a challenge and avoid such women, who they find intimidating and castrating. On the other hand, modern society has removed most of the challenges men used to risk in order to prove their manhood, i.e., their right to pursue, protect, and provide. While many women have enthusiastically embraced their new freedoms, some men have been unable to adjust to the new demands on them created by the economically and sexually liberated woman. Both sexes often are unfulfilled in their ad hoc relationships. Consequently, the relationship options for both boomer sexes are significantly more limited than they expected, without appropriate ways of meeting their biological roles.

In addition, cultural pressure on females and their biological system also push some women toward being wives of successful men and mothers of healthy children. The thought of relaxing any of their newly recognized career attributes to be mothers and homemakers makes some of them feel anxious, depressed and confused. As the confusion and ambivalence builds, both genders become numb to their own individual emotional needs. Such troubled men and women must ask themselves what they really want, how can they get it, and are they willing to pay what it will cost. Until the benefits and burdens of their options are sorted out, they remain in anxious conflict, possibly without understanding why. While a new standard of gender-based behavior is being worked out by the postboomers now entering adulthood, it is far from being universally established yet. In the meantime, role confusion and mutual frustration abound to stress gender differences.

There is just now the barest beginning of a comparable movement among men in this culture to balance the womens' equality movement. But the best mens' councils can do is try to recapture the hunter-warrior by going out to the woods on a weekend to beat drums and sit together naked in sweat lodges. When they return to their partners on Sunday evening, they resume their traditional roles of pursuer, protector, and provider and get conflicting signals from women about what they really want from their men. Some men are discovering mounting frustration, weariness and loneliness, and the statistical expectation of dying seven years before their female partners. While women rapidly have been changing their roles, boomer men have been replaying the adult tapes laid down by their fathers and grandfathers. Therefore, men often are confused about the roles they now encounter in intimate relationships. Boomer men who carry the behavioral tapes of their fathers and are thrust into the singles world through death or divorce may not know quite how to behave around the new woman. There is no longer a standard male role or behavior that is preferred by every woman. Each encounter with a new partner is an entirely new slate, with the opportunity for writing unlimited options upon it.

Implications for Change

Implications for changing lifestyles resulted from basic developments in morals, ethics, and economic aspects of social conditioning during the rapid changes of the last half of this century. Absolute authority for what was believed to be good, bad, right and wrong was questioned and repositioned in many areas of life. Your own beliefs about moral standards may be called into question and may need to be reevaluated considering the new gender reality of your life.

In the postboomer singles world, there are temporary ad hoc relationships, short-term ad hoc relationships, and long term ad hoc relationships. Any one of these types can be committed or uncommitted, sexual or platonic. Within these diverse relationships, the degree of intimacy can range from very little, as in business or professional encounters; to some, as in social encounters; to more, as in personal encounters; and to the ultimate, as in private encounters. The longer the term of the relationship, the more likely couples will experience challenges such as conflicts, despair, death, hard times, and peak enjoyment. The social removal of any stigma related to divorce has made it much easier for either partner to walk away when things get burdensome, i.e, when the burdens exceed the benefits.

Our geographic mobility and changing high-tech economy now force many people to search for intimate relationships more in short term friendships without the comfort of traditional long-term commitments. These ad hoc, disposable relationships can provide a certain richness to life. They provide new insights and perceptions in varied and unrestricted situations. They are like beautiful, fragrant flowers, to be enjoyed during their season, and then remembered for the joy they brought to us in their time. They are not burdened with the mutual dependencies of past committed relationships that were closed to outsiders. A certain erotic excitement, novelty, and zest for life are gained as we admit new people into our intimate boundaries.

However, the price children may pay for this repetitive excitement and individual freedom is the loss of traditional feelings of comfort and security that were obtained in the more rooted families of the past. Such a loss can cause mourning and a feeling of bereavement, extending into adulthood. Also, there is the need to replace transient relationships with new acquaintances periodically. We must develop internal resources of personal strength and courage to withstand the inevitable losses of these disposable relationships, if their benefits are to outweigh their burdens. As the stability of former roots is shattered, we must learn how to find new roots in transient relationships more quickly because of how temporary they are. Unfortunately, children do not have such resiliency, and often are harmed by disruptions of their nuclear family.

It also is much more difficult to choose a suitable intimate partner than it formerly was due to the many optional lifestyles now socially accepted. You might try to recall the social, political, economic, religious, and family aspects of your life during your teenage years. Compare those aspects to those of the people you sense as potential partners to understand them, and your new relationships, better. Only you can decide if the benefits of changing your basic beliefs that drive your behavior exceed the burdens involved – physical, intellectual, emotional, and spiritual.

All of life is meeting problems, solving some of them, and living with the others. We can only choose, accept the consequences of our choice, and choose again. The results are now ours to control. We are given the choice to withdraw to solitude and become a recluse, or to be open to a growing self, a renewing life, open to others, open to a new experience. All lifestyles have their advantages and disadvantages. Many famous, creative people marshaled their strength after dysfunctional parenting and troubling losses by withdrawing. In solitude, they produced some of the world's great art, music, and literature. Still others found the motivation for great creativity through loving, intimate relationships. Both options are painful and neither openness nor isolation can meet all of our needs by itself. Some of the choice is based on inherited traits now known to be transmitted through the genetic structure of human cells, where ultimate intelligence is thought to reside. Other aspects will be based on how we perceive the benefits and burdens of each choice as it is presented to us.

Moving Beyond The Past

Marion Solomon observes that everyone has normal dependency needs, and to seek mutual independence as a remedy for our family issues can often lead to isolation, unhappiness, and depression. She suggests that although recovery from codependency requires disengagement from unhealthy behavior, unfortunately, the important, primary, unchanging need for healthy dependency and for enduring, committed involvement has been lost in the recovery movement. As a solution, Solomon calls for a more balanced approach to mutual interdependence between partners who recognize that they can and must fulfill as much of each other's needs as possible if the relationship is to thrive and survive normal crises. Although everyone can point to significant dysfunctional aspects of their childhoods, it is only through the mutual caring (not care taking) of two committed partners that true self esteem and personal growth can flower. Psychic wounds develop within relationships, and healing of those wounds also requires relationships.

In recovery from dysfunctional role models, people can be divided into three groups: the eye-openers, the pioneers, and the mutual partners. A brief summary of these groups, provided by Emily Marlin, follows. Perhaps you may see yourself in one or more of them, because each of us usually exhibits some traits in all three categories.

Eye-Openers

- have decided to stop the old, self-destructive ways of thinking and behaving that gets in the way of healthy intimate relationships,
- have chosen to seek help in support groups, individual, or group therapy and begin a program of individual recovery,
- sometimes still deny the effects of a dysfunctional childhood and previous relationships and their effect on everyone close,
- no longer pretend there is not a problem,
- don't talk much,
- trust very little,

- begin to recognize both their positive and negative inner feelings,
- feel confused much of the time,
- feel angry much of the time, and
- sometimes feel ambivalent about their recovery process.

Pioneers

- have decided to look at themselves and focus on the qualities they already like and those they want to improve,
- continue to work on getting better through the help of their recovery programs,
- work hard to discover and establish their personal identities,
- are developing a deeper understanding of their dysfunctional life training and its effect on friends, family, lovers, co-workers, and spouses,
- wonder whether they have become too close or too distant from other people,
- often feel lonely and afraid,
- make mistakes but still feel ok about themselves,
- learn to accept themselves and others as they are,
- try to share their feelings with other people,
- persevere courageously through their recovery and growth.

Mutual Partners

- try to listen carefully to their own instincts as well as the voices of significant others,
- have internalized many lessons from their individual recovery programs,
- continue to grow and to change all the time,
- honestly and openly trust, talk, and feel;
- take action to try to resolve conflicts,
- take reasonable risks and make decisions,
- don't blame themselves or others for their circumstances,
- work on a healthy balance between closeness and distance, i.e., autonomy and belonging, with other people;
- are bound to significant others through commitment, common goals, and communication;
- enjoy themselves, their lives, and their progress, painful though it might be.

We have seen that all are shaped somewhat by cultural experiences, social conditioning, and religious beliefs. Theologians with conservative Christian beliefs describe us as born in a condition of separateness that can only be cured by a spiritual relationship with a Savior. New Age believers and modern ego psychologists say we are born whole and complete in the image of our creator. Very early, faulty parenting and adult role modeling cover our pure native essence with a defiled social personality and create holes in our makeup. They believe we get cut off from consciousness of our essence or complete being. Either way, the child within us is left with incomplete needs (psychologists call it unsatisfied narcissistic hunger) that we carry all our lives, driving our behavior like a tape recorder, trying to get our holes filled any way we can.

Hope for the Future

The experience and trends of the past are not necessarily trend lines into the future. John Naisbitt and Patricia Aburdene developed a method of looking at possible future social trends through what they call content analysis of the news media. They identified 10 trends that they think will shape our social world, as we move into the third millennium after the year 2000. Here is a list of the trends that Naisbitt and Aburdene see as the most important to our foreseeable future:

1. The Booming Global Economy of the 1990s
2. A Renaissance in the Arts
3. The Emergence of Free-Market Socialism
4. Global Lifestyles and Cultural Nationalism
5. The Privatization of the Welfare State
6. The Rise of the Pacific Rim Nations
7. The Decade of Women in Leadership
8. The Age of Biology
9. The Religious Revival of the New Millennium
10. The Triumph of the Individual

Certain words from the Introduction to this book are significant and I am given to quote them here for you, before going on.

> *"We cannot understand the Megatrends of the 1990s without acknowl-edging the metaphorical and spiritual significance of the millennium. – we must recognize its power to evoke our most positive, powerful visions alongside our most terrifying nightmares. – the millennium is reemerging as the metaphor for the future. Among nations, the desire for economic cooperation is stronger than the urge for military adventure with its huge human and financial costs. Like the ancient drama [of Eden] the modern millennium ignites our vision for a better world alongside our nightmares of the world's end. When we think of the 21st century, we think technolo-gy: space travel, biotechnology, robots. We are drowning in information and starved for knowledge. — many groups set their goals with reference to the year 2000, goals for ending hunger, a drug-free society, a cure for cancer. The wider our horizons and the more powerful our technology, the greater we have come to value the individual. The important thing is to craft your own world view, your own set of Megatrends to guide your work, ideals, relationships, and contributions to society. Though we will be guided by revived spirituality, the answers must come from us. Apocalypse or Golden Age. The choice is ours."*

The one trend I will comment on is "The Triumph of the Individual." I believe our technological successes have bred a generation of people starving for human contact. Robert Ornstein and Charles Swencionis have compiled a litany of the mind-body relationship as it is affecting some new thought in medicine. To quote them directly:

> *"There is no disease that kills people at the rate that loneliness does. At all ages, for both sexes and all races in the United States, the single, wid-owed, and divorced die at rates two to ten times higher than do married*

people younger than 70. People genuinely need each other. Yet, as a society we are moving away from traditions that have evolved over centuries to provide human contact and friendship for the lonely. The damage that social upheaval, conflict, and loss cause may be remediable by (medicine) to some degree, but such dislocation might also be prevented by improving social networks. When disconnected people band together and develop (intimate) ties, their health improves. Forming and maintaining social support is very important to our health."

Sometime ahead, men and women may learn to be more comfortable with the opposite-sex tendencies in each of them after this period of transition. Attitudes of both sexes may fall more in line with the social declaration of equality made by *Cosmopolitan* editor Helen Gurley Brown in 1963, although letting go of old expectations and replacing them with new ones is very difficult to do. In ancient Chinese philosophy, the Yin and the Yang describe this quality of opposites. Carl Jung called it the Animus in women, and the Anima in men. Being whole, balanced, and complete includes accepting that opposite sex part of us. Some beginnings for men are emerging, and these may grow dramatically during the next century. For that to happen, men must learn the lesson that women did long ago: it is OK to have intimate, noncompetitive, platonic relationships with other members of the same sex.

When we place responsibility for all our difficulties on our parents or somebody else, we think we are victims and powerless. When we become empowered enough to assume the responsibility for changing what we don't like in our lives, true growth really is possible. Although we are different, I believe men and women really are not enemies. The sooner we learn that, the faster we will be at peace with ourselves and at peace in our ad hoc relationships. We are only human beings doing the best that we can. Until both men and women feel good about themselves, we will continue to hurt each other. We all must put down our magnifying glasses and pick up our mirrors, then work on improving what we see. We are learning that we can only be in control of what we do and what we are. We cannot control others.

Some experts think that like attracts like and others say that opposites attract. It seems that our mental state is what sets up our relationships. If we come to a relationship with hostility, that is what we are likely to attract. If we come to another person with love and acceptance, we are more likely to attract love and acceptance. Our beliefs about them determine what we see in others. I believe our thoughts create our reality. If we believe that they are bad, we will see the bad. If we believe they are good, we will see the good, and when we give what we want, I believe we receive what we want; it is our choice. We may be surprised how our relationships improve when we become a lover instead of a complainer. An encouraging trend in healthy family development is the popularity of family workshops; demand is growing for knowledge about healthy families.

Encouraging as these hopes for the future may be, we must live in the present. When we look for an intimate relationship, we tend to be attracted to people who can fill the gaps in our own makeup, i.e., those who tend to make us feel whole and complete where we are now in our path of growth and development. Nevertheless, after her comprehensive look at human evolution, Helen Fisher forecasts that most women will continue to work and thereby assure their financial independence from marriage bondage. They will continue to confuse men by demanding both softness and vulnerability, as well as financial security and protection simultaneously. Men will confuse women by wanting their equal help in earning a living, while still being sexy, nurturing, and good mothers simultaneously. People will marry later than they did in the postwar recovery years of the late '40s and '50s, making it more difficult for the genders to compromise their wants with imperfect reality. Both genders will feel shame thinking they do not measure up. In response, both genders will act tense and controlling. Both may think there is no way out.

The longer they stay together and the more children they have, the less likely married couples will divorce, but they will have fewer children and defer them until careers and finances are relatively settled. More people will choose to remain single, and they will experience several ad-hoc relationships. Men will still say, "What do women want?" and women will still say, "They just don't understand." Women and men will realize their differences more consciously, communications will improve, and each gender will gain more respect and acceptance of the other. And yet, when our progeny look back on these times they may say, as we can, the more things change, the more they stay the same. However, if you learn what is in the rest of this book, you will be much better equipped to share in the healthy ad hoc relationships that you deserve.

In summary, the pre-boomer generation relied heavily on mutual complementarity in their intimate relationships. Most of them were consummated in a marriage wherein the husband was the main breadwinner and the wife was the main homemaker. Their boomer children added a lot of variety to their definition of complementarity and added a significant amount of romance to their relationships. They tested the feasibility of non-marital alternatives, but many found the burdens exceeded the benefits. However, their post-boomer children have carried these developments to another stage. Although they have redefined complementarity to be any variety of pairing that works in the short run, they still hang onto romance, but give both partners equal freedom of expression. In addition, Shervert H. Frazier has noted that they added a new dimension by seeking a new form of psychological wholeness in relationships. This new dimension of intimacy places more stress on men to reframe their behavior to meet the desires of women on their terms. Some might argue that women have lost more than they gained through achieving equality, but others claim there is still much need for continued pressure in that direction.

Mary Pipher illustrated the importance of having a well grounded sense of self in order to develop individually without being corrupted by the cultural influence of the times. From the many examples of troubled young women that she treated, her conclusion follows: "Early adolescence is when many battles for the self are won and lost. These are hard fights, and the losses and victories determine to a great extent the quality of future lives." Her analysis shows that only those with highly developed self awareness are likely to grow into well adjusted, productive, and happy partners in adult society. In that event, personality factors we are born with play an important role in intimate relationships.

In the next chapter, we will look at some very important aspects of human personality and discuss their meaning for relationships. The chapter concludes with some suggestions for making ad hoc relationships work although the couple sees the world quite differently. By understanding our unique inherited nature more completely, we can negotiate our differences more happily.

Three:
Blending Different Personalities

I have chosen to present in this chapter the most popular description of how persons who all have different types of personalities are likely to experience the process of relating with a significant other person (SOP). By understanding the material in this chapter, you will know yourself and others better. You will also begin to accept and respect the inherited differences in people, so your relationships will be more rich and rewarding, with more tolerance for disagreements and conflicts. Someone quoted Paul McCartney of the Beatles this way, "I used to think that anyone doing anything weird was weird. I suddenly realized that anyone weird wasn't weird at all and that it was the people saying they were weird who were weird."

To explain this personality model, the discussion will be based on the Myers-Briggs Type Indicator (MBTI) that, in turn, is based on the work of noted Swiss psychiatrist, Carl G. Jung (1875-1961). (MBTI is a registered trade mark of Consulting Psychologists Press, Inc.)

Unlike other models, the MBTI defines behavior in ways that permit a wide variety of behavioral preferences within the range of normal without making judgments about them. By understanding it and applying it to intimate ad hoc relationships, people will become more tolerant of their normal differences and more accepting of the benefits in the infinite variety of human personality gifts. While people can change their behaviors to a certain extent if the benefits of doing so are worth the burdens, application of MBTI modeling can make life a lot more effective and serene. And people who understand each other in this way may be much less judgmental of their differences.

When couples begin an ad hoc intimate relationship, many of the issues they encounter are manifestations of their deepest personality factors. Although much of human behavior is attributed by sociologists to learned role models, Jung concluded from his observations that people were born with certain personality preferences that were exhibited in their behavior and communications. If intimate partners understand and accept these aspects of themselves and each other, their lives together can be enriched and nurtured by their differences rather than being harmed by them. Knowing these fundamentals of personality also empowers you to make conscious choices about the type of person you might prefer or feel most comfortable with, and it enhances understanding of your behavior and communications. It will help you acknowledge, honor, and appreciate the differences between you and ad hoc partners.

Building upon Jung's theory, the MBTI supplies a vocabulary like no other similar psychological instrument to enhance intimate relationships. Its popular acceptance by the professional community gives it credibility that can no longer be overlooked. It can be combined with the holistic concept of personal wholeness comprised of physical, intellectual, emotional, and spiritual, to create deeper understanding of intimate relationships. I believe it provides a basis on which you can build better understanding and communication with each other. In my opinion, no couple who wants to improve the health of their relationship should make a commitment to each other without knowing each other's MBTI type preference and understanding the material in this chapter. To further enhance the power of the MBTI, this chapter overlays the 16-step model of behavior preference with a model of lifestyle shown in Figure 3.1. It takes a bit of explaining, so please be patient because I think the rewards certainly are worth the effort.

THE 16-STEP MODEL OF BEHAVIOR

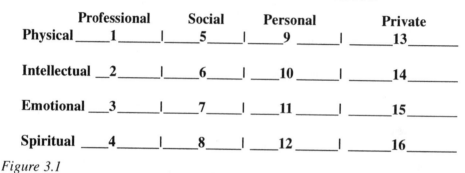

Figure 3.1

The matrix in Figure 3.1 illustrates four main classes of behavior and the four elements of personal wholeness. **Professional** describes what you do for money. **Social** describes how you relate to others off the job in recreation. **Personal** refers to behavior in family situations, and **Private** refers to time alone and in intimate relations with an SOP. Note that the elements of personal wholeness include physical, intellectual, emotional, and spiritual components. Each column created by the matrix represents one aspect of a relationship to which we bring the elements of physical, intellectual, emotional, and spiritual that make up human wholeness. The way a person ranks the priority of these elements varies with personality, as you will learn shortly.

The Myers-Briggs Type Indicator

The MBTI empowers people to cope with others and their differences more constructively than we otherwise could. It creates a climate in which differences can be seen as interesting and valuable, rather than disrupting, to any relationship. No type is more desirable than another, and each type makes a valuable contribution to society.

The MBTI is a questionnaire and reporting form designed to help people identify which personality type they naturally prefer. It measures the direction and relative strength of preference on each of four scales. Figure 3.2 illustrates the MBTI model of personality. Scoring of the MBTI results in the classification of people into one of 16 different personality types, but it does not limit their behavior to 16 options. In fact, the MBTI provides for the infinite diversity that is observed among humans. The result of these possible combinations is a four-letter description, i.e., **ISTJ, ENFP,** etc. (Note that **N** is used for iNtuition, because **I** is used for Introvert.) *Note: Please refer to the figure often as you read the following material to help clarify the details.*

MBTI MODEL OF PERSONALITY

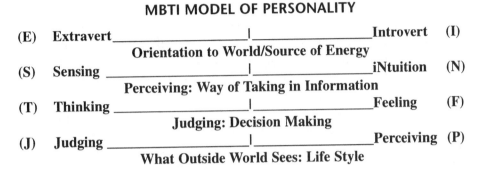

Figure 3.2

Within the MBTI model, each person exhibits unique behavioral traits that arise out of the combination of preferences for one or another side of each of the polarities (the four scales): Extraversion-Introversion, Sensing-iNtuition, Thinking-Feeling, Judgment-Perception. Although everyone seems to prefer one side or the other of each scale more than its opposite, every person exhibits aspects of both sides of each scale. No one is completely one-sided on any of the four MBTI scales. The most extraverted person uses introversion sometimes, and vice versa. The most introverted people need some human relationships and the most extraverted people need some quiet time alone, and a pattern and order in their lives. Both sides of each scale are used by everyone to some extent, although one side is preferred more and is therefore more highly developed.

How Your Brain Makes It Possible

Modern understanding of the physical human brain would place the left side of the MBTI scales with the left side of the brain and the right side of the model with the right side of the brain. Isabel Myers could not have known that when she aligned the scales as she did. Research by 1981 Nobel Prize winner Dr. Roger W. Sperry disclosed that the left and right cerebral hemispheres of the human brain perform different thinking functions. The left brain is verbal, logical, analytical, and sequential in processing information. The right brain is spatial and emotional and does more simultaneous processing, pattern recognition, and holistic thinking. People are driven by one side of the brain more than the other, although they tend to balance out as they get older. Once you understand this, all aspects of relationships take on new meaning. You can see brain dominance at work in the way people choose occupations. The fields of art, architecture, nursing, ministry, and psychology tend to attract right-brain people while the fields of engineering, accounting, law, manufacturing, and construction tend to attract left-brain people. When it comes to using a personal computer, left-brain people may prefer keyboard commands while right-brain people may prefer the icon, mouse driven approach.

Brain dominance seems to be apparent in entire civilizations. Since we inherit these traits through genetic transfer, it would be reasonable to assume that they are passed down through generations. For example, some of our forefathers in the east "knew" there was a better life out west and braved the Indians, weather, wilderness, and wild animals to push westward. They had the power of intuition, what Jung called the ability to see around corners. So, it is not unbelievable that more of the current westerners exhibit those same traits of adventure and intuition from their inheritance, while those who stayed in the secure comfort of the east passed along more of their conservative nature to today's generation.

Only since invention of the electroencephalograph (EEG) has it been possible to map the electrical waves produced in the brain, and thus analyze brain functions within a live person. New research made possible be magnetic resonance imaging (MRI) is mapping functions in the brain that were unimaginable just a short time ago. More recent brain mapping research has showed there are, indeed, physical explanations for psychological behavior. The fact is we behave as we do because we are made that way.

Schools emphasize left-brain thinking, and business decision making actually squeezes right-side thinking out of the management process. The fact that our government supports and encourages the arts is testimony to the influence of right-brain thinkers and doers, and the need for protecting their interests. More recently, psychologists have found that people who have access to and conscious control of their right-brain functions seem to live more successful lives. Daniel Goleman coined the phrase "emotional intelligence" to describe those people who exhibit the regulation of emotions in ways that enhance daily living in professional, social, family, and private relationships. This ability has been identified in pre-school age children and seems to be an inherited skill. They are adept at recognizing their own and others' feelings and responding in ways that make them endearing and trusted.

One concept of human wholeness includes the idea that a fully evolved person has the power of consciously using both brain hemispheres as each situation requires. Each part needs input from the others as appropriate in order to function at its best. Unfortunately, few people have achieved this level of integration, although it may be possible for many more. Most of us stay in the mode of our most preferred hemisphere while discounting and avoiding the other through prejudice and ignorance. When you become conscious of how your brain works, you can change it if you really want the benefits in achieving wholeness. We are not stuck with the patterns of behavior we inherited or were taught. By changing your thinking, you can change your behavior, and by changing your behavior you can change your thinking, although the process is not painless or free.

To apply the MBTI to human relationships, I need to take you much further along in your understanding of what the MBTI actually indicates. The description that follows is paraphrased, with permission, from a very useful booklet, "Introduction to Type," a publication of the Consulting Psychologists Press now out of print. It is also based on descriptions in a previous book I coauthored with Dr. Gary L. Harbaugh, Ph.D. (***Recovery From Loss,*** Health Communications, 1990.)

The Personality Function Scales

Jung called the middle two scales the functions of personality. To deal with any situation in life, people need both Perception and Judgment. However, these functions are not equally developed and can be ranked in their order of preference and then subdivided as to whether they are introverted or extraverted. Strictly speaking, Jung did not believe there were any introverts or extraverts, only introverted and extraverted functions. Following is a brief description of these functions.

Perceiving is a way of taking in information. Then judging is needed, which means a person uses a way of deciding which of the perceived options is most appropriate or desirable. Some psychologists believe that perception defines us as human beings and that we are what we decide we are, we are treated the way we choose to deserve, and ultimately we define the world we inhabit on the basis of the reality we create with these functions. Each person exhibits his/her personal behavior and communicates through employing the unique combination of these functions of personality. Reality, then, is the unique creation of each individual, is different for everybody, and is subject to change based on our will. A further explanation of these functions of personality may help you understand them better.

The MBTI assumes perception is of two types, either **sensing** or **intuition.** People who prefer sensing perception use their senses (touch, hearing, sight, smell, and taste,) for gathering the facts about the situation or their environment. They usually pay very close attention to these specific senses. People who prefer iNtuitive perception are not as present-oriented as Sensing people. They move rather quickly into what the facts mean and how they relate to overall possibilities. iNtuitive people are more likely future-oriented, looking for meanings, relationships, and possibilities that include but go beyond the physical senses. Sensing people tend to be realistic, practical, observant, and good at remembering facts and working with them. People who prefer intuition tend to value imagination and inspiration. They become good with creative ideas, projects, and abstract problem solving. You might say Sensing people like to look at the trees and iNtuitive people like to look at the forest. Most people use both sensing and intuition, but usually not at the same time and not with equal strength of preference.

Perhaps you can already see some ways in which how we perceive may affect how we respond to others in an intimate relationship. But before I explore these connections, let's be sure we understand what the MBTI means by **Judging.** In the MBTI, Judging refers to decision making. Everyone needs both a way of perceiving and a way of deciding. There are two methods of deciding or making a judgment, Thinking and Feeling. Each of these types of Judgment is a reasoning process (yes, Feeling judgment is a rational process, as explained by Jung). Use of the words

thinking and **feeling** does not imply that people who prefer feeling do not think or that people who prefer thinking do not feel. Nor do they refer to logic and emotion. Both logic and emotion can be applied when thinking and feeling, according to Jung. Actually, I think a better choice of words for these functions might be rationalizing for thinking and valuing for feeling, respectively, but thinking and feeling are the words chosen by the interpreters of Jung.

In decision making, Thinking people prefer to decide analytically, on the basis of cause and effect. They may see things mostly as black or white, right or wrong, with little tolerance for ambiguity or the gray areas of life. (They often make good accountants and engineers.) People who prefer Feeling are more likely to take into account personal values and emotions important to both themselves and to the other people involved in the decision, without requiring that the results be logical. (Feelers often make good care givers.) Therefore a Thinking decider is more objective, and a Feeling decider is more subjective. The person preferring Thinking strives for a just and fair decision. A rational decision by a Feeling person takes their own and other people's emotions and values into account, and is intended to bring about or restore harmonious interpersonal relationships. Can you begin to see the impact of these different preferences in a relationship?

If you prefer Thinking more, you tend to become more skillful in dealing with a world that behaves according to sequential order. You prefer a world in which there are few unpredictable events. If you prefer Feeling more, you tend to become better at dealing with the values that drive people, unpredictable as they may be sometimes. Feeling people may seem to be more sympathetic, tactful, and sensitive to the emotions of others, as well as their own. Thus, Feeling in the MBTI describes value decision criteria, not physical sensations such as hot, cold, etc. Those actually are sensing perceptions.

Each MBTI type has its own set of gifts and abilities, as well as deficiencies. Each brings its own strengths and weaknesses to an intimate relationship. *None of the MBTI types is either good or bad, the model merely provides a convenient form of understanding and communicating about our similarities and differences.* But those are very powerful skills.

A really good decision requires that we use all of the personality gifts in a balanced way even though only two of them are more natural to us. For example, you should use your **Sensing** for collecting facts, being realistic, putting aside all wishful thinking, and being an impartial observer. Use your **iNtuition** to discover all the possibilities, putting natural assumptions aside as you avoid assuming that there is only one obviously right thing. Use your **Thinking** to evaluate all the options logically, both pleasant and unpleasant. Count the cost of every option and examine every misgiving without letting personal loyalties interfere with the objective analysis. Use your **Feeling** to weigh how deeply you care about alternatives, which is closest to your primary values, what emotions are involved, to consider how other people will respond. Then, finally decide on a solution that will work out for the best, all things considered. This process creates a "Z" pattern on the scales, moving from sensing to intuition to thinking to feeling. A sign of maturity may be how effectively all the functions of personality are employed in making important decisions as appropriate to the situation at hand. Each situation will benefit most from the unique combination of functions that fits the circumstances best.

Conflicts in the use of this process possibly can lead to stress in decision making. For example, if your Thoughts and your Feelings pull you in opposite directions over a particular situation, it may be very difficult coming to a clear decision about the matter. If the consequences of the decision are extremely important, such as if you should marry a certain person or not, the tension caused by the internal **T-F** conflict can set up depression and anxiety. This is called splitting the personality, and can be very painful until you decide which side is going to prevail. Since none of us are likely to be perfectly developed, fully mature decision makers, you probably will use a decision process that primarily appeals to your favorite tendencies of perceiving and deciding in a specific unbalanced way. iNtuitive feelers may base a decision on some possibility without paying much attention to facts that might be crucial if the possibility is ever to come about. Sensing thinkers may settle for a faulty solution because they assume no better one is possible. **ST** deciders may overlook human feelings and values and **NF** deciders may ignore logical consequences and rational results.

It is amazing how different a situation can look to two people of different types, especially when they share an intimate investment in the solution. Better decisions are likely to be made by a couple with opposite preferences, if they can combine their strengths without letting their weaker functions cause conflicts. Couples with similar function preferences may make decisions more harmoniously, but they may duplicate the same kinds of mistakes by overlooking the aspects of the situation avoided by their similar less developed functions.

The **E-I** scale describes where you like to use your favorite function, either internally or externally. It also points to how you need to obtain psychic energy. Extraverts want to use their best, most developed preference in the outside world of things, activities, and people. Introverts prefer to keep their best in their inner worlds of interests, beliefs, or patterns of thought. Extraverts tend to become energized when interrelating with people and things, while introverts tend to be energized by activities that take place inside their minds, e.g., processing facts, ideas, concepts, and theories. A possible clue about the author is that researching information and writing books is an **I** type of behavior.

What The Outside World Sees

The scale on the bottom of figure 3-2, (**J-P**), identifies which personality function preference, whether it is perceiving or judging, the outside world is likely to see. If a person has an MBTI type that ends with a **J**, the outside world probably sees his/her way of judging or deciding. In our society, some people may be uncomfortable being classed as a Judging type. They may confuse the MBTI Judging type as meaning judgmental, which it does not.

Actually, the **J** stands for **Judging,** i.e., people who face the world from their decision process in a planned, orderly way, wanting to regulate life and preferring to be in control. The world is likely to see their **T** (Thinking) or their **F** (Feeling) behavior, whichever they prefer for decision making. **J** people like to make decisions and, if they are also extraverted (**EJ**), usually come to conclusions quickly. Sometimes, they decide too quickly and change their minds when new information or ideas intervene. They can appear to be jumping to conclusions to a person more oriented to perception, or even unable to make a decision and stick to it. **IJs** may mull over the possibilities longer before they come to any conclusions. Both may change their minds when new information comes along. Although a person with a preference for judgment and a deficit for perception may exhibit indecision, decision making is a valuable and indispensible function.

Perceptive P people prefer to rely on their preferred Sensing or iNtuition in dealing with the outer world and tend to live in a flexible, spontaneous way, wanting to understand life and adapt to it, rather than control it. Perceptives put off making decisions, sometimes too long, preferring to take in all the alternatives and not come to closure prematurely. If the **J** person has to be on guard so as not to come to a conclusion too quickly, the **P** person needs to be sure the decision is reached quickly enough. Remember, the **J-P** scale marker points to which of the center function scales a person prefers to use in external relations with others, either the Perceiving preference, whether it is Sensing or iNtuition, and the Judging scale, whether it is Thinking or Feeling. Your personality type may have either felt attracted to or repulsed by this explanation so far. If you work through the remainder of this chapter, I think you will be well satisfied with the new understanding you gain.

How Personality Functions May Effect Intimate Relationships

To apply the MBTI to the 16-Steps model of behavior in relationships, it is necessary to relate the functions of personality to the four energy resources or components of personal wholeness listed in *Figure 3.1* as follows:
1. **Sensing** preference relates to the physical resources,
2. **Intuitive** preference relates to the spiritual resources,
3. **Thinking** preference relates to the intellectual resources, and
4. **Feeling** preference relates to the emotional resources.

These pairings make it possible to discuss some powerful assumptions about how typical personality attributes might affect people in personal relationships. The following descriptions are compilations from several different sources.

(**Note:** *Since everyone exhibits behavior that is a composite of all four scales of the MBTI, some professional users of the MBTI believe it is a distortion to isolate any single scale or combination of scales without including all four scales simultaneously. Nevertheless, a brief discussion of the individual scales is useful, even though they are not actually exhibited by people in an isolated sense apart from each other.*)

S-N Scale – The **S** preference refers to people whose perception is based on the Sensing function, while the **N** preference refers to people whose perception is based primarily on iNtuition. **S** people look at life through eyes of realism, while **N** people look beyond the facts to the global possibilities those facts represent.

The **S** type person may be especially sensitive to the physical aspects of the relationship, those related to touch, sight, hearing, taste, and smell. When a couple separates, even temporarily, the memory of the physical presence may be very strong. There may be especially keen feelings of deprivation of the sexual relationship because physical presence plays a very important role in the life of the Sensing person. If some sensing connection is not made shortly, the sensor may feel the sensation of abandonment or loss keenly. Also, the Sensing person is observant of and responsive to any material, tangible connection with the partner. The personal "things" may be inseparable from the person and they can be very painful reminders of an absent loved one. When the partner is absent, the extreme Sensing person may mourn as though the absent person no longer existed.

It would be a mistake, however, to think of the physical relationship as only related to the sexual aspect for **S** people. The touch of the hand, the warmth of a hug, the sound of a voice, the smell of shaving lotion or perfume or of the couple's favorite meal cooking in the kitchen – any sensing input can be an important part of the physical relationship, in addition to sexuality.

In the pairing of MBTI traits with the 16-Step model in *Figure 3.1* above, you may have noticed that just as Sensing was paired with the Physical, so iNtuition was paired with the Spiritual. Since iNtuition is the opposite of Sensing, it might seem that iNtuitives are spiritual and Sensing persons are not. That would not be true. Gary Harbaugh has emphasized that every personality type can have a spiritual outlook and no one MBTI type is necessarily more spiritually minded than the others. However, spirituality for the sensor is more likely to be connected with concrete here-and-now realities, e.g., to be seen more in nature or science than in abstract faith. The Sensing person's preferred approach to spirituality could be more difficult to sustain in times of crisis. Furthermore, the iNtuition that might offer some spiritual comfort by moving the relationship to another dimension of intimacy is usually one of the less developed functions of the Sensing person. Therefore, in the situation of darkness caused by conflict or separation, the Sensing person has little light from iNtuition, since iNtuition is for the Sensing person mostly on the darker, less conscious, or what some refer to as the shadow side.

N type people may be more open to the subconscious spiritual aspects of relationships. The **N** type person may feel spiritually bonded to the partner or, equally possible, rejected without knowing exactly why. While there may be some comfort in this way of spontaneously knowing, the iNtuitive person may be much less in touch with the practicalities of life or the means to handle them. The whole area of self-care may be more of a problem to iNtuitives than it may be for Sensing types. If the partner is a Sensing person, probably that partner takes care of many of the day-to-day needs, perhaps financial as well as physical. The iNtuitive person may overlook the obvious physical (Sensing) aspects of life which need attention, including such basics as meals and keeping up with ongoing bills, repairing the car, organizing priorities, scheduling responsibilities, or even sleeping and personal care.

S people like to tend to the daily details of life while **N** people look out over the whole world from the top of the highest mountain. In extreme cases, **S** people can't see the forest for the trees, while **N** people can't see the trees for the forest. When **S**

and **N** couples get into conflicts, it may be possible to reduce the distress by following guidelines provided by Susan Scanlon, editor of the newsletter, "Type Reporter." To keep **S** partners from getting stuck in the specifics and refusing to look at the bigger picture, here are some suggestions for the **N** partner who wants the **S** to consider something new and global. Give the **S** a bottom line reason for your suggestion. Appeal to the sights and sounds involved in your suggestion. Make it practical with a specific plan of action. Relate your suggestion to something similar that already exists in the world of your **S**. Try out your suggestion informally first and give your **S** some time to raise objections before you claim defeat.

If you are the **S** partner, remember that your **N** partner does not like to be bothered with details, but is impressed with competence. So, encourage your **N** to talk about his/her personal vision and tie your details into that. Trace the details back to when they were a new and exciting idea. Give the framework of the idea before all the details. Don't judge progress by the lack of tangibles produced. Check instead for how your concept is being accepted. Don't demand a detailed rationale when your **N** is imagining possibilities. Just go with the dream. To get your **N** back to earth, don't shoot him/her down, but throw a line instead.

T-F Scale – This scale is the only one that has been observed as having a gender related tendency. The **F** preference describes people who emphasize the values and emotions of themselves and others in making decisions. Both are reasoning processes, but each has its own rationale. It may be somewhat easier for Feeling people to express their feelings verbally and for Thinking people to use their intellect more naturally because of the way their brains are constructed. Recent medical research indicates there are gender biological differences between the way male and female brains work that may affect this scale. Thus, differences that separate the sexes on the **T-F** scale may be determined more by their physiology than their cultural learning. Use of the left and right-brain halves and the communications between them differ with gender.

Women seem to show emotional sensitivity with both sides of their brain, while men concentrate emotional sensitivity more in the right side. These differences tend to make about 65% of men more Thinking and 65% of women more Feeling. Of course, that means that about 35% of men prefer Feeling and about 35% of women prefer Thinking. Thus, the minority of both genders exhibits behavior that may appear opposite to the majority of each sex. And, the probability is great that a **T** man and an **F** woman will pair up. This split could be the root cause of many relationship disagreements and conflicts.

Jung observed the cross-type behavior of some men and women and attributed it to the extraverted "anima" in men and the extraverted "animus" in women. These terms were used by the ancient Greeks who realized that both genders possessed elements of the other. Now, it is known that a fetus always begins life as female and only becomes male as hormones drive development of male characteristics. Both sexes possess equally 23 male and 23 female chromosomes. In any event, a man with dominant **F** preference may feel out of place in male company, and a woman with dominant **T** preference may feel out of place in female company. Likewise, they may not be fully accepted by their own gender because they do not quite live up to the stereotypical roles expected of them. The **F** male will have little difficulty making friends of both genders, but the **T** female may have difficulty with both sexes because she does not fit the expected role of either. Women may find her too different, and men may find her too competitive and insensitive. Thus, she may be rejected by both sexes, forcing her to act defensively and worsening the situation.

Regardless of gender, **T** people probably will do a lot of thinking in and about the relationship. They may over analyze the life they share with their partners, and intellectualize about the results of significant behavior. Thinking persons usually think ahead – they take a long range, step by step sequential view of things. They may do extensive thinking about their future life and appear to be unemotional and detached from the process of relating on an intimate level. Such apparent detachment might be infuriating or painful to a partner who prefers Feeling as the dominant preference. If they are reprimanded for it, **T** partners may feel guilty for not delivering what they do not have, i.e., a more Feeling nature.

T people may have difficulty dealing with the emotional aspects of relationships and feel stress when values are involved in behavior. The Feeling side of their personality usually is less developed so they may feel uncomfortable when emotions surface in themselves or their partner. Thinking people also may be befuddled and confused by events or emotional behavior that to them do not make sense. They assume a certain logical order to life, and when some happening destroys their logic, they may fear the loss of their moorings. They probably will be most at home handling the intellectual aspects of relationships and least confident with the emotional challenges. They may need to work a little harder at being sensitive to the emotional needs of a more **F** partner, and the **F** partner may need to be tolerant of their seeming indifference at times.

F people seek harmony in their lives and relationships with others, and base their decisions on emotions and values. They may be described as empathetic, compassionate, accommodating, accepting, and tender. They feel and express their emotions more naturally and spontaneously because they are willing to experience their feelings, which is the prerequisite for working them through. But areas of adjustment requiring logical thinking may cause them concern. They might avoid dealing with practical things, such as analyzing their current financial situation to fill out tax forms or logically thinking out the pros and cons of moving, and the possible consequences of other major decisions. They may also be susceptible to unethical or pseudo caregivers and others who can defraud them emotionally as well as financially. They may be too compliant and accommodating, too easily led for their own good. They have a trusting nature and will approach new relationships with open arms, possibly to their own detriment. However, they can be very assertive if their perception, especially intuition, tells them they are being exploited unethically.

T people are described as logical, reasonable, questioning, critical, and tough. They tend to trample over the feelings of F partners without meaning to hurt. So, **Fs,** don't respond when your feelings are strong. Wait a while. Prepare yourself to respond by getting clear about what upset you and why. Listen to the **T** and communicate some understanding of his/her logic. Explain your own feelings in objective terms and show the logic in them. Discuss your feelings with a neutral third party. **F** people don't like to deal with tough issues. So, the **T** partner should avoid giving any negative feedback when feeling critical. Prepare the **F** always by listing the things he/she does well. Express willingness to be cooperative and helpful. Show empathy for the feelings of your **F** partner by sharing a similar experience. Try to point out the impersonal forces at work in the world, but don't expect instant acceptance. Give your **F** time to experience the feelings and gradually introduce the logic behind your comments. If you are an **F** partner who must live with a **T** person, you may need to give yourself permission to be emotional without feeling guilty, and accept the relatively unemotional logic you get in return. Be specific when you describe or express your feelings, and don't take it personally if your loved one seems distant and unresponsive. If you pay attention to each other's needs, the **T-F** pairing can empower both partners to be more than either one could be without the other. Might you now see how these decision functions of personality can affect the way two people relate over the subject of love and sex?

Our unique type preferences cause us to see some things and miss others because no one enjoys balanced development of all four functions. Until our usual ways of deciding no longer work or cause intolerable stress, we go about decision making in ways that are most familiar to us, using our preferred functions in the normal ways. When our preferred method clashes with that of our partner, conflicts can follow. Such conflicts can escalate into breakups if the effects of personality differences are not well understood by the couple. Only by recognizing their differences and respecting each others' personality gifts can partners negotiate the disagreements caused by differing preferences.

The four combinations of functions, (**ST, SF, NF, NT**) lead to very different ways of experiencing life and to different ways of making decisions and relating to an SOP in intimate relationships. The way in which you employ these preferences will influence the level of comfort or feeling of fit that you experience with other people of different types. For example, if you prefer **ST,** you take in information primarily through the senses and make decisions primarily through logical, rational thought. If you prefer **NF,** you take in information primarily through intuition and make decisions based on feelings and values. If two such people team up, it will take a lot of respect, tolerance, and compromise by both of them to keep the relationship going because they are likely to experience a lot of conflicts.

A Look At The Other Scales

E - I Scale – The **E** preference refers to extraverted characteristics while the **I** preference refers to introverted characteristics. It is estimated that up to 75% of western culture is populated by **Es.** Couples who split on the **E-I** scale will need to understand the need for sufficient external stimulation of the **E** and the need for sufficient time alone of the **I.** The **E** partner may prefer to talk out issues while the **I** may prefer to process them internally and share only the solution. This difference can leave the **E** feeling left out and the **I** invaded. Misunderstandings can occur between **S-N** couples because they may see things quite differently. Intuitive partners with rapid insight may make sensing partners feel slow and mundane. Sensing partners with a solid sense of reality may cause intuitive partners to feel impractical and irrelevant. **J-P** couples may argue over issues of territory, lifestyle, and control, with the **P** partner preferring spontaneity and freedom to explore while the **J** partner wants to fit into social conformity. A counseling strategy with couples is to have each partner fill out the MBTI form, once for themselves and once as they picture their partner. The results usually are both surprising and illuminating.

Extraverts enjoy and like to be involved in the outer world of people and things because that is what gives them energy. They are the social planners of the world. When a breakup occurs, **E** people may want others around. They may want to get involved again with activities or another relationship as soon as possible. Extraverts seem to be more drawn to support groups and group travel opportunities, the kinds of activities that get them outside themselves. They may busy themselves with volunteer or avocational activities that will provide the needed contact with people and things. If they are forced to live alone, their quiet times can get quite oppressive to them. Sometimes they may walk through shopping malls just for the contact with people and the bustle that they perceive there. Extraverts enjoy talking about people, events, things, and activities, and they will miss conversational times with their partner when they are apart. People with the **E** preference are very responsive to what is going on around them. If they do not experience adequate support from their environment, Extraverts are likely to become depressed.

In contrast, the Introverted person typically is not drawn to large group activities because the **I's** energy does not come from outside them but, rather, from their inner resources. When an **I** person works in an **E** environment all day, he/she may want quiet, alone time in the evening to recharge and collect his/her energy. The Introvert may not enjoy reaching out for the support of other people or want to get involved in outside activities, even though it might be good if he/she did. It is not that the support of other people is unimportant to the Introvert, (in fact, it may be crucial to his/her mental health) but, rather, that reaching out is not easy or the usual approach of the **I**. When in group situations, the Introvert may be quiet and may appear to be on the outside of the group, more the observer than the participant. Even if an **I** makes the effort to get out among people, the **I** nature, i.e., observing and withholding, emphasizes the separateness of the **I** person.

An Introvert tends to be reflective, but can be talkative. However, the talk is more likely about ideas, concepts, and theories rather than people, events, and things. Can you see where a conflict may exist between two people who prefer **E** and **I** in opposing ways if they do not respect their differing gifts? **Es** may think **Is** are too withholding or manipulative when they don't share openly and consequently feel rejected. **Is** may think **Es** are too demanding and wish they could have more privacy to work out their thoughts in solitude. **E** partners may want to talk out their differences with a number of friends. **Es** need to talk to learn what they are thinking. So, **Is** must give them time to switch from speaking to listening, and maybe even be given a verbal message that it is time to switch. **Es** need to build in specific times for interaction during each conversation. On the other hand, **Is** need time to think before they speak so they can rehearse what they are about to say – maybe far too long for the **E** to tolerate. Is don't tell what they know and they don't ask enough about what others know. So **Es** should ask them direct questions to get them to open up more. Encourage him/her to switch from listener to speaker. And **Es,** always give your **I** time for reflection.

When a breakup occurs, the **I** probably will spend a good bit of time contemplating the loss and its meaning either logically or emotionally. This can be depressing as there is a limit to the kinds of answers that can come from contemplation alone. An Introvert may be more likely than an Extravert to research the cause of termination, and may be more motivated to read books such as this one on the subject of relationships. Social support is important to the **I,** but social support probably will be defined as involving one or two or, at most, a few close friends. With these trusted friends, the **I** may talk freely, something that would seem to be much more comfortable for the Extravert to do in a group setting. One of the primary supports for troubled persons, i.e., a group of persons who have had a similar experience, may not have the immediate appeal to the **I** that it might for an **E.** If someone the Introvert knows and trusts goes to such a group, that person may be able to extend an invitation that will have a better chance of being accepted. **I's** also need to be invited more than once with reassurance they are really wanted. **E's** may be likely to invite themselves, or to set up the activity themselves.

Extraverts are termed outer-directed. They may have a tendency to develop more sickness because of their feeling of being influenced by forces they cannot control. This tendency may account for some of the illness that widows and widowers are known to encounter within 18-36 months after the death of their spouse. Since the Introvert is inner-controlled, he/she may not be so likely to contract illness during the grief process as might the Extravert. If it were possible to identify the stressors and the probable results, then preventive steps could be taken by family and care givers that might offset some of the problems that occur during the grieving process. I think the perspective offered by the MBTI can be helpful in this way.

J - P Scale – People whose MBTI type ends in the letter **J** usually show to the outside world their preferred decision making function, i.e., their Thinking or their Feeling. People whose type ends with the letter **P** show their way of perceiving to the outside world, which either is Sensing or iNtuition. For Extraverts, what they show to the outside world is the favorite (Dominant) function. For Introverts, what is shown to others is their second favorite (Auxiliary) function. The Introverts keep their Dominant hidden, in their favored inner world.

J people prefer closure and control. They like to be on top of their situation. Js may be perceived as compulsively responsible because they set goals and deadlines and do their best to meet those commitments punctually, sometimes compulsively in the extreme. They typically do not like surprises or changes that alter their basic approach to life. They want to be committed and attached or to belong. They do not like open-ended situations. If being in love seems to wrest control away from them, the feeling can be very disconcerting and unbalancing so they may withhold to maintain control.

If their preferred function is Thinking (– –**TJ**), a Judging person may feel total frustration and a sense of befuddlement if unable to rationalize a conflict with their partner. If they prefer Feeling (– –**FJ**), and especially if they are also Extraverted (**E–FJ**), they may seek to avoid the pain of uncertainty and jump into new relationships prematurely. Certain types, like the **E – – J** or the **E–FJ,** want closure so badly that they are likely to be more vulnerable to connecting with someone not good for them. **J** people generally want to keep their lives in order and under control and they are extremely frustrated when they cannot. They want to move toward closure and usually appreciate assistance that helps them gain a sense of being on top of their situation.

P people show to the outside world their way of perceiving, whether sensing or intuition, rather than their way of judging, so they appear to be more flexible and adaptable. Not wanting closure, they find schedules and deadlines somewhat constraining, and they may undertake more commitments than they can comfortably handle, so they can feel overwhelmed. They prefer to approach life in a more open-ended way. So as not to close off any unforeseen option, **Ps** continue to look for possibilities and alternatives rather than risk a premature commitment. They may defer decisions while they seek more information or experience.

It may take longer for the **P** person to be ready to enter a new relationship after a breakup, since reconnecting necessitates acknowledging the termination as an ending. In order to move on to the new possibilities inherent in reconstruction, the **P** person who prefers **F** may need to work hard at giving up the emotional attachment to the previous SOP.

P people who prefer Sensing (–**S**–**P**) are likely to approach the options of dating on a day-to-day basis, with little thought for the future. They may need help and motivation to make the needed plans for their future lifestyle and security. If they are not financially secure, their future can be fairly uncertain. **P** people who prefer iNtuition (–**N**–**P**) can be ingeniously creative in looking out for themselves and dreaming about the future, but they may need some help in practical matters of life such as career planning or setting up a budget. Each of the other personality traits, Extraversion and Introversion, Thinking and Feeling, will also affect how the **P** person handles dating. An **E– –P** person is more likely to do something impulsively than the opposite **—J** type. A **– –TP** is more likely to have difficulty with the emotional steps of dating than the **– –FP.**

When a **J** and a **P** team up there may be a constant balancing act between process (**P**) and output (**J**). The conflict likely is to be over when do we know enough to make a decision, and when is the choice good enough to act upon. **Ps** may think **Js** jump to conclusions, and **Js** may think **Ps** never can make up their minds. So, **Ps,** give your **J** partner new information in advance of a choice so he/she can think about it a while when alone. Acknowledge that worthwhile decisions sometimes come out of the aggravating (to you) style. Make it clear when you are only speculating and when you want your **J** to speculate without jumping to a decision. Ask clarifying questions about the decision process being employed by your **J**. Let him/her organize the data-collection and review of options.

Since **Ps** like to seek more information and process data seemingly endlessly to the **J, Js** need to give the **P** plans in advance to think about. Acknowledge the worthwhile information that comes from all the options uncovered by the **Ps** style. When you make a decision, set a deadline, or intend to act, make it clear to your **P** what you want him/her to do. Even then be prepared for procrastination because a deadline is merely a signal to begin for a **P**. So, ask questions about process that will cause your **P** to think about order and schedule. Set up frequent feedback sessions so you can each talk about what you are thinking. Are you beginning to see the importance of the MBTI in maintaining healthy intimacy?

Ranking The Functions

The functions of personality, S/N/T/F, are not all preferred equally and can be ranked in order of their development. Extraverts use their dominant (favorite) function in dealing with the outer world, while Introverts keep their dominant function to themselves. This is an important distinction. With the Extraverts, what you see is their most favored function. But with Introverts, what you see normally is only their second best because Introverts use their auxiliary or secondary function in the outer world. They keep their preferred and usually most developed function hidden and only display it openly with people with whom they feel comfortable sharing their inner selves, or when it is demanded of them in a crisis.

Here is the most powerful aspect of the MBTI model. It is possible to rank the four functions in terms of the Dominant, Auxiliary, Tertiary, and Inferior preferences and to declare whether they are introverted, i.e., hidden, or extraverted, i.e, exposed. Since this ranking designates the functions in terms of their relative preference, it also points to their degree of development. Our least developed Inferior function may be the source of most of our stress because it restricts our creativity and originates a lot of our interpersonal conflicts. The concept of ranking the functions can be a little tedious, but learning it can be a powerful tool in relationship building.

If there are most-favored functions, that means there also are least-favored functions. Jung related the less developed functions to the less conscious side of personality. If Thinking Judgment is your favorite (Dominant) personality function, then the exact opposite of the Dominant on the same scale is the Inferior, i.e., Feeling and is likely to be least developed. The remaining scale contains the secondary or auxiliary preference and the third function, called the tertiary.

Jung observed that as people get older we naturally work harder on developing our less developed side. As we mature, Jung thought a natural development of the less preferred functions could occur in a few people whom he called "individuated." This development will require: 1) excellence in the favorite function, 2) adequate development of the auxiliary function, 3) admission of the less preferred functions into consciousness and partial relinquishment of the dominant and auxiliary functions, and 4) use of each of the functions in tasks for which they are best suited. Unfortunately, this development occurs normally after midlife, leaving younger people tilted toward their dominant preferences, and sometimes victimized by their inferior, least development function. After midlife, people often report they become more interested in developing a lifestyle that requires development of their inferior functions. Such pursuits sometimes disrupt longstanding relationships and surprise both partners. When one partner changes more than the other, breakups sometimes result if they cannot accommodate their new behavior.

Table 3.1 following shows the ranking of functions by type preference, grouped into couplets related to stress management. The table also shows whether the function is introverted (I) or extraverted (E) for each of the types. Further, they are paired according to opposites.

Functions By Type Preference

Function:	S	T	F	N
ESTP	1/E	2/I	3/E	4/I
INFJ	4/E	3/I	2/E	1/I
ESFP	1/E	3/E	2/I	4/I
INTJ	4/E	2/E	3/I	1/I
ESTJ	2/I	1/E	4/I	3/E
INFP	3/I	4/E	1/I	2/E
ESFJ	2/I	4/I	1/E	3/E
INTP	3/I	1/I	4/E	2/E
ENFP	4/I	3/E	2/I	1/E
ISTJ	1/I	2/E	3/I	4/E
ENTP	4/I	2/I	3/E	1/E
ISFJ	1/I	3/I	2/E	4/E
ENFJ	3/E	4/I	1/E	2/I
ISTP	2/E	1/I	4/E	3/I
ENTJ	3/E	1/E	4/I	2/I
ISFP	2/E	4/E	1/I	3/I

Table 3.1

Managing Stress

Under stress, a person may experience being beside themselves or "flipped out" if the dominant function is disabled and the inferior function takes over. It is as though one acts like a primitive version of the type directly opposite to normal, e.g., an ISTJ may act like a childish ENFP, an INTP can behave like a primitive ESFJ, etc. It is the inferior fourth function that exposes all the reasons why a relationship isn't working and cannot be redeemed. A person caught in the grip of his/her inferior or shadow is "standing in his own light" according to Jung.

Naomi Quenk has explained how people in the grip of their inferior function might behave or appear to others. When in the grip of their inferior function, Extraverts may be boastful, intrusive, and loud; Introverts may be aloof, inhibited, and withdrawn; Sensors may be dull, feisty, and obsessive; Intuitives may be eccentric, erratic, and unrealistic; Thinkers may be argumentative, intolerant, and coarse; Feelers may be evasive, hypersensitive, and vague; Judgers may be compulsive, impatient, and rigid; and Perceptors may be procrastinating, unreliable, and scattered. Obviously, being aware of these possibilities can help one to understand his/her own behavior as well as that of others when they are under stress.

Quenk proposes the key to managing stress is in calling upon the less preferred auxiliary or second function to work out of the malaise, much as a football coach sends in the second team quarterback when the lead quarterback is disabled. This process may require help and support from a therapist knowledgeable in MBTI application to couples in order for it to work. Failing such intervention by someone who can help invoke the auxiliary function, the partner in the grip of his/her inferior might just destroy the relationship.

Good type development implies the comfortable use of all the functions as appropriate to the situation. Quenk has described a fully adaptive form of each trait as follows: Extraverts are charming, enthusiastic, and sociable. Introverts are deep, discreet, and tranquil. Sensors are pragmatic, precise, and detailed. Intuitives are imaginative, ingenious, and insightful. Thinkers are lucid, objective, and succinct. Feelers are appreciative, considerate, and tactful. Judgers are efficient, planful, and responsible. Perceivers are adaptable, easygoing, and flexible.

Mature type development includes learning to identify the functions and attitudes we prefer, understanding their implications, using the functions appropriately, and overcoming any type falsification, reaching full development of our true type. Jung called this process of growth "individuation." If we keep type in mind when dealing with people, we are respecting their right to develop along lines of their own inborn preference, and also the importance of those preferences to our relationship with them.

Caution: It is possible to self-select your type preference from the information presented so far fairly reliably. In fact, a majority of such self selection is validated by actually completing the MBTI. However, it is not so easy to assume the type preference of another person from your observation of their behavior. Many complex factors are involved in your perception of another. So please avoid the temptation to assume that a friend or SOP is one type or other. Only by completing the MBTI and having it interpreted by a qualified counselor can a person's type preference be determined with confidence.

The Center for Applications of Psychological Type (CAPT) in Gainesville, Florida conducts research and provides education and training for those who want to learn more about specific applications of the MBTI. To promote the valid and ethical use of the MBTI, the Association for Psychological Type (APT) was formed. For more information about the MBTI and the APT membership, you can contact APT at 9140 Ward Parkway, Kansas City, MO 64114, or call (816) 444-3500.

Living in Harmony With Different Types

You might be wondering if type theory can predict which couples might be more likely to avoid getting divorced. Several investigators have studied this question, with mixed results. If you analyze marital conflicts, you may find a rigid, controlling, thinking type (usually male) paired with a self-righteous, indignant, morally outraged feeling type (usually female). Possibly the most congenial partners are those who were fortunate to have a childhood environment that encouraged their native personality preference to develop.

It seems people prefer mates who are more like themselves than different, although some people marry their opposites to reinforce their least developed side. However, cultural biases are indicated that make some groups prefer some types more than others. For example, in a particular study, one group of fundamentalist, traditional Christians preferred **ESFJ** while a more humanist, psychologically oriented group preferred **ENFP**. The single most common preference is for **E** over **I** in both genders, probably because most of western populations are estimated to be extraverts.

Men are supposed to prefer **T** and women to prefer **F** in themselves, but there is a growing preference for **F** in both genders. The two most popular preferences of women by men are **ESFJ** and **ENFP**. However, the most difficult relationship seems to be that of an **ISTJ** man and an **ENFP** woman. Women seem to be torn between preference for **SJ** and **NF** men, with the new-age liberated woman preferring **NF** more. My marriage was split on two scales, with Rosalene exhibiting **ENFP** against my **INTP**. Both of us apparently sought to fulfill our weakest function in the other. Her loss was excruciating for me as she made up the missing **E-F** half that I lacked. There does not seem to any evidence to indicate one combination of types between couples works much better than all others. Some researchers have looked at type and intimacy, and their findings will be presented later in chapter 8.

Margaret Hartzler concluded, after investigation of successful married couples, that if a couple is free to employ their different personality gifts to support the less developed sides of the other, without letting their differences create unbearable conflict, couples with any MBTI combination can enjoy a healthy, intimate relationship. Whether it works out that way or not may involve other aspects of behavior that are not measured by the MBTI. The process of searching, dating, and achieving commitment is affected by more than our personality type because other factors are involved as well. They include our value system, social experiences, cultural environment, and early life development, the physical, intellectual, emotional, and economic environment, as well as our sense of the existential meaning and purpose of life (spirituality). However, having this knowledge of personality factors can be very helpful in creating tolerance and understanding of the couple's differences.

Hartzler found that, while some types seem to connect with each other more often than chance would predict, there was no single combination of MBTI types that composed unusually successful marriages. While opposites tend to attract each other, they can feel very uncomfortable after the first stage of euphoria subsides and their differences emerge. On the other hand, where little difference exists nothing much new is learned from each other, and the relationship quickly stagnates. They do not enrich each other, they just blend together. Consequently most successful relationships are built between people who are somewhat different, but not totally opposite. What seems to be most important is how the partners relate to the differences that each brings to the relationship. The way people of different types who work well together do it may be based on **respect, acceptance, tolerance,** and **surrender,** (RATS) according to unpublished analysis by Gary Hartzler.

Respect implies unconditional love for the partner and even appreciation for differing gifts of personality. It comes from the type of "agape" love that forgives 70 times 7, as instructed by Jesus. (Matthew 18:21-22) Unconditional love knows no grievances because it is total at-one-ment with another. It is the fruit of the second commandment given by Jesus, i.e., to love your neighbor as yourself (Mark 12:31). It means to respect another as you respect yourself.

Perfect respect requires a complete, whole, healthy human being, and therefore, is not likely to be achieved totally since none of us are perfect lovers of ourselves. However, it is possible for introverts to respect extraverts, thinkers to respect feelers, sensors to respect intuitives, and judgers to respect perceivers, and vice versa when they think of others as just being different and not wrong. An intuitive type can appreciate a sensing type for presenting the facts, and a sensing type can appreciate an intuitive type for emphasizing possibilities so long as each does not judge the other. A feeling type can appreciate a thinking type for objective analysis, and a thinking type can appreciate a feeling type for harmony and sensitivity.

Each partner can receive benefits from the alternating leading and following that may occur if there is mutual respect for the separate desires and talents of the other. Both are willing to compromise their own desires sometimes to meet the needs of the other, if they are in conflict. It is important for respect to be mutual – a two-way street with both partners sharing in leading and following – because respect that is continually one-way in a relationship likely will grow thin with time. That way they share mutually the benefits of complementary contributions which each makes to the other without the rivalry of superior/inferior competition.

Acceptance comes from acknowledging different talents and ability, or stronger desire of the other partner for certain activity not shared equally by both. For example, one partner may defer to another who has some special connection with a local garage for his/her auto repairs. Or one partner may prefer to do inside house work more and the other may agree to do the outside work, so they respectfully apportion the work to the liking of each other. One partner may be trained more highly for financial administration, so the other partner may defer in matters of money management. One partner may have a burning desire to attend a concert or party not equally shared by the other, so they go to the concert or party together anyway. One partner may prefer a logical, ordered approach to life and the other may prefer a more spontaneous, here and now, freedom of expression. The range of possible differences is infinite.

Of course, we cannot love or accept another any more than we love or accept ourselves. If you do not love or accept yourself, that self rejection may be projected onto your partner who will feel it in the form of criticism, withdrawal, and attempts to control. If you accept yourself as you are, that feeling also is projected onto your partner in the form of nonjudgmental love, and that is what you likely will get in return. Although it is unlikely that perfect acceptance is possible in intimate relationships, I think the benefits of moving in that direction are well worth the effort.

Couples may get along in spite of their personality differences because of **tolerance.** Tolerance often is the response to superior power that is granted by one partner to another. It possibly is related to the controlling-dependent combination of relationship that is found often in dysfunctional families. If one partner is dependent upon or needs the other for money, housing, food, transportation, sex, or some deep emotional needs, he/she may tolerate significant differences with the partner who provides the thing(s) that are needed.

Thus, tolerance comes out of a sense of need rather than a sense of wholeness. If the more dependent partner has no alternative sources of needed self esteem outside the relationship, resentment for having no options can build up and fracture the relationship. With granted power from a tolerant partner, there may come a great deal of insecurity because the weaker partner may not think he/she is able to survive without the other. In time, the more powerful partner may grow weary of the imposed responsibility for care taking. Successful relationships based on tolerance must include the security of a reliable mutual commitment to survive for a long time.

In relationships that are sustained by **surrender,** one partner may be deluded or denying a master/slave relationship by belief in genuine love or acceptance, when hatred and rejection actually is working subconsciously. On the surface, things may appear to be running along smoothly between the couple while, subconsciously, the water behind the dam is rising steadily. Such relationships can survive for life if the pent-up resentment does not overrun the limits of pain. Sometimes other considerations, such as maintaining a home for children, may sustain this type of relationship for years. There actually may be very little acceptance, respect, or tolerance, and when one or the other partner realizes it consciously, he/she may leave. If they never get past denial, such couples may hang together for life in painful unhappiness. All the reasons why some couples with marked differences in the MBTI model function smoothly, while others do not, are not clearly known.

To summarize this chapter, a quotation from Otto Kroeger and Janet Thuesen seems appropriate: "Tension and disagreement are part of the human condition. It is out of tension and disagreements of our relationships that we move to more intense levels of love, to increased understanding and forgiveness, and to higher levels of sharing and growth. Believe it or not, the ultimate flowering of a relationship is not possible without the struggle. Typewatching, then, provides an exercise that can help you (develop) constructively and lovingly."

Transition

This concludes Part I. Now, you should understand the family, social, and inherited personality factors that make you what you are. Perhaps this material has opened up some painful memories that you have kept buried for some time. Maybe it will prompt you to begin the work of removing the barriers within that prevent you from bringing a healthy self to other people. Also, it may sensitize you to the differences among people and so give you more acceptance and understanding of why they are like they are. As you gain new insight from your observations, you may want to return to this material repeatedly to sift out more of the golden nuggets that it contains for you.

Now that you know how you got to be the person you are, we can begin explaining what the experts say about creating healthy ad hoc relationships. The next part presents the core material of the book in several chapters. It begins with a plan for searching and making decisions to meet your needs in intimate relationships with significant other people. Then we encounter alternatives about sexual behavior, and contrast them with the latest understanding of holistic love.

Later chapters cover communications, and gaining commitment and intimacy. I believe these are subjects that are crucial to establishing and maintaining healthy ad hoc relationships. After you understand them, I wager you will think so too. If you have been reading steadily this far, perhaps it is time to take a break to absorb what you have learned before going on.

Four:
Searching, Searching, Searching

This chapter is intended to improve your ability to search for intimate social contacts and make rational choices about your new ad hoc partners. It includes a description of several models of relationships that fit many real world conditions between couples. It also includes specific instructions on why to search, how to search, what to look for, what to do when you meet an attractive new prospect, and how to make rational choices so you won't set yourself up for a divorce later.

The genetic role of men is to pursue, protect, and provide while the genetic role of women is to stimulate, acknowledge, and nurture. Thus, men still seek women who present the appearance of successful birthing and mothering, and women seek men with the perception of fidelity, stability, and material resources, e.g., a dependable provider. (I exclude those unfortunate people who attach themselves to others and produce babies out of pathological disorders.) Reproducing the species and ensuring its survival have changed little from prehistoric cave dwellers. However, the techniques and standards for mating have shifted with the social values of recent years. There is far more freedom for both sexes to define the lifestyle they want to have with the opposite gender, including short term ad hoc relationships that are not based on procreation. But, both genders still want a partner who will appreciate them and make them feel good about themselves. Thus, a far wider range of searching methods and criteria are being used and will be described in this chapter. When you understand this material, you will feel more powerful and confident in your ability to control your selections in your new relationships to provide the kind of lifestyle you want.

Before we talk about searching methods, perhaps you should establish whether you are ready for a relationship or not. Some factors you might consider include: Your self acceptance and balance between independence and dependency, ability to respect your own needs and to say yes or no when appropriate, ability to face mistakes without shame and being aware of your limitations, knowing you have something worthy of offering another person, having a satisfying career and social/personal life, being clear about what you want in a partner, and being free from any grief from previous lost love affairs. Wounded adult children may or may not find the potential results of seeking intimate personal relationships worth the effort, depending on the strength of their needs. It takes a lot of work, it costs money, and it takes time to create healthy, intimate relationships.

Common sense says if you want to catch a fish, you have to go where the fish are biting. So it is with developing ad hoc, intimate relationships. You may feel awkward and even embarrassed the first few times you try to initiate a date with a new acquaintance. Making new social contacts can be a draining experience for certain introverted personality types, but extraverts actually may find it energizing. New relationships are developed more easily if you are not in dire physical or psychological need of the person you are meeting, but would like to relate to enhance both your lives. It is a good idea to inventory why you want an intimate relationship before you begin searching.

Why People Search

Some research indicates that men and women want different things from each other. In one study, in priority order, men reported wanting sexual fulfillment, recreational companionship, an attractive spouse (to boost their self esteem?), domestic support, and admiration (to boost their self esteem some more?). In priority order, women reported wanting affection, conversation, honesty and openness, financial support, and family commitment.

Each gender may have to compromise their needs somewhat during the search to meet the needs of the other. The dichotomy among the sexes may be the basis for much pain and many separations, divorces, and other conflicts in intimate relationships if it is misunderstood. One of the advantages to men and women of the equal opportunity movement is that neither gender must trade sex for financial or emotional security. When both sexes earn their own living they can meet each other on common ground of sexual needs and social gratification, which is a much more enduring, satisfying give and take. Well adjusted, interdependent people do not need to play games of control and manipulation. It does not matter so much what studies of random populations disclose. What matters is what you want from a relationship. This chapter is intended to help you find out and go for it.

Natural Sexual Drives

Exhaustive research in anthropology, reported by Helen E. Fisher and Willard Gaylin, point to both biological and social sources of this natural drive to reproduce. It seems to be driven by levels of a cocktail of chemicals and hormones that affect the brain. They include phenylethylamine, or PEA, the male hormone testosterone, monoamine oxidase (MAO), and serotonin. When PEA is low we are not so interested in mating, but when it is high, we are more susceptible to culturally determined desirable partners. Some anti-depressant drugs called MAO inhibitors affect the production of PEA that can be measured in the urine secretions. It has been found that high levels of PEA and serotonin are associated with any type of social activity that one thinks is exciting, including parachute jumping and emotional divorce court proceedings.

Serotonin and testosterone also contribute to the perceived ranking or dominance of males in groups such as military officers and college sports stars; it seems to be one of nature's biological attractions for sex in both males and females. It has also been observed that people who suffered a disease of the pituitary gland called hypopituitarism during infancy show few of the symptoms of rapture that comes with romance and infatuation, although they often marry and have families normally.

While it is generally agreed that thoughts create feelings that create behavior, now it may be assumed that chemistry controls thoughts. The question so far unanswered by medical research is what controls the production and level of these chemicals; i.e., which comes first, the thought or the chemical.

So, while evolutionary biology can help explain some of the source of feeling so "high" when we are in love, it does not explain other social and cultural factors that are very complex. Some people report never feeling lust or infatuation while others report falling in love easily and repeatedly. Time, place, and circumstance seem to have a large influence on our need and receptivity to intimate connections with the opposite gender. Fisher believes romance is driven from very primitive needs to reproduce that have been passed down through the generations for millions of years since man first evolved on this planet. It peaks and then wanes in a year or two when the brain switches from producing PEA to endogenous morphines (endorphins) that help create a feeling of contentment, security, safety, stability, tranquility, and reduced anxiety. That is the crucial time when partners must begin working on keeping the relationship alive and spontaneous before it becomes boring and even intolerable.

If primitive **biological needs** prevail, we may be attracted to people who merely fulfill the mating instinct. Men may be attracted to beautiful women and women may be attracted to handsome, successful men they can literally look up to. A trophy effect may be at work in such match ups as both partners seek, maybe unconsciously, to assure the most healthy, competitive offspring. If **social instincts** prevail, we may be attracted to people who will fit in with our perceived self image. We may seek people with the "right" career, the "right" family, or the "right" contacts. This is another form of the trophy effect at work. Social reasons found by Michael Broder for connecting intimately with someone also may include:

1. Improving your self esteem with the trophy effect of exhibiting your new catch.
2. Using the income of another to improve your financial security.
3. Valuing a coupled relationship higher than being single and unattached.
4. Using another to supply the missing parts of yourself.
5. Trying to make an ex-partner jealous of a new acquaintance.
6. Substituting to get over the grief of a recent breakup or traumatic loss.

Psychological Drives

Codependent people may want a partner to fill the void they feel in themselves. This need comes from childhood experiences that fostered helplessness rather than self-confidence. People who are void of their own self esteem or some other hole in their makeup may try to fill it through acceptance by another person whom they value. Sometimes, people run from one partner to another trying to do the impossible, getting self-worth from another. Signs of a codependent relationship, found by Sharon Wegscheider-Cruse, include the following types of behaviors:

> *Initiating most of the phone calls. Initiating most of the times spent together. Wanting to talk about the relationship more often than the other. Feeling uncomfortable and anxious during times of separation. Being concerned or unhappy when the other seems perfectly satisfied and*

happy, although not together. Wanting to know everything the other does, thinks, and feels. Carrying a disproportionate responsibility for maintaining the relationship. Thinking the other's wants and needs are more important than your own. Thinking you can't make it on your own if your partner leaves the relationship.

Codependents may look unconsciously for the ideal opposite parent, i.e., the one we did not have as a child. We may be attracted to the in-laws, if they represent a healthier family than the family of origin that we experienced. The relationship can become the center of living for a codependent person. It provides comfort and security that is reassuring and predictable. The person keeps returning to the relationship for the fix. Any threat of withdrawal by the partner brings a great deal of fear, anxiety, and stress. If the relationship ends, the codependent person can suffer excruciating grief, including physical symptoms similar to withdrawal by a drug addict. If this description speaks accurately to your situation, I recommend you get professional help or join a 12-step support program to become less dependent.

In contrast to those unhealthy reasons, Broder's healthy reasons for wanting an intimate partner include:

1. The desire to share aspects of your life with someone.
2. The desire for sensual or sexual pleasure.
3. Enjoying a sense of well-being with intimate companionship.
4. Enjoyment of feelings that come from sharing.
5. Giving of yourself to another person.

Whatever drives your need, whether it is conscious or subconscious, one bit of advice that seems appropriate is to first decide where you want to go with your life, and then seek a compatible partner to go with you. If you pursue these objectives in the reverse order, i.e., seeking a trophy partner who may or may not share your life goals, your chances for happiness and contentment may be at high risk.

Modern Mating Models

People get together for many different reasons and in many different ways. Sometimes it occurs when you least expect it and other times it follows a very carefully orchestrated plan. Writers have presented several descriptions or models of how relationships begin and evolve. An overall knowledge of these several models may be very helpful in your search and creation of healthy, personal relationships.

In all romantic connections, there must be the sense of meeting a need for social fit, sexual fulfillment, and trust. Proximity in terms of timing and location also plays an important part in stimulating all these forms of intimate connections. We must be "ready." Statistically, the most enduring matches are those between people of similar age, generation, and geography who share similar cultures and background. Those we choose as intimates reveal our own level of security, self esteem, wisdom, sexual development, and maturity. Although there can be strong attractions between opposites also, the initial attraction of opposites can wear thin if the necessary accommodation and compromise do not follow. As I explained in chapter 3, people generally prefer to connect with others who are more similar than different.

Intimate relationships seem to evolve through a rather standard set of phases. The first activity is a selection process, which is a ritual in our society. Both men and women use subtle and not so subtle forms of flirting or body language to express an interest in someone who appeals to their senses. After initial contact is made in the first phase of pursuit, the decision as to whether this is a platonic encounter or romantic seduction usually takes several dates. This phase can last one to three months. During this time, the one pursued may react positively only to find the pursuer turning cold and withdrawing in a switch of the roles. The sought becomes the seeker and the seeker becomes the sought. The relationship likely will terminate if the role reversal is not enacted by either party.

John Gray says women tend to move up and down in a wave-like rhythm or cycle, depending upon how they feel about themselves. "In a relationship, men and women have their own rhythms and cycles. A woman's ability to give and receive love in her relationships is generally a reflection of how she is feeling about herself. Men pull back and then get close like a rubber band, while women rise and fall in their ability to love themselves and others." If these gender differences are not understood and accepted, the seeker/sought cycle might be perceived as a threat to the relationship, a revolving door, as the couple gets stuck in seduction/switch and back again.

Thus, it is not appropriate for either partner to take responsibility or to feel guilty about the natural cycle of the other. There is no need to try and "fix" each other as this cycle unfolds. Both partners need to complete their cycles unimpeded. The last thing either of them should do is try to prevent or shorten the cycle from working through, even though it means they will have to tolerate some perceived threats to the relationship along the way. When either partner does not feel safe and secure enough to experience their cycles, their only alternative is to avoid intimacy and sex, to suppress their feelings and resort to codependent behavior such as drinking, overeating, overworking, or over care taking, none of which are healthy.

In healthy relationships, each partner feels free to assume either role of seeker or sought alternatively, with confidence that the other will not leave the relationship or impede their cyclic evolution. When this process is accepted as a natural evolution in every relationship, (which it often never is) the relationship actually begins as two individuals become a couple, and then coupling consists of three concurrent phases. One is a plateau when the couple enjoys each other physically and emotionally, begin to feel in love, and fantasize about the future together. Then comes a time of negotiating the resolution of inevitable differences that ends with the final phase of commitment or breakup, sometimes up to two years or more after the beginning of the selection. Couples can stay deadlocked in negotiations for years, move on to marriage, resolve into a less conventional, but committed, lifestyle in various levels of friendly intimacy, or break off the relationship and terminate all contact. Without adequate knowledge of how this process works, you can be in for a rocky path toward a new coupled relationship populated by repeated attempts and disheartening failures.

Potential intimate partners were classified into three groups by Lettie Pogrebin: (1) good enough, (2) good today/gone tomorrow, (3) and good for nothing. Since no one is perfect, she suggests that good enough is good enough and that people who search for a perfect mate likely are going to be looking for a long time. If you want commitment, people in groups 2 and 3 should be avoided. Unfortunately, you can't classify them reliably without the risk of getting involved to some extent, and testing their values. Further, relationships seem to move through five specific levels on the way to commitment. They can terminate at any of the stages. The five levels of relationships Pogrebin identified are described as follows:

1. Open dating, possibly with recreational sex, with several polygamous partners and zero commitment, ranging to
2. Steady dating, most likely with some meaningful sex to
3. A monogamous form of publicly going steady and having sex with only that person, to
4. Open monogamy-plus where the families and friends of the couple are brought into the relationship, to the final stage of
5. Mutual commitment and possibly living together with intentions of getting married.

If you are not very experienced with this process, you easily can confuse the behavior of your partner who is at a lower level with a more advanced level of commitment because the two people often are not on the same level at the same time, as noted above. Both parties can drift up and back in the levels with time at their own pace, as well, for various reasons. Pressuring or manipulating your partner to move up to a higher level of commitment before she\he is ready requires great sensitivity and tact. It is risky, and often leads to frustration, disagreement, and separation. This process of modern courtship is full of anxiety and ambiguity for both parties.

Relationships also can be scaled upward from acquaintances, through companions, to friends, to committed lovers, leading on into marriage. **Acquaintances** are people we know from repeated contacts, but for whom we take no responsibility. **Companions** are people we like to do things with. But, if they are not available, the activity takes precedence, and we find someone else to share it with or attend alone. The difference with **friends** is that they are people we want to be with. We will compromise or cancel plans to spend time with them. From friendships, the couple advances to being **lovers.** These are people described by M. Scott Peck who really want the best for their partners and are willing to sacrifice themselves to help their partners grow in every way. Achieving the transition from companionship to friendship to lovers may require that we weather one or more serious conflicts or disagreements together. In ad hoc relationships, sexual activity can and does get involved in all the lower level stages. However, it is not recommended by the Washington Ethical Society before reaching the state of being a committed couple, because the emotional aspect can cloud rational thinking prematurely. **Committed couples** represent exclusive sexual involvement in a monogamous situation, sometimes while living together. This stage used to be a prelude to getting married, but it often is sought as a goal itself now in ad hoc relationships.

Types of Relationships

Several basic ad hoc relationship patterns emerge from studies reported by Martin Blinder and Marlin S. Potash. They include validating relationships, structure building relationships, experimental relationships, avoidance relationships, fusion relationships, healing relationships, transitional relationships, compatible agenda relationships, and synergistic relationships. Here is a brief description of each type.

In a **validating relationship,** people choose lovers who can compensate for their own perceived deficiencies. It may be poor self esteem, physical inadequacies, low social or financial standing, deficient maleness or femaleness, that needs shoring up through mirroring by a valued significant other. Being accepted by a highly valued lover gives such people the affirmation that is missing from their own self image that probably was damaged in childhood. Buried beneath the aura from these glittering role models often is unconscious emptiness and anger. Validating relationships either make one feel lower than the mate and intimidated by their higher standing, or become boring and frustrating if we choose people just because they make us feel or look good. For these reasons, validating relationships most often eventually are abandoned. It is far more healthy to become self-validating and so less needy of the validation fix again and again from others.

In the **structure building relationship,** a couple works hard for the future. Often, they put their own emotional growth and personal satisfaction on hold while they build for their home and family life. Their individual preferences and values are subordinate to the relationship. They see themselves more in family roles than as passionate, intimate individuals. Commitment is more to the unit than to themselves or even to each other. The structure of the relationship fosters the choice of reliability over excitement and joy. It trades satisfaction in the moment for possible future returns, and it often imposes on the partners a life of quiet deprivation. Such couples need to give a higher priority to getting what they want for themselves. And they should put aside problems for a time to play more often.

Experimental relationships are entered to learn something we wish to know. They can be an informative kind of treading water. Adolescents often experience a fair number of instructive, short romances in the process of maturing and learning who they are. Sometimes a pattern of short-term flings can signal change itself as the desired constant. If you seem to be learning the same lesson over and over, with recurrent emotional pain, maybe the time has come to stop. Just say no to another fling and spend several months reflecting on what you are doing, why you are doing it, and where you are going.

Avoidance relationships provide the opportunity to be together without being connected, committed, or intimate. They avoid the risk of being close even though they can be erotically sexual. Avoidance relationships are founded on the need to escape feelings of vulnerability, loss, or responsibility, and threats to self esteem. They are characterized by emotional distance, busyness, superficiality, secretiveness, denial, withholding, and mistrust. Such relationships often form in times of crisis, fear, or emotional depletion. They provide safe havens because the partners need not change, mature, or even feel.

People with fuzzy boundaries and an undeveloped sense of self worth, whose greatest fear is being alone or abandoned, often develop **fusion relationships.** They connect with others only to survive, not to enrich each other. They will sometimes tolerate adultery, physical and mental abuse, and other aberrant behavior, while they go to any lengths to bind their partners to them. Neither closeness nor distance feels comfortable to them. They are two half-persons fusing together, trying to make a single whole. To be apart is to be incomplete, isolated, empty, and lonely. Fusion relationships are characterized by clinging dependency, hostile impulsiveness, and controlling possessiveness. They usually exclude any other relationships or activities. The partners view any wish by the other to be separate or individuated as a threat. They may have little in common except their mutual fear and insecurity, often expressed in hypersexuality.

Obsessive-compulsive relationships are an extreme form of unhealthy fusion relationships that are all too common. These connections often arise from unconscious needs to recreate bonding with the opposite sex parent that was absent at work, chronically ill, was an addict, or separated by divorce. If not actually physically abandoned, the pre-school child may have experienced emotional abandonment by the mother or father. Although maybe subconscious, the unfulfilled need to reconnect under conditions of total unconditional love and dependence can drive wounded adults of both sexes into obsessive-compulsive relationships to feed their attachment hunger. Often, the target of such uncontrolled desire is idealized, even worshiped as a sexual object, as the one magic person in all the world who can make the obsessor happy and whole. Obsessor behavior is characterized by intense longing and feeling abandoned when apart, irrational jealousy and possessiveness, spying and frequent telephoning, separation anxiety and panic attacks, uncontrollable desire to be an indispensable resource for money, sex, assurance, self worth, or any other need of the target.

Healing relationships are tender, caring, generous islands of intimacy that can serve a useful therapeutic purpose. They often occur after a period of suffering due to deprivation, divorce, death, emergence from an addictive love affair, or in response to dysfunctional parenting. The partners may have few of the qualities for endurance, but they can provide a soothing, healing environment to enhance recovery from psychic pain. They can be extremely fulfilling sexually as well as spiritually. Such relationships usually run their course and wither as the partners experience healing, unless they develop a more synergistic basis for continuing.

We often are not equipped to replace bad relationships for good ones in a single leap, so we may seek **transitional relationships** to help bridge the gap. People involved with each other on this basis may sense they are in transit and tend to isolate their partners from the rest of their lives, family, and associates. When such relationships run their course, goodbyes are fairly easy. They are life changing experiences that represent growth and movement toward a more enduring love relationship.

Compatible agenda relationships can be based on open, hidden, or automatic subconscious agendas we have developed to maintain psychological stability. They depend upon two people filling each others' holes in their makeup and depend upon input from one another. These agendas may be in the form of unspoken, unilateral contracts. If two people believe they can get what they want from each other, they can embark on a relationship that lasts so long as they get their needs met from each other. If and when one of their needs changes and the other does not respond as before, the hidden contract may rupture, along with the relationship.

Life script relationships are subconscious attempts by couples to play out unfinished business from their childhoods, reenacting scenes or complex patterns they may not even recall. In this mode, there often is the need to repeat patterns of behavior that can be traced back through the family tree for several generations to learn lessons that were never completed. We either try to duplicate dysfunctional family circumstances or choose to seek fulfillment without knowing what we really want. We may either choose partners who are much like our role models or opposite to them and transfer all the old scripts onto the new relationship.

Synergistic relationships are created by people who have substantially completed their personal growth after working through several of the previous types above. They continue to change and to grow, but their sense of worth, place in life, and self esteem are maturely established. Their relationship supports individual growth, even if it means periodic separation. However tight their connection, room remains for individuality of both partners. Neither partner is locked into traditional gender roles or family patterns. They have developed significant tolerance for ambiguity and neither partner expects the other to change very much. The relationship is not static; they learn to negotiate the terms of their relationship as both of them change and grow differently.

Robert McKinley says a new kind of **equals relationship** can emerge from the self awareness that liberates us from the perpetual discontent of our learned interpersonal habits. Mutual agreement determines the events between them. One can take care of the other, and then the roles can reverse while each retains responsibility for himself. Both partners remain nondependent, separate, and fully themselves while the relationship fulfills wishes for presence, for sharing, for touching. Each holds the other as a precious privilege and not a necessity. Except for sexual monogamy, each expects and treasures that both have social relationships with others. Sex is shared between equals as an intimate end in itself, as the ultimate pleasure and secondarily for procreation. They agree to share sex without deforming it into a means for other ends. Each can ask for their wishes from the other and accept a yes or no response without feeling rejected. Recognizing the preciousness of each other, both accept the fact of impermanence.

Having escaped their infantile interpersonal habits, both grasp that all relationships are temporary. The two may agree to end the relationship if other contingencies take priority. An equals relationship begins with each giving the other up. Relating as equals and personal peace go together in such enlightened partnerships, according to McKinley.

Barbara M. Fishman discovered three forms of relationships during her career as a marriage and family therapist. She calls them exchanges, mergers, and resonances. People in an **exchange** use the relationship as a background to their lives, not its center. There personal interests, career, friendships, and social lives come first. Their goals are separateness, freedom from traditional gender roles, personal autonomy, and equal contributions to the relationship. People in a **merger** make togetherness their primary interest, leaving their personal, career, and social activities come in at a distance, if at all. These couples follow traditional gender roles and pursue a lifestyle that emphasizes family and security. According to Fishman, couples in a **resonance** relationship recognize that both separateness and closeness have their place. They acknowledge that traditional gender roles can be shaped according to the talents and desires of each other. Their kind of relationship allows for personal freedom, intimacy, and compromise. Obviously, the resonance model is more likely to be sustainable over long periods than either the merger or the exchange.

Another model of relationships by Dorothy Tennov is based on phases from initial attraction to some relatively permanent bond. **Phase 1** is one of sampling, initiating, or auditioning as we try to find out what we have in common with the other person. In this stage, people determine whether they will find a deeper involvement desirable. **Phase 2** involves bargaining or exploring in which the partners invest time, energy, and money to see if the benefits are worth the burdens. If the returns are not sufficient, the relationship will not develop further, will stagnate, or will deteriorate. **Phase 3** is one of integrating or revising, or intensifying with some form of commitment being established. This is a very euphoric phase as the partners gradually begin to stop dating other people and begin to fantasize about a permanent coupling. In **Phase 4,** a bonding takes place as the couple formally ratifies their commitment. It can be marked by an event such as moving in to live together or getting married. This stage can then exist for life, or some extended period. But, if the relationship does not nurture the growth of each partner, it can begin to deteriorate. If that happens, in **Phase 5,** the couple experiences a reduction of tolerance for each other and more touchy problems limit their sharing of feelings and ideas. More and more unresolved conflicts begin driving a wedge between the couple. They ultimately begin drifting apart in **Phase 6,** as the relationship begins stagnating and the partners begin avoiding each other. Finally, the relationship is terminated in **Phase 7** as one or both parties asks for a formal ending.

While these models are all somewhat different, they all have a common pattern. The common thread that pulls people together involves filling holes in each other left from their incomplete, distorted childhood. Incomplete people find each other, they express attraction, they begin spending time together, they test their compatibility, they decide to develop a relationship, a decision to make a commitment is made, and they work to build permanence, sometimes successfully, and sometimes not. If not, the cycle may be repeated. The reason for the repetition may be that we have not worked out our own holistic health enough to bring wholeness to anyone else. We cannot give what we do not have. The first task for everyone is to work out our own health so we can create not one, but many healthy intimate relationships. That is the theme throughout this book.

Where People Do It

If you have been single and dating actively for some time, this section may seem somewhat fundamental to you. If you are exceptionally sophisticated at meeting new people and making friends easily, you might prefer to skip lightly over it. If you are re-entering single life after being married for some time, or are just entering single adult life, this material may help meet your needs. Further, please note that searching at the workplace now is very risky, albeit more so for men than women. The new sexual harassment laws can be interpreted just about any way a complainer wishes to, so it is safest to keep your search activities outside the workplace.

When you are ready to meet a significant other person, unconscious forces may take over the task of getting you in the right place at the right time. Some people may call them coincidences, but Carl Jung observed that the unexplainable meetings of life seem to be driven by an unseen force that he called "synchronicity." Jean Shinoda Bolen described many chance meetings between couples that seemed to happen on their own, but in reality may have been driven by a higher power than either partner realized at the time. Eastern mystics call the unseen matchmaker of such seemingly happenstance meetings fate, destiny, Tao, or Karma. It may be simply that one's hormones just trigger the human need to mate, or that one's psychological need to bond or connect overrides the need for independence and freedom. If you prefer you may call such coincidental meetings between two people "Godincidences." Conversely, if the relationship later turns sour, you may attribute the initial meeting to the Devil, as in the famous line by comedian Flip Wilson, "The Devil made me do it."

Whatever drives you, when you decide that you want to develop new intimate relationships, you will need to get acquainted with the kind of people whom you seek. There are many opportunities for meeting new, single people. They range from casual pick-ups at public places to singles clubs, church and other social activities groups, newspaper or magazine advertising "In Search Of (ISO)" columns, and more professional matchmaking, such as video tape dating services. You can associate with groups likely to involve people with views, interests, and values similar to yours or you may seek growth and challenge by participating with people who involve patterns of behavior differing from your traditions.

There probably are many activities in your area for getting acquainted dates. You may enjoy theater, hiking, tennis, bowling, parties, restaurants, museums, or other types of activities together. It is always a good idea to ask a new acquaintance what he/she likes to do so you can plan mutually acceptable dating activities. The Washington Ethical Society (WES) recommends that your first few outings together should be activities that permit you to interact and get to know each other. Avoid passive activities at first such as movies, theater, concerts, etc. They do not provide an opportunity for closely communicating and getting acquainted with each other. Also, WES recommends that you avoid private time in romantic settings at the outset to reduce the erotic stimulation that might begin too early. That means avoid meeting in either of your residences on a weekend night the first few times.

If you want to meet somebody new, here are some of the options for making singles contacts that might be available to you in your area:

1. Clubs for various types of activities from hiking and dancing to book reviewing.
2. Sporting events.
3. Classes that are conducted by local service groups, churches, parks, and schools.
4. Co-ed health clubs that offer exercise, dancing, swimming, tennis, and racquetball.
5. Vacation and travel groups.
6. Business networking groups in the field of your career.
7. Singles night clubs and bars are even OK if they are run as legitimate business establishments.
8. Dating services and personal ads in search columns of local news media.
9. Social clubs for widows and divorcees such as Widowed Persons Service and Parents Without Partners.

Dancing has such a high priority in the social life of this country that I think it deserves special mention. Fisher has connected dancing to the mating ritual among many human cultures as well as animal groups. It is practically a universal indication of mutual acceptance when two searching partners get into a physical rhythm with each other, whether on the dance floor or in a singles bar. For some, dancing is an essential step toward choosing a mate. They believe the opportunity to move as a couple in time with music is a prerequisite to love making. So, a good way to meet eligible single people is to attend social dances.

How easily a woman follows a man might say something about her level of assertiveness or need for autonomy. How well a man leads could have something to say about his self esteem, courage, and will power as well as his sense of rhythm and coordination. However, just because two people dance well together does not prove that they could live happily together forever after. That takes knowledge and practice of the behaviors explained in the second part of this book. If dancing is not for you, then it is counter-productive to meet someone there who likes such an activity. Obviously, you will start off on the wrong foot. *(Sorry!)* Choose some other activity that attracts single people where you feel more comfortable attending, where you can demonstrate ability to get into physical rhythm with a partner.

You can find all such outlets for singles in the local newspaper section that describes weekend activities. Attend activities that you will feel positive and good about whether or not you make a new contact. Go to places you like to go, and do things you like to do. That way you will enjoy yourself and not think you have failed or wasted your time if a new contact does not develop.

Learn To Talk Properly

Making connection with a new partner requires conversation. Few people ever take lessons in this skill as it relates to relationships. When it comes to intimate conversing, most of us learned ineffective methods from the adults who were our role models. This situation was recognized in the late 1960s by a group of counselors headed by Sherrod Miller. They found that couples who were happy together knew how to and spent more time in effectively talking to each other, using skills that troubled couples did not. They formed Interpersonal Communications Programs, Inc. (ICP) to teach better conversing. Their work was documented by Carol Saline. You will make a better impression on a new connection if you learn the skill of conversation because it is the quality of our conversations that creates happy, intimate relationships. Saline identified four fears that keep us from being candid with new partners. If you seek more intimacy with a partner, these fears must be faced, shared, and overcome:

1. Fear of Speaking Out - afraid of being disliked for something we've said. Afraid of sounding dumb or silly. Afraid that if we are honest and forthright we will hurt our partner's feelings, insult them, or wound their pride, or receive criticism or anger in return.

2. Fear of Fighting - because we never learned to fight for what we want without attacking another in a relationship. Fear that arguments always end in a stalemate or deadlock.

3. Fear of Self-disclosure - if we reveal our real selves, point out the location of all our soft spots, our deep dark secrets, we are afraid that we will look foolish, even perverted. We might lose respect and love of our partner and be rejected.

4. Fear of Entrapment - if we get too close we may lose ourselves and our freedom. Our boundaries may be breached. The risks of intimacy outweigh the benefits. We fear failure to be able to keep a promise because it will cause blame and criticism.

The result of all these fears is that we tend to use a defensive talking strategy to avoid being hurt or to get some space between us for protection or to take control. We may protect our boundaries with defensive maneuvers that include lies, half truths, omissions, and cover-ups or we resort to manipulation. These are all reasonable options when we feel threatened. The problem is that our feeling of fear may not be based in reality. When both partners act on it, true intimacy is prevented and some form of distortion is substituted for a real relationship. What is worse, we may seek to maintain control of the situation and unintentionally lose it in the process. Some people just clam up and avoid talking about crucial issues at all.

ICP recognizes two components of talk: content and style. The style must be matched to the content if intimate connection is to be achieved. Four styles of talking were identified in the ICP meeting groups: small talk, control talk, search talk, and straight talk. Behind these styles are intention and behavior. Having the ability to apply the appropriate style to your intention creates choices between the styles that are available. Matching up intention, content, and style is a skill that can be learned. It is a very important component of intimacy in close relationships.

Small talk is a chatty, sociable style that is suitable for casual content, when you meet someone for the first time, and in opening conversations with friends or business associates. The content is common, ordinary, everyday topics. Little or no tension exists and emotions are on an even keel. Feelings are not openly expressed or described. The tone of voice and pace of speech are normal, relaxed, friendly, and even-handed. The operating pronoun in small talk is "IT." There is very little risk in small talk. Small talk is the appropriate style for reporting events and factual information, keeping informed, joking and storytelling, routine questions that begin with who, what, when, why, where, etc., simple descriptions, making unelaborate statements about yourself, your habits and preferences, your opinions, your physical state, your actions and your friends. Small talk is not appropriate for handling strong differences or important issues. Much of our cocktail-party small talk is based on who we are, what we do, and what we have. Intimacy could be enhanced in small talk if we learned to share more of who we are earlier in new relationships.

There is a certain skill about making small talk that you can learn to make a better first impression on meeting people you would like to know better. It is facilitated by asking questions that begin with who, what, where, when, and why that will encourage your partners to express themselves. Consider learning to make small talk a great investment of your time. It is easy to small talk when you give yourself naturally to the dialogue. Small talk is a way new acquaintances can give to each other without undue risk at the beginning. There is no shortage of things to talk about and you probably have lots of interesting things to say, if you give yourself the chance. If you can begin conversations easily with a new acquaintance, small talk can lead to bigger things.

Information is the new currency of society and small talk is the way we exchange it. When you enter a social group be prepared for small talk with a personal agenda of your own, written down in advance if necessary to help you remember it. Emphasize what you hope to get and to give in first encounters with new people. If you don't know what you want from a small talk encounter, you can't ask for it and the other person will not be able to give it to you. If there is no exchange, there can be no relationship. So, plan out your strategy, write a script in advance if necessary, and give responsibility to the other people to plan out theirs.

The principles for winning friends and influencing people presented by Dale Carnegie back in 1936 are powerful talking tools for creating intimacy quickly in small talk. Here are some of the important points scattered throughout his world famous book, *How to Win Friends and Influence People.*

"The deepest desire in human nature is to be important to another person. Everybody likes a compliment. We spend about 95 percent of the time thinking about ourselves. If we stop thinking about ourselves for a while and begin to think of the other (person's) good points, and be lavish in our sincere praise, (and show verbally that we are concerned about their problems and opinions) people will cherish (us) and repeat our words over a lifetime. If there is any secret of success, it lies in the ability to get the other person's point of view and see things from his angle as well as your own. People are not interested in you. They are not interested in me. They are interested in themselves. You can make more friends in two months by being interested in other people than you can in two years by trying to get other people interested in you."

Carnegie encapsulated his principles for effective relationships in several groups of talking principles. Here is the way I would summarize them: Become genuinely interested in your partner; smile; remember that a person's name is to him/her the sweetest, most important sound in any language (even if he/she doesn't like it); be an active listener; encourage your partner to talk about him/her self; respect your partner's opinions and boundaries; talk in terms of the other person's interests; make the other person feel important, and do it sincerely; give truthful compliments that are based on I statements, e.g., "I really like the way you look in that dress/suit"; try honestly to see your partner's point of view; ask questions instead of giving direct orders; praise the slightest improvement in behavior of your partner and praise every improvement; be courteous and pay little attentions to your partner; avoid monologues. No one likes a person who only talks about him/herself. If you have that much to get off your chest, find a third party to dump it on or invest in some professional therapy.

Control talk is well known to most of us because it is the style we experienced most of the time as children. The operating pronoun in control talk is "YOU". Our parents and teachers thought they had to control us at all times, so control talk is what we usually heard from them as children. There is little wonder it is the style we are most likely to use as adults. In situations requiring clear, authoritative leadership, control talk is appropriate. Control talk is troublesome in intimate relationships when the partners struggle over who is in charge. Light forms of control talk are effective to persuade, to direct or lead, to seek but not force agreement, and to use legitimate authority. Light control talk is preferred when it instructs, it cautions, it establishes expectations, it leads, it signals rising tension, it praises, and it advises.

Untrained people often move from light to **heavy control talk.** Heavy control talk always wounds when it expresses blame and causes guilt. When we accuse or attack, the victim usually becomes defensive and counterattacks to justify his/her position. Heavy control talk can be active or passive, direct or indirect. Active heavy control talk involves labeling, name-calling, mind-reading, blaming, accusing, threatening, demanding, evaluating and putting down, ventilating, ordering, taunting, ridiculing, criticizing, nagging, lying, and sarcasm. Active heavy control talk is fairly easy to spot because we feel its cutting edge, and it usually destroys intimacy.

Passive heavy control talk can be even more destructive to a relationship because its users employ weakness and dependency to get their way. They may make themselves appear victimized or inadequate. If you are the recipient of passive heavy control talk, your reaction may be anger, but you might not know why. You may be hooked by either guilt or pity and you are confused about responding. Passive heavy control talk is exposed by these behaviors: complaining, whining, denying, disqualifying, withholding, pseudo-questions, poor-me, foot dragging, assuming blame, playing the martyr, self putdowns, excuses, changing topics, self-righteousness, sweetness and light, and keeping score. If this list sounds like the undesirable product of codependent behavior, you are on the way to recovery.

Saline emphasizes that control talk is the most common talking style of our ad hoc culture, in spite of its obvious negative impact on intimacy. In unhealthy modes, it often is motivated by anger, frustration, broken expectations, fear of threatening situations, desperation, sadness, and the cultural need to win, to make someone feel guilty, and to force or to resist change. If these motivations sound like traits of your dysfunctional family, there might be a connection between your learned talking style and the difficulties you have now in maintaining healthy, intimate relationships. The mark of a weak or troubled relationship is concentration by the partners on using small talk and control talk. The aim is to build intimacy not destroy it, so a better way is recommended by ICP.

Search talk is the style to use when you want to test the waters, when there is an issue of concern around or mutual plans to be made. Search talk seeks information, but without the judgmental accusation of control talk. Search talk is an intellectual, nonjudgmental fact-finder. Search talk uses many qualifiers to maintain a tentative environment. The operating pronouns in search talk are WE and US. Search talk is preferred when your intention is to check out uncertainties, share impressions and hunt for explanations of behavior, examine possible causes, and pose tentative solutions. Search talk is low risk.

Straight talk begins inside yourself, where the other styles never venture. In straight talk, we lower our boundaries and expose the real inner self that is normally concealed, often even from our conscious mind. By agreement, straight talk is a safe zone where all attacks are outlawed. Straight talk is needed when you have something personal or special to share about an emotional, highly charged issue or conflict. You bore to the core of an issue without blaming, demanding, defending, or deceiving. Straight talk is for dealing with negatives, handling tension, expressing dissatisfaction, resolving broken expectations, expressing hurt without laying on guilt, getting beyond anger to deeper intentions, asking forgiveness, sharing vulnerability, resolving a harmful pattern, dealing with impending change, affirming yourself, your partner, and your relationship, using your partner as a consultant, and appreciating your partner. The operating pronoun in straight talk is I. Straight talk is for building intimacy, but it is also extremely high risk.

Matching these styles to the situation is appropriate in healthy ad hoc relationships. The one exception is that heavy control talk never works and should be avoided, always. Light control talk is appropriate in situations calling for accepted leadership. Parents, bosses, and teachers need light control talk. Heavy control statements beginning with "you" almost always are intended to tell others how to act. They make people feel trapped, guilty, and angry. Instead of saying, "You make me mad." own your feelings with an I statement by saying, "I get mad when you accuse me of something I did not do."

Small talk will not help solve major issues. To stay in small talk when denying major issues will not build intimacy. Search talk is fine for exploring a sensitive issue, but it won't help solve an emotional, ethical conflict. Even in straight talk, you cannot assume your partner knows what is going on inside your head. Saline defined six basic talking skills that you can use to help share your full awareness of yourself with an intimate partner. These skills may be more or less difficult for codependent people, depending upon their personality preferences described in Chapter 3.

1. Speak for yourself - begin sentences with "I" instead of "you." Use the pronouns I, me, my, mine to claim ownership of your perceptions and actions without attempting to control. Many of us were raised to think that such I statements are improper because they seem vain, ego-centric, even arrogant. But speaking for yourself establishes you as the authority on your awareness. It declares that your thoughts, feelings, and intentions have great value. In terms of personality preferences, introverts may have more difficulty expressing themselves verbally than extraverts.

2. Say what your senses tell you that you see and hear. Sensing observations provide a frame of reference so people understand exactly what you mean. "I guess you don't like my fancy cooking" becomes much more effective in the form, "I notice you did not eat much of my gourmet veal dish. I would appreciate knowing what you think of it." People with introverted sensing may find it difficult to experience their sensory input and describe it to others without seeming to be hostile.

3. Say what you think. If you don't express your thoughts, you deny your self-worth, and you shut your partner out of your head. Your ideas are valuable, and statements beginning with "I" state your personal view of things without making authoritative or controlling generalizations that make people defend themselves. "I thought the movie was great." "I don't think you understand my

meaning." People who prefer introverted thinking may have to work a little more at this than those who prefer extraverted thinking.

4. Say what you feel. Behind every feeling usually is a wish for something or someone to change. Statements such as "I feel — when you —." illustrate this rule. Give yourself permission to describe your feelings, and give your partner responsibility for his/her own reaction. It is all right to feel terrified, sad, glad, mad, lustful, sick, depressed, guilty, etc. Feelings are just feelings, they are not "beings." It is healthy to say, "I feel terrified, and I am OK." Putting both good and bad feelings into words is not easy for many people; it may be nearly impossible for male codependents with introverted feeling preference. In our culture, real men are supposed to be stoic, unemotional, rational, logical, scientific, and objective. Many women who are extraverted feelers think otherwise. What many women may mean when they complain that their men are not "intimate" is that men really do not verbalize their feelings. This conflict will be explored more deeply in Chapter 7.

If you prefer introversion, these talking skills may not be natural for you and the practice of them may consume more energy than they naturally do for an extravert. An extravert talks to think, while an introvert must think much more to talk. To offset some introversion, you may act as though you are a designated hostess or host and quietly match up people by introducing them to each other or being helpful in other ways, such as serving refreshments or helping with other arrangements. This diversion will take the emphasis off your own nervousness a bit and help you to mingle more easily.

Dealing With Shyness and Rejection

You will incur the risk of rejection as you begin reaching out to others. Codependents may be reluctant to make an opening invitation to a stranger for fear of being rejected. They may feel too shy or think they are uninteresting. We may feel that a rejection indicates something is wrong with us, because of our low self esteem. Not true. There may be all sorts of reasons someone new says no to your invitation, and most of them have nothing at all to do with you. On the other hand, shyness can prevent us from creating healthy new relationships.

Shyness often is projection of a negative self image that is not supported by the facts. Blaming themselves for failures and giving credit for successes to outside circumstances is part of the baggage codependent people carry. Anything you can do to help bolster your self esteem will help overcome shyness. The secret to overcoming shyness is in learning to like yourself more as you are, even if you can't dance, swim, fly, sing, lift 200 pounds, or do any other thing you demean yourself for not doing or being. The prescription for overcoming shyness begins with learning relaxation methods to overcome the physical symptoms. They can include sweating, shaking, pounding heart, tense stomach, urge to urinate, tight breathing, dry mouth, blushing and dizziness.

Overcome a low opinion about yourself. Turn negative self descriptions such as inept, unlovable, insignificant, unwanted, weak, stupid, useless, inferior, inadequate, withdrawn, etc. into positive self descriptions such as self-assured, confident, worthwhile, relaxed, adequate, likeable, significant, attractive, secure, valuable, capable, lovable, effective, etc. You can stand in front of a full length mirror and repeat such positive affirmations (beginning with "I am —") to yourself. While looking at your image, maybe while nude, repeat, "You are self assured, attractive, likeable," etc. That might sound a bit ridiculous, but remember that we tend to act like we think. If you repeat these thoughts enough, you actually will begin to believe them.

Also, you can learn the social graces that make shyness go away. Take some courses or read up on what people in social situations need to know. Something so fundamental as how to dress or use makeup to appear attractive is important. Then, if you find someone you would like to know better, walk up and say so, in your own words. You can do it in spite of feeling shy, although it may take more energy if you prefer introversion to extraversion.

The way to manage (you may not be able to overcome) the fear of rejection is to develop higher self esteem. Then, actually experience rejection and live through it to try again, and again. It just takes practice to get used to hearing no. Of course, you may be the recipient of an invitation, as well. Then, it will be your turn to say yes or no.

A key skill in making new connections is the ability to make small talk with a new acquaintance. You can use small talk to engage a new acquaintance and make that first response a yes. Rejections are the necessary first stages required to get to acceptance. It is just a numbers game. The more rejections you get, the more acceptances are likely. Can you accept that as a mathematical probability?

Go to some function where you are likely to meet other single people with interests similar to yours. Never share everything about your personal or professional life on the first date. It may take up to 12 weeks or 6-9 dates to decide whether or not you want to pursue a relationship. During that time, it is wise to avoid making a major investment in the relationship, either financially or emotionally. Use the opportunity to get to know the person, to share yourself, to see how well he/she meets your criteria. A person who tries to seduce you in the early dates probably is not acting in a healthy manner. Be aware that premature sexual involvement can abort an otherwise healthy process. Sexuality can distort your perception and cloud your decision making ability with its addictive quality, especially if you are codependent.

Each of these search methods demands lots of self confidence, social poise, and the ability to tolerate rejection. There always is the chance that new relationships will abort after you have invested time, money, and emotional energy trying to achieve intimacy and commitment. The risk of getting hurt is always there any time you expose your self to someone and get rejected. It seems that we must risk being vulnerable in order to seek love. But, as with other new skills, it gets easier with practice. When you try to meet new people, confidence and motivation may follow if you apply the practices recommended throughout this book.

What To Look For

If you want a new, committed relationship, Judith Sills suggests you take a rational approach to the search to avoid confusing your decision making with emotional baggage in your makeup, i.e., the tendency dominant feelers have to get carried away with romance. She suggests that the basic relationship needs of most people boil down to security, companionship, intimacy, and love. She suggests three major rules for picking a partner. **First** is availability; the person must be without professional, personal, social, or emotional entanglements that would make it difficult to get together in the way that you want. **Second** is benefits; everyone brings baggage or burdens to every relationship. In general, the older the person the more baggage. The benefits must outweigh the burdens in your value system. **Third** is feelings about your self; being in the relationship should make you feel good about yourself. It should enhance your self esteem and not degrade it. If any of these criteria are missing in sufficient amounts, the chances for intimacy and commitment are diminished even though short-term casual sexual attraction or physical chemistry may be strong.

You might begin your rational planning by writing out a description of the ideal person and lifestyle you seek to meet your needs. Be as specific and as complete as possible about such aspects as character, assets, behavior, activities, and moods, in addition to visual appearance. Making such a list will help you realize a lot about yourself, your needs, wants, and values, that may need further analysis. Visualizing the person will help you to fit people you meet into your model more easily, or eliminate them more quickly. Your compatibility check list might include the following descriptions of what you want in a partner:

- Personal interests (hiking, art, raising animals, music)
- Practical information (age, physical appearance, family, debts)
- Health practices (exercise, diet, smoking, drugs, alcohol)
- Philosophical and moral attitudes (politics, religion, spirituality)
- Education and cultural background (travel, occupation, taste in art, entertainment, clothing)
- Social style (outgoing, quiet, wild, inhibited, spontaneous, party goer)
- Love style (affectionate, caressive, aloof, romantic, uninhibited, undemonstrative)
- Communicating style (kinesthetic, audible, visual)
- Goals (professional, family, children, personal, social, relationship)
- Personality - (MBTI type as explained in Chapter 3)
- Professional or career financial success and stability
- Decision making style in a committed partnership
- Companionship, emotional acceptance, and social network

This description should also include all the aspects of any new relationship that are important to you in terms of the holistic personhood; physical, intellectual, emotional, and spiritual. They can be combined with the four elements of your preferred life style in professional, social, personal, and private dimensions. Structuring the two dimensions of lifestyle and personhood, as illustrated in *Table 4.1,* may help you to fill out the specific details about the kind of relationship you want. This matrix illustrates four main elements of relationships and the four components of personal wholeness. Taken together, they make up a compatibility model.

This model can help you sort out the complex aspects of relationships and deal with the many complex issues involved when you describe criteria for making choices. **Professional** means the work one does for a living; **social** means what one does for fun; **personal** means relations with family and relatives; **private** means what one is like alone or with a lover.

   Physical elements are those aspects related to the senses such as feel, hear, see, smell, and taste; **Intellectual** elements relate to rational thinking and logical reasoning. **Emotional** elements relate to feelings and values. **Spiritual** elements relate to the intuitive side of life that knows we are more than biochemical creatures, although scientific proof is lacking. The latter is not a matter of religion in this context. It is more a matter of metaphysics, i.e., the knowing that we are more than physical. It is the connection between people that occurs at the energetic level of the soul, transcending time and space. Few people ever develop fully their consciousness of the spiritual/intuitive side of themselves. Those who try to do so enjoy a greater richness in life, because they approach a unity with the universe that transcends all the physical senses. The healthy individual seeks a balance in all four quadrants of life, neglecting the use of none in his/her search for wholeness.

THE 16-STEP MODEL OF BEHAVIOR

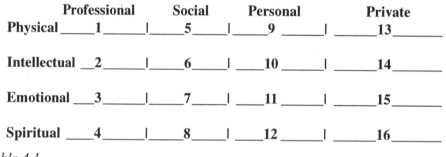

	Professional	Social	Personal	Private
Physical	1	5	9	13
Intellectual	2	6	10	14
Emotional	3	7	11	15
Spiritual	4	8	12	16

Table 4.1

   Once you know precisely what it is you want, you will automatically move toward it, as though the Universe has already granted your desire, and the energy you need will be focused in that direction. Dedication and tenacity are two indispensable ingredients for getting what you want out of life. If you do not have what you want, it just means you are still on the journey. You may recall the old saying, "If at first you don't succeed, try and try again." But I suggest you add, " – and then try something else because there is no sense in making a fool of yourself." After you read the rest of this book, you may want to come back to this task and revise your statement as you will probably also do after you apply it to a few real life situations for practice.

   If we can develop the imaginary visual image of the ideal type of person we seek, and drive it into our subconscious minds, it may be possible to attract people like that into our lives. Jesus said, " – all things are possible to him that believes." (Mark 9:23) Which would you rather have, a dysfunctional partner like your faulty role models or one more closely approaching an ideal person? If you believe without a doubt that you can, maybe you can. But, if you live with doubt and disbelief, guess what? It is unlikely that you will get your dream. People have an uncanny ability to act in ways that prove their beliefs to be true. Some counselors imply that we get exactly what we want out of life, even though our goals may be subconscious. It seems we attract people who are just about as holistically healthy as we are. We may create our own reality. So why not try to create the best one you can?

Conversely, do not get carried away with your model of a perfect mate after you create it. It may eliminate too many prospects who can provide the security, intimacy, love, and companionship you need to be happy. It may not be possible to meet all your requirements among the people available to you. Stay open to possibilities with everyone you meet who is available, who comes with benefits to offset the burdens, and who makes you feel good about yourself when you are together. If you do not reject people on first appearances because they seem to fail some aspect of your ideal model, you may find many more prospects than you thought possible with whom you can be happy. Avoid the idea that there is only one perfect person out there for you. Use the model as a guide, but don't let it eliminate people who may not be a perfect fit at first sight. Give yourself and them some time and the opportunity to demonstrate the potential benefits before you make a final decision.

Developing several platonic, unconditional friendships among both sexes is an excellent way of boosting your lagging self esteem, and feeling the benefits of being needed and useful to somebody else. That way, you get the much needed practice in getting reacquainted with your own new self. Some writers estimate there are 70 million single adults in this country. Many of them report a lack of nurturing friendships, although most people have plenty of acquaintances. Women seem to have more close friends than men do, possibly because men are taught to be more competitive, stoic, and self reliant. Women who are career oriented often find it difficult to make close women friends. The competitive work environment prohibits close friendships for them as it does for men.

In general, men do not have buddies except in the context of groupings for mutual defense, such as on athletic teams or in war, or for mutual self indulgence in fraternal clubs and the like. History shows it to be extremely difficult, although not impossible, for platonic friendships to be maintained between opposite sexes. Men may need women more than women need men for maintenance of self esteem. Although half of all friendships occur between people within five years in age, people of all ages can develop beautiful and fruitful friendships with each other. Both sexes can benefit from having a group of close friends of either or both sexes. Maintain a community of friends at various levels of intimacy and commitment with up to 10 people at a time, because no one person can meet all your needs all the time.

Platonic relationships have been observed by Lettie Progrebin in seven degrees of closeness. They range from acquaintances, neighbors, confederates, pals, close kin, and coworkers, to friends. A true friend is someone who exhibits loyalty and trust, is generous with time, effort, acceptance, and money; is truthful, open, and honest. Necessary ingredients of friendship include physical proximity, similarity, reciprocal liking, and openness about self-disclosure. Friendships with these ingredients often last a lifetime. Although romance and sex are enhanced by friendship, friendship is often diminished by romance and sex. Platonic friendships should be morally pure, free of the whiplash of libido. The greeting of a platonic friend warms the heart; when it quickens the loins, the rules change. When a friendship crosses that line, it becomes a love affair albeit possibly a sexual friendship.

Making Decisions Confidently

Throughout the process of working through the various models presented in this chapter, people must decide and redecide whether or not to pursue the situation further with a new partner. We cannot avoid decisions because no decision is a no decision. One of my goals is to help you make more healthy choices in a condition of freedom, without the baggage accumulated from negative experiences of the past, even though their influence may be unconscious. Even though you may prefer emotional, feeling-oriented decision making, I believe applying the rational decision model described in this section can help you toward that goal. However, it may take considerable effort and time to resolve a conflict between your thinking and your feeling decision processes and to mitigate the subconscious forces involved in making rational choices.

We require time, money, and energy to invest in relationships. We can replace the money and energy, but time is irreplaceable and nonrevocable. Obviously, we can use time only once in this life. While we are with one person, we cannot be with another. I think it is crucial to use your time wisely when developing new relationships.

For every benefit that is gained from a new connection often there is a compensating loss in other relationships to consider, such as giving up time with cherished friends to be with the new beloved. If we only have one relationship, the decision is easier than when juggling multiple relationships simultaneously. Even then, we must consider alternative optional uses for our time, energy, and money. For example, you might have to decide whether to spend time in a family activity, pursue a career goal, or date your partner.

Unconscious or conscious practices of deception also await the unwary. To be fair, when in doubt men seem to infer sexual interest by women when they may only mean to express sincere friendship or desire for intimacy. On the other hand, David M. Buss has pointed out that women often are aware of the sexual affects their willful deception has on men, but they still choose to flirt to get something they want, be it taken to a favorite theater or sports event, or to gain favors and attention to validate their desirability. Buss says that while women are likely to be sexual deceivers, men are likely to be commitment deceivers, faking emotional interest when none exists to gain sexual favors. So humans sometimes deceive each other to gain access to resources the other gender possesses.

Recall from Chapter 3 that decisions are made based on logical, rational thinking and on emotional, value-based feelings. Although they use both, people generally prefer one or the other approach, i.e., thinking or feeling, and thus rely upon it with more confidence. The one preferred is more highly developed and reliable.

No matter which combination of decision processes you prefer, a balance between thinking and feeling is needed to avoid poor decisions. In other words, both the heart and the mind must be engaged. Sometimes, they can pull us in opposite directions, causing a great deal of stress until one side or the other prevails. Sometimes we can stay on the razor's edge, see-sawing from one side to the other indefinitely. This condition can be very painful and even lead to depression until the decision is resolved.

The following method of compiling a benefit/burden ratio can help to improve your comfort and confidence when deciding about investing in relationships.

Begin by setting up a sheet of paper for each of the optional choices being considered. Divide the sheet in the shape of a "T" by making a vertical line down the middle and a horizontal line across the top. Label each sheet at the top with some identification of the option, i.e., the person's name, event, or other description of the option being considered. One possible option is to label one sheet "Staying As Is" and the other "Choosing Commitment." Label the left column of each option sheet "Benefits" and the right column "Burdens."

List all the factors of the situation that you can think of and put them in the columns according to whether you classify them as benefits or burdens. Try to group your factors into sections describing your perception of the physical, intellectual, emotional, and spiritual aspects of the relationship. Further, match them up to professional, social, personal, and private realms of your preferred lifestyle. Refer to the statement you composed before for completion of the lifestyle matrix in *Figure 4.1* above. Some other issues you might consider include: the circumstances surrounding past relationships, influence of parents and family of origin, financial management and generosity, relations with friends, how you spend quality time together, how mistakes and hurts are handled, attitudes toward children or pets, the role of humor in life, balancing home life with work life, communicating and loving styles, and overall holistic health.

Then considering your personal values, give each factor a numerical weight on a scale of 1 to 100, with 1 being least important and 100 being the highest importance. When you total the weights of each column, the sum will show you whether you value the benefits or the burdens more highly. Subtract the lesser from the higher column and you will see whether that option comes down on the side of benefits or burdens and by what weight. Although it may seem to be a sensing, thinking device, the elegance of this method of valuing options is that it employs your preferences for perception and choice in the way that is unique to your personality. You can employ both your logical, rational left brain preference as well as your intuitive, emotional right brain preference in whatever proportions are unique to your makeup.

By comparing the results for all the options being considered on other sheets of paper, the decision that you prefer at that time will be more clear. Of course, new information gathered at some future time could change the result. Sometimes the choice will boil down to the lesser of the burdens. Sometimes, you may feel ambivalent about all the choices. When that happens, an honest decision usually falls out on the side of a no. A yes hardly ever is clearly without any ambivalence either. Sometimes the choice is so balanced between benefits and burdens it will cause severe stress until you decide to come down on one side or the other. If the distress threatens to become disabling, I recommend you seek professional help in sorting out your feelings and thoughts. When you have analyzed your benefit/burden options this way, you will have more confidence about the outcome of your decision.

There is one basic rule to observe in this decision process. Whatever the ratio of benefits to burdens is, do not expect your partner to change it. People do change, but only if they want to. No one can force another to change their behavior or values.

When your partners describe their likes and dislikes, believe them. Only the person, including you, can decide to change and then only when their (your) threshold of pain prompts one to take action because the burdens are sufficiently worse than the possible benefits of the change. Change is stimulated by fear of loss or ambition for gain. People change only when they perceive the anticipated gain or loss as more valuable than their present set of circumstances. They must be sufficiently discontented with their present situation to motivate action. Contentment is very difficult to overcome, because it causes us pain and energy to change. So, with the benefit/burden ratio, what you see is probably what you are going to get. If you try to make it into anything else you probably will be disappointed.

Once you have made your decision whether to continue in the relationship or not, it is best not to look back. You can always play "what if" games with yourself, but they provide very little new growth. Hindsight can always disclose another viewpoint or some new insight or perception that might have tilted your decision in the opposite direction. We can work ourselves into a state of depression by always second guessing how things might have turned out had we taken another optional choice. Recrimination and self doubt can become a habit that will stifle the hope in all future possibilities. It is best to assume that the decisions we make are the best ones at the time we make them. Of course, all decisions are subject to change as new perceptions are gained.

Whatever your choice, you can believe it is the correct one at the time, and go on from there. Life merely provides the opportunities to choose and to choose again. As Yogi Berra says, "Sometimes we come to a fork in the road and we have to take it." Perhaps there are only choices and consequences. Perhaps it is in the search itself that we find fulfillment and happiness. So, perhaps it is best to continue the search and leave the outcome up to the universe.

It may be that the task of living abundantly is merely to go with the flow as the universe inevitably unfolds. To be open to new possibilities as they emerge without putting boundary conditions in front of yourself may be true happiness. If you have no preconceived notions whatever, then there are limitless possibilities just around every corner in the ad hoc culture of today. Every instant and every encounter may be the very one that will bring you the most bliss. So, prior to commitment, close yourself off to no opportunity, say no to no invitations, and decline no new adventures in your search, so long as they do not violate your moral values or risk your mental and physical health. It is only as we extend the envelope of our experience that we grow, even though it often is painful to do so.

With your search plan in place and with confidence in your decision making process, we will work next on the issue of sexuality. After an explanation of holistic love comes discussion of communicating effectively with your partner and how to identify and observe healthy boundaries in your intimate relationships. These are core chapters of the book.

Five:

The Sexual Question

Nationally syndicated newspaper columnist Ann Landers conducted a poll on sexual values among her readers during 1995. She reported that 72 percent of women respondents would rather be held close and treated tenderly than perform "the act." In contrast, out of 67,588 replies from men, only 5,600 males, (8%) almost all over 60 years old, agreed with the women and said they would be willing to settle just for cuddling. What sex means to you will be explored in this chapter. The issue of sexual behavior must be worked through by each reader for your own physical, intellectual, emotional, and spiritual well-being. The options that are possible range from absolute celibacy to extreme perversion. This discussion may help you sort out the options and make a decision about your lifestyle that is healthy for you. It also will help you to evaluate the behavior of intimate partners, and manage the stress resulting from differences in gender related sexual attitudes that you likely will encounter.

By the end of the 1970s we had experienced a swing toward liberal attitudes about sex, including experimentation with open marriages and communes. As we near the end of the century the cycle is once again moving back toward sexual restraint and increased romanticism, possibly driven by the rampant rate of divorce and the real danger of AIDS. More recent random sample surveys reported by Robert T. Michael, et al, indicate that sexual behavior among people in America is far less exciting than the popular literature indicates. They quote Lord Chesterfield, "Sexual intercourse is grossly overrated as a pastime; the position is undignified, the pleasure is momentary, and the consequences are damnable."

This chapter discusses the issue of human sexuality from prevailing opposite viewpoints and provides understanding of gender related differences. Unlike romantic love that emanates from the Greek god, Eros, sexuality stems from the Greek god, Pan, the god of pure sensuality and physical pleasure. Either Pan or Eros may be honored by humans but, apparently, only at the expense of the other.

The mechanics of sexual performance have become common knowledge, thanks to the open press granted by the Supreme Court in 1957. However the morality involved in sexuality still is very controversial. On one hand, Ernest Hemingway reportedly said, "What is moral is what you feel good after." By that measure, sexuality can be a very moral act under certain conditions to some people some of the time. Ruth Westheimer and Louis Lieberman called for more open discussion of the morality aspects of human sexuality in all its forms from masturbation to adultery, to homosexuality. The people they surveyed usually stated they got no instruction in the moral aspects of sex, neither from their parents, theologians, or schools. Instead of positive encouragement toward healthy sex, these people got only negative prohibitions that do not reflect reality.

Our sexual behavior today probably has roots handed down for millions of years from our earliest ancestors, through biological mechanisms we are just beginning to discover. Helen E. Fisher proposes that the "silent" ovulation of women served an important function among our pre-historic ancestors. Although some women report feeling increase in libido, most modern women do not become sex-crazed at mid-cycle when the egg is released from the ovary. Their behavior among cave dwellers got the females more of what they wanted - males - to protect and provide, and males got more sex, thus assuring more variety of the species when it was initially evolving. Unchained from the ovulatory cycle of animal females, and a sex drive that peaked and waned, humans now can choose to copulate at any time for many reasons, including power, spite, lust, love, or pleasure, in addition to procreation. For some, sex is the ultimate pleasure.

Cultural Standards Affect Your Attitudes

If you enjoy an active social life and modern dating, at some point you and your partner will have to decide how to conduct your sexual lives. Sexuality is a natural part of humanity, but it carries great emotional stress for most of us as we try to reconcile the Pan and Eros within. We must strike a balance between our physical urge to procreate, social standards, and moral beliefs that demand commitment, and mutual responsibility between sexual partners. Healthy ad hoc couples integrate a natural form of appropriate sexuality that does not violate the boundaries of either partner.

Traditional sexual attitudes include a belief that the sole purpose of sex is procreation and it should be strictly limited to married couples. Enlightened asceticism acknowledges that sex is not evil per se, but that it needs to be carefully controlled. Relational beliefs describe humanistic liberals who believe sexual behavior should be based on the relationship of the couple or "situational" ethics. Radical humanists permit any type of sexual behavior so long as neither partner is harmed by it. Recreational beliefs assume the main reason for sex is to enjoy the pleasure and have fun. In sexual anarchy, no limits are placed on any type of sexual behavior. Thus, sexual behavior is seen to vary by age, education, location, sex, race, religion, and other social variables.

Moral, ethical, and religious values in our culture now range from the purely uncommitted, recreational extreme to conservative religious views which still sanction sexual relations only in marriage. The contrast in values between preboomers, boomers, and postboomers (defined in Chapter 2) reaches a climax with their sexual behavior. Most preboomer females were taught that "nice" women do not make sexual overtures to men or behave freely in bed. But many postboomer women think nothing of inviting a desirable man to share their beds and bodies on the most casual, recreational basis. Many boomer women are caught between the sexual freedom of their liberated peers and children and the traditional behavior of their parents.

Research indicates there is a lot of sex going on among single adults in the 1990s over a wide age range. Studies among high school students in the District of Columbia found that two thirds of the 10th grade boys and one-fifth of the girls had four or more sexual partners. That is quite different behavior than their parents and grandparents adopted. Recreational sex also is reported more among singles over age 50. Some of it may be to make up for lost time in dysfunctional marriages. Sex among younger single adults now is practically universal, although it is not always equally satisfying for both partners. Some of it may be healthy fun, but some of it is dysfunctional manipulation and a substitute for boredom. For many people, sex is more of a barrier to intimacy rather than a part of it. There still seems to be considerable confusion between men and women about intimacy and sexuality that causes much unhappiness and frustration.

Men and women interviewed in research studies often define love and sex in different ways. Many women prefer love to be shown in deep sharing of feelings through intimate dialogue. They see sex more as a demeaning expression of physical lust unless it is accompanied by sincere sharing intellectually, emotionally, and spiritually as well. Some codependent survivors who are driven by a need to reinforce their lagging self esteem may feel a compulsive desire to find one or more sex partners to provide the nurturing parenting they never got. For others it just may be a simple, hormone driven, lustful, biological itch that wants satisfaction.

Others may consider sex to have far more deeper significance as an expression of love and commitment. There is no commonly accepted standard of sexual behavior anymore. In its healthy form, sex may be a form of communication, cooperation, expression, love, bonding, play, ecstasy, fun, closeness, joy, power, warmth, and physical intimacy. In its unhealthy form, sex becomes controlling, fearful, angry, empty, "icky", manipulative, crazy, addictive, distancing, using, overwhelming, and isolating.

Whether or not you find an active sexual relationship satisfying without being married has roots deep in the resolution of your physical drives, your values, and your religious training. Your sexual behavior also is affected by your cultural circumstances and your overall psychological maturity. There is a wide variety of opinion about what may be right or wrong in sexuality among consenting adults.

Considerable divergence of opinion about singles sex also exists among the various religious denominations and church leaders, depending on how they interpret Biblical instruction. As with most personal values, there are no absolute authorities, only interpretations. Opinions of religious leaders on fornication range from "definitely not" to "maybe" to "OK."

I don't mean to imply any particular religious authority in this matter. It is a choice of behavior that you must decide for yourself. However, I think it is important to base the decision on a concept of personal wholeness, involving the emotional and spiritual aspects as well as the intellectual and physical aspects. Without connecting on all four of these levels, most couples will find that a sexual relationship based on physical lust alone is difficult to sustain very long.

A study of the affect of personality preference on the timing of sex in a new relationship was reported by Marvin Rytting and Roger Ware in the 1993 Conference Proceedings of the Association for Psychological Type. It showed that those who preferred **NTP** in their makeup are more in favor of beginning sexual relations early on, while those preferring the **SJ** makeup were more inclined to be sensitive about the need for sexual restraint. They stated, "It may be that to ask an **SJ** to adopt an open, free, spontaneous lifestyle in relationships which come more naturally to the opposite **NP** would be as unwarranted as to demand that the **NP** adopt the constraints that are more natural for the **SJ**." So knowing your own personality type can help you to avoid stressful ambivalence if your partner wants a sexual lifestyle that would be uncomfortable for you.

The Washington Ethical Society suggests that premature sex before a couple achieves monogamous commitment can block intimacy and prevent a relationship from developing in a healthy, holistic way. When sex is the complete experience of connection, physically, intellectually, emotionally and spiritually, that it can be, each becomes everyone to the other and neither needs or wants any other substitute. On the other hand, some might say that no healthy, intimate relationship can survive without good sex because it releases and empowers the primal male and female in each of us.

The Changing Sexual Times

The roles of men and women in sexual relations have changed dramatically since World War II. The womens' liberation movement is pursuing equality into the bedroom, where equal pleasure between men and women now is expected as the divine right of both genders. Feminist leaders gave women permission to be assertive and aggressive lovers. Some may say, "And why not?" Sex was removed from the dark, and all the better for those females who know no more about their potential for sexual pleasure than dysfunctional families model for them. The introduction of "the pill" gave women unilateral control over birth control. Women were relieved of the life-long consequences of unwanted pregnancy, and sexual liberation was born. But, as the record of unwed mothers attests, the pill did not diminish their genetic role of reproduction. It did relieve irresponsible men of their obligations to protect and provide for their offspring, however, because promiscuous women could no longer proclaim the paternal identity of their impregnators.

Many young men initially thought the turn-about in the late 1960s was heavenly as males and females began sharing equally in sexual participation, if not responsibility. Monogamy and commitment were challenged by the avant-garde leaders of the times. Open marriage, free sex, and communal living were tested by youths during the late 1970s. In place of the sacrificial commitment without freedom of the 1950s, they substituted personal freedom without commitment. People maturing during that time who were involved in that movement made a significant and lasting impact on all of society. Male-female roles shifted permanently. Men began finding themselves being sex objects of assertive women who believed in their own right to the pleasure of orgasm. Turn about was fair play. Sexual performance became a legitimate field for scientific enquiry, self-help books, movies, video tape and Dolby sound. A new role for professional sex therapy began. Professional sex surrogates became available for enhancing pleasure of the sexually dysfunctional.

Women expected men to perform better as lovers in addition to performing well as wage earners and fathers. Women also became wage earners as well as mothers as a new form of social equality between the sexes emerged during the 1970s. Some men jumped into their new role appreciatively with support for womens' equality. Other men with shaky self esteem were intimidated by the more assertive women and withdrew apprehensively from the new form of commitment. Still others played the new game, although confused and bewildered.

With the new sexual permissiveness, there came dramatic rises in divorce and a general unrest between the sexes. Both sides began developing a new definition of happiness and personal fulfillment. More recently there came the new threat of Acquired Immune Deficiency Syndrome (AIDS). The threat of AIDS has caused many people to be more cautious in technique and choice of sexual partner. Relationships between the sexes still are changing as we approach the new century.

Many people of both sexes are learning what they really want and how to ask for it. They also are learning when to say "no" or "not now." In fact, unless there is a definitely articulated "yes" a man may find it necessary to defend himself in court on charges of date rape after a mutually satisfying night. Some women cannot tell the difference between rape and second thoughts that occur the morning (or weeks or months) after a bungled lovemaking session in which there was not mutual pleasure. Sex is becoming a dangerous game for men who misread the intentions of their partners. No longer does silent acquiescence mean yes. The legal definition of rape is being redefined. The more radical feminists would define rape as any sexual encounter in which the female feels remorse afterward.

Perhaps the extremes in both directions from conservative to liberal are changing into a more middle-of-the-road approach to sexuality. One common theme runs through the current research: members of each sex are becoming more sensitive to their own needs and that of their partners. A more satisfying form of sexual communication is becoming available to people who can step out of rigid, traditional values into the light of healthy mutual sexual expression. But, for some of the boomers and postboomers, the light still takes some getting used to.

The Addictive Power of Sex

Production of the hormone, testosterone, makes sex a compelling drive among healthy men and women from puberty to old age, although it varies among both genders. Some experts believe that the sex drive is more physical in males, and more social, cultural, and psychological in females, but it seems to be driven by testosterone in both genders. Abraham Maslow placed sex as a fundamental basis for the pyramid of needs he developed, next to the basic drive for food and shelter.

Simon LeVay reported studies that show laboratory animals that are wired so they can self stimulate pleasure centers in the brain will defer food and drink, swim moats, jump hurdles, and cross electrified grids to repeat the pleasure. He says, "One would not be surprised if human brain regions concerned with sex were connected with such a system." From the sea horse that mates in a hypnotic underwater ballet, to the rodent who copulates to death, to the female mantis who chews off the head of her mate while copulating (presumably so he won't have to think about what he is doing,) there is astonishing diversity among the ways life forms pass on their genes to their offspring. A few rare species reproduce asexually but they are the exception. Some species live to nurture their young into adulthood and some parents die soon after mating, leaving their offspring to fend for themselves. One species of bird stealthily inserts its single egg, which hatches earlier than the others, in the nest of a different species. Then it actually pushes the unhatched eggs out of the nest and proceeds to enjoy the instinctive protection and provisions of its "adoptive" parents.

Unfortunately, some humans are not as discriminating in their mating as are most animals. There is no process of natural selection among us. For some, the exhilaration that comes with sexual acceptance by any other human being triggers their basic needs for self esteem so deeply that addiction is an appropriate word for the compulsive-obsessive desire that results. When erotica culminates in orgasm, the high can be as exhilarating as a drug hit. Orgasm does have similar chemical affects in the brain, stimulating desire for another euphoric "fix" again and again.

LeVay reported biological studies which indicate that a small gland deep in the brain called the hypothalamus may be responsible for sexual arousal. When it is removed from a male animal, its sex drive is also removed. Of course, no such experiments have been conducted on humans. Nevertheless, LeVay has reported many studies which show that human sexual behavior, including courtship and parenting, apparently is driven by secretion of chemical hormones from various glands that are converted into physical behavior.

Moreover, scientists have been able to trace the chain of oxytocin secretion and distribution from the brain to the nipples that causes the excretion of milk from nursing mothers. Some nursing mothers describe intense pleasure akin to orgasm while nursing. It is little wonder that female breasts are significant in sexual foreplay, and that new fathers can become intensely jealous of their nursing infants. The oxytocin that is secreted by the pituitary gland at orgasm and during breast feeding and giving birth may be responsible for the pleasure of sexual arousal and orgasm. In men, it may be secretion of other hormones, viropresson, and nitrogen oxide, that drives their sexual behavior. Test rodents have been observed to become sexually aggressive with nitrogen oxide and highly protective of their mates and their turf after given high doses of viropresson. It seems that nature uses chemistry to ensure pair bonding between sexually active couples.

During the anticipation phase, you can experience heart palpations, sweating, dizziness, nausea, shaking, compulsive urination and bowel movements. These are all physical symptoms of a rush of adrenaline the body is automatically producing to stimulate the "fight or flight" response that occurs when people anticipate any mortal danger or exhilarating event. They should act as signals that something may be dangerous for you in what you are about to do. According to Stephen Segaller, Carl Jung took note of this phenomenon among his patients and attributed the result to projection of the inner anima, the female in man, and the inner animus, the male in woman, onto a sex object.

Jung described the results this way: "You see, you have a certain image inside yourself, without knowing it, of woman, of THE woman. Then you see that girl, or at least a good imitation of your type, and instantly you get a seizure and you are gone. And afterwards you may discover that it was a hell of a mistake. So you see a man is quite capable, or intelligent enough to see that the woman of his choice was no choice at all, he has been captured; he sees that she is no good at all, that she is a hell of a business, and he tells me so, and he says, 'For God's sake, Doctor, help me to get rid of that woman' - and he can't, he is like clay in her fingers. That is the archetype; that is the archetype of the anima, and he thinks it is all his soul, you know."

The demand for orgasm can be excited by just the look of the opposite sex in a movie, a magazine advertisement, an erotic book, smells of perfume or body odor, fantasies, or of course, a partially clothed person at a night club, beach, or even on the street. When they cannot control or resist their urge for orgasm from such stimuli, some people can truly be classified as addicted. It doesn't mean they chose it or that mentally they do not hate it. But, like the drug addict, it feels so good to their body, and they like it so much, they want it again and again even though the results may ruin their lives and create untold suffering for their offspring.

The first step in kicking any addiction requires acknowledging that one is out of control and that phase of life has become unmanageable. In fact, several 12-step sex anonymous support programs throughout the country are based on this affliction, which at this level is considered a disease as powerful as alcoholism. Sometimes it persists into the middle and later years of life, even though people are married and have children. Frequently, another movie is produced around this theme of passion out of control because it is a fairly common phenomenon. People in the grips of a sexual obsession may need professional help in addition to support groups to help regain control of their lives.

The sex drive urges even the poorest, sickest, and the most ignorant to continue making babies when they are likely to suffer starvation. Some women in dysfunctional families have a baby to obtain unconditional love and meet their need for self esteem. Once the child begins expressing autonomy, another baby may be needed to fulfill that role. Thus, more and more single mothers require government financial aid and remain only slightly more than children themselves. Then, there are the millions of abortions and thousands of abandoned babies that also attest to the powerful drive of sex in humans.

The desire to enjoy the pleasures of sex and fulfill the parental instinct is so urgent that the painful results do not matter to many people. Sex addicts often risk their professional, social, and family lives, and even their physical and psychological health to pursue the high fix of sexual accommodation. Once the addictive sexual hook is set, the only choices remaining are very painful, like a fish caught on the line. If you fight it, you do severe damage to yourself, and if you don't, your ending will be even more unpleasant. Withdrawal from sexual addiction can be as painful as the symptoms of a drug addict, and requires professional therapy to escape its magic attraction.

However, if there is a healthy holistic commitment, sexual sharing bonds two people like nothing else. For some, it becomes a special, personal, only-we-two-can-share-it secret. One can learn whether his/her heart, head, and genitals line up together or operate separately. Sex allows participants to make assessments quickly that would have taken earlier, less liberated generations many months of formal dating. Things happen very fast when you get naked and start sleeping with someone. If you pick a sick partner, things can get pretty oppressive, soon. Some people can "lie" with their genitals as with any form of communication, but it definitely is more difficult.

The urge to mate and reproduce is so great I think we all are born sex addicts to some extent. Most of us learn to control that drive in socially accepted ways, but many do not. The basic text for Sex and Love Addicts Anonymous contains the following description of sex addiction: "The basic human need for a close (physical) relationship with another, combined with the realization of one's (reproductive) sexual capacity as an expression of commitment in a relationship, can be debased by addiction into a compulsive search for sex and romance, or obsessional entrapment in relationships characterized by a personal neediness and hyper-dependency - in patterns that can forever prevent really meeting the underlying need for authentic experience of self and other."

When they discovered orgasm, many people of the boomer generation immediately pulsated with the popular cultural standards of the "new morality", "guilt-free sex," and the "sexual revolution" of the 1960s. They dived into situations where they could experience sexual contact without any emotional involvement, i.e., sex without commitment. They created a mass market for sexually explicit films, videos and books. Many found that they can become addicted to these sexual substitutes, also. The issue of feminism introduced a conflict for both women and men who wanted professional equality. Now, many of the boomer generation are worrying about trying to merge sexual freedom and independent professional goals with a traditional family life they recall as children, while they keep their own teenagers from repeating their mistakes.

Many adults in our current society exhibit characteristics of sex addicts. The result for many is a dysfunctional sex life. When the sex and love addicts ultimately face the truth about themselves, they can know authentic terror. The only solution is to replace the faulty infantile programming with a more mature, adult concept of self worth that is not based on who one is sleeping with. Unfortunately, that is a lot easier said than done. The first step is in recognizing this dysfunction and committing to overcome it. If this description of sex addiction has spoken to you, perhaps it is time for you to seek the help of a Sex Addicts Anonymous support group in your area or to see a professional therapist.

Two Opposing Moral Beliefs

To practice a healthy sex life, one needs a fairly clear understanding of his/her own moral boundaries, and one's behavior must match one's values and beliefs. To help you sort out your views about sex, following is a brief essay presenting opposing descriptions of the sexual options that I was assigned to compose by a therapist to help me sort out my own values. One extreme view is based on traditional, conservative, legalistic values. The other extreme is based on a more liberal humanistic, social view of sexual relations among modern consenting adults. Perhaps these divergent viewpoints will help you to set healthy guidelines for your own behavior, before the circumstance for choosing arises.

GIVEN: Sexual Relations Between Consenting Single Adults Is a Symbol of Serious Commitment with Deep Religious Constraints

The Pro Argument:

The role of sex in life basically is to reproduce the species in a committed relationship that guarantees a measure of security and nurturance of offspring during the crucial years of their dependency. Conservative interpreters of the Bible consider every act of sexual mating to be an act of potential procreation. Thus, sex should not be part of a relationship unless it follows a commitment to create and maintain a family. Such commitment should only evolve from the sharing of mutual love. Sex is the ultimate expression of that love in its highest calling of procreation of the species.

Religious morality argues against liberal sexuality. Absent procreation, the Apostle Paul said that it was better for widowed people (and presumably divorced) to marry than to burn with lust, but he preferred the unmarried and widows to remain single, so they could serve God freely. (I Corinthians 7:7-9) The Ten Commandments includes specific prohibition of adultery, and Jesus reinforced that commandment. He noted that a man who even looks upon a married woman with lust was committing adultery. (Matthew 5: 27-28) He also said that marriage was sacred and that anyone who engages in sex after divorce engages in adultery, which is prohibited by one of the Ten Commandments. (Matthew 5:31-32) St. Paul also definitely rejected the option of fornication, i.e., sex outside of marriage (Corinthians, 7:1-2).

Since sex originally was intended only to beget children, it follows that engaging in sex should carry the potential for begetting children, with no artificial means of contraception. The responsibility of caring for children is a complementary job of both parents, with each one carrying defined gender roles - the mother being the nest builder and the father earning the income to support the family.

Since families represent blood relationships with instinctive love and devotion among the members, it follows that sex is a prelude to creating this type of family unit. Sex signifies the willingness to take on this lifetime family responsibility by each of the partners. It is a natural consummation or expression of love between potential parents.

Sex is the ultimate form of sharing of the most sheltered, valued, and sensitive parts of human bodies. Human production of sex hormones determines our separate gender qualities and should be protected from sexually transmitted diseases. Sexual relations imply a highly significant evidence of pair-bonding that sets the couple apart from all others, and makes their relationship more intimate than any other relationship they can have with others. It is more significant than social relations with acquaintances, neighbors, coworkers, friends, and relatives. The physical bonding of sex also signifies a personal caring for the other that transcends the mere connecting of bodies and shared orgasms. It signifies a concern and responsibility for the holistic wellness of the other and confirms the wish to be together and to share in all of life's lesser experiences. It says to the world, "this is my partner in life and love and parenting" - even if children do not result from the mating.

Sex is the supreme act of pair-bonding and should not be shared with anyone but the person one has selected as the life partner. It is the symbol of the utmost in commitment to another. Without such commitment to parenting and life-long mutual support, the sex drive should be sublimated and single people should remain celibate. This is the ideal of a healthy, moral approach to human sexuality, with sex as the culmination of a commitment to another person for life. Only in this mode are self esteem and emotional health assured for the human race.

The Con Argument:

The role of sex in human life actually is twofold. One is to propagate the species. The other is to provide the ultimate pleasure that comes from sharing with another person this most sensuous aspect of intimate human relations. With birth control methods and abortions easily available, pregnancy is no longer the unwanted potential outcome of sex that it once was. The responsibility for parenting of children that might result from sex no longer is an issue in the decision whether to engage in singles sex or not. With the economic liberation of women, neither is it any longer necessary for men to assume responsibility for the financial support of their sexual partners. The feminist movement has advanced and encouraged women to seek sexual freedom and satisfaction more openly. Federal laws on abortion also place the use of their own bodies completely in control of women, who are freer to choose the sexual behavior they want.

To stimulate thinking people to take on the responsibility of parenting, the creator placed sexual needs just above the drive for food and shelter. Therefore, functional people have a high physical drive to mate. In this culture, that drive is emphasized by the communications media, which uses sexual appeals to sell all sorts of products and services. Our culture also holds physical beauty and virility in high esteem, again due to the youthful models used in the media, at the expense of holistic bonding.

The primary criterion now is the physical desire and inclination of the partners to enjoy this form of sharing in the physical act of ultimate pleasure that sex is without deep emotional bonding. So long as there is no physical force or emotional coercion applied to the other by either partner, engagement in sex is the free choice of each person. The only proviso is one of law that allows adultery as grounds for divorce among married couples, and the protection of ones self from physical harm and sexually transmitted diseases.

Two people can maintain as much or as little pair-bonding and sharing of lifestyles as they choose while enjoying pleasurable sexual contact when the desire is mutual. Commitment to each other need not go beyond the agreement to be monogamous so long as the relationship exists on that plane of intimacy. There need not be any further commitment to future marriage, economic or financial responsibility, or future obligation to maintain the relationship. If either partner chooses, each is free to maintain an active social life with co-workers, friends, and relations, while engaging in monogamous (or even polygamous) sex on occasion with the preferred partner. Since sexual desire is hormonally based, it is not necessary to be "in love" or cathected with the partner, although being friends with one's sexual partner enhances the relationship. On the other hand, becoming sexually active with a platonic friend changes the relationship into a sexual affair and the rules then often change, with commitment possibly being added.

Commitment derives from one's investment in the object or project of commitment. If the investment is of little value, then the commitment is also. If the investment is of high value, then the commitment will be more highly esteemed. This is not the same as saying that the agreement to engage in sex together implies a foregoing commitment in advance. It is not likely that both partners to singles sexual friendships will value their investment in exactly the same way, so it is possible that one partner may feel more committed than the other. This can result in uneven emotions and some cognitive dissonance on the part of the more committed partner, with simultaneous feelings of attraction and repulsion. The sense of values and behavior must be brought into some level plane if both partners are to be satisfied equally with the relationship. Commitment is a unilateral act and neither sexual partner can impart his value system to the other.

Unless it is explicitly stated, enjoyment of sexual relations with a consenting and willing partner is not of itself an act of commitment, nor does it imply responsibility at any level. In fact, further commitment beyond the willingness to enjoy sex may be overtly avoided by many single couples where marriage is not a consideration. If both partners are fulfilled in the sexual aspects of the relationship, there need be no assumption of any further responsibility on the part of either one for the physical, intellectual, emotional, or spiritual welfare of the other. In such relationships, neither party is immorally exploiting the other, and no guilt need be attached to the sexual enjoyment of each other for its own sake.

The Moral/Social Balance

Somewhere between these two extreme views there lies a holistic, rational, ethical, and moral approach to the question of sex that is right for you. In a healthy, intimate relationship it should lie about in the same place for both partners. If either one or the other partner sees sex as something more or less than the other one does, sexuality will not be the source of pleasure and joy many believe the creator meant for it to be for either one. Undoubtedly, some readers may wish for more specific instructions on what is right or wrong regarding their sexuality. Unfortunately, as you read above, the opinions vary from one extreme to another. There is a lot of sexual ambiguity in our culture.

On the one side, people are blasted with the benefits of freedom and self expression. On the other, conservatives shout sin and damnation, decry destruction of family values, and loss of human dignity. Feminists cry for equality while they simultaneously demand legislative protection. The political government tries to straddle the fence to avoid losing voters on both sides, while taxpayers pay to raise illegitimate children and provide abortions simultaneously. School children are taught how to use condoms, but not how to be parents. Meanwhile, deaths from AIDS increase at an epidemic rate. It is a mess.

Instead of groping for what is "right" or "wrong," a more healthy approach may be to stay within legal bounds while seeking sexual complementarity with a partner. John and Linda Friel found that healthy sexual people are able to :

1. Be turned on to each other some of the time.
2. Initiate sex some of the time without making the other just a sex object.
3. Respond to sexual advances freely and openly without losing self or feeling like an object or thing.
4. Say no when they don't feel like it and not feel paralyzingly guilty.
5. Accept a no said to them without feeling paralyzingly ashamed, afraid, or angry.
6. Tell each other what they want and need in bed, including protection from disease.
7. Mutually cooperate so that each feels satisfied they are getting what they want or need.
8. Enjoy variations in sexual expression limited only by the needs and wants and creativity of the people involved.

A sexual partner can be your friend, your confidant, your most trusted ally, your lover, and pal because we are most vulnerable during sexual expression. If the child within you feels safe to come out and play spontaneously with such a partner, your sexual parts will work just fine. Perhaps you can see why the suggestion that a mutual commitment to monogamy as a prerequisite to sex has many benefits to recommend it, besides the moral and spiritual ones. People who can have sex without any meaningful connection to their partners may learn little about their partners or themselves. No intimate relationship can endure without respect and trust. Aside from its potential shield against AIDS and other sexually transmitted diseases, sexual monogamy preserves the couple's energy for recycling and renewing their relationship.

However, monogamy can be constricting if it is based on a contrived agreement to predict the future commitment or adhere to a secret unilateral contract. Unlike their grandparents, modern postboomers consider monogamy as a choice and not a rule. When monogamy is imposed externally by social standards, it chafes and itches and many people are all too inclined to scratch. One new approach to sexuality discussed by therapists on a TV talk show was described as VENIS - Very Erotic Non-Insertive Sex - as a solution to the goal of orgasm without AIDS issue. In a society with no rules about sex, how does one establish his own boundaries?

Meeting Your Needs – Ethically

Sex and love are not the same, even though we often call having sex "making love." Although sex can be one form of expressing love, sex cannot satisfy love needs and love cannot satisfy sex needs. I believe the sex act can have any meaning we choose to place on it or no meaning at all. Basically, it is a physical act to procreate the species and give pleasure. It can even be enjoyed solo, but for purposes of this book we are assuming a partner. For some, it is used to affirm their self esteem if they do not have a well-established identity based on self affirmation and a sense of competence in professional or social areas. Such people may seek sex compulsively to reconfirm their self esteem, provide security, and meet their addictive needs.

With all the divergent views now existing in our culture, each person must be responsible for his/her own sexual actions. Invitation or social pressure for casual sex from your more liberated friends may create tension and stress if it violates your moral behavioral standards. The resulting emotional turmoil is called "cognitive dissonance" by psychologists. This disorder results from a lack of harmony or agreement between belief and action, a discordant, incompatible, incongruous situation.

So, beware of the potential for mental suffering in ad hoc sexual friendships if your partner takes a less committed, more casual approach to sex than your values support. You may need to change your values to match your behavior, or control your behavior to match your values, if you are to avoid painful emotional conflicts. If your feelings and beliefs are deep, professional counseling may be needed to make the adjustment to more liberal modern values. You should not indulge in singles-sex unless you can successfully balance your erotic needs with the dissonance that may be involved so that the benefits exceed the burdens. If your values are based on a more conservative upbringing, you may need to rid yourself of moral barriers to a free enjoyment of pleasurable sex. You may need to break free of hidden emotional restraints, such as guilt or fear. Either your behavior or your thinking must change to bring both into congruence if guilt is to be avoided and sex enjoyed to its fullest.

If it is consistent with your values and religious beliefs, and the opportunity develops, an active, satisfying sex life may contribute to your well being. Sex as a compulsive way of replacing your self esteem should be avoided because sex is hormonally based, while love is more than physical. Platonic love can occur without sex and sex can occur without love. When the two are experienced together, the emotional atmosphere is beautiful, living poetry. Sexual love reaches its peak when partners know and care about each other intimately, and it is enjoyed without guilt. Then, sexual love can be the prototypical act of intimacy well into mature age.

Friendships can blossom out of sexual compatibility and mutual fulfillment of one another's erotic needs. Some people believe uncommitted sexual relationships can imply a certain amount of emotional bonding, caring, trust, and loyalty between two friends who complement each other physically. However, all experts do not agree with this view. Premature sex actually can preclude real emotional intimacy in fledgling relationships. Real holistic intimacy includes open communications, caring, and sharing with each other in many ways including intellectual, emotional, and spiritual besides just the physical. Feelings between sexually active friends may or may not include the romantic interludes of first love or the eternal love sworn by married couples. They can range from general liking, tenderness, fellowship, and romantic fusion, all the way to synergistic love and can be the basis for developing deeper intimacy. If two people find sex mutually satisfying, there can be an emotional and spiritual response involved. Such friendships may go beyond common social, career, or cultural interests.

Sexual friendships can develop even when other interests are not shared. Sexual exploration and indulgence of erotic fantasies about the other can come first, leading to emotional closeness and discovery of other common interests. In fact, unless the beginning romantic, erotic, and lustful aspects of sexual friendships develop into a more enduring emotional intimacy, it will be difficult to sustain such a relationship on sex alone. Influences from the external environment can overcome the filters that fresh lovers use to blot out the burdens in any sexually driven relationship. These include such intrusions as work overload, conflicting demands on time and energy, other suitors, power struggles, and family commitments. People who do not develop sustaining emotional pair-bonding can drift into and out of sexual friendships. They may seek to renew the physical stimulation with new partners when the excitement of fulfilled genital fantasies wears out and the relationship becomes predictable.

Couples who are sexually active but only lightly committed must work to sustain friendship and avoid burnout by injecting variety in their time together. They must make arrangements for erotic activities that each of them can enjoy. They also must convey appreciation for the other in their respective lives. They can find self actualization through the combined resources and mutual support in the relationship. But, beware of the pressures for temporary connections in sexual friendships. You can avoid the likely pain of disappointment and loss if the relationship deteriorates without developing into genuine love with true intimacy. If love and intimacy do not develop and the relationship stays on the purely genital level, it likely will be difficult to sustain if the initial erotic excitement deteriorates into boredom and familiarity.

You should not use sex to satisfy other needs or to mask problems that should be dealt with differently. Such behavior is not being honest with yourself and it is not fair to your partner. Obviously, you should practice safe sex to protect the health of both yourself and your partner. AIDS currently is the greatest danger associated with promiscuous sex, but it is not the only health danger to be avoided. There are 30 or more other sexually transmitted dangers ranging from simple infections to more serious diseases.

There are many different nonsexual behavioral factors that can distort and blunt the sexual act and interfere with healthy relationships. Your partner also may bring nonsexual baggage into the bedroom, and that, too, should be discussed openly and solved outside of the sexual relationship. These nonsexual factors, described by Frank Hajcak and Patricia Garwood, that cannot appropriately be met in sexual relations, and thus cause unsatisfying results, should be identified and removed from the bedroom:

- sex to gain affection
- sex to control
- sex to avoid intimacy
- sex for revenge
- sex to avoid loneliness
- sex to overcome jealousy
- sex for atonement

- sex to overcome boredom
- sex to safeguard fidelity
- sex to dominate
- sex to confirm sexuality
- sex as a haven
- sex to build self esteem
- sex for social pressure
- sex to overcome guilt
- sex to buffer depression
- sex to mask anger
- sex as rebellion

If any of these objectives is carried into the bedroom, even though subconsciously, it will confuse the sex act. Neither the nonsexual objective nor sexual needs will be satisfied. Both sexual and nonsexual needs will be frustrated and the relationship will be flawed. A careful analysis may disclose that you carry over some of them from your family of origin, unresolved and still powerful enough to mar your adult relationships. These nonsexual needs should be identified and resolved outside the bedroom in an atmosphere of open communication between the partners so that sex can be the undistorted pleasure it was intended to be.

Avoid Gender Misunderstanding

Since Sigmund Freud first developed psychotherapy, differences have been reported between the way men and women express love. Whether these differences are learned through family role models or are transmitted genetically has not been proven. John Gray went so far as to say, "Men are from Mars and women are from Venus." There probably is something of both earth and the stars at work. We know the moon controls the tides, so it is no great leap of imagination to assume that other cosmic forces affect human lives in ways we cannot yet sense or measure. There has always seemed to be a social struggle for power going on between the sexes, in addition. With the traditional complementary roles of men and women now being redefined by more economic equality, a new dimension of competition for power and control has entered intimate relationships. It is as if competition in the factory or office between men and women who both are employed is taken home and carried into the bedroom or living room or wherever. The actors only shift the drama from work life to love life. Some couples seem to persist in confusing the differences between gender roles at work and at home. True maleness and femaleness are given full expression from the depths of human ancestral inheritance through the sexual elements in relationships.

Since few people ever reach deeply enough to uncover their natural essence, relationships often manifest our confusion and adolescent development. When each partner is mature enough to be who they really are, rather than what they think society decrees them to be, true sexual intimacy can elicit the highest good in both. Until that level of awareness is achieved by both partners, interpersonal conflicts are likely to be expressed in sexual terms because of their lopsided development. Unfortunately, neither men nor women in our culture experience many fully developed adult role models in their families. Without healthy modeling of female and male roles we cannot hope to grow into mature adult sexuality until we become aware of our dysfunction. We must make the investment of time, energy, and money it takes to find our pathway to completion.

The evidence of our sexual dysfunction abounds in studies reported by Shere Hite, Michael McGill, and William Novak. Women complain that the men in their lives do not know how or do not choose to express love and affection sufficiently, apart from sex. Women commonly complain that men are not ready or capable of a full, equal, and supportive emotional relationship. Women say they want more attention from their men, more active listening, more emotional sharing and less intellectualizing or rational talking. Their men may be successful professionally and even sensitive or willing to be committed, but they somehow lack completion as whole human beings. Talking about work and current events is desirable but it does not equal sharing of emotions for women in these studies.

Women studied expect a commensurate depth, an equal emotional exchange, with each party bringing comparable communication of self to the relationship. When they feel shut out and prevented from knowing their men in depth, they feel unloved. Many men apparently do not understand this need of women for intimacy at all. Only among their women friends do women experience the emotional equality they seek. Said one woman in the McGill survey, "It really is unfair. A woman lays herself open to a man (note the sexual innuendo), she is willing to tell him anything and everything about herself, and what does she get in return? She gets screwed, that's what. Literally and figuratively screwed!"

Novak quoted one of his female subjects as follows: "Most men just are not all that tuned to women. We need a lot of strokes, warm hugs, and plenty of time. Men have a different outlook. They are used to getting quickly to the point and coming up with the right answers. For women, it's the process that is important. Women usually want more feeling, more talking, more touching. Men can separate the sexual from the emotional, but most women can't. It's incredible to meet someone at the door you've slept with and he doesn't even want to hug you. I want somebody who knows how to be tender and physical out of bed, too. "

From a man in the McGill study we get the other side. "I guess I do use sex a lot to substitute for my feelings, or at least to substitute for talking about my feelings. There are a lot of reasons. You have to start with the fact that sex is a lot more fun than anything else I can think of. It sure is easier than trying to talk things through. Then, too, it gets to be a habit. You get used to using sex to make up after a fight or to make you feel good when you're depressed or to celebrate when there's something to celebrate. What it really comes down to is I am not very comfortable expressing my emotions — I don't think many men are — but I am pretty comfortable with sex. So I just sort of let sex speak for me."

The confusion between sexual roles and intimacy is seen in this perceptive quote from one of McGill's female respondents. "Sex changes everything. Once you start sleeping together you can't be as close, you just can't. Good friends talk about sex, men or women, talk about sex. They ask questions, share their feelings, try to figure what it's all about. People who have sex together never talk about it. They get into performing and proving, none of which was there when they were just friends talking about sex. Every close friendship I've ever had with a man sooner or later became an affair, and the friendship ended when the affair started. Once you've been to bed with a man, he won't let you into his head and he stops sharing, he stops being a friend and starts being a lover." Some women obviously want more than just intellectual talk from their intimate men, even though that is about the best many can expect.

The confusion that some men experience can be felt in this remark, "I think women have this need to analyze everything, talk it through down to every little detail, no matter how private it may be. If you don't do the same thing, they accuse you of not loving them enough. If I don't talk about my feelings, it may be I am not feeling anything. Do you think she will accept that? No way, not for a minute. She gets all over me for not being 'feeling' – whatever that means. It's one of those areas where you just can't seem to win with a woman. You're damned if you do and damned if you don't." This opinion may not be far from reality for many men.

Of love and sex, another woman said to McGill, "I have a husband who is a great lover. On the other hand, I have a lover who is terrible in bed, but he talks to me. He talks about himself, about us, we even talk about sex. Because he is so open with me, I have the feeling that he is giving much more of himself to me than my husband, and in a lot of ways I love him more. Believe me, sex is great but it's no substitute for real love." For many women such as this one, intimacy is evidenced by the depth of feelings expressed in conversation. Suffice it here to say that talking styles have as much to contribute to or detract from intimacy as does the content of the messages. It is obvious that many women view sex as only one dimension of an intimate relationship. For them, it is a dimension that contributes no more to the development of closeness than do private and personal self-disclosures.

Unfortunately, some men still confuse sex with love. They end up aggravating their women, which only adds to their stress, and the cycle repeats. She wants verbal intimacy, he responds with sex minus verbal intimacy. She withholds because she feels unloved. He demands more sex because he feels rejected. She demands more verbal intimacy because she feels rejected. Soon, they can be deadlocked, each in their own isolated pain. If they can't talk about it, breakups or multiple affairs often result. Of course, this conflict can work in reverse as well, with a man being the emotionally deprived or sex-abused partner. But those couples do not appear often in the published studies.

The qualities that make a man or woman successful in business, and thus desirable from the viewpoint of professional success, counter the desire for intimacy in private. Said one of Novak's male subjects about women, "They want us to be two different people at the same time. Women want us to be successful at work, tough, aggressive, and earning a good income. They want me to be driven at work, but sensitive, emotional, and vulnerable, and intimate at home. Society just does not permit you to be that integrated. Something has to give; either you end up being too soft at work, or you are too tight and controlled at home. There is very little place in business for emotional honesty or for caring. You have to be realistic about this, but women who want soft men are anything but realistic. And whenever women are faced with a kind and nurturant guy who isn't very successful professionally, they often still choose the man of power and achievement."

Men often complain about the hypocrisy of modern women; and they feel duped and angry. They maintain that despite all that women say about wanting sensitive, loving men, these same women are quick to flee when they encounter men who actually have these qualities if they are not accompanied with the macho image and male dominance of the past. Some women seem to want their men to be two different people, one who is professionally driven and successful for material comfort and security, and another who is sensitive, vulnerable, emotionally open, and intimate. For them, sexual fulfillment requires equal elements of both material success and sensuality. That is too tall an order for many men to fulfill, but it seems to be the recipe for successful relationships for many women.

Of course, the preference for intimate sharing could be reversed, with the man being more feeling, and the woman being more thinking. But, as I noted above, such couples rarely show up in the studies that have been published. Recall from Chapter 3 that women who prefer thinking and men who prefer feeling are a minority in our culture. Many couples are suffering needlessly because the situation is not apparently improving very rapidly, and they can't seem to talk about it. However, to be fair, there also are many men who do feel comfortable sharing their emotions with women, but apparently they were not encountered very often by the women in these studies.

There are many good reasons for developing intimacy along lines of sharing outside of sex. In fact, sexual deviations may be related to lack of true intimacy. Studies among animals show inappropriate sexual behavior among insects, birds, rats, and dogs that have been reared in isolation. Their behavior improves when they are given intimate nonsexual social support. Social, nonsexual intimacy may be a path to improved mental health for humans also. Close, intimate relationships provide a sense of security, a predictability, a certainty that improves decision making. Nonsexual intimacy can increase ones self-awareness and can offset feelings of meaninglessness in our high-tech culture. It can provide a psychological safety net in a risky world. Most importantly, it would mean that we might know love. Neither sex wants to be abused, and they both want to be loved. Neither partner is going to think the other is very loving if he/she seeks only his/her physical satisfaction. One of McGill's male respondents put it, "I never knew how much I was loved until I loved."

Although we have mastered the physical mechanics of sexual connection, many have lost the joys of sexuality in a strange confusion between personal wholeness and physically intimate ways of relating. Often, sexual problems among couples really mask problems of expressing personal wholeness. When we express ourselves with another totally, sex becomes far more than "screwing." It becomes the "making of love,". The Malones expressed it this way, "After orgasm, we feel more together, more alive, and more connected even though we have just ended. We feel closer. That is the important difference between making love rather than screwing." We can learn how to add the closeness of love, with its intellectual, emotional, and spiritual intimacy, to the physical connection. When we combine such intimate closeness with the physical thrills of sex, intimacy can be elevated to the awareness of God and universal peace that was the original Garden of Eden. If we ever experience that level of wholeness with another, nothing less will suffice.

Sex On The Rebound

The feeling of deprivation from loss of the physical body contact with a partner may be difficult to deal with when an ad hoc relationship ends. For many grieving people, especially those whose dominant preference is sensory perception, the empty bedroom is far worse than the empty living room or kitchen. Sexually relating is connected to self esteem. It definitely plays a part in how we value ourselves. Once enjoyed, loss of sexual connection in your life can bring excruciating longing. For codependents, grieving for lost sexuality amounts to the work of completing your own self image. At first, you may recoil from the loss and deprivation of her/his physical presence, with no need whatever for sex. After several celibate months, your production of testosterone may again begin to assert its need for release of sexual tension. This can be an excruciating loss for many, setting up conflicts that are difficult to resolve.

The feeling of physical deprivation and need for substituting physical contact for lost intimacy may be so acute as to drive anyone into a sexual relationship with any available volunteer prematurely. Sometimes, such relationships blossom into synergistic partnerships, and they can be temporarily healing in their own right. They also can generate grief on top of grief, if they break up. Over two thirds of rebound marriages that occur prematurely during this time of grief end in divorce. If you have the opportunity of dating or intimate relationships soon after a significant loss of a lover, try to avoid too much emotional investment until you have completed most of the task of detachment from your previous partner.

In this situation, there really are only three possible sexual alternatives: (1) celibacy, (2) masturbation or (3) casual dating encounters. Your intellectual, emotional, and spiritual condition all will be involved in the decision, in addition to your physical body image. If you are active socially, there may be some assertive volunteers who generously offer to fill the sexual role for you, who "know what you need." You will need to guard against such volunteers during your period of vulnerability if you suspect their motives. Under normal conditions, people often can sense the motivation of others and use this knowledge to protect their sexual boundaries if need be. In the depression of grief, this discretionary sense often is dulled. Survivors sometimes can be lured into rash activities that are not good for them at that time. Many grieving survivors have found themselves entrapped into a sexually driven rebound relationship before they were intellectually, emotionally, and spiritually ready. If you fall into such a trap, the resulting dissonance can be a major setback in your grief work. It may not be healthy to engage in a sexual relationship purely out of the need for a physical substitute.

The euphoria of sexual arousal and orgasm at this stage of your recovery can set up an altered state of consciousness that may become addictive and destructive. It can provide a temporary escape from grief like the temporary escape from anxiety that can be provided by alcohol or drug abuse. You live for the next hit or fix to offset your painful discomfort and feeling of abandonment. If you are sexually vulnerable during grief, it is easy to get in over your head without understanding what is happening.

When sexual behavior becomes compulsive or gets out of control, you may need to seek professional help. Recognizing it as a symptom of your need for physical substitution or an attempt to deal with anxiety, lowered self esteem, loneliness, and other basic feelings of loss may be the first step in recovery. Healthy, active, sexual relationships can be a part of your reconstruction. But, unless you can renew sexual activity without addictive compulsion, anxiety, or guilt, perhaps abstinence may be the best course for a while until your wholeness has been perfected.

Underlying all these sexual issues is the possibility that social trends from liberal to conservative sexuality is cyclical over time. Jonathan Gathorne-Hardy documented such repeated cycles for the past 400 years of history in Western cultures. However, these cycles take from 80 to 100 years to complete, so our choices may be determined by the phase of the cycle that we presently experience. It appears that we may be completing another such cycle and that sexual liberalism is once again peaking, to be followed by another cycle of conservatism. If so, the trend may be away from a sexuality that has little basis in emotional bonding, toward a form of expression that involves a return to balance between romance and animalism. This trend toward a spiritual form of sexuality may be expressed in these words from her interpretation by Marianne Williamson.

"When you equate yourself with a body, you will always experience depression. Equating another person with a body will bring up the same anxiety. One of the ways the body can be used to manufacture depression is through loveless sex. Our sexual impulses become canvases onto which we extend love or project our fear. When sex is of the Holy Spirit, it is a deepening of intimate communication. The Holy Spirit uses sex to heal us; the ego uses it to wound us. Sometimes we have thought that sex with another person would cement the bond between us, and instead, it turned out to manufacture more illusion and anxiety than there was before. It is only when sex is a vehicle for spiritual communion that it is truly loving, that it joins us to another person. Then it is a sacred act."

If this chapter was a bit heavy for you to read, you might wish to take a short break before you begin the next chapter. Next, we will discuss the implications of holistic love between intimate couples. It may be that love does, indeed, make the world go around, even in the ad hoc society.

Six:
Holistic Love and Self Esteem

Are there differences between romance and love, infatuation and lust, attachment and commitment? Many writers and human experience seem to indicate there are; sex can exist without love, and love can exist without sex. Somerset Maugham observed cultural differences about love when he wrote, "In France, a man who has ruined himself for women is generally regarded with sympathy and admiration; there is a feeling it was worthwhile, and the man who has done it feels a certain pride in the fact. In England, he will be thought and will think himself a damned fool. The English are not an amorous race and are only sufficiently sexual for purposes of reproducing the species. That love should so absorb a man has seemed to them unworthy."

Carl Jung wrote, "I have again and again been faced with the mystery of love, and have never been able to explain what it is." It is a mystery that requires exploration. So, in this chapter, I describe a new holistic model of love that incorporates both rational and emotional aspects with roots extending back throughout history. It adds the latest in spiritual and psychological insight to those ancient models. When you understand and practice this new model, you may appreciate the mystery and begin to grow through love to others and to the overall universe, of which each person is an equal part, and perhaps divorce will be less likely in your ad hoc future.

Recent discoveries about our brain chemistry seem to relate our feelings of longing, searching, finding, and linking to changes in the levels of chemicals called endorphins in the brain. This romantic "wiring" of our systems may account for the psychological and physical abuse many people are willing to endure for fear of losing "him" or "her." Robert Johnson spoke of confusion about love, "Hardly anybody in our world knows the difference between loving someone and being in love with someone. We have the language for it, but we don't have the concept for it, collectively speaking. To love someone is to draw close to that person as a human being. To be in love with someone is to make a divinity out of one's beloved, which neither he nor she, nor oneself, can ever live up to." The pathway of holistic loving may seem miraculous when its many benefits begin to manifest in your life, as they surely will if you prepare the way. So let us begin.

Love as Both Noun and Verb

"What is this thing called love?" Cole Porter wrote that question into a song for the 1929 production of his Broadway play "Wake Up and Dream." One of the earliest celebrations of romantic love was written in the Song of Solomon, recorded in the Old Testament. The cry for love was expressed by St. Paul, (whom many scholars think never married) "If I speak with the tongues of men and of angels, but have not love, I am only a resounding gong or a clanging cymbal. If I have the gift of prophecy and can fathom all mysteries and all knowledge, and if I have faith that can move mountains, but have not love, I am nothing. If I give all I possess to the poor and surrender my body to the flames, but have not love, I gain nothing." (1 Corinthians 13:1-3) Historical literature depicts a paradox for lovers who are driven to experience the ecstacy and life changing moods of romantic, erotic love while also fearing the profound deprivation and sorrow when it ends, as it often does.

If an addiction is anything that becomes compulsive enough to destroy your freedom of choice, then romantic love will do nicely. According to Ethel Person, "The aim of (romantic) love is nothing less than to overcome separateness and achieve union or merger with the beloved. The longing for union and for the elusive complex gratifications it promises is so compelling that the lover willingly forgoes lesser pleasures and endures any pain. The peremptoriness of the wish is such that the lover will sacrifice anything whatsoever to fulfill it - even his reason. So it is that (romantic) love sometimes appears to be related to madness. Romance is at once both the most enriching and liberating experience life can offer and a curse and storm of the blood that makes us all victims of its control."

Experts in human relations disagree about the role of love in our modern lives. David Viscott and Abraham Maslow expressed the opinion that love is a valid need of the human being. In contrast, David Burns wrote that love is not a necessary factor in achieving mental health or happiness. He proposed that seeking after love when it is not available only contributes to depression when it is not found. Jed Diamond and Stanton Peele went so far as to lump a neurotic need for romantic love and the addiction to drugs in the same class. Tim Timmons and Charlie Hedges proposed that seeking love exclusively in one other person actually grows from a primal need for finding God or returning to our original oneness with the universe. In their view, searching for ultimate intimacy in another person is the humanist way of searching for the original spiritual oneness with our creator. Through love, the I may be transcended and the reunified WE exposed in life. To share love like this with another person often is life's supreme joy and also its supreme suffering.

John Welwood referred to romantic love as, "The most powerful agent for growth and transformation - a change of heart." "The meeting of two personalities is like the contact of two chemical substances; if there is a reaction, both are transformed", said Carl Jung. Person concentrated on the emotional highs and lows of romantic love as the essential drive for transformation and transcendence of the self. Although she acknowledged that modern psychology is recommending a more rational approach, she says, "Rationalists regard romantic love as a foolish if not downright dangerous illusion which creates impossible expectations in people and makes them unable to just accept the good that is possible in relationships." Rationalists fault romantic lovers for their insecure insistence on monogamy and exclusivity, their encouragement of mutual dependency, their confusion of love and possession, their jealousy and need to control the other, their self-destructiveness.

Romantics, on the other hand, see the rationalist view as love with the heart cut out. "The heart has reasons which reason knows nothing of," contended Blaise Pascal. Romantics tend to regard rationalists as emotionally shallow or inhibited, fearful of their passions and imprisoned in caution. These experts approach the rational and emotional components of love as two coexistent and contradictory traditions. I see them more as complementary components of the same phenomenon that are emphasized by different personality factors. Those who are more thinking in orientation, i.e., more left brained, may prefer the rational approach, while those who are more into their feelings, i.e., more right brained, may prefer the romantic approach.

Unfortunately, the literature of romance leaves much of love's positive components unexplored. I shall try to broaden that limited view with a more holistic approach. In this approach, love can become the whole connection between many whole people, the change of dual "I"s into the unified "We", where it becomes impossible to separate who is giving and who is receiving. Holistic loving meets needs for physical, intellectual, emotional, and spiritual mutuality and communion as no other human activity can. Holistic love permits both sexes to experience the oneness of self that existed in the womb before sexual differences emerged in the fetus while, paradoxically, maintaining their unique separateness simultaneously without being totally submerged addictively in another.

In a relationship between two truly mature people, both the rational and the emotional aspects of love can merge into peak holistic bliss. When the two sides of ourselves, rational and emotional, merge with another in balance, true passion is achieved without addiction or loss of self. To achieve that bliss, we must continually dance on the razor's edge of individuation and dependence, first tilting one way and then the other, much as a sailor continually tacks to one side and the other of the course to his destination. For many, the continuous stress is too intense to maintain. It unmasks all our fears and weaknesses. Few people may ever reach this level of maturity in their relationships, but I think it is the highest and most joyful form of life.

John Gray explained love in terms of a metaphor of a garden through the four seasons as follows: "Falling in love is like springtime. We feel as though we will be happy forever. We cannot imagine not loving our partner. It is a time of innocence. It is a magical time when everything seems perfect and works effortlessly. Throughout the summer of our love, we realize our partner is not as perfect as we first thought. He or she is a human who makes mistakes and is flawed in certain ways. Frustration and disappointments arise, weeds need to be uprooted and plants need extra watering under the hot sun. We discover we are not always happy, and we do not always feel loving. It no longer is easy to give love and get the love we need. Many couples at this point become disillusioned and stop working on the relationship. They unrealistically expect it to be spring all the time. They may blame their partners and give up. If we tend the garden during the summer, we get to reap the harvest in the fall. It is a golden time, rich and fulfilling. It is a time of thanksgiving and sharing. We experience a more mature love that accepts and understands our partner's imperfections as well as our own. Then the weather changes again and winter comes. This is a time when we experience our own unresolved painful feelings, when our own lid comes off. It is a time of solitary growth when we need to look more to ourselves than to our partner for love and fulfillment. It is a time of deep healing. This is a time when men hibernate in their caves and women sink to the bottom of their waves. After loving and healing ourselves through the dark winter of love, spring inevitably returns. Once again, we are blessed with the feelings of hope, love, and an abundance of possibilities. We are then able to open our hearts again and feel the springtime of love."

A Model Of Holistic Love

J. A. Lee defined six styles of love and gave them Greek and Latin names: Eros (passionate romantic love), Ludus (game-playing love), Storge (friendship love), Mania (possessive, dependent love), Pragma (logical, practical love), and Agape (all-giving selfless love). It is possible to relate these models of love with the personality preferences explained in chapter 3 by concentrating on four of them.

Healthy ad hoc relationships involve components of the four classes of love in various situations to some degree, based on the personality preferences of the partners and their needs at the moment. When sensing prevails, Eros rules; when thinking prevails, Pragma rules; when emotions and feelings prevail, Storge rules; and when spiritual intuition prevails, Agape rules. When all four elements come together in a single relationship between two people, they may experience the most complete merger of two selves, physical, intellectual, emotional, and spiritual that is possible in human experience.

The four separate forms of love are identifiable in all cultures, and can be related to the concept of personal wholeness we are using throughout this book (which also includes four elements as was taught by Native Americans: physical, intellectual, emotional, and spiritual). A healthy society benefits from all four forms of love. Erotic romance stimulates propagation through satisfaction of a need for physical connection, familial love assures family security for nurture of young, philios maintains fraternal groups for belonging to a wider community, and agape provides spiritual nurture of the soul by unconditionally giving to those in need. Obviously, we experience different forms of love with different people and with the same people in different situations.

Sufi philosopher, A. H. Almaas, described the experience of loving this way: "Understanding love doesn't mean knowing love is this or that, love is good, love is sweet, love affects you in this warm way, love nourishes you (although it does all these). Understanding love is to be love in the moment, to feel what it is like. If you understand this completely, which means you are completely and totally love, with a discriminating consciousness of the state, understanding automatically moves to a deeper level. The moment there is completeness in that state, when the insight is there, this is love. And you always know it, though sometimes you may not be able to say what it is. It is not as if you realize love, you understand it, and then you are done. It is much larger and richer. You might be always feeling loving, but not know consciously what love is, what it does. Love will arise in your experience only if your environment needs it. You don't have to feel it all the time, because you know it is there whenever you need it. The unfoldment of all the levels and manifestations is what is beautiful."

The Process Of Love

Donald Montagna, leader of the Washington Ethical Society, offered this 4-stage model of human growth. After the infant stage of symbiosis with mother, we experience Stage 1 of life, in which we are basically alone. This is a time of life when we learn who we are and develop our own sense of autonomy to balance the infantile need for dependence. It is a time of developing our self esteem, a time when we establish the ego boundaries that will define our sense of identity for the rest of our lives. It is when we develop the certainty of who we are as individuals.

The latter part of Stage 1 is a time of life when some may experiment with a variety of lifestyles that are different from the home life in which they grow up. It can be a dangerous time if it is used to become addicted to drugs, alcohol, tobacco, gambling, overeating, sex, or other compulsive, harmful behavior. This stage of learning to be alone, of separating from mother while still being dependent, is an essential step toward building a good relationship with another. If our self-love is not developed enough to create the autonomy we need to become independent of our parents, we may not achieve the capacity to be fully loving and committed to another in a healthy way.

By being with healthy others we learn that the opposite of dependency is not independence, but rather the ability to be interdependent. In a stable, interdependent family, children come to understand, accept, and respect their differing gifts and values. With ideal parenting, perfectly emotionally healthy children would develop a balance between nurturing self with autonomy and nurturing another through belonging. As adults, they choose to be connected, understanding neither can meet all the needs of the other all the time.

Most people find it difficult to balance their needs for autonomy and belonging and tilt one way or other. They are unable to overcome their fear of the obligations that come with commitment or their desire for independence. This imbalance can result from faulty or incomplete separation from the opposite sex parent that each adolescent must experience when they confront sexual interests in the opposite sex parent. At puberty, boys and girls must wrestle with the unconscious urge to maintain connection with the opposite parent. They must begin to relate more to the same sex parent as an adult role model and move outside the family for their opposite sex fulfillment. This is a significant departure for most young people of both sexes and sometimes they get stuck in the process and cannot move on. They may exhibit unhealthy, and even neurotic behavior, the rest of their lives.

The normal function of teenage dating (to explore what type of person one may want as a mate) is distorted as the young adult clings unconsciously to hope for connection with the opposite sex parent. Then it may manifest later in all manner of troubled adult behavior, including outright rejection and hatred of the opposite sex parent. Lovers can be chosen who offer the same kind of relationship with the idealized parent that was impossible, or the opposite can happen when the youth chooses harmful lovers in a subconscious attempt to make the desired parent jealous.

There are many additional childhood complications that can thwart development of the ability to love maturely as an adult. They include perceived and actual rejection by parents, other adult role models, and even peers. If social adjustment is distorted in any way during adolescence, an unhealthy adult emerges. Unfortunately, many people in our modern culture grow up with holes in their makeup for such reasons. Eventually, healthy people let go of their dependence on their parents and peers, and they develop adult-to-adult relationships with them as they mature into becoming their own person. They grow from being their parents' love-child to being their same-sex parent's rival for affection of the opposite sex parent, to being their own person. For various reasons in our ad hoc culture, many people do not make this transition completely. Since very few people get the personal therapy it may take to recognize and outgrow such early experience, they may help account for the ubiquitous dysfunctional families and divorces.

At the core of our existence, we all feel the basic ache of feeling separate from mother. We long to be connected to someone so we will not feel this ache so sharply. A predominant desire to connect with someone eventually predominates in most people, to belong to someone whom we can care about and who will care about us, who can fill up the holes in our faulty makeup. If we make that hurdle, we are prompted to enter Stage 2, that of "falling in love." This is a state of irrational and unconditional symbiotic merging with another. It is a state of complete ego collapse and places us in a situation we are powerless to control.

Falling in love may be a necessary first step to gaining rational, unconditional, holistic love. Falling in love requires at least the partial collapse of all our boundaries in terms of money, self-disclosure, touch, proximity, and sexuality. Psychologists call it "cathexis" or "limerance." This powerful attraction may be nature's way of ensuring procreation. Cathexis may be necessary to get people past the trauma of the wedding vows, because responsibilities of marriage and child rearing are so monumental. Only in a state of total vulnerability and psychic defenselessness can we permit another to get close enough to merge physically, intellectually, emotionally, and spiritually.

We don't seem to have much control over who we fall in love or cathect with. In the early stage of new romantic relationships, you are likely to feel temporarily omnipotent. It seems that nothing can happen the two of you cannot handle together because all your holes seem to be filled by that one magic person. This is an illusion, of course, but it helps you get past decisions that might otherwise scare off rational, thinking people. When two incomplete people fall in love, they join as two halves to become one in a symbiotic bonding or merging. The symbiosis occurs as two people meet basic belonging needs of each other so that alone, neither feels complete. By filling our holes, the person who is object of our affection may make us feel more whole and complete. In that case, "I love you" may really mean, "I need you." A more healthy couple may experience falling in love differently, as mutually sharing the ultimate power and energy of the universe. Sometimes people who are ready to make a connection just happen to be in the same place at the same time.

At its best, falling in love is an extremely risky endeavor. John Welwood says, "Love between the sexes is, of all things, not safe. Intimate relationships are not safe. That is not their nature. We sit on the razor's edge, directing our love toward an object we can never completely possess. Wholehearted devotion is a powerful transformative energy that can work magic on the human soul. When we romantically idolize someone, we project all the power, beauty, and richness of our being that we failed to recognize was within us." The longing to devote ourselves to something we regard as greater than ourselves is a beautiful quality. But, when we fail to recognize its essential nature, falling in love can leave us feeling helpless and tortured. This agony can itself become addictive because its burning intensity makes us feel so alive. While struggling to win the beloved, the lover keeps the fire of passion burning at a feverish pitch. Thus we often choose partners who are unattainable, because of marriage, age, distance, or other incompatibility. In this way, our unconditional passion, which is genuine longing to connect with the vastness of life, gets converted into an addictive obsession.

The experience of romance can be exhilarating and depressing simultaneously, as we both revel in the intoxicating euphoria and panic at the loss of rational control. Addictive passion is thus a riddle without a solution. Paradoxically, passion that starts out making us feel so intensely alive, brings us to the consideration of death. At this level, the addiction to anyone we use to make ourselves feel high must eventually lead to its own destruction.

People who are in love may think they know each other to the core though they may know relatively little about each other. We often do not really know the other person at this stage. Our feeling of bliss may have no basis in reality, as we fabricate an idealized image of the beloved. The partners experience each other in a variety of different situations, and really get to know each other as time passes. Some of what they learn may be difficult to accept when they wake up to reality. They may find that their secret contracts, i.e., those deals they make with themselves about the expected benefits of the relationship, are wishful thinking. They may awake with the sickening thought that their commitment was a mistake, that their desires, tastes, behavior, and needs are too different.

After a while, usually in six to eighteen months, sensory familiarity may reduce the initial erotic romantic bonding. All the previously collapsed boundaries of money, touch, proximity, self-disclosure, and sexuality may snap back into place. Activities outside the relationship such as school, work, family, etc., again demand priority attention and time. We start tallying up the benefit/burden ratio. When the honeymoon period (whether married or not) wanes, we face the question of doubt. We may wonder if the burdens are worth the benefits in the relationship. Although they can last for years, eventually most honeymoons end, and the realities of life return. A new form of familial love must then develop if the relationship is to survive. When the symbiotic honeymoon ends, the relationship either ends or we move on into Stage 3, that of a power struggle. In this phase, the previous feeling of unconditional loving transitions to conditional loving based on the simultaneous needs for belonging and autonomy.

We grow up with unbalanced needs for either connection or separateness. People whose parents were too remote or unavailable often fear loss of love and human contact. They fear being neglected or abandoned. People whose parents were to invasive or controlling fear losing their psychic space as individuals. They fear engulfment. From incomplete development of the self in Stage 1, we all have the opposite basic needs to be dependent, to love and be loved (Ethel Person refers to it as the need to surrender), the need for belonging. It may be related to incomplete separation from the security of the womb. No one experiences a perfectly balanced development of needs for autonomy and dependency in childhood. Welwood noted, "Moving smoothly and gracefully between such opposite poles is not an easy thing to do, for it calls on us to develop and integrate very different sides of our nature." Giving ourselves to a loving partnership while remaining true to ourselves, learning to balance we and me is the central challenge of intimate relationships. In Stage 3, the imbalance in these needs that we all possess drives us to force the other person to give us more of what we want, whether it is more belonging or more autonomy. Our anxiety about meeting these needs often causes us either to turn against them or to exaggerate them.

Problems and conflicts emerge then because the partners inevitably have unequal and opposing needs for belonging or autonomy, and these needs shift with time. Deborah Tannen and John Gray attribute these divergent needs to gender differences. There is a gender component involved as men who want autonomy may feel invaded and women who want belonging may feel evaded. Men often are depicted as wanting more autonomy and women as wanting more intimacy and feeling of belonging. But, I think this is an over generalization that does not hold up in real life. Social values are changing and with more women in the workforce, the gender roles may not be so distinct. In any event, because opposites attract, a person with a fear of abandonment may pair up with a person who fears engulfment. One may value autonomy or independence more highly than belonging, while the other may value belonging more highly than autonomy. Some people grow up fearing both abandonment and engulfment if the parents erred in opposite directions. Further, we continually tread the razor's edge between these two needs, and we fall to one side or the other moment by moment. *The more healthy a person is, the more conscious are these conflicts, and the better he/she is able to tolerate and manage this ambivalence between wanting belonging and autonomy.*

Most, if not all, conflicts between couples are unconscious expressions or symptoms of these underlying, primary motives for autonomy or belonging, i.e., to get our holes filled. The magnitude of the dichotomy can make the autonomous beloved feel trapped or the dependent partner to feel abandoned. Both may long to escape the frustration, and that may cause guilt which creates resentment, which fuels more conflict. When people act in destructive ways, it usually is because they are being driven either by an accusing self critic or a wounded child within them.

The strategies of engulfment employed by a dependent partner rely on manipulation and control. They often consist of making excessive demands for time and attention, violating the partner's proximity boundary. Or, they may involve attempts to rescue or save the target partner from issues and responsibilities rightfully their own to meet. Such demands can stifle the more independent partner or make him/her feel entrapped in a strait jacket, or possibly being suffocated or forcibly drowned. The defending partner reacts by demanding more free space and time to themselves or with others. In turn, the more dependent partner then feels abandoned and makes even more demands for time and attention. In their confusion, each misunderstands the other. The initial attraction of their difference may become the criteria for their conflict. Strategies of abandonment involve threatening to leave if we don't get what we want, or withdrawing some behavior the partner values very highly. People who fear abandonment often feel ashamed of their desire to connect with another. They may find it difficult to accept the complementary needs of others to spend time alone, to have their own space. The basic weapon of more independent partners is withholding; the basic weapon of engulfers is guilt. If each responds by giving in to what the other wants, they carefully keep score to be evened up later.

The partner who favors independence may perceive the partner seeking more belonging as being too needy or clinging. He/she fears for loss of self, if the need for belonging is granted. The partner seeking belonging or connection may fear the emotions of abandonment and perceive the more independent partner as intentionally withholding intimacy. Unaware of the unconscious forces from imperfect childhood driving them, the couple is embroiled in a great drama. They become combat ready and obsessed with the high intensity of energy and attention that is, somehow, perversely rewarding. All communication becomes a form of conflict and resolution of minor differences seems to be impossible as both sink into a compulsive, obsessive mode. Stage 3 begins to wane as the partners become more and more polarized over their opposing, unmet needs. There may be a feeling of futility, until their polarization becomes isolation from each other. Most of these situations result from unresolved issues developed in childhood that neither may be consciously aware of without professional therapy.

If either partner decides the pain of abandonment or engulfment is beyond his/her limits of tolerance, stage 3 may end in termination of the relationship. Each partner concludes that he/she is being punished for seeking personal, legitimate needs for independence or closeness in the other. If either partner wants out of the relationship for other reasons, the symptoms of this struggle for power make good excuses for termination. If they terminate, each partner goes back to Stage 1 of being alone again. Eventually each may pick up a new partner and the cycle may repeat. If these childhood wounds are not brought into consciousness and healed, they can create conflicts in relationships forever by inducing controlling, manipulative behavior.

If they wish to go on together, the partners must renew their faith of Stage 2 that joy, pleasure, tenderness, and love are possible in their relationship and accept their respective needs. If the couple never experienced the romantic connection of Stage 2, there may be little foundation on which to build further development. Both partners must give up some of their immature demands on the other. They must learn to tread the razor's edge between satiation and frustration, moment by moment. The partner who values autonomy most highly must change the need for independence to more negotiable interdependence. The partner who values belonging more highly must let go of dependency, and become more self-confident in being separate. There is a need to settle for less than utopia.

If they continue the relationship, they enter Stage 4. It is a conscious effort to recognize and dissolve their individual barriers to unconditional, "no-fault" agape loving. In the view of M. Scott Peck, this is a mutual interest in developing the spiritual growth of each partner by the other. This goal evolves as each of them experiences their own life path separately, and yet remain interdependently committed to each other. The relationship then includes a series of negotiating experiences and compromise agreements which cements the two into "us." The couple solves conflicts by trial and error and by remodeling and redecorating the relationship as time passes. The couple develops a mature interdependence in which reasonable autonomy and belonging needs of both are met, although imperfectly. No love can be sustained without intermittent moments when a sense of complete holistic merger is achieved, when they feel truly one as soul mates. However, each lover must maintain enough of a separate identity to serve the other's needs for belonging and autonomy without loss of self. They solve the paradox of achieving merger and maintaining autonomy. In effect, they give each other the permission to hurt them within the relationship.

In a healthy Stage 4 relationship, the partners learn to move freely back and forth between the opposing two poles of autonomy and connection in a continuous cycle that embraces the full ranges of fusion, companionship, community, communication, and communion. Rather than being an addictive form of togetherness, it becomes a ceaseless flowing back and forth between joining and separating. After moments of intense connection, they naturally begin to fall back into aloneness. When they feel most separate, an intense desire to come together again is reborn. The electricity in the relationship is sustained as they feel themselves as two separate poles, man and woman, alone, but together. They become conscious of the other, not only as person, but as a whole being, physically, intellectually, emotionally, and spiritually.

The process in Stage 4 requires stepping back from the attachment and energy of the power struggle, and discovering the true feelings underlying every complaint about surface behavior. The partners translate their needs into specific requests that can be negotiated to the satisfaction of both partners. In Stage 4, erotic symbiosis is embellished with familial bonding in a healthy relationship. This process can be helped along often with the intervention of a professional counselor or a trusted friend who can mediate the differences of the partners without emotional entanglement. As the relationship matures into a family of two, agape enters to produce unconditional, nonjudgmental acceptance of each for the other. Sometimes, a spiritual component is brought into conscious focus. The couple become true consorts, empowering each other to grow toward the best they can be physically, intellectually, emotionally, and spiritually in all dimensions of life, professional, social, personal, and private.

In Stage 4, we learn how to encourage each other to be interdependent while meeting the mutual need to belong. Unmet childhood needs are not justification for threatening to abandon or engulf your partner. Each person can feel both free and belonging. They learn to negotiate appropriate ways of meeting the adult needs of each other. Freedom to seek unmet non-sexual needs elsewhere among a wider group of friends and associates is part of this stage with mature people.

These four stages of love are presented here in linear fashion for explanation. I perceive them more as life situations than as timed phases, because they often overlap and they can exist at any time in life. Couples can get locked in one phase or another and never really move on to the mature, holistic loving that can be life's supreme joy. By understanding this model of the development of rational love, and sensing where you are in it, your journey to wholeness may be less traumatic and painful. Nevertheless, I think it takes a lot of work and effective communication between the partners for a lifetime to maintain healthy love.

Love and Addiction

Some modern psychologists have related falling in love to the prototype of addiction, as with sexuality. Here are some symptoms of love addiction listed by Howard Halpern:

> *A compulsive drive to be with the object of addiction, panic at the con-templation of a breakup followed by total devastation when it happens, withdrawal symptoms that include physical pain, weeping and sweating, stomach and abdomen disorders, sleep changes, and a feeling of no way to end the suffering except to return to the addiction, followed by a sense of liberation and triumph after surviving the loss. Underlying all these issues is a sense of incompleteness, emptiness, despair, and being totally lost without the connection to someone outside oneself. If you are deeply unhappy with a love relationship but cannot leave it, give yourself rea-sons for continuing that balance or exceed the valid reasons for leaving, feel dread and terror at contemplation of loss that makes you cling even harder, suffer to reestablish contact when you are apart, feel lost, alone and empty without your fix, chances are good that you are caught in a love addiction.*

Romantic attachment and rational love apparently are two different facets of a complex human phenomenon, with roots going back to separation from the womb at birth, and maybe even further. There is an unconscious urge to achieve symbiosis with the opposite-sex parent to duplicate the idealized relationship of the same-sex parent. Although it is politically incorrect now, Freud referred to this drive as the Oedipal complex. Jung also took note from his own experience that the essence or innermost soul of an individual mediated between the conscious and collective unconscious. He called it the anima in men and the animus in women - terms he took from Plato. He proposed the process of falling in love consisted of projecting the inner anima and animus onto a real person who must be obeyed, either for good or evil. During his most agitated confrontation with his own anima, his wife permitted him to take a mistress who sometimes even lived with them, according to John Kerr. But even she was no substitute for the real anima of his life, one Sabina Spielrein, a romantic Russian aristocrat whom he encountered as a youthful patient when he treated her for hysteria. She spent her entire life in a reverie about the romance with Jung that was not to be. Thus, the call of the anima for the animus and vice versa creates an attachment hunger that gives all romantic relationships elements of uncontrollable addiction, the call of Adam's rib wanting to reunite with its source.

Classical literature and films are full of accounts of people who gave up their own selves to live vicariously by submerging their identity in another. They became gripped in an all-consuming passion that took precedence over mere happiness. Until this century, public opinion favored such alliances for women, extolling the virtue of self-abrogation and self-sacrifice in the interests of some (or several) successful, powerful man. The master-slave relationship is reversible. I think men are just as capable as women of using unhealthy love relationships to gratify their longings for humiliation, self-punishment, or self-destruction. In extreme cases, it becomes enslavement, obsessive, self-destructive masochism or vents sadistic aggression to cause the beloved humiliation by demanding slavic subjection. There are many cases where a highly charged mix of love and distorted power keep couples together, although painfully, for years.

Shakespeare described such a relationship between Demetrius and Helena in "A Midsummer Night's Dream" with the following dialogue:

> **Demetrius:** *Do I entice you? do I speak you fair? Or, rather do I not in plainest truth tell you I do not, nor I cannot, love you?*
> **Helena:** *And even for that I love you the more. I am your spaniel; and Demetrius, the more you beat me I will fawn on you; Use me but as your spaniel, spurn me, strike me, neglect me, lose me; only give me leave, unworthy as I am, to follow you. What worser place can I beg in your love, and yet a place of high respect for me, than to be used as your dog.*
> **Demetrius:** *Tempt not too much the hatred of my spirit; for I am sick when I do look on thee.*
> **Helena:** *And I am sick when I look not on you.*

Unrequited love is an ideal vehicle for addiction, because it can so exclusively claim a person's consciousness, separating us from a full life as we concentrate on the isolated satisfaction of the next "fix," that of being with the object of our physical affection. The healthiest, rational response to that feeling of chemistry that draws us irresistibly to a physically attractive, but unhealthy, other actually may be to walk away. Few people have such control when romantic love attacks their rational logic. Many have fallen to its emotional power to overrule thinking that results in painful, unrequited love or physical and emotional abuse. The goal should be a more holistic form of mutual love in which two whole, complete interdependent people choose to share their lives and the world together.

Compulsive, obsessive romantic attachment to a person can be an expression of unhealthy behavior by codependents. It can take one of two forms: the urge to be possessed and the urge to possess. In both forms, total submerging of self in complete fusion with another is the goal. Stanton Peele defined addiction as "an unstable state of being, marked by a compulsion to deny all that you are or have been in favor of some new and ecstatic experience." Falling in love can meet that criterion for many codependents who become addicted to the love partner. They can become obsessed and preoccupied to the point of becoming dysfunctional in jobs and social life. The love-sick mind becomes distracted from its other duties and is overly preoccupied with desire and longing for the beloved. There is no sense of wellness except in the presence of the lover, who is granted great power over the dependent addict. This is in contrast to holistic love, which transforms both lovers and creates mutual transcendence of selves, providing a lilt to the voice, a smile on the face, and a spring in the walk. It is the creation of a new, better self.

Psychologists warn against being driven by attachment hunger in our search for love that comes from childhood, when we were appropriately dependent on others for our security. Your infantile need for attachment may lead you into relationships where such dependence is inappropriate as adult behavior, and potentially damaging to both you and the relationship. Dependency may appear to be love because it forces people to attach themselves fiercely to one another. It seeks to receive rather than to give. It nourishes infantilism rather than growth. It traps and constricts rather than liberates. Ultimately, it destroys rather than builds healthier relationships. Most writers on love agree that the destructive impact of dependent, addictive infatuations is harmful to one's general development as a person. It induces its victims to attempt to control the relationship through manipulating sexual power, exhibiting weaknesses, irrational servitude, provoking guilt, and stimulating jealousy. Although they may seem to be effective in the short run, all these tactics designed to hold the relationship together are doomed to fail ultimately.

If you aren't sure if you are entrapped by addictive love, here are some more of its characteristics, developed by Terry Gorski.

1. Belief in magic or unrealistic expectations. We assume the relationship will make us better without the need for us to think or act better.

2. Expecting instant gratification. The beginning bells and whistles lead to immediate erotic sexuality. We expect immediate, intense, and continual satisfaction from each other. We confuse fear for passion, because in both we experience loss of self.

3. Difficulty being honest; we prefer dishonesty. We believe the relationship will be destroyed if we know too much about each other. "No talk" rules keep fear, excitement, and pseudo-passion alive.

4. A compulsive need to over control, for without intense, continuous effort, the relationship will self-destruct. We become obsessed with it.

5. Trust is lacking. Alternating doubts abound about which partner is at fault if the relationship is failing. We have to manipulate our partner to give us what we want. Shame, guilt, blame, scape goating is the pattern.

6. Social isolation. There is a need to hide the relationship from others to protect the source of our happiness and to close out potential intruders who may expose the unhealthy aspects of the union.

7. A cycle of pain repeats. Desperate action is followed by short-term intense pleasure, followed by disillusionment and another blowup, followed by blaming the partner, and then self. The cycle repeats.

Dorothy Tennov is given credit for coining the word "limerance" to describe the attributes of being in love, being infatuated, or crazy about someone. While not necessarily addictive, they are symptoms of romantic love. She developed the following characteristics of limerance:

1. Intrusive thinking about the limerant object (LO);
2. Acute longing for reciprocation by your LO;
3. Your mood depends on your interpretations of LO's actions with respect to the probability of reciprocation;
4. Inability to react limerantly to more than one person at a time;
5. Fleeting and transient relief from unrequited limerant passion through vivid imagination of reciprocal action by your LO;
6. Fear of rejection and incapacitating, unsettling, shyness in LO's presence, especially in the beginning and whenever uncertainty strikes;
7. Intensification through adversity, at least up to a point;
8. Acute sensitivity to any act, thought, or condition that can be interpreted favorably, and extraordinary desire to invent "reasonable" explanations for why neutrality that a disinterested observer might see are, in fact, signs of hidden passion in the LO;
9. An aching in the heart chakra (a region in the center of the chest) when uncertainty is strong;
10. Feeling of buoyancy when reciprocation seems evident from LO;
11. A general intensity of feeling that leaves other concerns in the background;
12. A remarkable ability to emphasize what is truly admirable in LO to avoid dwelling on negatives, even responding with passion for the negative and rendering it, emotionally, if not perceptually, into a positive attribute; and
13. Sexual attraction is almost always an essential component of limerance.

There are some positive, and maybe necessary, aspects to the addictive quality of love. It may be necessary to get us past the marriage vows if the potential responsibility of commitment and family obligations are too fearful. In fact, M. Scott Peck suggested it may be a necessary genetic inheritance to assure human procreation. It also may provide necessary bonding to keep couples together when times get tough through sickness, financial reverses, and the many conflicts that can develop between intimate partners. Addiction may be harmful when it keeps people victimized in an abusive, unhealthy, restrictive relationship that prohibits individual growth and destroys personal freedom through unrequited love. Its worst intrusion may occur when love addiction causes infidelity and creates a triangle that splits a committed couple if one of them cannot control its influence from a third party. If you are caught in a love addiction, you will have to decide whether to live with it, try to improve the health of it, or leave it.

Moving Toward Holistic Love

We can move from addiction to a more holistic, healthy love although the process can be lengthy and painful. Here is a self-help method from Brenda Schaeffer to help move from addiction to more self affirmation. Her plan includes the following seven

steps:
1. Awareness: admitting that love addiction plays a significant role in your life.
2. Assessment: discovering the extent and roots of your addictive behavior in childhood deficiency.
3. Decision: using your personal Higher Power to move from dependence to rational love.
4. Exploration: examining your personal fears, myths, and social and emotional history.
5. Reprogramming: letting go and grieving for the old beliefs and behaviors and embracing a new healthier set of values.
6. Renewal: moving toward development of mature love relationships.
7. Expansion: developing personal uniqueness and the ability to genuinely love yourself and all others.

Can we love emotionally and passionately without being addicted? How can we care for each other and take care of ourselves also? Can we belong to another and still set personal boundaries and look out for Number One? What is functional, healthy love all about? Do we really know the answers? Perhaps it is in the search for these answers that life evolves. Perhaps it is only possible to live out the role in which we are cast, or to play the cards which we have been dealt. Awareness, courage, and gentleness with ourselves are needed to help us trust life enough to love through our imperfections. We can learn to recognize destructive thoughts that lead to dysfunctional behavior. By choosing to work at changing our behavior, we can affect the feelings that destroy holistic loving.

I believe that humans can experience a form of healthy love that embodies all four elements, familial, philios, eros, and agape in an unlimited number of healthy, platonic relationships. It can be romantic and rational simultaneously. It can also be polygamous. Indeed, it must be polygamous to be holistic. This may be a shocking idea to you, if you are confusing love with sex. Most people confuse monogamous sex, which is desirable, with love and avoid loving, really loving, beyond their immediate families. They confuse the taboo against polygamous sex with love. When one partner stifles the other's natural tendency to love others out of jealousy, fear, or insecurity, the stage is set for possibly breaking up. Eric Fromm wrote, "The affirmation of one's own life, happiness, growth, freedom, is rooted in one's capacity to love." As I note above, Jesus said, "Love your neighbor(s) as yourself." He made it the second greatest commandment of all. (Mark 12:31)

Holistic love is described in the Bible this way:

> *"If I have no love, I am nothing. Love suffers long, is patient and kind; it is not jealous or conceited or proud; love is not ill-mannered or selfish or irritable; love does not keep a record of wrongs; love is not happy with evil, but is happy with the truth. Love never gives up; and its faith, hope, and patience never fail ... These three remain; faith, hope, love; and the greatest of these is love. (I Corinthians. 13:2, 4-8,13)*

When we love for the sake of being loved, we are human; but if we can love for the sake of loving, we are being God-like. "Beloved, let us love one another: for love is of God; and everyone that loves is born of God and knows God. He that loves not does not know God; for God is love." (1 John 4:7-8; Today's English Version.) James F. Masterson defined true love as "a union of two people, each for the good of the other, where the other's best interests become at least equal to one's own - it is to like, approve of, and support another's real self and to encourage the other to activate, express, and nurture that real self, (thereby) enlarging, enriching, and completing the experience of the self." If this type of love does not develop in marriages or between committed couples, when the excitement of erotic love fades divorces and breakups often result.

Brenda Schaeffer set up the following characteristics to define people who are holistically loving in healthy relationships:

"They allow the individuality of their partner. They experience both oneness with and separateness from their partner. They bring out the best qualities in each other. They accept endings as inevitable. They exhibit openness to change and exploration. They invite growth in the other partner. They share true intimacy but do not panic when the partner is occupied elsewhere. They feel the freedom to ask honestly for what they want. They experience giving and receiving in the same way. They do not attempt to change or control the other partner. They encourage self sufficiency in each other. They accept the limitations of self and other. They do not seek unconditional love. They accept commitment, but do not demand it. They have a high self esteem that is not dependent upon acceptance by each other. They trust the memory of the beloved and enjoy solitude. They express feelings spontaneously. They welcome closeness, risk vulnerability. They care without compulsive care taking. They affirm equality and personal power of self and other."

Holistic love is not cathexis, it is not dependency, it is not self-sacrifice, it is not obsession, and it is not only the erotic ecstasy or feelings associated with passion. On the other hand, holistic love includes the work of attention, of listening actively to the needs of the other as they manifest in all four elements of life. Often, our own ego needs get in the way of hearing what our partner is saying until her/his need to be heard becomes a scream. Holistic love is far more sensitive.

I believe holistic love is an unconditional, unilateral act on your part. If you need or intend to get something in return for your love, it is dependency, exploitation, manipulation, infatuation, attachment hunger, cathexis, limerance, addiction, or something else. It is not unconditional, nonjudgmental, holistic love. One who has distorted love by emphasizing only the erotic or sensual aspect while denying the emotional and spiritual aspects often hopes that his/her lover will not meet new people and enjoy the world. To do so implies competing ties and interests that would make her/him less dependent on the relationship.

When holistic love develops out of friendship which, in turn, develops out of companionship, it is likely to be more enduring than when love is sought through compulsive sensual or erotic bonding only. The process of developing holistic love cannot be rushed. It takes time for companionship and friendship to mature into agape love. All new acquaintances do not develop into companions. Neither do all companions develop into friends, nor do all friends develop into lovers. Give yourself permission to experiment and make mistakes in your new relationships. You may have nagging feelings of loss, guilt, and bone-deep unhappiness as you try to reconstruct your life anew after a traumatic loss. The influence of a dysfunctional childhood and adult losses can linger throughout life, disrupting all aspects of new intimate relationships, if faulty behavior is not changed.

The model of relationships provided by Terry Gorski includes a description of healthy, holistic love which he states as follows:

1. It is realistic and rational and does not change the rest of our lives. First a healthy self, and then the possibility of healthy intimacy. Each partner builds a self-protection policy into the relationship.

2. It builds slowly for long term contentment, security, and peace of mind. Each partner practices "share and check" self-disclosure to test if future sharing is safe. New partners take 10-12 weeks to decide if they really want a committed relationship. Sex may be avoided prior to commitment to monogamy.

3. Rigorous honesty and openness is practiced to share the nature of who we really are with each other, to know we are totally accepted, unconditionally.

4. There are no secrets withheld about the relationship, but extensive self-disclosure is not made on the first date.

5. There is voluntary, free-flowing cooperation. The relationship is comfortable and secure, with normal brief periods of problem solving together, then back to the norm of comfort.

6. Rational trust exists, with expectation that partners are acting in accordance with their own nature without games, seeking their own best interest.

7. The couple integrates socially with old friends, but they also make new friends together. His, hers, and ours problems are worked on progressively for growth of each.

8. Because they are satisfied with each other, there is a deepening sense of contentment. Problems are addressed through rational resolution. Intimacy is heightened by confidently shared feelings without threat of abandonment or engulfment.

The kind of commitment and will demanded of holistic love is possible, and also desirable, with more than one other person at a time. This is not to say that there is no value in your having a primary commitment, a primary life-sharing "special only person" who is number one in your life. I am not suggesting that exclusivity is impossible or undesirable in your intimate sexual relationships. In fact, I believe healthy marriage requires a commitment to someone who can be number one in your life. However, you may have to consciously and willfully allocate your available store of love among many new friends who are brought into your life. Having a primary relationship with only one person, even a marriage partner, at the expense of other loving friendships is very narrowing, besides obviously being risky, because all marriages ultimately end in either death or divorce. I think holistic love brings a richness when it is shared with several others, rather than being stifled in a restricted environment between two people exclusively.

There is a poignant quality of love that leaves us feeling unfulfilled until we learn that only by sharing it with as many people as possible will we ever be happy. Love must flow through us continually from its eternal source. Closed couples who only look inward and cut off relations with their outer world use each other up. Unhealthy people fear that love will fly away if it is shared. Only by staying open to its flow can we be assured of a continued supply of love. One of the miracles about holistic love is that it can expand to meet the opportunity.

Here is an important concept about holistic love from A Course In Miracles. The Course distinguishes between "unholy" and "holy" relationships. I offer the definitions at this point by quoting directly from the Text. (chapter 22, page 235.)

— *"an unholy relationship is based on differences, where each one thinks the other has what he has not. They come together, each to complete himself and rob the other. They stay until they think that there is nothing left to steal, and then move on. And so they wander through a world of strangers, unlike themselves, living with their bodies perhaps under a common roof that shelters neither; in the same room and yet a world apart.*

"A holy relationship starts from a different premise. Each one has looked within and seen no lack. Accepting his completion, he would extend it by joining with another, whole as himself. He sees no difference between these selves, for differences are only of the body. Therefore, he looks on nothing he would take. He denies not his own reality because it is the truth. Just under heaven does he stand, – For what is born into a holy relationship can never end." (Thus possibly explaining the feeling of continuing connectedness widows and widowers describe with a deceased beloved spouse.)

Jealousy and Wholeness

Jealousy is the green eyed monster of Shakespeare that caused Othello to commit suicide after killing his wife for a mistaken belief that she was unfaithful. Although some liberal folks attempted to experiment with open marriages during the late 1960s and into the 1970s based on equal rights to cheat, these experiments often resulted in divorce. Sure, the baby boomers adopted a more liberal lifestyle than their parents, and there are single folks who sometimes can get enjoyment in a polygamous lifestyle, but they are not a majority. A poll in 1997 by "USA Today" disclosed that 79% say adultery is "always wrong" unless a married couple is legally separated, even though 52% said they knew a close friend or relative who had an extramarital affair. In addition, 55% said that an employee who has an affair with a married boss should be dismissed from the job. Most ad hoc couples require sexual monogamy to keep the relationship together. When a breach of that taboo arises, jealousy results.

What constitutes a legitimate trigger for jealousy and an appropriate response has changed over time and varies from culture to culture. Ayala Pines reported studies that show wide extremes in what constitutes a trigger for jealousy and appropriate reactions in cultures throughout the world. Social values have changed dramatically in America since 1970 when feminism began giving women more freedom to explore their own needs and create financial independence. Confinement to a man is no longer necessary for their security. Many married people of both genders now admit to sexual infidelity in pursuit of the exciting variety and thrills of conquest that often come with it. A few even claim that it adds zest and passion to their marriage. Only a minority of young people are virgins when they get married, often having many partners enroute. And more people are choosing a swinging single lifestyle or being unmarried lovers in these times of occupational uncertainty and economic risk. People of certain personality types (mostly SP) find it difficult to make long term commitments because they always wonder whether the next one might be better in some way, or they just don't want to miss out on any possible new opportunities.

Jealousy is a strong emotion that combines feelings such as rage, humiliation, despair, and panic that results from a perceived threat to the existence or the quality of your highly valued relationship. It stems from real or imagined actions between your partner and a third person, and defends against loss of what one finds most attractive and desirable in a partner. The most jealousy-provoking third person is one you know personally and envy, i.e., someone you think is more successful or brighter or attractive than you in ways that you would like to be. Moreover, it is well known that, in general, men and women feel differently about sexual infidelity. Men react with anger at the forbidden sexual event because it potentially deprives them of exclusivity in transmitting their genes to their offspring. In contrast, women react with anger because the forbidden sexual event represents a loss of their exclusive emotional involvement with the partner.

Jealousy may have a primitive purpose in assuring a man that his offspring will not be contaminated by another man's seed, and assuring a woman that she can depend on the security of protection and provision of her mate while she is raising their children. Also, intentionally provoked jealousy can serve as an aphrodisiac with some couples who possess a certain genetic tendency to take risks and to seek the ultimate pleasure. It may increase their mutual libido when they know they are attractive to someone else, if both partners equate high drama with passion. Such people may unconsciously collude to keep the jealousy problem alive so the passion will not fade. These people may find a mate who is neither unfaithful nor jealous actually boring. Some people actually enjoy a jealous reaction from their mate because they think it indicates a sign of protection and commitment to the relationship. They mistake jealousy for love and concern, even though it may provoke physical abuse.

Sometimes, one partner will intentionally, though maybe unconsciously, provoke jealousy with sexually illicit behavior to send a message that all is not well in the relationship. When the intended jealousy is triggered, communications can begin to correct what is wrong and provide for the changing needs of each other within the relationship if the commitment to each other is maintained. If not, and trust is destroyed, the relationship may rupture when that was not the intention. If you slip up unintentionally, it may be an indication that something is wrong that could be fixed by talking it through. Open, honest discussion to confront whatever issues separate the couple can prevent or overcome some very serious infidelities and prevent a divorce in many cases. A loving relationship can withstand many mistakes, but it cannot withstand much dishonesty because commitment is rooted in trust.

Jealousy also can be a sign of envy of the third party, i.e., wishing that you were that attractive, youthful, sexy, muscular, successful, wealthy, or whatever seems to be lacking in you that is more attractive in the intruder. So, part of the response to romantic jealousy should be reinforcement of your own worthiness, desirability, and value as well as that of your partner. Sometimes, it is necessary to let go of a philandering partner who prefers somebody else. Some people say if you really love someone, you will want to see them happy, even if it must be with someone else.

Halpern and Pines suggested that a certain amount of normal jealousy exists in all relationships because we all fear rejection and loss to some extent. However, obsessive stalking, spying or imagining, groundless repetitive interrogation, accusation, and suspicion actually are thought to be signs of emotional immaturity. In the extreme, these reactions may indicate some form of mental disorder in need of professional treatment. The difference between self esteem that is based on self worth reflected from a situation, social position, or relationship, and self esteem that is based on unshakable self worth derived from our creator seems to be crucial in managing jealousy realistically. Self esteem that is based on what you do, or what you have, or who you have sex with, is not built on solid ground. All those attributes are temporary.

Perhaps the greatest trigger for jealousy is adultery, or the suspicion of it. Some people seek affairs to prove to themselves they are not imprisoned in the relationship and can indeed be free of its bondage. The more unfaithful you have been to your lover, the more likely you will feel jealous when your partner behaves in a similar manner. Oscar Wilde reportedly said, "The chains of marriage are so heavy it takes two people to carry them, and sometimes three." Projecting your own desires for infidelity onto your mate makes you jealous. Monogamy can eliminate the projection of infidelity, and thereby reduce the tendency to be jealous, but nowadays monogamy has come to mean serial relationships rather than marital sexual fidelity. Jesus said that a married man who even looks at a woman with lust has committed adultery in his heart (Matt:5-28).

Nevertheless, adultery is common in all cultures, no matter how it is punished. Monogamy is enforced in only a few societies around the world as a social and legal standard. In fact, only 25 states have laws prohibiting adultery, although all of them permit it as a cause for divorce. Bonnie Eaker Weil makes a persuasive argument for adultery being the "forgivable sin." She cites data indicating that 65 percent of marriages marred by infidelity end in divorce, whereas only 2 percent of her clients so inflicted end their relationships. And it was Alexander Pope who said, "To err is human, to forgive, divine." Forgiveness is a gift you give yourself after you decide you have suffered enough pain.

Eaker Weil has deduced that adultery is a genetically inherited behavior, sometimes passed on for several generations as individuals try desperately to meet emotional needs that were unmet by their parents. She has found that people who are not in some kind of pain do not commit adultery. Many recent popular studies indicate that both genders just about equally like the taste of variety now and then for the stimulating effect it provides. She says that one partner will have an affair in 80 percent of all marriages. There is a gender difference, however, as men more likely say infidelity provides fun and excitement, while women more likely say it provides love and intimacy they are missing. But, it often, although not always, is followed by remorse and self-incrimination in both cases. Thus, adultery has a devastating effect upon the whole family system.

If you hold on to the illusion that your life will be horrible, empty, and unhappy without that one and only partner, it will only lead you into misery if they are unfaithful. Now, you have the adult power to create and generate your own happiness no matter what happens outside you. When your adult sense of self worth is unshakable, jealousy cannot invade your serenity. But, if it does, it can cause you to overvalue your partner and confuse you about what you really want from the relationship. The infantile fear of abandonment can be a tormenting obsession. The codependent mind perceives being dismissed or left for another as being undesirable or worthless, and is utterly devastating. Like all emotions, for jealousy to continue it must be fueled by thinking that intentionally, although maybe unconsciously, keeps up the tension. Thus, by changing your thinking about the situation, you can change your feelings and that will make it easier to change your behavior.

Basically, the cure for abnormal jealousy lies in accepting two ideas: there is no absolute one and only partner for you, and you can survive and thrive after the loss of a love. There are likely many people with whom you could have a healthy relationship, even into mid-life and beyond, and you can enjoy the single life. Without this self assurance, you may swing from joy when your partner behaves as you wish and to depression when he/she resists your control. It really is impossible to control the feelings and behavior of another. Continual attempts to do so may smother the relationship and create resentment. Ultimately, they generate a self fulfilling prophecy if the partner leaves the relationship to escape the attempts at control and manipulation that jealousy motivates. You can only take care of yourself and your own needs. The antidote to jealousy is unshakable self worth that is built only upon the unshakable relationship you have with your Higher Power, God, or Inner Self.

Building holistic love is a lifetime endeavor. The way is not always smooth, and the rewards are not always assured. Since each couple is unique, we all are pioneers on this journey through unexplored territory as life unfolds. Nevertheless, many codependent people and adult children find that the benefits of building healthy, intimate relationships based on holistic love are well worth the effort. You can decide to let go of the dysfunctional behavior of the past. You did the best you could under the circumstances, so you need not feel guilty or ashamed for that. You can put the past to rest and enjoy the abundance of life your creator intended for you.

The next chapter deals with the issue of communications and the one following is devoted to creating true intimacy and commitment. Without appropriate dialogue, true intimacy cannot exist, and with it jealousy has little chance of flourishing. Few people really know how to communicate effectively or negotiate win-win outcomes to disagreements. I think you will find the following material very interesting and extremely useful in relations with the SOP in your life. It is the key to avoiding getting divorced and enjoying ad hoc relationships.

Seven:
Intimate Communications

This chapter contains the latest instruction about communications methods between human beings useful in dating and relationship building. Since every ad hoc relationship is based on communications, this material is absolutely necessary for every single person to understand if you are to avoid getting divorced.

Communication is so important between doctors and patients that the National Institute of Mental Health found it accounted more for successful therapy and physical healing than any other thing, including medicinal drugs, for treating depression. Better and shorter treatment requires empathic communications, so managed care companies are requiring their doctors to take courses in communicating. Intimate communications might be summed up with these three traits: Know what you feel, say what you mean, and take responsibility for your choices. Easy to say, but much more difficult to do when relations between ad hoc couples is at stake. The next three chapters contain specific ways of achieving this goal.

Before babies develop language, they communicate their distress and pleasure very effectively. We learn that we get more of our needs met by displaying anger, suffering, or fear than we do by displaying joy and contentment. As we get older and develop use of language, these tactics for getting our needs met become less effective as they conflict with the needs of care givers. The words we learned to negotiate for our needs as children often are carried into adult relationships and cause problems if they no longer are appropriate. Therefore, this chapter is intended to help you avoid the pitfalls in dialogue that you probably are not aware of.

Studies by James J. Lynch, reported by Robert Ornstein and Charles Swencionis, resulted in this conclusion: "Communication is vitally linked to our bodies and is probably the single most important factor that influences our health or lack of health. — our bodies are inextricably bound up in the most peculiar of all human functions - communication." From the quiet comforting of a dying person to the cuddling of an infant, in single, widowed, divorced, or married people, in neurotic, schizophrenic or normal people, one factor unites us all - dialogue. Dialogue is the essential element of all social interactions. In its most general meaning, dialogue consists of reciprocal conversation between two or more living creatures, whether written or spoken. It involves sharing of thoughts, physical sensations, ideas, ideals, hopes, and feelings. In total, dialogue involves a reciprocal sharing of any and all of life experiences through words. Without such sharing there can be no intimacy in any relationship.

The Pitfalls in Language

We all learn to talk, i.e, to put words together that make up sentences, but few of us really learn to communicate, i.e, to understand, and to be understood. We learn certain meanings of words and sentences and to deliver them in habitual fashion, what linguists call semantics, dialects, and registers. When all of these ingredients are combined, no two people possess the same definition of many significant words no matter what the dictionary may say. What is worse, we assume the recipient of our transmissions learned the same criteria for meaning that we did. Unfortunately, nothing could be farther from the truth. You may be surprised to learn the only meaning your words have is that in the mind of the receiver. Your intended meaning has nothing to do with it.

People actually dialogue together within the framework of a consensus as to the meaning of words, symbols, and gestures, since no one knows what objective reality is for sure. Unless we have received special training in the art of intimate communications, most of our interpersonal transactions depend upon trial and error. When the changing gender roles discussed in chapter 2 and the personality differences discussed in chapter 3 are laid over faulty communications, you have the ingredients for misunderstanding, frustration, anger, and breakups. So it is important to clarify the meaning of every transmission before you jump to conclusions about your partner's intent.

Recall from Chapter 4 that throughout our youth we also create a "dream lover", according to Polly Young-Eisendrath, from our same-sex conversations and exposure to the opposite sex. We also unconsciously develop an image of our own self from the way we are treated by primary care givers. Either of these can be realistic or unrealistic stereotypes and carry over into our intimate relations in the form of projection of the undesirable aspects onto our significant other to avoid claiming them as our own. Then, both partners become confused, overwhelmed, and frustrated about the relationship that sometimes ruptures when they do not understand each other.

Many couples live for years in disillusionment, blaming each other for their unhappiness, when both lack the capacity for effective dialogue. Actually, the process of learning to communicate with each other as equals is fairly recent. Learning to hear and translate the gender style of language between the sexes began in Western cultures just in the past few decades. Before then the complementary roles of men and women did not present as many pitfalls in dialogue as exists among the boomer generation. Research on how the brain converts concepts into language began very recently, in the 1970s, practically in parallel with the feminist movement. In 1981, the Nobel Prize winner, Dr. Roger W. Sperry, created the new science of neuropsychology that is now producing fantastic new findings about the brain and communicating styles. His beginnings in brain dominant theory have now become a world-wide movement.

The renowned Swiss psychiatrist, Carl G. Jung, believed that a committed relationship through adulthood could provide "individuation" for both partners. By this term he meant the gradual unpacking of the baggage of our own lives, coming to see both the conscious and unconscious meanings and motives of both partners. When you can communicate better with your intimate partners, all aspects of your relationships will be enhanced remarkably and the more likely you will be to get what you really want. A committed relationship can provide our own psychological development and make us more conscious of the other gender side within each of us, what Jung called the Animus or male in women, and the Anima or female in men.

Few of us are ever trained in the form of verbal dialogue that takes place between intimate couples. We just pick up both the good and bad habits from adults before we enter school and continue a personal style that is driven by our preferred brain dominance and personality. Consequently, people use words differently and assign different meanings to identical words unless some intervention changes things. What they say and how they say it reflects their values, beliefs, assumptions, expectations, biases, prejudices, experiences, and brain dominance preferences. Internationally, our differing communicating styles are expressed by saying England and the U.S. are two countries separated by a common language. Henry Ford applied this idea to business this way, "If there is any secret to success, it lies in the ability to get the other person's point of view and see things from his angle as well as your own."

More recently, Linda McCallister quoted Lee Iacocca, then chairman of Chrysler this way, "Motivation is everything — and the only way to motivate people is to communicate with them — It's important to talk to people in their own language. If you do it well, they'll say, 'God, he said exactly what I was thinking.' And when they begin to respect you, they'll follow you to the death." Language is a way to power and control. Everybody wants to be the master of the meaning of their words and impose that meaning on others. Consider this dialogue from *Through The Looking Glass*, by Lewis Carroll: "When I use a word," Humpty Dumpty said, in a rather scornful tone, "it means just what I choose it to mean — neither more or less. "The question is," said Alice, "whether you can make words mean so many different things." The question is," said Humpty Dumpty, "which is to be the master — that's all." Recall that the master is the receiver, not the transmitter.

Several writers have classified communicating styles into groups. Ned Herrmann discovered that personal dialects can be divided into four groups corresponding to the four quadrants in brain mapping. There is the language of logic and reasoning (**NT**), the language of structure and control (**ST**), the language of feelings and emotions (**SF**), and the language of intuition and imagination (**NF**). You can probably guess which of these are likely to be used more by males and females if you recall the personality factors from Chapter 3.

Couples can turn issues into problems and conflicts without knowing why if our partners use a different style, or one we think is not appropriate to the situation. No matter what style we prefer, if our partner uses a different style we most likely will feel irritated by it. To make it even more complicated, we often use different styles in different situations, or a combination of styles.

What you hear is an example of semantics, dialect, and register. You can imagine how difficult it is to communicate feelings and ideas with someone with a different dictionary than yours. Moreover, people also use non-word forms of communicating including facial gestures, body language, dress, voice pitch, volume and rate, all of which leave less than twenty percent of communications vested in words alone. Yet, we depend largely upon words to convey our intentions, feelings, and meanings. It is not the words themselves that cause problems so much as the perception we have about the meaning behind the words. Note it is not the meaning per se, but the perception of the meaning that counts.

No matter what they say or how they say it, there appears to be a gender-based power struggle expressed in conversation between men and women. Social conditioning practically assures that men and women will each find the other confusing in their use of communications. Men and women learn different forms of communication as children that follow them into adulthood. Suzette Haden Elgin explained the way genders suffer through faulty communications because of their social conditioning and lack of training. She illustrates many words and dialogues that men and women perceive as having different meanings. She explains how complicated the art of communicating really is and how difficult it is to design research projects to explain the reasons behind human linguistics. She also expresses the potential for increased happiness and intimacy when faulty ways of communicating are identified, and gives specific instructions for improving. I have included her most powerful concepts in this chapter but I, too, must assume the meanings you attach to my words are the same as mine since I have no way of verifying your understanding. Since my background is different from all readers, chances are excellent some of you are going to misunderstand my meaning.

In their microscopic analysis of social conditioning, Deborah Tannen and John Gray both found that men are programmed to use conversation as expression of their autonomy, control, and status. Men usually prefer to use conversation to exchange official information competitively, while challenging each other for power. Although there are exceptions, women more likely talk with each other in order to exchange information about events and details of their lives. Women develop close friendships by exchanging their secrets and feelings, while friendship between men more often is related to some competitive activity where they can exhibit their skill or display their knowledge.

Gray went so far as to use the metaphor that men are from Mars and women are from Venus in describing their differences. Men almost always are assumed to be the more powerful by both sexes. Neither gender is motivated by conversation that is interpreted as rejecting, demeaning, abandoning, blaming, or controlling. Not only do boys and girls grow up in different conversational worlds, they tend to judge each other's behavior by the standards of their own gender after they grow up. Even when women gain economic equality, if they speak as leaders they often are seen as inadequate women and when they speak as women they often are seen as inadequate leaders by both sexes. It seems that gender differences are built into our language to stay.

Conversation in a close intimate relationship continues to be more important to women than it is to men. A couple can spend time together, share touch, sex, and space, but if they do not share rapport through verbal, visual, and kinesthetic (touch) communication, intimacy remains undeveloped. All manner of relatively minor differences often are exploded into major conflicts when communications are faulty.

Women have regularly described their frustration and anger at being unable to elicit more open harmony and intimacy through communications from the males in their lives. They often give up trying to get their men to communicate more openly. They either settle for a dissatisfying relationship, leave to seek a better one, or give up and choose to live alone. They often find more close relationships with other women who share their interests and ability to communicate on a deeper level, both intellectually and emotionally.

Men often report that their closest friends often are women, possibly because there are so few men who know how to, or choose to, be deeply communicative. However, social conditioning can be modified if we choose to work at it hard enough to have more strategies at our disposal. Both partners can learn more about meeting the communications needs of the other if they communicate about it. We can learn to accept the differences in gender conversational styles that sets us apart, rather than being separated by them. However, our learned patterns of faulty communications may be so deeply imbedded and unconscious that only professional therapy can help remove the barriers of understanding and help change our behavior.

Communicating Affection

People differ in their preferred ways of communicating affection. From my observation and study, the four main methods seem to be cuddling, gifting, talking, and sex. Cuddling refers to all manner of fondling, from holding hands to back rubs and full body massages, to hugs and intimate caresses. Gifting refers to either doing favors for the partner or buying things for her/him. Many men prefer to gift their loved ones rather than talk or cuddle. Talking means spending time in relating to the problems, concerns, and issues facing the other. Women with husbands who do not understand this aspect of their makeup can feel abandoned and unloved when they need the support of dialogue and do not get it.

All expressions of affection should be undertaken slowly at the outset of any new connection. Be careful to assess the potential for further intimacy before committing yourself with a heavy emotional, financial, or physical investment. However, the order and level of preference of these expressive methods varies with a person's training, personality, role models, and personal values. Unless partners prefer these expressions in perfectly identical priorities, some accommodation will need to be made by each person to meet the preference of the other. You must develop and sustain an environment in which sensitive feelings on these and all issues related to the relationship can be discussed and removed from concern. If open communication about these issues is not maintained, hidden grievances may cause feelings of hostility that can lead to damaging behavior which in turn can result in unwanted separations or breakups.

The principal senses used in communicating are sight, hearing, and touch. The scientific terms for these forms are visual, audible, and tactile or kinesthetic. Each person prefers these methods in a specific order or priority, although every healthy person uses all three methods. Further, our preference for them varies with time, circumstance, and mood. Not only that, but we use them to create mental references or images that define all of life's experiences and memories in a way that is unique to each of us. These references or models or images are composed of the content, the volume, and the sequences in which we use these communicating senses.

The importance and power that preferred communicating senses hold for building affection with another should not be underestimated. If you want to communicate effectively with a person most affectionately, you must use the same combination of senses, volumes, and sequences that is most natural for that person. When two people with similar sensing preferences connect, they may feel a kinship immediately that creates significant rapport and bonding. Like opening a combination lock, if you use the right combination you will gain access to the person, and if you don't you won't.

As intimacy develops, each partner tends to concentrate on the sense that is most important or preferred. At the outset of a new contact, the most preferred sense usually is the one that grabs or hooks us into getting closer. It might be the sight, sound, or touch of the person, how she/he looks, talks, or feels, or even smells. Something about the sound, sight, or touch of the person may remind you in some way of an ex-love, fantasies about your dream lover from your alone period, or desirable traits of your opposite sex parent. There may be very deep psychic or energetic connections from previous lives or unseen universal forces that fuse people together at first sight. Or, it may be a person with traits opposite from your experiences who is most attractive to you. Whatever the trigger, sensory communications and intuitive, psychic influence will be involved from the outset and will steer the relationship through to its conclusion.

If you can be aware of your own sensing preference, and can tell where your partner places her/his communication priority, you can modify your approach to meet her/his needs. In fact, you will have to use compatible communications styles for the relationship to develop into deeper intimacy. The truth of this statement is proven when parents respond to a newborn baby with cuddles, cooing, and babbling that mirror the infant's only available communicating skills. If your partner is oriented to audible communication and you are the silent type who prefers visual images or the written word, you can become more talkative. If your kinesthetic partner prefers touch, you can be more caressive, and include feeling descriptions in your conversation. If your partner is a visual person she/he will appreciate more sight images in your verbal conversations and more written words.

Here are some words Michael Brooks found that people use in everyday conversation that might be clues to their sensing preferences.

> **Visual** *people may say: see, look, birth, picture, colorful, illuminate, clear, flash, appear, focused, foggy, form, etc.* **Auditory** *people may say: hear, listen, loud, sound, melody, tune in, crescendo, discuss, express, harsh, resonance, etc.* **Kinesthetic** *people may say: feel, touch, pressing feeling, exciting, fits, firm, spike, aware, hands-on, secure, clumsy, angle, etc.*

You may be able to detect your own sensing preferences from the way you react to these word lists. Try to rank them in terms of your preference and you may have the pattern of your own communicating style. You can also listen to yourself speak to detect the pattern of words you use that may indicate your personal preference. By listening for these key words and observing behavior, you can detect the sensing preference of your partner to some degree. However, beware that your preference may shift according to many variables. Among these may be the time of day, your overall mood, and the circumstances of the encounter. For example, some people wake up audibles, become visuals during the day, and transition to kinesthetics in the evening, but not every day.

Experts generally agree that from infancy we all need to have our feelings mirrored back to us in order to feel affirmed and acknowledged. If you use a communication process of mirroring the sensing preference of your partner, you are able to reinforce agreement in the relationship and provide a means to greater intimacy when moving toward commitment.

Mirroring is the replication of like or similar forms of communicating you detect in your partner. It is demonstrated in infancy as a mother coos to her baby and a father does baby talk with his toddler. It may be the use of certain descriptive words, the use of visual stimuli, body language, or embraces and caresses. Sensing and replicating the communicating mood of your partner, whether it is visual, audible, or kinesthetic, rational or emotional, can be a powerful way of achieving and maintaining instant rapport. It might be what your grandparents referred to as "getting on their good side" or being on the same wavelength. If you want to talk shop or sports when your partner wants to pet or share feelings, you can see the obvious harm to communications and intimacy. If a thinking man wants to intellectualize when a feeling woman wants to relate, you can see the communications dichotomy that is created. Each must learn to accommodate the other, at least somewhat. You must be careful not to let mirroring deteriorate into mimicking. If it is obvious to the other person that you are intentionally mimicking, you easily can make your partner feel belittled. And, of course, you will want to avoid being critical of the other's communicating style.

On the other hand, you can drive people away if you insist on meeting your own communications sensing priorities without adapting to theirs. Communications priorities often shift with time and the professional, social, personal, or private situation of the person. If you prefer to be silent, talk shop, see sights, or caress your partner, when she/he prefers a different approach, you may abort the relationship without either partner understanding why. People who decide based on Thinking or who read this book may figure it out. People who base decisions on Feelings may just walk away without wondering why, only reacting to the angry, negative turn off that results.

Other barriers to communications are injected by a wide variety of distortions, filters, external noise, and one's personality preference for thinking or feeling, or left and right brain dominance. The message usually is distorted in both the process of transmission and reception. A person cannot accurately get into the mind of another only with the mechanical senses. In addition to the five senses, a sixth sense has been proposed by people throughout history. Referred to as the "third eye", intuition may refer to sensing of the energy fields between people as they engage in close dialogue. If two people are on the same "wavelength" their communications are enhanced and if they are not, mutual understanding and acceptance are thwarted.

By encouraging feedback, i.e., asking for confirmation of understanding, (Example: "Would you please tell me what you think I just said?") a return path can be inserted intentionally in the communications process, making a closed loop. Although feedback loops can improve understanding, they also can insert additional barriers and filters, adding further distortions to the process. Soliciting such feedback also can anger people who are not aware of their communications barriers if they perceive your intentions incorrectly as judging them negatively.

Good communications skills do not come naturally to either gender, but men need to work on their ability more often than women who begin practicing with their female friends in early childhood. So, here are some suggestions by Martin Blinder to help make a relaxed environment for more effective communications in a healthy ad hoc relationship even better:

1. Arrange situations on a regular basis during which positive communication about the relationship is most likely to take place without the distortions of intrusions by daily outside events.

2. Keep discussions open-ended with the focus on enhancing the communicating process between you; solutions can come later.

3. Start all serious dialogue with an expression of some wonderful experiences you have shared together.

4. Share your hopes - what each of you wants from the relationship.

5. Learn the terms of the unwritten contracts that each of you expect from the expectations you have hidden unconsciously.

6. Use I statements that own your own feelings and thoughts to avoid criticizing your partner's shortcomings or transgressions. When "You are being too quiet" becomes "I am feeling shut out of your thoughts" more positive results may be obtained.

7. Listen actively and with full attention for the feelings and unmet needs of your partner, especially if there is nothing you can do about them. Put whatever thoughts are going through your head aside for the moment, and concentrate on what your partner is saying. Do not try to fix the unfixable, but affirm and acknowledge the feelings of your partner. Without such acknowledgment and affirmation, your partner will feel rejected and, worse, that his/her feelings are signs of some defect or are inappropriate.

8. Find ways of meeting the needs of your partner without building resentment by cutting into yourself or being untrue to yourself or violating your boundaries. (Boundaries are limits to intrusion including proximity of time and space, touch, sexuality, money, and self-disclosure.)

9. Acknowledge and reinforce any changes your partner makes on your behalf. "I really appreciate the way you saved up the money first instead of using the credit card." "I really felt better when you acknowledged how I feel about that incident."

10. When your partner criticizes, defuse testy critical judgments with adult clarification. Ask for the meaning behind the words. "Can you tell me what I did or said that makes you feel (think) that way about me?" When you get to complete

understanding, then clarify what is desired of you. "So, if I —, then you would —. Is that correct?" After such clarification, then you will be prepared to negotiate a way out of your difference.

11. Sometimes, lavish attention on your partner unexpectedly just because of who he or she is, not for what he or she does.

Get In "Touch" With Your Partner

If you are kinesthetic or tactile, there are good medical reasons for your preference for physical touch. Studies at UCLA, reported by Helen Colton, showed about one third of all the nerve endings responding to touch exist in the palms of the hands, and the largest area of brain surface that responds to touch is devoted to the hand. Therapeutic touch, or the laying on of hands, has been demonstrated as a healing method by religiously oriented practitioners for centuries. This method has been so refined by Dolores Krieger, a professor of nursing at New York University, that more than 50 nursing schools now teach it to their students. Many nurses now are being encouraged to touch sick patients in hospitals and nursing homes because it hastens their healing. Researchers at UCLA reported finding increased production of hemoglobin, the oxygen carrying substance of the blood, and reduced blood pressure as a direct result of meaningful touches. They concluded that people need several intentional, meaningful touches per day to avoid reducing life expectancy.

Unfortunately, our modern Western culture has attached meaningful touching and hugging primarily to sexual foreplay and, thus, has made it a taboo among non-attached people. Touching is the seductress of nature to assure procreation. The most sensitive areas of our bodies are those assured of attracting us to sex; the fingertips, lips, tongue, nipples, clitoris, and penis. It seems to me to be a contradiction to prohibit social touching in a society that condones freedom of sexual relations among consenting adults. Some people are so disconnected with their touch sensors because of the social taboo that they are not comfortable with nonsexual caressing. Some adult children seem to have a lower need for caressing and being caressed, possibly derived from disturbing events of their childhood or genetic or socially learned preference.

If you are a dominantly tactile person, i.e., kinesthetic, without the opportunity to meet your touch needs, the sense of physical deprivation can be eased a little by getting nonsexual hugs from people who care about you. However, even close friends and relatives may be reluctant to get that close to you, if hugging was not a regular part of their family relationships previously. You may represent a threat to their own ego boundaries. You may need to ask for hugs from those whose physical contact you want, but remember to use an I statement when you do so. Example: "I would like to share a hug with you, may I?" Not: "Do you want a hug?" That is a form of passive control that can lead to resentment if your partner responds reluctantly.

Unfortunately, even a light display of affection between members of the same sex often is prohibited in our sexually "liberated" society because of its homosexual implications. Even members of some churches often avoid public hugging because they are afraid of the negative cultural implications. Men are more likely reluctant to show affection in this form than are women, for the same reason. Too bad. I think hugging is a valid and effective form of communicating and sustaining your self esteem.

When asking for hugs, you will need to be sensitive to the touch and sexual boundaries of others. There is a definite difference between a therapeutic hug and a romantic embrace. Don't force yourself onto a person who absolutely recoils at the idea of hugging. With some people, a handshake is about all you can expect. But, that still is touching. If you are open to the opportunities, you may find yourself getting healing hugs more than you expected.

What You See Probably Is What You Get

If your partner prefers visual stimulation, you may need to provide dinners by candlelight, scenic encounters in the city or the country, unexpected written love notes and greetings, occasional flowers, and conversation that emphasizes visual images. Even the type of pictures on your walls or the color of clothes you wear can make a difference in the level of intimacy you achieve with a visually oriented person.

It may be that our etheric body of electromagnetic energy is more compatible with certain parts of the visible light spectrum than with others. A new medical finding connects Seasonal Affective Disorder (SAD) with the apparent feeling of depression when daylight is restricted to an increased discharge of dopamine from the pineal gland, which has a known relationship to depression. Although usually associated with cosmetic needs of women, the science of color now also includes the needs of men. If you can find a competent color analyst in your area, having your skin tone analyzed and creating a wardrobe and home and work surroundings that match your color preference can improve your overall spiritual peace. When you are surrounded by colors that clash with the nature of your spiritual energy, (or the needs of your pineal gland?) the result is a discordant, stressful, reaction.

People also send us visual clues to their level of involvement with the way they position their body during communications. Body-language has been explored extensively for its usefulness in nonverbal communication. Some experts suggest that intent and understanding are derived more from visual input than audible input. How we perceive a person through the tone of voice and body positioning may be more significant than the words they say. Ralph Waldo Emerson said, "What you are doing speaks so loudly I cannot hear what you are saying." He may have been a visually oriented person. Sitting back, crossing arms, and looking away, or frowning, can be signals of withdrawal, disagreement, or rejection. In contrast, leaning forward, touching lightly, smiling or nodding can be signals of acceptance, agreement, or acknowledgment.

It is easy to misread body language because what may appear to be an invitation or a rejection may just be getting physically comfortable. If you detect such body language responses from your partner, it may be useful to check out their meaning by noting them and asking your partner if, in fact, his/her body language is being used to send a nonverbal message. For example, saying something like, "I sense that you may be feeling uncomfortable right now by the way you are frowning. What did I say or do that is causing you any discomfort?" may help to clarify unspoken intent of your partner. The action may come from subconscious needs of which the person is not aware. Calling attention to it may help to clarify the underlying meaning, and showing your concern also will illustrate how sensitive you are to your partner's feelings.

Share Your Beliefs and Feelings

In addition to checking validity of your verbal perception, the skills of sharing your beliefs, opinions, and feelings, and handling conflicts are important to successful intimate communications. When people find that their partner shares similar beliefs, opinions, and feelings, they often experience closer rapport. The opposite also is true because intimacy suffers when these elements are withheld by either partner. Opinions and beliefs are derived from your Thinking or Feeling judgment. They usually are extensions of a rational process of sensing observation, intuition, logical reasoning, factoring emotions and values, and drawing conclusions through learned interpretations.

People whose dominant decision making process is sensing-thinking (**ST**) find sharing ideas and information quite comfortable either verbally or visually, but feel stress when involved in emotional dialogue. People who prefer the intuitive-feelings (**NF**) decision process might experience more stress when asked to express opinions or beliefs requiring logic. For them, the expression of feelings and possibilities through emotions and caresses comes more naturally and spontaneously. A couple may prefer opposite modes, such as the likely combination of a male **ST** paired with a female **NF.** Again this dichotomy could be expression of right-left brain dominance. They might find it difficult to sustain intimacy if their differing communicating styles are not understood, and accepted with love by each other.

Thus, men and women often are frustrated by their partner's way of responding to feelings, and further hurt by the other's frustration. However, two women who prefer feelings are more likely to express understanding of each other's problems and, thus, build a sense of sharing and intimacy. When two people of like preference, whether thinking or feeling, talk, the result is more likely to be one of symmetry with greater understanding and less conflict. However, similarities do not stimulate much growth or creativity in either partner. And, if partners respect their differences, complementarity can provide a much richer communicating environment for both.

As being used here, Feelings does not refer to a sensation received through the sense of touch, e.g., hot, cold, rough, or smooth. These are sensations. The feelings referred to here are the results of an emotional state or inner values and intuitive reaction to a perceived condition. Adult children often learned to disown the parts of themselves that feel in order to survive their ordeals at home. To avoid expressing feelings is to be cut off from other people. If people do not share their feelings, we may go through life confused and overwhelmed. If we permit ourselves to feel the anger, guilt, shame, depression, and grief as well as the joy, elation, and happiness that are parts of real living, we will recover more quickly and heal more completely from each distressful experience. However, I believe there is a healthy way and an unhealthy way of communicating our feelings.

We can choose to express our feelings by displaying them openly and spontaneously in both verbal and non-verbal means. Positive feelings can be expressed by smiles, squeals of delight, a pat on the back, a hug, applause, or other graphic means through use of appropriate body language. Open expression of positive feelings usually is good for us and for the partner in an intimate relationship. You may have had the experience of enjoying a cat purring when it is rubbed affectionately or the delight of sexuality with an uninhibited partner. If so, you know what it feels like to get that positive feedback. Expression of positive feelings leaves no doubt that we are pleased with the situation. It is very reinforcing and encourages our partner to deliver more of the same treatment. Withholding the expression of positive feelings may be considered an insult by people with dominant extraverted, feeling preferences. They may feel anger or resentment at being rejected or guilty for wanting to share feelings more spontaneously. The relationship can be stifled because withholding positive feedback retards further intimacy.

On the other hand, expressing negative feelings openly and spontaneously may be good psychologically for us but unhealthy for the relationship. We should resist projecting judgmental criticism or personal rejection directly onto an intimate partner. Infantile negative feelings might be expressed by crying, pouting, withholding, screaming, and throwing things. Such displays are likely to be met with defensiveness, regret, guilt, and loss of self esteem by the person to whom they are directed. They can stimulate equally negative expressions in return. Physical fights may begin this way when tempers flare over simultaneous, spontaneous expression of negative feelings. No one needs to accept physical abuse, but expressing negativity too much might be its cause.

A more appropriate way to describe negative feelings is by making I statements that put them into words. This suggestion requires that you have the necessary vocabulary to make your point accurately and effectively and that you own or take responsibility for your negativity. Describing your negative feelings in this way will not guarantee that your partner will change behavior more to your liking or cease behavior you don't like. Healthy people will behave as they choose, according to their personality preference and their system of values. However, you may increase the chances of obtaining positive outcomes if your partner knows what you are feeling.

If fear of a rejection or defensive reaction is keeping you from opening up, begin practicing to communicate by taking small steps. When sharing feelings, we do not have to let it all out at one time. We must be true to ourselves and observe the limits of our boundary of self-disclosure as well as the proximity boundary of the partner. The safest rule is to share a little and then check with your partner to see what kind of reaction you obtain. Checking means asking the partner how she/he is reacting to the shared feelings. If the relationship moves forward, you can share a little bit more. But if the partner becomes defensive, fearful, guilty, manipulative, or pulls back, it may be a signal to slow down the pace of sharing.

As you work through sharing feelings, self-disclosure takes place. Here again, a sexual difference shows up. The more women know about a person, the closer they feel to them. However, men often feel uncomfortable in deep self disclosure because they fear it may show up their fears and weaknesses. However, without such an exchange, there can be no deep, intimate relationship.

Unfortunately, with such openness there also is risk. Self-disclosure makes us vulnerable to rejection as the danger builds that our partner may learn things about us he/she does not like. As you disclose more of yourself, your partner has more information on which to decide to stay or breakup. So, there must be some balance between risk and self-protection if optimum communication is to take place. Women must compromise their desire for closeness and men must compromise their desire for self protection. Self-disclosure does not come naturally to members of either sex who prefer introverted feelings in their personality makeup. They may appear an enigma to the partner seeking more intimate sharing. Introverted feelers will need to work harder at extraverting their feelings if intimacy is to be served.

Learn How to Ask For What You Want

Learning to ask assertively for what we want from an intimate partner is a crucial skill in verbal communicating. As infants, we may have only learned to get what we want by displaying anger, suffering, or discontent even before we learned to talk. As adults, these tactics often fail leading us to conclude that our relationships are flawed when the real problem is our communications skills. If we persist in their use and do not get what we want, we abandon our personal peace. On the other hand, by denying our legitimate unmet physical, intellectual, emotional, and spiritual needs because we fear rejection or violating boundaries or causing conflicts, we build up resentments against our partner that inevitably drive a wedge in the relationship and destroy intimacy.

However, you must know fairly clearly what you want in all quadrants of life, physical, intellectual, emotional, and spiritual. In some instances of a specific situation, what you want might be very simple and plain. In other situations, there may be a vague awareness that something is missing that would make your life more fulfilling, but you don't know exactly what it is. That is the normal condition of many adult children who sacrificed so much of their needs for their family of origin that they lost themselves. If that is your situation, I suggest that you take some time out for yourself to find out what you really want, and don't want, in life.

We may not always get what we want and we must respect the legitimate boundaries of our partners. It may be more effective to ask for what we want without complaining that we aren't getting it. Complaining or attacking may only generate guilt, resentment and anger, causing defensiveness, and driving people away. Straightforward asking invites them into partnership with you. As in expressing feelings, the art of asking for what we want includes learning to phrase your needs in I statements. If you preface your request with a sincere and honest compliment, you may get a lot more of your wants satisfied. Saying, "I like the way you look in that dress/suit, and I would be pleased if you would wear it out with me this coming weekend." is much more powerful than saying, "That is a very pretty dress/suit. Would you like to go out with me Saturday?" Can you see, feel, or hear the difference between these two sentences? The latter is a global statement that might or might not be true, while the former is an honest description of your own opinion.

The more sentimental, romantic approaches to love may prompt one to conclude that people in love should be able to meet the needs of each other intuitively. I don't think it is fair to expect your partner to be a mind reader about your needs. By using I statements, we can acknowledge ownership of our needs and feelings and take responsibility for getting our needs met. Good I statements begin with a phrase describing what the "want" will mean to us, if it is satisfied. Example: "I will feel very comforted right now if you would give me a brief back rub for about 10 minutes." You can also begin by expressing empathy: "I sense that you have a lot to do right now, but I would like to spend about 3 hours with you (be specific) as soon as your schedule improves." Remember to ask without injecting a complaint. Complaining about your partner's behavior or lack of it will only cause him/her to become defensive to justify the existing behavior or feel guilty and withdraw. It will do little to gain the change in behavior that you seek.

Even when we ask in an appropriate way, we may not always get what we want because everyone has the right to choose how they will behave toward another. Everyone will behave in accordance with their personality preference, value system, previous experience, training, and a host of other issues carried into the relationship from our family of origin and life experience. Therefore, the ability to accept a no lovingly without taking it personally also is very important.

If our self esteem is sufficient, we can give our partner permission to protect his/her boundaries by refusing our request without serious damage to the ego of either one. If our self esteem is deficient, a no can be perceived as a sign of personal rejection and cause feelings of abandonment when it may be only a temporary deferral. We can confirm the no by asking for clarification. (Example: "I hear you saying no at present. What can we do to make it easier for you to meet my request?")

The Washington Ethical Society suggests that you employ a 7-step dialogue before you finally accept that you are not going to get that need met from that person. This procedure injects an element of negotiation that may get more of your needs met, but you must do it in a way that is not perceived as manipulating or over controlling by your partner. The seven steps to getting your needs met suggested by the WES are:

1. Be specific; "I would like it very much if you —."
2. If you get a no response, restate the meaning of fulfillment to you. "If you —, I will —."
3. If the answer still is no, ask why it is not possible for the person to meet your request right now and if it might be possible later.
4. Actively listen to the response and try to empathize, understand the position of your partner.
5. Test the boundaries of your partner but don't confront, complain, or argue with your partner. "I sense that my request is violating your boundary of (touch, proximity, sexuality, or self-disclosure). Can I modify my request in some way to protect your boundary?"
6. If the answer still is no, ask again (maybe at another time) by restating your

need in a different way or with an option that will avoid violating the boundary issue.

7. Accept the next no response as final, and state your gratefulness for being given consideration.

If the final answer still is no, then you have the choice of sublimating the need, substituting another deliverable need in its place, or trying to get it met in another relationship. That may sound a bit cold and too rational for emotional readers, but those are the options. As with other suggestions in this book, you may need to practice this one for some time to make it a regular habit.

Being able to give a loving no to requests made of you that violate your present boundaries also is important. It is natural to respond to the needs of a friend, but I think there are limits to what anyone can give. We can say no to manipulation and pressure and still say yes to meeting their needs. We cannot be free to say yes in a healthy manner until we can be free to say no lovingly as well. If we can't say no lovingly we can feel guilty, and then angry or resentful at the person who made us feel guilty.

So, it is important to be able to set limits to the beginning and ending of our giving. We must learn to be content with giving as much as we can give comfortably. You can choose to deliver a no with or without encouragement for possible future compliance. If you feel no for now, but believe it is only temporary, say so. (Example: "I love you but I can't grant your request right now. If you ask me again [when] I will be glad to reconsider and try to meet your need then.") If to grant the request really is a non-negotiable violation of a sacred boundary, give the reason and then continue your life without guilt or assumption of any responsibility for your partner's need. (Example: "I cannot ever grant that request because it would be an unforgivable violation of my (money, touch, proximity, sexual, or self-disclosure) boundary.") If that is your unalterable position, then you must grant your partner the right to choose either to sublimate the unfulfilled need or try to satisfy it with somebody else. We must also accept that true giving is giving without expecting or wanting anything in return.

It also is permissible to reject a gift (this includes the gift of sexuality) if to accept it you would feel indebted to the giver. Saying, "I love you, but no thanks" can work miracles for your self esteem. The appropriate response to a gift you choose to accept is to acknowledge it and express appreciation for it. That is all that is necessary to close the loop. No further obligation on your part is due.

Practice Active Listening

Listen, actively listen to your partner. Really listening is to make sense or give meaning to what we hear and, equally important, to ask for what we do not hear or understand. Failure to actively listen is a root cause of many problems counselors encounter with troubled couples. When we do not pay attention and give undivided priority to listening, our partner can feel frustrated and even infuriated at being demeaned by our apparent lack of interest. When people realize they are heard, they feel validated and affirmed. Obviously, those are necessary to maintaining intimacy.

Here are some suggestions by Verderber for improving your reception and under-standing of what is being transmitted to you by actively listening, assuming that your physical hearing mechanism is working properly:

1. Give attention to listening. Often, we are so occupied with what we plan to say next that it gets in the way of really hearing what our partner is saying. If we interrupt another and give the impression of attempting to dominate the conver-sation or impose our will or control inappropriately, communications can be halted. Observing appropriate conversational priority, speaking and listening in turn, is crucial in social encounters of all kinds.

2. Clarify the meaning behind the words. When a person uses a word you do not understand, ask for its meaning in the way the person is using it. Do not assume that your understanding of the meaning is the same as your partner intended. Often people use words we think we know the meaning of in different ways, so it is always good to check on the meaning and intention behind the words. Worse yet, we may assume we know what another really means based on our own interpretation that may be entirely wrong.

3. Withhold making judgments or evaluating what is being said until you receive the entire message.

4. Listen with empathy for the position occupied by your partner. This is more dif-ficult if you have very little in common with your partner, or if you prefer thinking judgment. Your capability for empathy can be increased if you concen-trate your attention on your partner, exhibit genuine caring, become a skillful observer of his\her state of mind, and practice. While none of us actually can walk in the shoes of another, we can move in that direction.

5. Give feedback to clarify the meaning of what you think you heard, by para-phrasing the statement for confirmation of its meaning. This means restating the message in your own words (paraphrasing) with emphasis on clarifying the meaning of both the content and the feelings behind it. Of course, making a dis-tinction between the content and the feelings behind it is difficult when the transaction is very stressful.

6. Ask for the thoughts behind silence. It is said that if you do not know something about an extravert it is because your haven't listened, and if you do not know something about an introvert it is because you haven't asked. Introverts some-times do not say all that is on their hearts unless they are certain you want to hear about it. Both introverts and extraverts can be introverted feelers, so give your partners confidence in making self-disclosure by showing concern for their feelings and encourage them to say what they really mean without being judg-mental about the content. It is by asking questions that they understand you really care and you will learn a lot more about your partner in the process. It isn't always necessary to have answers or solutions to their problems, just lis-ten. As stated previously, men sometimes want to fix the unfixable when their partners only want affirmation and acknowledgment.

7. Avoid overlaying your own thoughts and issues onto the speaker. He/she proba-bly does not want to hear your assessment or monologue and to force it upon

him/her is a violation of personal boundaries. Merely acknowledging that you have heard what was said and share in the feelings of the person may contribute more to intimacy at such times than anything bright or cute that you could say.

Also, it may be necessary to actively ask your partner what he/she wants you to do or say in response to a statement. Codependents often do not know how to ask for what they want, so it may take some loving prompting to get it out of them if they don't think they really deserve to be heard. The socialized differences in conversational styles between men and women also pose barriers to response. In addition, personality factors, such as the dichotomy between feeling and thinking, inject distortion and misunderstanding in conversation. If we acknowledge a statement with a question such as, "I heard what you said; what would you like from me in response?" you show your empathy while expressing your willingness to give unconditionally. If you just assume a response, and say or do what comes to mind, it may not be what your partner expects. That can cause a breach of the relationship.

Negotiating Compromise Solutions

Negotiating is a special communicating skill that all intimate partners must learn well to maintain a healthy ad hoc relationship. Negotiating styles derive unconsciously from the interactions between infant and mother before language is developed, according to Robert L. McKinley. We learn to get our needs met as infants by negotiating, i.e, we balance expressions of joy, satisfaction, and contentment, with discontent, suffering, angering and neediness. After language develops, we use words to get what we want based on the pattern of negotiation we developed as infants. McKinley calls this our "interpersonal operations." A better way is available if we can break the interpersonal habit that drives adult behavior unconsciously from infancy. It consists of stating a position in adult terms of "I want ——— " and being able to trade concessions with your partner until a compromise is reached that is satisfying, although possibly not ideal, to both partners.

This process in a relationship is not unlike settling a labor negotiation or major business contract. It is as important to your intimate future because it determines how major and minor decisions are made as a couple that can affect your intimacy, and how resources are used for daily living, as well as creating security for your long term future. People who are not trained in negotiating will likely use infantile tactics that are harmful to the relationship to achieve their goals or that gum up the relationship so neither partner is satisfied. These tactics include making excessively high unrealistic demands, disguising true feelings and wearing a mask, discrediting legitimate claims of the partner, and using control tactics to keep the partner off balance to achieve a win-lose outcome or lose-lose outcome. A win-win solution is more to be preferred.

Kenneth W. Thomas and Ralph H. Kilmann established that negotiating styles follow two dimensions based on a tendency to aggression or cooperation; one on a scale from unassertive to assertive, and the other on a scale from uncooperative to cooperative. Researchers of business negotiations estimate about 60 percent of all negotiators use a cooperative style and 40 percent prefer an aggressive style. There are effective, average, and ineffective negotiators of both types.

The aggressive style employs words to emphasize and exaggerate the differences between positions. Aggressors routinely use intimidation, accusation, threat, sarcasm, and ridicule to pressure the other side. They view cooperative negotiators as weak, naive, and deserving exploitation. Although they are not unwilling to compromise, the disadvantage of this strategy is that it generates a lot of tension and mistrust that often causes misunderstanding and deadlock over trivial issues. It also threatens the intimacy needed to sustain commitment to each other and to the relationship.

The cooperative style is based on seeking some common ground and demonstrating shared interests, attitudes, and values. Cooperative negotiators regard aggressors as manipulative, exploitative, and overbearing. Cooperators generally feel an obligation to seek an agreement that is fair to both sides. They seek a trusting, open atmosphere in which to negotiate. They avoid threats, use rational, logical persuasion, seek impartial analysis of the facts, show good faith and trust, and admit the weaknesses and problems in their case. The disadvantages of cooperation are that it makes one vulnerable to exploitation by skillful aggressive negotiators, causing over granting of concessions, and over reacting to the emotions of the situation and losing objectivity.

To be an effective negotiator requires skill, perception, and self control because there are five styles that must be carefully applied to different situations. For example:

Competing may be appropriate in an emergency requiring quick, decisive action, on an important issue where the right course of action is painful, or to protect yourself from being victimized.

Collaborating may be appropriate to find a common solution that will satisfy important issues on both sides, to merge two different viewpoints, to gain commitment, or to work through hard feelings.

Compromising may work best when goals are not worth major assertion, when partners have equal power, to achieve solutions quickly, and as a back up to collaboration.

Avoiding may be okay when there is little chance of agreement, to buy time when needed, when the benefits of solution are not worth the burdens, and when the issue is trivial.

Accommodating can be useful when you are wrong, when the issue is more important to your partner, when continued competition would be damaging, and when appeasement is appropriate.

The most effective negotiating strategy in ad hoc relationships is a selective combination of both the cooperative and aggressive styles that results in a win-win outcome. The challenge in a personal relationship is to use the best of both approaches in a positive manner, without injecting threats of engulfment or abandonment to either partner. The overall objective is for each partner to be seen as cooperative, trustworthy, and consistent by the other. Each partner must convince the other that he/she has a strong position and that any concessions are in the best interest of the overall relationship. Power and rights are subordinate to the legitimate interests of the partners. The negotiating goals are: (1) to reach a desirable and durable result in a reasonable time, (2) to reach agreement efficiently and fairly, and (3) to keep the relationship intact and healthy.

Personality factors enter into negotiations quite specifically. I cannot emphasize too strongly how important it is to recognize the differing negotiating approaches that will be used by people who prefer thinking or feeling decision processes. Thinkers will be more logical and rational and feelers will be more emotional and harmonious. Similarly, judging types who prefer immediate closure may force a negative agreement when taking a little more time at a more leisurely pace would permit a naturally acceptable solution to emerge. Conversely, some who prefer delaying a decision may stall for time while they continue to explore alternatives endlessly. Deadlocks and breakups often occur when partners do not acknowledge and accept these differing approaches to making decisions.

Otto Kroeger makes the following suggestions for resolving conflicts for specific personality preferences:

1. Extraverts should listen more carefully and attentively to the other person's view and resist trying to talk their way through or out of conflicts.
2. Introverts should tell their side of the story repeatedly until the other person has heard it and they should avoid stifling their own opinions.
3. Sensors should look at all the circumstances of the issue and not concentrate so much energy on the few facts of the issue that pertain to them.
4. Intuitives should stick to the issues and avoid clouding them with the overall big picture that avoids the specific details and complicates resolution.
5. Thinkers should allow some emotion to be expressed by their partner even though they are unable to do so with comfort.
6. Feelers should be more direct and confrontive than normal, say what they really mean even if it sounds harsh or negative, and don't feel guilty for doing so.
7. Judgers should respect the opinions of others and accept on faith that they may not always be right, or that every issue is one of black and white, right and wrong without accepting the gray areas of life.
8. Perceivers should take a clear position even though they can see both sides of every issue, which can only prevent them from taking a stand and defending it.

Both partners can achieve their needs through win-win negotiating. Both partners can choose to help each other achieve legitimate goals. Open and frank discussion about thoughts and feelings can expand the options for both partners if the following negotiating principles are employed: Focus on the problem and not the person. Focus on the interests and rights, and not the positions and solutions. No one option is exclusively acceptable. Some objective standards are used to evaluate the options. If a strong foundation of trust exists, neither partner needs to be bound by any option that they suggest to the other. There is a lot more to negotiating through a healthy ad hoc relationship, but this brief introduction may help you understand the negotiating skills a partner must have to assure a happy future.

To summarize this chapter, your success at going from casual, polygamous encounters with acquaintances, through polygamous activities with companions, to monogamous dating, to romantic commitment, cohabitation, and possibly marriage, depends a great deal on how effective you are at reaching mutual understanding with the other person. This skill depends on the compatibility of your respective verbal and nonverbal communicating styles and your ability to uncover and negotiate the unconscious boundary conditions, both your own and those of your partner. Boundary issues and the conflicts they create will be discussed more deeply in Chapter 9. In the next chapter, we shall discuss the movement from dialogue to intimacy and commitment.

Eight:
Holistic Intimacy and Commitment

The degree to which commitment is achieved with your partner will depend a lot on your understanding and practice of the behavior we will discuss in this chapter. It also includes basic guidelines for creating a happy marriage and healthy family life, if that is your goal. When two people are intimate, it suggests a warmth and a delicate inter-communication of a very holistic nature. True intimacy develops continually over time if the couple enjoys mutual commitment. Without commitment, each partner may feel a continuing sense of pending separation, with the attendant anxiety, anger, and aggression needed to maintain a defense of their self image.

Intimacy validates our self esteem through full disclosure of who we are, if we tell the complete truth about ourselves. We forfeit the chance to feel loved for ourselves, not who we are, what we do, or what we have, if we withhold or lie about our full identity. It is through deep sharing of self that "I" becomes "We". When all four elements of wholeness (physical, intellectual, emotional, spiritual) are involved, mature holistic intimacy is the feeling we get when we mutually open our minds and our hearts in total acceptance of each other. At its best, it is the sense of human connection at the level of the soul.

The word intimate in the verb form means literally to make known ones deepest nature. It implies a very close association, contact, or familiarity. People who need a third, fourth, or other affair to keep their primary relationship going usually are afraid of intimacy. They may be afraid that making a commitment will prevent them from continuing to grow or may threaten their need for independence. There is little doubt that intimacy is a healthy goal, because of its many proven benefits to mental and physical health. It is through intimacy and commitment that the fullest potential of human relationships is achieved. Unfortunately, few really know how to achieve true intimacy because intimacy is very misunderstood in our culture. Intimacy is so often confused with sexuality that its real meaning and, therefore, its benefits in relationships are practically lost for many people. Consequently, men usually give conversation in order to get sex, and women usually give sex in order to get conversation. And both genders forfeit the joy of intimacy for its own sake. That is why understanding this chapter is so important.

Roots of Intimacy and Commitment
Common sense may place intimate communication secondary to sex as a way for

two people to share their most intimate feelings. Many women, although not all, would reverse that ranking and put communications first. However, Suzette Hagen Elgin describes the learned gender barriers to intimacy in verbal American Mainstream English (AME) this way: "Men are afraid that if they become involved in intimate conversation with a woman they'll find themselves showing emotions that aren't on her list or in ways that are forbidden by the rules, or both. The last thing they want is to have that happen in front of a woman who might use it against them at some later time, and who, every time they see her, will be a reminder that she's seen and heard them being unmanly. How in the world, under these circumstances, can men be expected to let down the barriers to intimate communication that have been trained into them over an entire lifetime?" How, indeed.

It is not surprising that intimate communication between the genders goes so badly in ad hoc relationships. What is surprising, says, Elgin, is that it ever happens at all because so many men are afraid that the women they value most will not respect them after emotional intimacy, and there are enough women who act that way to validate this fear. She says the only remedy to this problem is to build mutual trust that is deep enough and strong enough so that a man will know that violating the AME manliness code in front of the woman he shares his life with is not going to make her despise him or give her a weapon to declare him a wimp later. And the opposite is also true. The same trust and confidence that neither will betray or criticize or belittle the other is needed to make women feel open and free to make intimate self disclosure to their men also.

John Gray observed that men usually need trust, acceptance, appreciation, admiration, approval and encouragement. He says women primarily need caring, understanding, respect, devotion, validation, and reassurance. However, both need some of the opposite too. These needs are ongoing and require responsiveness on a continuing basis. Ironically, when one's needs are being met, we are more highly motivated to meet the needs of our partner. Unfortunately, each gender is most likely to offer what they want for themselves to the other, without realizing the difference. Without an awareness of what is important to the opposite sex, men and women can inadvertently behave and speak in ways that often are counterproductive.

Each partner must feel free to express themselves in their own way. However, to be really known, really vulnerable, really exposed, to be so open, so raw, risks being declared unlovable, unworthy, unacceptable in our culture that admires independence and self assurance. Complete self-disclosure of our needs is fearful. It means we expose ourselves to possible rejection and ridicule. The risks of intimacy are real, but it seems the benefits are impossible without the risk. There is a delicate balance between our need for intimacy and our fear of it. When a couple faces their fears together, they become mutually vulnerable and that honesty helps create deeper intimacy. To seek intimacy and commitment, we must value the potential benefits more than the potential burdens.

A commitment is an agreement or pledge to do something in the future. It is the state of being obligated or emotionally impelled. Commitment to another also requires being open and vulnerable to risks of many types. They are experienced as fears that must be tolerated. Fears of commitment include the fear of failure ending in separation or divorce, the fear of restriction from pursuing other relationships and life goals, and the fear of pain arising from inevitable conflicts. These fears can be addressed by the information in this chapter, but they can never be completely eliminated. We must learn to live with fear, because we cannot escape it, whether we are alone or committed. Throughout a committed relationship, each partner must assume that the other will honor his/her trust in spite of deeper self-disclosure. The fear of this risk can make an uncommitted affair seem more preferable.

Commitment also requires the honoring of our promises, whether the burdens seem worth it or not. An obligation is a formal contract, a promise, or demands of conscience or custom that binds a person legally, as well as morally, and ethically to a course of action. No society can endure for long if its people do not honor their commitments. Interpersonal commitment requires that we desire belonging more than autonomy. We must value the perceived benefits more highly than the perceived burdens.

Holistic Intimacy Promotes Mental Health

If intimacy and commitment are to develop in ad hoc relationships, it is absolutely necessary that dating partners share verbally, unconditionally, and nonjudgmentally their deepest thoughts, ambitions, and emotions with each other. They must collapse their boundaries momentarily and let the partner in without concern that deep self-disclosure in the model of wholeness — physical, intellectual, emotional, and spiritual — will create rejection or withholding. In addition to expressing appropriate self-disclosure, the boundaries of money, touch, proximity, and sexuality all must be collapsed, momentarily. Intimate partners must believe they are accepted for who they are, as they are, without needing to wear a mask as they might in other less private relationships. We show whom we love by whom we trust with our real selves. When we risk showing another our selves, we honor them and the relationship. Without the trust that must accompany being honest, the relationship may gradually starve for intimacy after the glow of initial erotica and romance is replaced with the routine of living and working together.

Commitment is served best when we assume that by giving what another wants, we get what we want. The WES teaches that when we elicit the best in another, we get it for ourselves. If all I am interested in from you is having my needs met and all you are interested in from me is having your needs met, then it is quite likely that neither one of us will have many of our needs met. However, if I sincerely choose to meet all your needs that I comfortably can, and you sincerely choose to meet all my needs that you comfortably can, then it is likely that both of us will have many of our needs met.

Unfortunately, no partner can consistently and continually meet all of our needs, no matter how much she/he wants to. Merle Shain said it so realistically, *"There is no perfect person who can make you whole. You have to do that yourself, and if you wait for someone to fill you up you always wait in vain, because no one is ever equal to the task. Waiting for another to give to you always makes you feel vulnerable and insecure. The only way you ever feel strong and sure is when you are giving to others instead of wishing that they would give to you. It is very hard to learn that lesson and to stop hoping to get from others what you must provide for yourself. It is even harder to start looking instead for what you might have inside that you can give to someone else. But giving is the key."* Jesus taught this same principle as follows: *"Give, and it will be given to you; good measure, pressed down, shaken together, running over, they will pour in your lap. For by your standard of measure it will be measured to you in return."* (Luke 6:38)

Research at Loyola University of Chicago by McAdams and Bryant (Journal of Personality, September 1987) showed a difference in the way men and women perceive the benefits of intimacy. Women in the study reported associating intimacy with greater happiness and gratification. Men reported associating intimacy with lack of strain and lack of uncertainty. Women living alone who possess high needs for intimacy reported lower levels of gratification and more uncertainty in their lives. The need for intimacy seems to decline significantly with aging for women, while it actually may increase for older men. This tendency could be proof of the theory posed by Carl Jung that older people become more conscious of their anima and animus respectively.

Jung observed that men and women tend to adopt roles and orientations of the opposite sex as they move from middle age to older adulthood. He thought that the female part of man, that he called the anima, and the male part of woman, the animus, each strove for recognition with age. If so, women would tend to become more like younger men as they get older, needing less intimacy and more autonomy. That is an interesting way for nature to compensate for the likelihood that men will die earlier than women. Men would tend to become more like younger women as they get older, needing more intimacy and sense of belonging. Thus, men and women may exhibit an increasing mismatch between their needs for intimacy as they get older. Now, researchers know that production of the male hormone, testosterone, declines in males with age, and the female hormone, estrogen, declines in the female with age. The result is a physiological change that permits the proportional increase of estrogen in the male and of testosterone in the female. Thus, science has found a biological explanation for the process Jung explained intuitively. The unanswered question, however, is what triggers these changes that occur with aging. How do the cells of our bodies know that it is time to change their activities? The answer may be found in our genes, i.e., it may be an inherited process.

High intimacy contributes to women's overall happiness and satisfaction with life, while it makes for less strain in life, fewer emotional symptoms, and greater sense of certainty for men. Intimacy may help women to define their self-image in terms of relationships with other people. Warm, close, communicative relationships may provide men with self-assurance, confidence, and security. Such ties may enable a man to venture out into the world, much as the boy needs a secure base with mother to explore the neighborhood. Low intimacy may be expected to lead to greater levels of anxiety, isolation, immobility, strain, and even physical health problems for men. These could be indirect signs of lack of support for the self in interpersonal relations. Intimacy may function less as a secure base for women and more in the manner of providing a sense of identity through which their concept of self may be built up.

Personality factors also affect how we pursue intimacy. In the 1993 Conference Proceedings of the Association for Psychological Type, Marvin Rytting and Roger Ware reported studies that relate concepts about trust, authenticity, and commitment to the MBTI personality types explained in Chapter 3. For people who prefer **SJ** temperament, the commitment comes first; thus, they prefer a form of unconditional love and personal regard that makes intimate sharing possible. People with the **NP** perspective preferred a more personal and conditional relationship that emphasizes self-disclosure, authenticity, acceptance, and similarity as a basis for commitment. Those with an **F** preference emphasized self-disclosure and mutually supporting behavior, while those preferring **T** emphasized rational acceptance and a positive regard for one another.

Commitment Is A Unilateral Decision

Making a commitment to someone or some personal goal can be terrifying. It means you close out options and possibilities for other ad hoc relationships to some extent. Every choice means you give up some control of other choices. Also, you must surrender some of your personal self image and, often, some of your plans and goals for the benefits of the relationship. If the commitment includes cohabitation or marriage, you will need to negotiate and compromise many aspects of living together that are your own personal choices as a single person. You also may lose intimacy with some close friends who sense your new commitment as a threat to their own self interest. If your time and attention are concentrated more on your partner, they may leave your social circle. In making a commitment, we say yes to the benefits of the relationship and yes to the burdens as well. The perceived benefits must outweigh the perceived burdens, if commitment is to be made freely.

Commitment carries risk that must be offset by an equal amount of trust. We say to our partner, "I trust you enough to place our future together in your hands." Without enough trust, the tendency for one partner to demand commitment from the other in return for favors granted may result in a feeling of psychological entrapment. A psychological trap is a situation that is easy to enter, that can only get deeper, that can only be exited with a painful sense of loss, and that seems to have no way to retreat to save face or maintain self esteem. Therefore, I think it is futile to demand commitment when it is not voluntarily forthcoming. If there is one dominant need of humans, it is that of sovereignty, the ability to freely make choices. Coerced, enforced commitments, no matter how evoked, are the most illusory forms of security. Both partners in an ad hoc relationship must be free to make their own decision without pressure of any kind if the relationship is to stand on a solid foundation.

Personality factors also may be involved in making a commitment. A Sensing-Thinking person may require a logical, rational approach to the facts before commitment is natural, while an Intuitive-Feeling person may be more willing to make it as an act of faith. If you are matched in a **JP** relationship, the **J** partner may be frustrated by reluctance of the **P** partner to commit. The **P** partner may feel rushed by the **J** partner into making a premature commitment. One **P** type I know lives by these words on her T-shirt, "Life is uncertain, so eat dessert first." Two **P** types may scarcely be able to decide what to do on a date, and two **J** types may continually make and remake decisions, often regretting their premature choices and correcting them repeatedly.

People who prefer to employ their perception in the outer world like to keep things open. They don't enjoy making decisions that close out potential opportunities. Many people of the **SP** type personality temperament have varying degrees of resistance to making serious commitments, even to themselves. In relationships, **SP** people may think that a better partner for them is just around the corner, always. They may let wonderful opportunities for a lifetime, healthy, intimate relationship go by as they wait for another one that might be better. In contrast, **SJ** people who prefer using their decision function in the outer world want to come to closure and reach resolution quickly. If they cannot reconcile their opposing feelings and thoughts, they may feel a state of confusion. Being in that painful state is part of their makeup. But to avoid the pain, they may make decisions on the slightest amount of information. Sometimes, new information will prompt them to change their minds later, again and again. That can make them appear very indecisive or undependable, the very image they dislike the most in others.

In any event, making a commitment to another person in an ad hoc relationship is an imperfect process. To add more risk, there are the legal, ethical, and moral implications of commitment involved in cohabitation and marriage. When these concerns are added to the decision, most of us enter commitments with great stress and uncertainty. However, we make choices all the time. No decision is a no decision. So even when we don't make commitments, we are making no decisions about a partner and yes decisions about alternatives, including remaining uncommitted.

The process of initiation, becoming acquainted, developing companionship, friendship, and moving on into commitment is not a linear one. The parties can move forward and backward in this process on different schedules. If either partner does not accurately confirm where the other partner is, the relationship can be disrupted and may even break up if they misunderstand the intentions of each other. The commitment can be stabilized at the level of acquaintance, companion, friend, lover, or spouse. Sexuality may be involved at all levels. Each partner can make a unilateral commitment to the other at any level, and that level may not be the same for the other partner. Codependents are often overtaken by their need for care taking. They may commit from compulsion and later feel intense cognitive dissonance, as they confront the split between their thoughts and feelings that might pull them in opposite directions, until they come down on one side or the other. In the meantime, their partner may feel abandoned and confused, not understanding the powerful inner war that is being waged.

The concept of unilateral commitment may be difficult to accept if you are more conservative, or if your traditional ethical, moral, or religious beliefs dictate otherwise. If you place a high moral value on a sexual friendship, becoming attached to a person with a more casual attitude can be painful. It can cause you considerable suffering if commensurate commitment is not forthcoming as you might expect and want. In a state of limerance, we can project onto our partners an image of idealism that we actually desire. We can delude ourselves into assuming that their behavior means more in terms of commitment than it actually does to them. Something as simple as doing personal favors, holding hands, hugging, kissing, petting, and of course ultimately sex, can be misinterpreted as signals of commitment when they are not. It pays to ask how much commitment is involved in such behavior. I have found some people value their autonomy and freedom even more highly than orgasms.

A person who values autonomy very highly may confer affection, such as buying presents, doing personal favors, or hugging and cuddling, even sex, onto a person who values belonging very highly. The more dependent person may misinterpret the gifting behavior as a signal of falling in love or commitment when it is not. Even the people bestowing such favors may not be aware of the underlying motives that drive their behavior. Adult children without effective parenting may be so needy that the first sexual encounter with a new partner triggers their feeling of commitment unilaterally. **Kisses are not contracts.** They may declare genuine love when it is merely the overwhelming need to belong and to feel attached that is driving their feelings. When a codependent recipient of such favors wakes up to the reality, he/she may be thrust into remorse and grief, even depression.

If the more needy or dependent partner persists in demanding upgraded commitment, the more autonomous partner may be compelled to withhold, withdraw, or leave the relationship to avoid feeling engulfed. The healthy response by the codependent is to give the less committed partner reasonable time and space to evaluate his/her behavior and possible future involvement. If a breakup occurs over this misunderstanding, the unrequited lover can suffer the pain of rejection and loss deeply for a long time, and the other may feel guilty for causing the pain.

If your ad hoc partner is not ready to make a commitment according to your needs, try not to take it personally. The partner may be dealing with personal, family, career, or other issues that are not even related to the relationship, or to you, at all. The process of gaining commitment cannot be forced. Neither can we control the timing of it.

Each partner must give the other partner permission to move forward and backward at the pace that is most comfortable for them. Neither partner should force the other into a level of commitment he/she is not ready to make. Neither partner should be manipulated or controlled. The resulting emotional stress can force a breakup if a partner is not ready to make a commitment, or the more committed one is not tolerant and patient enough. On the other hand, if you are unable to make a commitment it is best to be honest and truthful with your partner so you do not encourage unrealistic expectations.

Once made, commitments always are subject to being recalled in ad hoc relationships. Commitments must be renewed continually between the partners if they are to last a lifetime. A commitment that is derived from healthy behavior is a conscious choice by a person who has considered the benefits and the burdens of the situation. He/she has decided that the benefits outweigh the burdens sufficiently to make the commitment desirable within the preferred decision making process.

It can all get very complicated and cause a great deal of emotional suffering. One or the other partner can feel rejected and bewildered in the relationship, if it does not move along as he/she wishes and expects. It is important for both partners to be scrupulously honest with themselves and with each other as each phase of the relationship drama unfolds. Personality differences again will become significant as partners with differing preferences for thinking and feeling try to work out the decisions they must make about commitments.

A means of compiling terms of a covenant for discussion and negotiation of a commitment might be helpful. The Washington Ethical Society offers the following covenant to ad hoc partners as a statement of moral, ethical, and healthy commitment. I recommend that you apply it to each and every one of your ad hoc relationships as appropriate to the level of commitment involved with each partner.

MY COVENANT WITH YOU

To: _____   Date: _____

1. I will not abandon you, although there may or may not be a renewable time frame for this obligation.
2. You are the most important other person in my life.
3. You are my sole and only sexual partner.
4. I will develop and maintain other intimate supporting friendships so that I will not attempt to get all my needs met within our relationship, and I will encourage you to do the same.
5. I will not talk about you negatively with any third party, except to explore my own feelings and choices about us.
6. I will honor all my obligations and agreements with you.
7. I will tell you the truth as I know it and I will not intentionally mislead you.
8. I reserve the right to say no at any particular time with or without encouragement and I accept your identical right. The only exceptions are items in this covenant, once promised.
9. I will make time for us for: warm contact when meeting or separating, to check in with you each day whenever proximity permits, to be together each week for an intimacy date, a planning/searching conversation, a recreation date, and to be alone, and to enjoy other people together.
10. I respect you and I will honor all your boundaries. I will not abuse you physically, emotionally, or intellectually. I will not threaten abandonment, engulfment, physical abuse, suicide, or murder. I will not call you uncomplimentary names or intentionally create conflicts between us. (I will get outside help if I am feeling desperate about an incident or conflict.)
11. I will translate your complaints into wants and all our encounters into either a call for help or an expression of love. I will remember our basic intentions and express myself clearly when something is not going right for me in our relationship. I will complete an Awareness Wheel (to be explained in Chapter 9)

before I ask for discussion of any ethical incident.

12. I will encourage your leadership by being a good follower and I will offer leadership myself. I will share small talk, straight talk, search talk, and light control talk as appropriate.
13. I will be responsible for chores and activities that I agree to accomplish.
14. I will love you as myself, and respond to your expression of fear, or hurt with empathy. I will not discuss private intimate details of our disagreements with anyone who knows you.
15. I will take turns in leading and following, communicate, and attempt to empathize with you in any arrangement that we make.
16. I will appreciate all our differences as unique ways that we can contribute to each other.
17. I will see your beauty, goodness, joy, creativity, and spontaneity. I will do my best to encourage your growth in all components of wholeness — physical, intellectual, emotional, and spiritual.
18. I will give and seek amends for both of our transgressions. I will forgive you in response to feeling hurt or damaged.
19. I will express all my positive feelings to the limit of my comfort and I will describe my negative feelings in words of communication.
20. I will not insist that you do anything that is dangerous to your health, is embarrassing to you, or that will violate any of your boundaries.
21. I will resist any request from you that will violate my boundaries and cause resentment if it is something that is embarrassing, dangerous, or unhealthy for me.
22. I will seek my own physical, intellectual, emotional, and spiritual growth, and I will encourage and support you in doing the same.

_____

Signature

Changing Attitudes About Marriage

Traditional thought assumes no adult relationship can match marriage for the formation of strong and intricately woven bonding. In the fundamental Christian and Jewish traditions, marriage is the ideal culmination of romantic love. However, studies of happiness have ranked married men, single women, married women, and single men, in that order. In a study reported by Stan J. Katz it was found that longevity was promoted by marriage for men and by close female friendships for women. Single men had death rates up to three times higher than married men. So it is not surprising that men usually pursue women, and more women end relationships than men. It is becoming more difficult to achieve mutual security in marriage successfully in our culture, so ad hoc relationships are more likely.

Gary Zukav has observed that marriage, when it does occur, may be approaching a new archetype in the 21st century. Western culture may be awakening to a more spiritual balance in marriage where both partners agree it is appropriate for their souls to grow in an equal relationship. Marriages that succeed will do so because both partners are conscious of their spiritual partnership in addition to their physical and emotional commitment.

Unfortunately, the likelihood of that happening diminishes rapidly with age. Research at Yale and Harvard, reported by Linda Levine and Lonnie Barback, indicated that only 20 percent of single women over thirty statistically can expect to marry; this figure drops to only 5 percent over the age of 35, and to only one percent over age 40. The odds for men may be somewhat better because limitations are placed on the marriage options for midlife single women as men tend to die younger. From analysis of 1980 census data, William Novak estimated that there is a 39 percent surplus of single women under age 30, a 42 percent surplus of women age 30-44, and a 56 percent surplus of women age 45-56. That leaves many single, searching women for whom no available male can be found.

Many women who delayed marrying while they developed their professional careers want to marry a man who is their economic equal or better, which increases the odds against older career women still more. As people of both sexes age, they come to know and to accept themselves better. Often, they are less willing to negotiate or compromise their differences with an intimate partner. Finding someone close enough to their ideal model becomes more difficult. They may experience ambivalence in every new relationship that throttles romance as they learn more about their differences, after the sexual fireworks of eros subsides. Thus, for a variety of reasons, single women must compete aggressively for the available men in practically all age ranges.

Second marriages of older partners may not work as well for many in modern times as compared to when few people lived long enough to seek a second partner in middle or old age. Some couples, who are well suited to living together, are reluctant to get married because their combined incomes are greater if they remain single due to taxes or other financial aspects. Some single parents are restrained from marriage by their children, either for moralistic reasons or to protect their expected inheritance. Sometimes older couples just are not flexible enough to permit the compromises and negotiations demanded in all marriages. And many older couples bring a series of previous romances and sexual affairs to the new union, making for constant comparisons and lingering jealousies. Some people live acceptably with ghosts of the past, and others do not. Marrying later in life places all of one's past, and the self-image it represents, at risk to develop a new sense of partnership, and that can be a fearful experience. It is much different than marrying young when there is little past to lose and much future to gain, with time to overcome any mistakes that might be made.

Marriage later in life is much more complex than marriage in early life because experienced partners bring a whole lifetime of unsatisfied wants, likes, and dislikes into new relationships after midlife. The partners may be at vastly different stages of recovery from dysfunctional families of origin or severe loss, such as divorce or death of spouse. Some may decide that sorting out the common threads of life with another person is too much of a burden in comparison to the benefits, even if they include ecstatic sex and overcoming loneliness and isolation. Some may fear they must give up too much of their own lives and possessions to combine with another.

When the final commitment approaches, desire for autonomy often wins out over need for belonging.

Reconstructing a healthy lifestyle based on platonic idealism or ethical values with several significant other persons may be more gratifying than marriage. Because no two people are perfect for each other, all intimate relationships exhibit some tension and stress. Infatuated romances continually teeter on the razor's edge between euphoria and despair. You may realize that both you and your partner are changing continually. You can either choose to attempt to meet your partner's changing needs without losing yourself, or you may decide to pursue a lifestyle without a full time, committed partner. You can just "go with the flow" for a while, making the most of friendships or companions the universe brings to you, and even learning to manage being alone and lonely, difficult as that may be. There are advantages to being single. They include having freedom to explore your self development without compromises, being able to choose your lifestyle without consideration for another, and spending your money however you wish, etc.

If you decide to marry, many issues should be settled to make a marriage last and be happy. Some of these issues can and should be openly discussed before you get seriously involved, but some of them may not be anticipated before they arise. These issues include the following topics, proposed by Richard Stuart and Barbara Jacobson, for discussion with your partner:

CONSIDERATIONS FOR A HAPPY MARRIAGE

1. Coming to terms with the positive and negative aspects of previous relationships, letting go and detaching from the investments in the past, overcoming lingering jealousy, and idealistic comparisons with previous lovers.
2. Identifying criteria for selecting a new mate. Love may no longer be a necessary reason for getting married, although it is a sufficient condition.
3. Uncovering and negotiating "secret contracts" or "hidden agendas" (expectations that are not openly communicated to each other) in the relationship.
4. Managing the merger of separate estates, homes, furnishings, and incomes for current enjoyment and long term security.
5. Learning to really communicate and understand each other's personality preferences, fears, and lifestyles.
6. Resolving conflicts and making them work for the couple instead of against them.
7. Balancing homelife and worklife, especially in two-career marriages where time together may be difficult to arrange.
8. Resolving the status and roles of parenting with step children and other relatives.
9. Establishing sexual loyalty and compatibility and learning to communicate about jealousy.
10. Developing the most enjoyable, exciting and enriching aspect of marriage, that of true intimacy.
11. Planning for mutual enjoyment of leisure time separately and together.

12. Learning to identify and resolve boundary issues where no-nos really exist.
13. Negotiating use of time and talents to make a partnership work professionally, socially, personally, and privately.
14. Sharing responsibility for money, earning it, spending it, and saving it.
15. Comparing likes and dislikes for such a variety of issues as erotic stimulants, entertainment, food, and housing.
16. Resolving the combination of separate incomes, establishing financial responsibility, and estate planning. Where step families are involved, resolving this issue through a prenuptial agreement would be wise, striving for win-win results for both partners and their heirs.
17. Combining personal possessions, family keepsakes, and housekeeping styles into a single integrated household.
18. Developing mutual trust and confidence in each other to the extent that fear of possible divorce or conflict can be reduced to insignificance.
19. And, of course, you will want to know your partner's background, recognize his/her dysfunctions, and know and share ambitions, hopes, and dreams.

Of all these issues, money seems to be a high priority. Victoria Felton-Collins wrote about why money interferes with love and what to do about it. She says, "When money is seen in the proper perspective, it can be a tool for enhancing intimacy and a catalyst for growth." Two keys for financial peace and contentment are embodied in her money bill of rights as follows: We will honor our differences and hold them as potential strengths, and we will defend our love no matter what happens to our money. Differences in learned values, ambitions, and preferred decision making process will undoubtedly cause some conflicts about making money, handling credit cards, spending habits, and savings and investments. When two careers or blended step families are involved, the issues become even more complex, requiring mutual respect, and ability for accommodation. As in all conflicts, honesty and open communications will help you to reach an accommodation that is comfortable for both partners.

The Healthy, Integrated Family

Whether first, second, or third marriages are involved, three inter-related functional units must be successfully coordinated to create a healthy family system. These are the **spousal unit** that defines relations between the adult partners, the parenting unit that defines relations between the partners and children, and the **sibling unit** that defines relations between brothers and sisters. A set of guidelines by Delores Curran for each of these units in healthy families follows:

> In the **adult spousal unit** of a healthy family, the partners respect and support each other, they nurture each other, they practice tolerance, they have fun together, they are sensual lovers, they share significant interests, they are intimate confidants, they are financial partners, they are each other's primary social partner, and they resolve conflicts and work out problems.

> In the **parental unit**, parents provide adequate food, clothing, shelter,

and medical care; they provide adequate protection from hazards, they are appropriately affectionate, they understand and accept normal stages of child development, they assign responsibility and grant privileges according to stages of development, they establish and enforce clear and reasonable rules and behavioral guidelines, they validate the child's thoughts and feelings and teach appropriate forms of expression, they respect and encourage each child's uniqueness, they support each other's authority, and they encourage their children's growth toward independence.

*In the **sibling family unit**, siblings teach each other valuable social skills, they form a natural peer support group, they form a society of near equals, they provide a social setting for learning, they help each other develop and define an accurate personal history, and they stimulate a healthy circle of friendships.*

Another model of healthy modern families was compiled from research conducted by Delores Curran. She surveyed over 500 professional family therapists to find out what they thought were characteristics of healthy families. Following are the most popular 15 traits chosen by the experts out of a total of 56 optional traits offered in her survey:

1. Members of a healthy family communicate effectively and listen actively to each other.
2. The healthy family makes time for regular meals at table that stimulates intimate conversation.
3. The healthy family affirms the self esteem of each member and supports one another in their separate goals.
4. The healthy family demonstrates and teaches respect for each member and for members of other families.
5. The healthy family develops a sense of mutual acceptance and trust, with confidence that each member will fulfill his/her individual role in the family system.
6. The healthy family makes time for and has a sense of play and humor.
7. The healthy family maintains a balance of interaction between members that encourages each one to feel accepted and belonging.
8. The healthy family makes time for leisure activity both separately and together.
9. Members of a healthy family assume and exhibit a sense of shared responsibility for each other.
10. The healthy family learns and exhibits a sense of moral and ethical right and wrong, sometimes delaying or foregoing personal gratification in loving sacrifice for the whole.
11. The healthy family creates and perpetuates strong rituals and traditions.
12. Members of a healthy family share an interest in a common core of religious beliefs.
13. Members of a healthy family respect the privacy of one another.
14. The healthy family values and practices a concern for service to others outside their relational boundaries.

15. The healthy family admits to and seeks professional help with interpersonal and individual problems.

John Rosemond, a family therapist, provides these guidelines he and his wife have learned are the most important stabilizers of their 25-year marriage.

- Express your unhappiness in simple, straightforward, but nonjudgmental statements such as, "I really wish you would not do that." or "Like it or not, this is the way I feel about what you did."
- Accept the big reality that neither of you is a perfect match for the other and that everyone is difficult to live with sometimes. The diversity in emotional commitment, childrearing, financial responsibilities, housekeeping, sexual drives, and differing likes and dislikes do not always mesh.
- Compromise as little as possible to resolve conflicts because it may mean that neither partner gets their needs met. It is better to resolve differences by allocating ultimate authority for crucial decisions to the partner best equipped with knowledge, experience, and motivation.
- Accept the probability that neither partner is likely to change very much with time. Although people can and do change their behavior and opinions as they get older, their basic genetic makeup usually does not change in revolutionary ways.
- Husband and wife should put each other first and make the children second. Keeping the adult focus on the marriage allows children to develop their own sense of autonomy and promotes their emancipation as individuals.
- Be stubborn and tenacious about being determined to make the marriage work, survive, and grow. So many marriages might be failing because the couple never has learned to work hard for anything, never had to persevere, never been forced to hang in there during difficult times. Mature couples avoid boredom and value the marriage more than either one values him/herself.

If single parents remarry, they may be surprised at how long and difficult is the task of merging two families, whether or not the ex-spouse is alive. Patricia L. Papernow explains how a new family can be created by working through several developmental stages. She calls them the fantasy stage, the immersion stage, and awareness stage, the mobilization stage, the action stage, the contact stage, and finally the resolution stage. If this sounds like it can be very complicated, you got it. It can also be very painful to all the parties involved and take several years to work through.

Step couples who are not prepared for the persistence and tolerance required to integrate their families can sometimes give up and go through another divorce. Even the best of adjustments often include having to accept less than perfect integration of the step siblings with each other and with both stepparents. Some members of the binuclear family may always choose to remain outsiders. According to Papernow, fast step families can move through these stages in three or four years. For average step families, it can take seven years for all members to feel comfortable in the resolution stage.

When older single people choose to marry or live a committed lifestyle, other issues are involved in addition to all that has been discussed above. Older people must contend with their awareness that time for a healthy life is shorter and that recovering from mistakes may be more difficult, or even impossible. Also, issues of merging assets, retirement living, preparation for chronic illness, and long term terminal care are added. Adult children of older singles may be both assets and liabilities to the relationship. Some adult children may oppose any intruder they perceive to be making a claim on their inheritance, or who may be adding additional concerns about elder care. Blending of adult step families can be practically impossible for senior singles. Tax laws also favor couples living together rather than being married, and that issue can raise moral concerns for many traditional couples. Estate planning and prenuptial agreements can throw a wet blanket over an ardent love affair among senior citizens. And, of course, there are the accommodations to physical aging that must be resolved. On the other hand, older committed couples may enjoy some of the most happy times of their lives if family responsibilities no longer interfere with the opportunity to enjoy each other and life together.

E. Kent Hayes suggests that the key to all healthy family dynamics is developing a relationship in which each participant feels free to bring up the most stressful topics for open discussion in a nonjudgmental, honest dialogue. In his experience rehabilitating juvenile delinquents, the most important factor in healthy families is training of parents to participate, really participate, in the development of their children. However, Hayes says that successful families all have kinks and faults, and that healthy families are not especially pretty. They argue when they have to make a point. They shout when they need to be heard. And they cry big sloppy tears all over each other when they are hurt. But, each member does his fair share to help each other develop their full potential.

Since few us ever had any training to be good parents, most of us grew up without competent parenting and pass that legacy on to the next generation, even though we may possess advanced college degrees. With so many of today's kids being raised in professional daycare centers, there is no forecasting what kind of families they are being taught to create. However, if relations between parents are healthy, chances are good that children will get the message and respond in a healthy manner. When you clear away all the fantasies and remove the distortions, a clean slate can emerge upon which you can write the script for a happy, though imperfect, marriage. One such script was supplied to me by an ad-hoc partner of mine in the form that follows, and I offer it to you as a model affirmation to set as your goal in marriage or other form of committed healthy, intimate relationship.

OUR PARTNERSHIP

I am creating a true partnership with a person who is a coming home for me; one with whom I can relax and "be", rather than having to be something that I am not; and I desire that this be true for her/him also.

Our relationship is:
- spiritual, physical, intellectual, and emotional and is based on the principles of conditional love

- joyful, often playful; we are able to access the "child" in each other; open and totally honest
- expressive, communicative; we learn and practice the art of making I statements, and let each other know our feelings, without judgment, so that we can continue to know each other and ourselves better
- appropriately committed, so that trust is built day by day
- sensitive and sensual - with our lovemaking expressing the joy of, and being the symbol for, our unity
- able to consider new ideas, growing, expanding, maturing, peaceful
- mutually supportive, even if working on difficult situations, or on significant and unequal changes
- a vehicle for sharing, expressing, becoming more empowered than we could possibly be alone
- committed to negotiation and compromise, to help us through the difficult times, rather than making demands, or harboring anger, or walking out; we are committed to finding solutions that work for both of us, even it takes a lot of effort
- a commitment more to us and the relationship, and to our lives together, than to anything outside the relationship
- positive, we look for the good, the perfect in each other, and each helps to support the other in that outlook
- mutually appreciative and respectful of the other's many talents, abilities, families, friends, strengths, and weaknesses
- a great friendship, as well as a great love.

Together, we are:
- in love with life as a grand adventure rather than a sentence to be served, living it with style and great joy
- able to work together, yet retaining our separate identities, nurturing of each other, both physically and intellectually
- responsive to each other, even when the other's ideas seem foreign
- happy at doing things together: cooking, fixing, earning, creating, homemaking, dancing, playing, lovemaking - and we understand that it takes both of us to create these harmonies
- involved together on a path to live more spiritually, more fully, more joyously, more lovingly, on a common path to higher consciousness and spiritual enlightenment
- in tune with one another - we create harmony rather than discord by accepting each other's native, infinite worth, and we are committed to keeping it that way so long as we are together
- financially prosperous because we make a good team, although we can feel whole and complete in temporary separations from each other
- concerned about bettering the world in which we live, if only by brightening the corner where we are.

Transition

Now, we have finished Part II of the book. The next chapter begins Part III, the last section. So, it might be a good time to pause for a rest and then go back over chapters 4 through 8 for a brief review. Perhaps you now will agree with me that this is not just a book to be read quickly and returned to the shelf or discarded. It is a living reference you can refer to throughout all your ad-hoc relationships and even your marriage. To make it most useful, you need to be familiar with its overall organization and content so you can find what you need when you need it. Review the Table of Contents to see how the material is organized and where you now are in its development. But, as I said in concluding the Foreword, there is too much here to absorb quickly. Take your time to digest it one chapter at a time, while you are learning the healthy behavior you never learned from your adult role models.

Since no two people are perfectly matched, differences normally will be experienced as conflicts in every relationship. There is no such thing as a relationship will all benefits and no burdens. Since they are bound to occur in all ad hoc relationships, it is important to learn how to deal with conflicts. In the next chapter, we will work on means of avoiding unnecessary stress and possibly even inadvertent breakups by learning to handle inevitable conflicts in a healthy manner.

Nine:

Loving Through Conflicts

Apparently, it is only through attempting to solve problems that we can learn and grow. Current conflicts often stimulate memories of events long forgotten and angry feelings long suppressed that have nothing to do with the matter at hand so they can be resolved. Most anger has some fear lurking deep underneath its thunder and lightning. Those who are mentally ill seek to avoid emotional suffering by withdrawing from current reality into a protective cocoon of defense. Healthy partners accept life as it is and seek to negotiate their way through all the barriers to happiness by exploring their needs together in an environment of mutual respect and acceptance, if not total understanding. In this chapter, we will explore sources of conflicts and offer some proven methods to approach effective solutions to them. When you can use these new skills to enhance your commitment and intimacy, your ad hoc relationships will be elevated to a higher level of bliss beyond your expectations.

Bonnie Eaker Weil said, "Where there is no fighting, there is not passion." It appears that people require both allies and enemies in their lives, else natural selection would have removed one or the other from human evolution by now. Even the cells of our bodies sometimes work at odds against each other, and death is the ultimate result. Jesus said there would "always be wars and rumors of wars." When two people become intimate partners, the problems can lead to separation and divorce if they cannot work together for solutions that fit both their needs.

Sometimes people just feel feisty and like a fight to discharge energy, so they choose to work toward making war rather than peace. This benign mood is illustrated by a TV comedienne who said to her husband, "I feel like fighting tonight, so you can pick the subject." However, Marion Solomon showed that sometimes chronic fighting actually is a symptom of deeper psychological issues that may need help from a therapist to resolve. Paradoxically, she says, "the deeper the emotional connection between partners, the more likely that wounds from the past will emerge in the relationship." If one partner chronically picks a fight, that partner may actually be harboring deep unresolved emotions from preverbal childhood. By projecting what cannot be tolerated or resolved alone onto the partner, one actually may be trying to eject unconsciously rejected parts of self.

Elizabeth Kubler-Ross has said all of us possess both a Jesus and a Devil. The Jesus may evoke a messiah complex that attempts to solve all problems with unconditional self sacrifice that looks like masochism. But, the Devil may seek only maximum self fulfillment at the total expense of others that looks like sadism. It is possible for two partners to adopt complementary behavior unconsciously that assures and perpetuates conflict as both seek to resolve inner issues through the other. If the couple can make these issues conscious, the relationship can be a safe harbor in which to heal infantile wounds that could fester for a lifetime.

Sometimes a fight is beneficial to clear the air and reset the relationship after resentments have built up. By themselves, disagreements between intimate partners are neutral; they just are. It is what we think about them that gives them power in our lives. Most fights probably are disguised symptoms of unconscious and unresolved issues dating back to our prehistoric ancestors that were never resolved. Life poses an endless series of problems that demand our attempts to solve them. Just as we learn one lesson, the universe presents another problem for us to solve, and continually balancing the ambivalence between peace and war seems to be one of them.

Sources of Conflicts

If we were perfectly ego-less people, without any opinions or judgments, there would not be any disagreements. However, because we are not perfectly reformed creatures and we have opinions and make judgments, there is conflict in every intimate relationship, even the most loving, co-creative ones. Also, every conflict indicates that a relationship exists, because people without any connection usually do not experience any conflicts. Resolution of conflicts always requires some compromise and negotiation. There are no solutions that are ideal for both partners, and each settlement results in benefits and burdens on both sides. Only with perfect balance between wanting to belong and simultaneously to be free, which is impossible, could resolution of conflicts be flawless.

Ironically, when we make deep self disclosures that may expose our fear and anger, codependent partners may try to "fix" us to protect themselves. Instead of merely acknowledging our feelings and supporting us while we work out our own solutions, such a partner may cause harm or create a conflict by either discounting our plight or making a judgmental response. Then we may respond defensively and set off a round of miscommunication that can end in a real conflict where none existed at the beginning. Whenever our boundaries are breached, feeling hurt and angry is a natural result. However, many codependent people and those with introverted feelings are not consciously aware of their emotions, so they are suppressed. It may take such people some effort and time to get in touch with their feelings and bring them into consciousness to motivate action. On the other hand, some people are too quickly motivated by their feelings and may take negative actions, sometimes including emotional and physical abuse, without stopping to anticipate the consequences. Neither approach is a good way to handle conflicts. Both suppression and unbridled anger should be avoided to preserve the partnership, which is very fragile and easily damaged during conflict.

If a partner feels accused, discounted, or demeaned by criticism, he/she may be driven to rationalize the action for self defense. Dominant feelers may be motivated to seek harmony and accommodation, even though conformance to the wishes of an intimate other brings resentment into the relationship. By handling our conflicts with mutual respect for our differences, relationships can actually become stronger and our mutual commitment deeper. If not handled effectively, unresolved conflicts build upon one another until they create irreversible tendencies toward breakup. Therefore, it is wise to welcome the legitimate suffering and pain of problems, as well as the joys of life. To avoid conflicts also is to avoid the growth that suffering the pain of solving them brings to us.

Every interpersonal conflict may be a signal of some wounded places hidden inside ourselves that needs attention and healing. Underneath all conflicts may be unmet essential needs that are being expressed in distorted or unconscious ways. John Welwood suggested that relationship conflicts can be used as paths to greater intimacy and commitment if we shift our focus away from the heat of the struggle with our partner and explore its source within ourselves. Conflicts often are mirrors, reflecting back to ourselves some unfinished business of our own that needs attention. They can point to ways we need to grow or to heal.

Conflicts can also be created if we do not understand and accept the gender differences in communicating styles. When a misunderstanding of words and actions is fueled by a faulty response, the situation can easily escalate quickly into a fight that benefits neither partner. John Gray identified four strategies people use to avoid getting hurt in such encounters. They all are counterproductive. *First,* we can choose to move into an offensive stance and strike out at our mate by blaming, judging, criticizing, and making the partner look wrong. Such intimidation always weakens the relationship. When attacked this way, women are likely to close up to protect themselves, and men are likely to shut down and stop caring as much. *Second,* we can choose to flee the situation by refusing to talk to avoid the confrontation. The silent partner hurts the other by withholding love and thus receives less in return. They can resort to overworking, overeating, or other addictions to numb their unresolved painful feelings. *Third,* we can pretend there is no problem, put a smile on our face and appear to be agreeable and happy to fool ourselves that everything is OK. That way, we sacrifice or deny wants, feelings, and needs to avoid any possible conflict. *Fourth,* we can fold up, take the blame and assume responsibility for whatever is upsetting our partner, and end up losing ourselves. Eventually, this tactic results in resentment for having to give up ourselves to retain love.

What works best is to recognize these faulty behaviors and take a time-out to cool down and then come back to talk again at a selected time and place. While on your time-out, it is a good idea to write a love letter to your partner explaining your feelings, anger, sadness, fear, regret, and love. These are the five main aspects of emotional pain. Then, write a second letter pretending you are responding as you would like your partner to. Later, after you have cooled off, you might share your letters with your partner and conclude by asking for what you want. When hearing such a love letter, Gray suggests it should be with the following attitude: "I promise to do my best to understand the validity of your feelings, to accept our differences, to respect your needs as I do my own, and to appreciate that you are doing your best to communicate your feelings and love. I promise to listen and not correct or deny your feelings. I promise to accept you and not try to change you. I am willing to listen to your feelings because I do care and I trust that we can work this out."

In this way, intimacy is enhanced and each learns how to please the other, and to change so as to become more of what the other wants, thus giving and receiving more love. In any event, working out your feelings alone, or with a same sex support group, or an objective third party can prevent a serious breach in your relationship due to misunderstandings.

People often invoke primitive needs for self protection and security in their close relationships. In conflict, romantic or rational love is never enough to resolve important issues. During negotiating and compromising, logic and realistic reasoning must be employed, as well as emotions and values. Under the stress of conflict, even co-committed couples often discover they really don't understand each other. The shock of this awareness can be devastating and, itself, causes breakups when real communications seem impossible. How you fight is more important to the survival of the relationship than what you fight about.

Some people seem to need to prove they are right in every conflict. Maybe you only need to allow your partner to get a grievance off her/his chest without taking it personally. In doing so, you make the leap of growth that is possible in the situation. People who truly love each other unconditionally, and have adequate self esteem, may be more free to openly face conflicts than those who fear their love will not survive candid expressions of differences. When the issue of who is right and who is wrong loses its importance, the couple can really hear the pain of each other. If feelings arising from conflicts are not acknowledged and worked through together, nursing a grievance in private only creates distance and causes resentment rather than encouraging intimacy to grow. Sharing, communicating, and growing through conflicts together are absolutely necessary for a happy marriage or committed ad hoc relationship.

Conflicts often arise when we become conscious of boundary issues. Everybody has a certain need for defense of their boundaries. You may not be able to tell exactly why, where, when, or with whom you may fall in love. But you can be aware of your ego boundaries and you can control your actions to a great extent in response to stimulating, stressful ethical incidents. The primary boundaries we should guard are limits to health, money, touch, sexuality, self-disclosure, and proximity (space and time) that we all prefer for maintenance of comfort, peace, and security. You can become sensitive to your vulnerability if your ego boundaries are not under control. As intimacy and trust develop between couples, the defense of their boundaries is less fortified, and they become more open to each other. However, the intimacy that develops with openness of boundaries is risky. As partners learn more and more about each other, the information can be used to justify withdrawal, manipulation, and control. We also become more compliant and accommodating to wishes of our partner and that can set up resentment if we do not control our boundary limits.

Conflicts also arise from unfulfilled contracts that partners expect each other and their relationship to honor. Contracts are agreements the partners make that stipulate what they will get from each other and from the relationship for what they put into it. Contracts can be of three types: conscious and communicated, conscious and uncommunicated, and unconscious. The contracts that are uncommunicated and unconscious cause the greatest conflicts when they are not consummated. When values that come from basic beliefs clash or expectations are unmet, conflicts can emerge from seemingly unrelated incidents that are but symptoms of the unsatisfied contract. Partners must become more conscious and communicative about their differences to solve such problems in a cooperating environment.

Co-committed loving does not mean being victimized. In fact, you can live in victory over life if you change the way you think about adverse events and disagreeable people. You can learn to avoid being entrapped into relationships with people who only want to exploit the neediness, compulsive care taking, or savior complex parts of your makeup. You can say no lovingly to anyone who attempts to violate any of your boundaries, even though unintentionally. Everyone deserves to get their needs met, but everyone does not get what they deserve in this life. It is natural to be angry when we are frustrated. If you are a whole person yourself, you do not have to assume responsibility for the needs of others, unless you freely choose to do so. Even so, I don't believe you can be responsible for another person's happiness. Setting limits to giving is a difficult task for codependents, but it is healthy to do so.

Establishing and Honoring Boundary Issues

Although we may not always realize it, conflicts usually occur over violations of personal boundaries based on role models that were set during our childhood. Boundaries enable us to maintain a balance between the need for belonging and the need for autonomy, or dependence and independence. It is as though each person is encased in a balloon of boundaries in each of these five areas: money, touch, proximity (time and space), self-disclosure, and sexuality. Through communications, we let our partner know the size and shape of these balloons, which vary considerably from person to person, and even with time and circumstance. Some people are encased in very large balloons and others display very small ones. The size of the balloon also can vary with our reaction to conditions or to the person we are with. Sometimes, we may be very open to reshaping our balloon depending upon the person we are with, the environment, and the mood we are in. Sometimes, the shape of our balloon is more rigid and unyielding.

We compile most of our boundaries by the age of twelve from what we picked up verbally and visually from our surroundings. We are fed a steady diet of cliches, inconsistencies, contradictions, and blatant lies in addition to some truths. As our condition changes through adulthood, all that we learned needs to be constantly reevaluated for its relevance to the present. Many of the reasons we set the boundaries we do are buried deeply within our unconscious, especially if it would be painful to recall them consciously. We must guard against the use of selective memory, the harboring of beliefs that are distortions of reality from the past filtered by faulty role models. Old tapes learned from childhood and past experiences may not be appropriate now, requiring that we introduce new limits on behavior, and remove old, obsolete limits.

Successful management of boundaries is very important to codependents and adult children, people who may have very poorly defined balloons. They may be invaded easily and victimized for the sake of belonging or connecting with another. They can permit their boundaries to be violated up to the point of panic. Then they may react by exploding in anger or fleeing relationships or staying and being victimized in a self destructive way. If we do not honor our boundaries, we can either build up resentment and rage over being victimized or we despair and become depressed for lack of control. In any event, I think harm is done to the relationship if boundary issues are not successfully managed. Healthy people sense the limits of their own boundaries more realistically. They are respectful of and honor the boundary limits of others, while they acknowledge that everyone carries around some obsolete and utterly dysfunctional beliefs. Remember how important it is to say no lovingly to intrusions of your boundaries. It is only as we can say no that we also can say yes in a healthy manner.

Victims, Offenders, and Messiahs

Clinical observations led Carmen Renee Berry to conclude that dysfunctional families lead adults to act out roles of victim, offender, and messiah. Faulty scripts learned in childhood can set negative beliefs about ourselves that drive our behavior in self-defeating ways. Some negative life scripts described by John Welwood are:

I don't deserve love.
I have to earn love.
I can never get what I really want.
I will only be loved if I play hard to get.
If others see how needy I am, they will run away.
I don't trust love - it is a form of control.
I must save women (or men).
I must always be pleasing to men (or women).
No one will ever love me if I show myself as I really am.

Modern psychology attributes such thinking to the result of highly emotionally charged, irrational, fixed ideas beneath adult consciousness. Negative ideas that are acquired in our early years, under stress, take over and control a person's behavior, according to Michael Franz Brasch. He demonstrated that the picture we have of ourselves literally determines how what we see and hear is interpreted as reality. If our self image is flawed, so will be our perception. **Victims** may think the only choice they have is between the pain of commitment and the pain of separation. That is the condition in which pessimists live most of their lives unless there is some intervention that corrects their self image and improves their self esteem. They could just as easily assume optimistically that the choice is between the benefits of commitment and the benefits of separation. When in the victim role, we may unconsciously assume that we deserve to be treated badly as we were in childhood, and actually invite attacks on our boundaries by offenders. **Offenders** assume they are entitled to violate the rights of victims, as their role models did, and proceed to defile personal boundaries of others.

In this context, being victimized is not the same as suffering inevitable human problems such as getting sick, losing a job, losing a loved one, or making a costly financial mistake, etc. These types of problems do not mean that we are weak, incompetent, unlovable, or stupid. All such experiences in life merely call attention to the facts that humans do not control everything in their lives all the time and none of us make perfect decisions all the time. The victims I am referring to here learned in their families that defending themselves against boundary attacks was not appropriate. Their self esteem is wrapped in the opinions of more powerful family members who may use any of the unhealthy roles to control them. Their childhood experience taught them it was useless to complain or to expect their needs would be met.

Messiahs are selfless super care takers who assume they have the responsibility of protecting victims and neutralizing offenders, as they did in childhood. Messiahs can assume roles of pleasers, protectors, givers, rescuers, counselors, teachers, and crusaders. Most dysfunctional adults assume one or more of these three roles in various situations. Some people seem to play all three roles from time to time with different people. Messiahs often use care giving as a tactic to keep people beholden to them and, thus, under their control. Their apparently endless, sacrificial giving may be a screen for insecurity and need to maintain connection with an intimate partner.

Healthy people recognize and accept these imperfect traits in themselves, but do not let them become compulsive behavior. They strive to be responsible for their behavior in ways that usually elicit the best in others because, in so doing, they obtain the best for themselves. Unfortunately, victims, offenders, and messiahs all instinctively rely on the weakness of others to enhance their own self esteem. You must guard against being victimized by your own need for self esteem and defend boundary issues that will inevitably occur. Sometimes, it is appropriate to be indignant, defensive, and angry, but many codependents find it very difficult to confront people who breach their boundaries until the situation becomes a crisis. People who were abused in childhood, those who are middle children, and people with certain personality preferences exhibit a tendency to be over compliant and too accommodating, even to their own detriment.

If you are over compliant or too accommodating, (a trait of people in whom feelings are dominant and extraverted) you also may have learned that proper behavior included being selfless and even sacrificial in the service of others, i.e., being a martyr. Certain fundamental religious teachers often instill sacrificial giving in children as highly desirable behavior. As children, we may have been taught to put kindness and consideration of others before ourselves, that being selfish is unacceptable and putting our own needs first is wrong. One of the lessons we may not have learned is the necessity of adequate self-care. As adults we may not recognize the validity of our own needs and feelings. Needs denied can increase feelings of helplessness, worthlessness, anger, and resentment toward those to whom we grant power over us. While considering the feelings and welfare of others, we also need to learn good self-ishness, that "me too" is okay. Many people from dysfunctional families can take the undeserved role of childhood victim into their adult relationships. As a result, adult children can be defrauded easily by manipulative people, controlling family members, and needy intimate partners. I think we can learn to balance meeting the needs of others with our own needs.

Our boundaries may be either too tight or too loose. If they are too tight, we don't permit people to get close enough to develop loving intimacy. We cannot be giving, caring, sharing, and nurturing when such behavior is appropriate. If boundaries are too loose, we may rush headlong into a victim role with anyone who pays the slightest attention to us. If they pay significant attention, including sexual advances, we may lose all boundary control with regards to sexuality, self-disclosure, proximity, money, etc. The needs of adult children for self esteem and acceptance can lead them into relationships with compulsive people who are exploitative, manipulators, liars, cheats, and addicts.

There may be those offenders who purposefully, or unconsciously, tend to use your needy emotional condition to meet their own needs, without contributing significantly to yours. Some humans can be very predatory when it comes to preying on the weaker neighbors of society. Some people we cannot resist are downright dishonest, and may act illegally. Not only are physical assaults common in our country, but so also are emotional assaults that never make the news. Some people seem to be natural-born users. Some people who exhibit pathological antisocial behavior can habitually victimize others, even to the point of physical harm, for years before they commit some illegal act worthy of criminal prosecution. Often, the legal system only turns them back into society to victimize again, and again.

Berry perceived that compulsive victims, offenders, and messiahs often are inclined to get together because of the way they complement each other. It is uncanny how people can get together to play complementary roles, i.e., offender-victim, victim-messiah, messiah-offender, etc. Each of us has the potential for all these roles and we probably play all of them from time to time. Neither compulsive, obsessive giving nor taking is healthy behavior, obviously. Healthy people exhibit a balance between isolation and over-dependency. We can learn to share and to care within healthy limits, unconditionally and freely from a position of personal wholeness. People with a history of repetitive divorces, unstable work record, drug or alcohol abuse, criminal convictions, migratory residency, or other signs of anti-social behavior should be held at some distance until they are thoroughly proven to be rehabilitated. Even law enforcement professionals can be fooled by the charm and seeming good will of dangerous people who go on swindling, robbing, dealing, defrauding, and even murdering their fellow human beings.

Setting limits may require that we acknowledge and recognize that some problems have no solution that we can provide. We may have to accept that life is unfair in many ways, when severe losses or needs arise among acquaintances, companions, friends, and even relatives and lovers. After you have mustered all you can of your available resources and options, you may have to face the fact that there is nothing more you can do comfortably within your limits. Do not let your over-dependent intimate friends and family smother you with their problems. If a safe balance is not achieved between giving and receiving, you may have to choose the lesser of evils. i.e., losing such a friend or living as a victim of your own messiah complex.

We must deal with the emotional consequences of saying no to someone we care a lot about, if saying yes will make us feel exploited and resentful. We can apply this guideline: "Will I respect myself more if I say yes or no?" Try to settle that question before you make any commitment that threatens one of your boundary issues. That test applies to relations with your siblings and parents as well; give yourself permission to say no to them also. Unhealthy, manipulative or controlling family members also can be potential bullies or victimizers, sometimes unknowingly. Family relationships often are the hardest to keep within healthy boundaries. Sometimes it is necessary to make what may appear to be ruthless decisions to protect your boundaries, but you can learn to deliver them compassionately, with love. "Darling (or whomever), I love you, but that violates my _____ boundary, and I just am not going to do it."

Positive, reinforcing exchanges should be the goal of all your intimate relationships and your choices should be based on mutual benefits, rather than mutual burdens. Without a balanced exchange between giving and receiving, I don't believe there can be any healthy, intimate relationships. Achieving the balance between protecting yourself from negative victimization to achieve self esteem and learning to give from unconditional, nonjudgmental love poses a challenge that demands great courage. That challenge is part of the razor's edge of healthy, intimate relationships.

But, to be fair, this may be easier for those with certain personality preferences. You may recall from chapter 3 that certain people prefer an open approach to life, while others prefer coming to closure more rapidly. This preference is shown on the **JP** scale of the MBTI. Those who prefer the **J** side may commit before they think it through sufficiently. Also, it is possible for a person to be pulled in one direction by his/her emotional feeling process and in the opposite direction by his/her rational thinking. If you are caught in such a **T-F** dichotomy, making a decision to protect yourself when in such a place is very difficult and may require professional support. This is one time when stopping to count to ten is very appropriate, taking time to work through the painful cognitive dissonance that such conflicts arouse.

As you take more responsibility for your decisions, conflicts will be created with those who would use you for their own benefit at your expense. Dealing with those conflicts, both internally and interpersonally, is part of living a mature life. As you develop more control of your boundaries, you may find the intentional users in your life drifting away when they realize you are no longer their victim. But, when you defend your boundaries, conflicts are sure to occur.

Dealing With Conflicts Lovingly

When you share opinions, beliefs, and feelings, draw boundary limits, and reject victimization, conflicts are likely to develop in every ad hoc relationship. It is important to sense when a conflict has occurred and to give yourself permission to feel and express your feelings to a degree that is appropriate to the incident. The Washington Ethical Society defines an ethical incident as "something that happens to one or both parties that negatively affects the way they relate to each other." They can evolve from unfulfilled contracts or invaded boundaries. Sometimes, the triggering incident is not plain or clear, and sometimes it is very specific. Sometimes an incident is clearly related to deeper issues and sometimes the real underlying problem is more difficult to discover and work out. An incident that is evidence of a deep personal matter of self-development needs to be clearly framed before it grows into a serious crisis that threatens survival of the relationship. Sometimes an incident is the result of a minor problem or issue that was not settled before it escalated.

Incidents can be framed into three different types of complaints: those related to topics, personal matters, and the relationship itself. Topics include things, places, events, ideas, and people. Some typical topical incidents arise from housing, friends, careers, money, children, leisure, contraception, drugs, work, clothes, and time alone or together. Some personal issues can include self esteem, identity, values, energy, responsibility, success, appearance, goals, habits, health, and recognition. Relationship issues can include matters of sex, trust, jealousy, affection, commitment, decision-making, control, communication, boundaries, and cooperation.

Often the incident will be accompanied by physical sensations of stress such as heart palpitations, a knot in the stomach, sweating, feeling hot or cold, or maybe even shaking. Once a triggering incident is apparent, the grieved partner has the choice of confronting the other with the grievance or stuffing his pain. If partners are not confronted, conflicts cannot be resolved, resentment builds, and a breach is created in the relationship. Confrontation is a positive act, when it is used to work through an incident. Unless that step is taken, (and it is difficult for introverted feelers) the couple either stays in a state of denial or the grieved partner stays in withdrawal and the conflict is not resolved. The grieved partner then lives with resentment, anger, and frustration as the likely result. The repressed emotions may be expressed in other dysfunctional ways that are harmful to the relationship. However, confrontation should be postponed until a preliminary analysis of the internal source of your reaction to the incident has been completed. The rule about counting to ten before you confront your partner is good advice. But, a better plan is to work through the Awareness Wheel that will be presented shortly.

After they overcome denial that a problem exists, people usually deal with conflict in one or more of five specific ways. These are withdrawal, surrender, aggression, discussion, or persuasion, according to Rudolph Verderber. **Withdrawal** is physical and/or psychological removal from the situation. Withdrawal can be appropriate if it provides a temporary cooling off period for close inquiry into the deeper motives underlying your reaction, or if it is used by people who are only acquaintances who seldom communicate. Again, counting to ten first is a good idea. But, permanent withdrawal usually is not healthy as it can lead to a stalemate, leading to resentment, deadlock, and, possibly, breakup if the issue is significant enough. Many dysfunctional families only practiced permanent withdrawal, so you may not have learned the more healthy styles of conflict resolution. It is much healthier to recognize an incident leading to conflict in its incipient stage rather than to wait until it grows into a full blown deadlock that can cause a breakup.

Surrender is giving in immediately to avoid stress. Although surrender is a common tactic among codependents, it can infuriate a healthy partner because there is no testing of the situation. Unwillingness to stand up for your position can cause even more conflict born of disrespect. **Aggression** is the use of physical or psychological force to get your way. It does not deal with the merits of either position, only with who is bigger, stronger, louder, etc. **Persuasion** is used in discussion and may include trying to motivate through reason, use of emotional language, and impressing with superior knowledge or credibility. Discussion is an adult, rational way of defining the problem, analyzing it, suggesting possible solutions, selecting the one that works best for both partners, and working to make it work. **Discussion** involves willingness to negotiate and compromise. I think that is the key to handling conflicts.

Handling Ethical Incidents – Fighting Fair

I want to emphasize again that in our culture it is quite probable that a woman who prefers feelings (they are 65% of the population) will be paired with a man who prefers thinking (they also are 65% of the population) in their decision processes. Of course, the opposite combination can also exist. In addition, socially learned styles of communicating often separate women from men. The result often is a dissatisfied woman who wants more intimate sharing with her man than he is willing or able to give, or vice versa. He may even not be aware of her need, and vice versa. Consequently, many incidents may be a reflection of this basic dichotomy in the relationship. Often, it is the woman who brings up her reaction to a conflict and wants attention to resolve it, with the man avoiding the confrontation or pretending no such incident exists, or defending his actions by discounting his partner's complaint. Simply realizing that what seems like intentionally spiteful behavior merely is a different style of personality may help to reduce the tension.

What is really being sensed may be loss of ones power, or at least the perception of threats to it. Power can sustain romantic interest in a partner or it can become a controlling device warped with many kinds of unhealthy manipulative behavior. Partners deprived of their power usually compensate by using or abusing the controls that remain available inside the relationship.

Discussions on sensitive boundary issues must be handled very carefully to avoid imparting guilt or shame to either partner, either for causing the painful situation or for being sensitive to it. How conflict situations are handled and how compromise solutions are adopted will be crucial to the outcome of the relationship. If unconditional, nonjudgmental love is the basis for the relationship, necessary compromises can be openly and freely negotiated, since the highest good for each partner is the primary goal of the other. If these matters are successfully navigated, then the relationship is more likely to weather the unfair, disabling, and emergency crises that are inevitable in every ad hoc partnership.

This is what a healthy relationship is all about: allowing conflicts to be described openly to a partner you trust, putting them in proper perspective with your own background, resolving them directly, and putting them into the past, without penalties of withholding, abandonment, guilt, or engulfment. Remember this principle of attitudinal healing: We can always perceive ourselves and others as either extending love or giving a call for help.

People either prefer to seek a solution to conflicts or to avoid the confrontation that is required. From the various combinations among couples, three possible scenarios result. They can be grouped into collisions, collusions, and collaboration according to Robert Langs. **Collisions** are confrontations between two seekers out of control. The goal in collisions is for one partner to win and the other to lose. Each partner brings out all the dirty wash in the relationship. The main issue is lost in all the unrelated argument. The real issue is one of control. They can go on until someone surrenders, both withdraw in disgust, or some superficial resolve is adopted, though unhappily, by both partners.

Collusions and silence are maintained when two avoiders team up. The goal in collusions is not open, but it amounts to loss for both partners. The issue is denied until the pressure gets too much for one partner, who may abruptly leave or blow up. They may set up substitute ambiguous issues to avoid confronting the main, central issue of conflict. Instead of confronting unpleasant issues or expressing taboo feelings and thoughts, collusion only perpetuates conditions that are harmful. Neither of these approaches obviously is healthy. The stress they invoke can cause physical illness and, maybe, even death.

Collaboration occurs when one or both partners seeks a reasonable accommodation. The couple seeks a negotiated compromise that meets some of the needs of both. The solution assures the benefits exceed the burdens for each one. The goal in collaboration is for both partners to win equally. For collaboration to begin, we must first interrupt the learned patterns of collision and collusion.

Naomi Quenk described the very intricate process normal people use to defend ourselves against traumatic and emotionally charged events and fantasies by unconsciously encoding all types of messages, even to stretching the truth and telling lies. Much of what passes for communications during a conflict actually is a dialogue between the unconscious of the sender and the unconscious of the receiver.

Quenk attributes such dialogue to being in the grip of the fourth or least developed function of personality. When ad hoc partners fall into the grip of their inferior sides, both express their least effective, primitive traits, leaving their more developed sides confused, drained, and disabled. Quenk poses the following possible symptoms when each type person is in the grip of the inferior function of personality. (Refer to Table 3-1 on page 57 to review the MBTI ranking of personality functions.)

Inferior Extroverted Sensing:

INFJ and INTJ   Obsessive focus on external data

Overindulgence in sensual pleasure

Adversarial attitude to outer world

Inferior Introverted Sensing:

ENFP and ENTP   Withdrawal and depression

Obsessiveness

A focus on the body

Inferior Extroverted Intuition:

ISTJ and ISFJ   Loss of control over facts and details

Impulsiveness

Catastrophizing

Inferior Introverted Intuition:

ESTP and ESFP   Internal confusion

Inappropriate attribution of meaning

Grandiose visions

Inferior Extroverted Thinking:

ISFP and INFP   Judgments of incompetence

Aggressive criticism

Precipitous action

Inferior Introverted Thinking:

ESFJ and ENFJ   Excessive criticism

Convoluted logic

Compulsive search for truth

Inferior Extroverted Feeling:

INTP and ISTP   Logic emphasized to extremes

Hypersensitivity to relationships

Emotionalism

Inferior Introverted Feeling:

ENTJ and ESTJ   Hypersensitivity to inner states

Outbursts of emotion

Fear of feeling

Since the runaway inferior has effectively disabled the dominant function, it falls to the auxiliary or second function to mediate the outcome. By invoking the auxiliary, a person in the grip of the shadow can work toward balance again while the inferior is being strengthened. Quenk proposes that the experience of working through these defensive reactions can result in positive growth if the couple allows each other the chance to work through the episode. When completed, such a transition actually can strengthen the relationship. Obviously, a person without this knowledge may well try to compensate with the good old dependable dominant function, only to find it useless or locked in psychic combat, and therefore feel panic and out of control. Then, professional therapy may be needed if the victim is to recover a sense of balance and control.

Under the stress of conflict, the sender uses encoded messages to avoid the pain and confrontation with the inferior or shadow side of personality that would be called for in open, truthful dialogue. If the inferior function of the receiver is "hooked", he/she plays the game by accepting the encoded message as real and returns equally encoded responses from his/her inferior side. Then, you have a dialogue between the two undeveloped, unconscious, inferior sides of both partners and nothing can be resolved. Each partner may confuse the truthful meaning of their messages and may be perceived as dumping on each other, and that only makes matters worse. If they stay in that mode, the partners soon become deadlocked and further communication becomes impossible.

In order for a couple to communicate within a truthful system, both partners must have the capacity to tolerate emotional pain, to delay immediate responsive reaction that might discharge the situation but destroy the relationship, and to draw upon the strongest, most dominant functions of their personalities. Each partner must defer a considerable amount of automatic self defensiveness and the automatic search for immediate relief to permit resolution of the incident. Relating meaningfully to another, therefore, involves the decoding of encoded messages and identifying and working through of the incidents that trigger them. Although confronting the extremely painful realities about themselves and others can be risky, Langs suggests that sending and receiving the truth about a disturbing trigger event fosters healthy forms of relating after the possible anxiety and depression are worked through.

A very useful tool to help us collaborate by stopping to analyze why we are upset over some triggering incident is called an Awareness Wheel. It permits a logical way of looking at the situation from a rational viewpoint. Sometimes, anger is an appropriate emotion, but few of us have any training in communicating it in a healthy manner. The Awareness Wheel, described by Miller, et al, can help you manage your anger more constructively. The Awareness Wheel consists of several segments. They are: Trigger Incident, Actions, Feelings, Interpretations and Resolution. Instructions for using it are as follows:

First, write a description of the triggering incident in terms of what the unbiased facts were. Avoid any subjective judgments in the description. Consider what actions took place by yourself and your partner during the incident and write them in the segment titled **"Actions."** Add how you sensed the situation with specific physical reactions in the **"Sensations"** segment. Describe the **"Feelings"** that resulted from your sensory input or your thoughts surrounding the incident. Write some **"Interpretations"** both about yourself and your partner concerning the incident. This step can take some time if your review points to deeper issues surrounding the incident. Often, a complaint is but the symptom of some deeper inner lesson that we can only learn by working it through. The complaint may be an inevitable confrontation with your own issues that the behavior of your partner triggers into consciousness. What actually did they mean and what were the underlying values or thoughts from your training and experience that caused them? When you peel off the layers of self deception, you may discover how much concern is appropriate to the current relationship, and how much of it actually is unfinished business from your previous experience. If you find out, the behavior of your partner may be seen as an opportunity to seek solutions to your own inner issues. Finally, itemize precisely what you want in terms of **"Resolution,"** from yourself to yourself, and from your partner to you.

By the time you finish writing down all parts of the Awareness Wheel, you probably will have defused the initial emotional reaction and found yourself better able to deal rationally with the issues involved in the incident. You will understand more of your own subconscious contribution to the incident and why you reacted as you did. You may discover unfinished aspects of your own development that need more work. You may identify the way your inferior fourth function is likely to jeopardize even trivial conflicts. You may realize how your encoded messages have confused the situation and added more emotional distortion than necessary. But, be cautioned that merely knowing these skills does not change your basic makeup, and that conflicts are likely to emerge periodically throughout your relationship. If your partner also uses the Awareness Wheel to communicate issues, they likely will be less damaging and provide opportunities for even more understanding and bonding as they are safely resolved.

Only after these steps have been completed privately should you then engage your partner in a discussion of the incident. By then, your feelings probably will have cooled down somewhat so you can work out a solution more effectively, based on truthful, open communications undistorted with encoded messages.

When you are ready, ask your partner for a time and place to discuss the incident and its resolution. Make a specific appointment, even to the point of reserving the amount of time you think it will take. Present your grievance in this four-part pattern: *"When (describe the incident), I feel (or felt) (describe your emotions), because I believe (or think) (describe your interpretation of why you feel as you do). I want (turn your feelings into a specific request)."*

Your intention should be to share the experience of your reaction in a positive way, not to blame your partner or prove your case. Give the other person the opportunity of sharing an incident on their agenda that may help clear the air. Equal sharing can encourage generosity, acceptance, and partnership. This process may be new to you if you are from a dysfunctional family or have a long history of collisions or collusions. It may take some practice and you may have many setbacks before it becomes a natural part of your behavior. If you keep practicing, soon you will be the way you act. The object is not to change — we probably couldn't even if we wanted to — but to be honest with your partner in dealing with your emotions.

First, you must be impeccably honest with yourself. Understanding your values and character traits and how they interact with your partner will help you have more effective communications and allow you to accept and support each other more completely. Unresolved grievances can fester and erode any relationship if you do not deal with them openly. Understanding how you react to such events is the first step to their solution. One caveat is appropriate here, however. Sometimes compulsive honesty can be cruel if it is used, even unintentionally, to create jealousy or to elicit some reassuring guarantee of your partner's commitment.

For example, it may be harmful to the relationship to tell your partner graphically every time you feel lustful about someone you see or work with. Although most experts agree that having fantasies about other people is normal, if there is a good chance you could actually carry out your fantasy, then it might be more humane and loving to keep such temptations to yourself. The one exception is where you think your desires are caused by some resentment you carry against your partner or some behavior you want him/her to change. Then, it may be good for your relationship to voice your wishes, citing the fantasies as reason for bringing up the issue. This is especially sensitive when you are dissatisfied with your sex life and think it might be better with someone else for whom you feel lust. Although adultery is a forgivable insult to your partner, carrying out a sexual temptation usually creates resentments that are difficult, and sometimes impossible, to heal. Remember that if either partner thinks there is a problem, there is a problem.

Be Forgiving...and Assertive

Relationships can stabilize at any level of involvement from polygamous dating to monogamous dating to committed cohabitation as long as both partners are content with the situation. Couples can agree openly or implicitly to be acquaintances, companions, friends, or lovers, without ever working on becoming more. It seems that romantic, sexual relationships either proceed toward commitment, or recede toward breakup when either partner is not satisfied. Along the way, both partners are likely to make some mistakes of action or judgment which hurt the other. The realization that we cannot control the behavior of others, only that of ourselves, can be very painful if we have made a significant emotional investment in a relationship. If conflicts are not reconciled through effective communication, they can add up and cause serious doubts about continuing.

The only solution to such pain is unconditional, unilateral forgiveness. Sharon Wegscheider-Cruse said, "Forgiveness is the healing gift we give ourselves." It implies that we admit that we do not know the complete circumstances of the people who have had an impact on our lives, including our parents and other adult role models during childhood. We choose a happy life for ourselves and others when we forgive them all. We relieve ourselves of the burden of carrying around hurt, anger, pain, and loneliness. We give someone else the freedom to live their life and work out all their own behaviors, feelings, and consequences. Jesus knew about the self-healing power of forgiveness. He advised that we forgive those who hurt us "seventy times seven" times. (Matthew 18:21)

Forgiving is not tolerating unresolved grievances or intentional abuse, however. I think your partner should acknowledge the painful behavior and attempt to change it after you communicate your feelings and offer to negotiate a compromise. If that doesn't happen, then you may consider leaving the relationship for your own health. Although he wrote a great deal about extending unconditional love with no expectation of return, Leo Buscaglia also wrote, "If a relationship becomes destructive, endangers our human dignity, prevents us from growing, continually depresses us - and we have done everything we can to prevent its failure - then, unless we are masochists and enjoy misery, we must eventually terminate it. We are not for everyone and everyone is not for us." When the burdens of staying in a relationship outweigh all the benefits beyond your level of tolerance, you have every right, possibly the obligation, to consider leaving the relationship. It may be a necessary step to maintain your mental health.

No one deserves to be abused, physically or emotionally. You should not have to endure real pain and suffering through disrespect, neglect or indifference, being deprived or exploited, abandoned, or engulfed. To continually repress resentment, rage, and humiliation over such abuse is as bad for you as swallowing poison. However, I think you should carefully test your decision before you terminate a relationship in which you have made a significant investment. Always complete a benefit/burden ratio before you make any significant decision, as I described in Chapter 4.

Learn to Think More Clearly

Your feelings of rejection or abandonment and engulfment may be a valid reading of the situation when your partner habitually abuses your boundaries. Unfortunately, wounded adult children often employ faulty logic that distorts the truth. This behavior can result from applying old childhood tapes that stunted our self esteem to current situations when they do not actually apply. Unless they are dug out of our subconscious and revised to meet current reality, twisted thinking and perceptual distortion can cause your feelings to be invalid. We can continue to employ techniques of crisis avoidance and pleasure seeking that we learned in childhood when they no longer apply. They can reflect your own poor self-image and lack of self esteem, rather than intentional misbehavior of your partner.

Because of the imperfect aspects of human perception, it is imperative that we check our thinking against reality when conflicts boil up into threats of abandonment or perceptions of abuse. Faulty thinking also can occur due to personality preferences when we are under stress. You may recall that thinking as a decision process is the least preferred function of people who prefer emphasis on feelings. When feelings are running out of control, rational thinking often is disrupted. Thinking also can be distorted when we are in crisis or feel anxiety or panic in a tense situation. Aaron T. Beck, David D. Burns, and Gary Emery, and Marlin S. Potash demonstrated how helping clients straighten out their twisted thinking through cognitive therapy often improves their feelings and relieves depression more quickly when it accompanies medication. If your family of origin encouraged any kind of faulty thinking, it may be useful to check with a professional cognitive therapist for help in your recovery.

For centuries metaphysics has taught that we create our own realities by our beliefs. The ancient proverb says, "As a man thinks so is he." In modern terms, believing is being. Before you can do anything, you must first believe that you can. If you believe that you cannot make your relationship work and mitigate your conflicts, chances are you won't even try. First century Greek philosopher Epictetus wrote, "Man is not disturbed by events, but by the view he takes of them." In this view, finding the solution to conflicts requires a change in the way you think about the issues involved.

In directed cognitive therapy, the counselor forces the client to test the factual basis or evidence for reaching false conclusions that create negative feelings that stifle fulfillment. Therapists Beck and Burns call it "reality testing." Here is their description of faulty thinking patterns, called cognitive distortions, found to be common among depressed people. You will benefit highly by working toward avoiding these mistakes of logic (they are impossible to eliminate entirely) in sensitive, intimate relationships to prevent unintentional breakups and to minimize your grief over justified losses.

DESCRIPTIONS OF COGNITIVE DISTORTIONS

1. ALL-OR-NOTHING THINKING – You see things in black-and-white categories. If your performance falls short of perfection, you see yourself as a total failure. If your partner fails in one instance, he/she fails in everything.

2. OVER GENERALIZATION – You see every single negative event as a never-ending pattern of defeat that you are powerless to change. You convert specific "I think –" statements into global principles that set you up for certain conflict instead of recognizing them as your isolated opinions. And you fail to realize that global statements by others really are "I think –" statements of their own opinion and not a general principle.

3. NEGATIVE MENTAL FILTER – You pick out a single negative detail and dwell on it exclusively so that your vision of all reality becomes darkened, like the drop of ink that discolors the entire beaker of water.

4. DISQUALIFYING THE POSITIVE – You reject positive experiences by insisting they don't count for some reason or other. In this way, you can maintain a negative belief that is not contradicted by your everyday experiences.

5. JUMPING TO CONCLUSIONS – You make a negative interpretation of events and comments even though there are no definite facts that convincingly support your conclusion.

6. NEGATIVE MIND READING – You conclude arbitrarily that someone is reacting negatively to you, and you don't bother to check this out to confirm it.

7. NEGATIVE FORTUNE TELLING – You anticipate that things will turn out badly, and you feel convinced that your prediction is an already established fact. You could just as easily anticipate that things will turn out well and assume that is an established fact.

8. MAGNIFYING OR MINIMIZING – You exaggerate the importance of things (like looking through a magnifying glass) such as your mistake or someone else's achievement. Or you shrink things until they appear tiny, including your own desirable qualities or the other person's imperfections. This is also called the binocular trick.

9. NEGATIVE EMOTIONAL REASONING – You assume that your negative emotions necessarily reflect the way things really are: I feel it, therefore it must be true.

10. *SHOULD STATEMENTS* – You try to motivate yourself and your partner with shoulds and shouldn'ts as if you both have to be whipped and punished before you will do anything. Musts and oughts also are offenders. The emotional consequence is guilt. When you direct ineffective should statements toward others, you feel anger, frustration, and resentment.

11. *NEGATIVE LABELING AND MISLABELING* – This is an extreme form of over-generalizing. Instead of describing an incident or error factually, without criticism, you attach a negative label to yourself or the other person: Instead of "I made a mistake," you say, "I am a loser." When someone else's behavior rubs you the wrong way, you attach a negative label to him or her instead of to the specific action. Mislabeling also involves describing an event with language that is emotionally loaded.

12. *PERSONALIZING* – You see yourself or your partner as the cause of some negative external event which, in fact, neither of you was primarily responsible for. You take responsibility for things beyond your control.

Psychologists and medical scientists now commonly accept the age-old premise that our feelings stem from our thinking. Not only does faulty thinking cause emotional stress and create unnecessary conflicts, it also can cause psychological illness such as depression and even physical disease, maybe even death when it restricts our immune system. We cannot control the behavior of anyone else without physical coercion or mental abuse. We can only communicate, attempt to persuade, and be willing to negotiate. It follows that if our feelings are hurt by someone's behavior, to change our feelings we must change our thinking first. The longer negative thoughts are hosted, the more physical and emotional damage they cause.

But, we can become aware of these faulty thinking patterns and strive to counter-attack them with positive, rational logic whenever we sense we are being soured by our own internal negativity. We can learn to counter every automatic negative thought by searching for the evidence to support our feelings. We can stop our negative thoughts and talk back to our negative schema with more positive affirmations. A simple way to practice that skill daily follows with the worksheet of Figure 9-1. It is done in five steps. After developing this skill, then we can communicate hurt feelings openly to our partner, using the Awareness Wheel as a tool to organize the process and obtain confirmation or even amends. Here are the steps:

1. Write down the troubling incident.
2. List your negative feelings and rate them as to intensity on a scale up to 100.
3. Insert your automatic thoughts about the incident in the left column.
4. Identify your distorted thinking in the middle column, selecting from the list above.
5. Challenge your thinking with more positive responses in the right column. You may have to practice this exercise daily for a while until it becomes a natural part of your makeup. Or, you may need the help of a cognitive therapist to develop the arguments needed to offset your negative thinking patterns.

THE DAILY MOOD LOG

DESCRIBE THE UPSETTING EVENT *(1)*

_____

NEGATIVE FEELINGS - Record your emotions and rate each one on a scale from 0 to 100 (most). Include emotions such as sad, anxious, angry, guilty, lonely, hopeless, frustrated, etc. (Scaled 0-100) *(2)*

_____

AUTOMATIC RESPONSES *(3)*	DISTORTIONS* *(4)*	RATIONAL THOUGHTS *(5)*

All or Nothing, Overgeneralizing, Mental Filter, Discounting the Positive, Jumping to Conclusions, Magnifying or Minimizing, Emotional Reasoning, Shoulds, Labeling, Personalizing Blame, Mind Reading, Fortune Telling.

From: Burns, David D., Feeling Good. NAL Penguin Inc. New York 1980

Figure 9.1

If we can recognize when we are employing one of the cognitive distortions above, and dig for the subconscious sources of our negative thoughts, we may find fear at their base. We may bring our conversations more honestly in line with our reality, and be able to negotiate through our conflicts more easily. With such powerful unconscious forces driving people, you can see why it is useful to probe very carefully for the real meaning behind seemingly observable conflicts. Also, with complete understanding of our native personality type through the MBTI, (Chapter 3) we may become conscious of the underlying stream of undeveloped, primitive distortions that drive behavior during crises in close relationships.

If you cannot improve your relationship with the techniques explained in Chapters 8 and 9, perhaps a counselor who specializes in relationships can help mediate your differences. Having an understanding of these methods and carrying them out with your partner are two different matters. Your partner must be willing to work on his/her own dysfunctional training and experience as well, and to learn these methods. If that is not forthcoming voluntarily, a third party counselor may be able to elicit the needed change. But, if you enter couples counseling, be prepared to meet the possibility that your partner views the situation differently from you and may see you as the uncooperative source of your problems.

Unfortunately, when all else fails to limit intentional abuse by your partner, termination may be a healthy solution. Warning signs that your relationship is terminally ill can involve both rational and emotional factors, depending upon your preferred decision style. Some questions posed by Barry Lubetkin you might ask yourself to check your situation are as follows:

> *Are you feeling anxious, depressed, or in a panic, with a sense of impending doom? Are you and your partner keeping secrets from each other? Have either of you just stopped caring about the physical, intellectual, emotional, and spiritual happiness and growth of the other? Do you feel disconnected and lonely, even when you are together? Do you find ways of avoiding sexual encounters, such as watching late night television, feeling too tired, or sleeping excessively? Do you feel emotionally or physically abused? Do you feel devalued, cheated or untrusted; does your partner lie to you? Is an addiction or serious behavioral problem obviously intruding on your relationship? Are you fantasizing about how much better it would be with someone else or even being alone; are you actually having an affair with another person? Have you exhausted the potential of couples counseling with a qualified professional? If your answer is yes to even a few of these questions, perhaps it is time to consider the possibility of terminating the relationship before you get married and face a divorce later.*

Some dysfunctional relationships can survive for years if there is a complementary need being met between the partners, i.e., when a compulsive giver and a compulsive taker team up. You may be fearful of the outcome or loss of whatever you are getting from the relationship despite the burdens. You may reject termination to avoid the possible negative consequences that you think may be worse than continuing. You might be put off by fear of the confrontation and possible reaction from your partner. Or, you may fear rejection of your self for imposing the pain of termination upon your partner. Deciding to leave an abusive or dysfunctional relationship is not a mark of personal failure. It might be a very healthy thing to do for the long run, even though it poses painful contemplation of the immediate change in lifestyle that likely is involved for you and your partner.

Only you can make the determination whether it is time to bail out of an ad hoc relationship. However, I suggest that you carefully evaluate the potential benefits and burdens of both staying and leaving in order to arrive at your decision. Even with all your good intentions and new skills in seeking intimacy and commitment, all intimate ad hoc relationships will terminate eventually in the fullness of time, either through breakup, divorce, or death. When they do, we must experience the loss, give up the past, and let go of wishes by our wounded inner child that things should be different among mortals. Then we must go on to the next challenge of growth in adult life, dealing with loss and recovery, as discussed in the next chapter.

Ten:

Healing Inevitable Losses

Just as it is common to change careers several times during our lifetimes, it is not uncommon to change ad hoc partners as well. Although breakups are extremely painful, the primary goal of western culture is to avoid pain. From infancy, we are taught to seek immediate relief from all discomfort. Therefore, we must learn how to suffer when the pain of loss is forced upon us.

Oscar Wilde reportedly said, "There are two great tragedies in life, losing the one you love and winning the one you love." And, after observing the impact of bereavement, John Bowlby said, "Loss of a loved person is one of the most intensely painful experiences any human being can suffer." Sigmund Freud wrote, "We are never so defenseless against suffering as when we love. — There is no treatment for grief, only tolerance." There may be no escaping the pain of inevitable loss, but there is more than tolerance available for healing, as you will learn in this chapter. Loving embraces potentially losing. But, if you really love someone, you will want them to be happy, even if it is with someone else or being alone.

I believe that our unconscious needs draw people together to accomplish a purpose, either to learn a lesson or to experience psychic growth. We can choose to believe there are no mistakes and that each relationship has some definite teaching purpose in the lives of both partners. When our lessons are learned or our growth step is completed, we may go on with our pathway either through separations, divorce, or even death.

You cannot own or control another human being, no matter how much you may wish to or assume that you do. We can only be ourselves and hope our partner adjusts as we change through the stages of life. Letting go of our attachment may feel like letting go of a life preserver in deep water when you don't swim. But if you can let go, you may find the benefits well worth the effort. Insisting upon grasping onto an unwilling partner can only cause more of the pain we are trying to avoid.

Why Breakups Occur

There are endless reasons why one partner may leave the other. Our billions of ancestors may all have felt the ecstasy of infatuation, the serenity and security of attachment, the tension of philandering, and the agony of abandonment. One biological reason may be a low level of an enzyme in the brain called monoamine oxidase (MAO). People with this condition seem to crave drama and excitement in their lives, including a varied and active sex life. Most Americans disapprove of infidelity, yet many engage in extra-marital affairs and take serial lovers regularly.

Theodor Reik was quoted by Ethel Person as commenting, "Wise men warn us again and again not to expect permanent and serene happiness from (romantic) love, to remember that it brings misery, makes one dependent upon an object, has downs as well as ups, like any human creation. It is not love's fault that we demand too much of it, putting all our eggs in one basket. We should know that there is no heaven on earth." At its most blissful, romantic love stimulates sexual relationships that allow us to realize our infinite selves, physically, intellectually, emotionally, and spiritually. It may also satisfy deep infantile needs for the kind of nurturing connection provided by mother. But, it cannot be sustained and must be replaced in another object if that feeling of ecstacy is to be recovered.

Sometimes personal needs change quite rapidly, and often. People grow in differing paces in differing directions. Neither partner can control the direction or pace of the other. Changing roles are part of the evolution of a relationship. It is difficult for some people to negotiate significant changes in a relationship as changing needs of each partner evolve. If we cannot accept imperfect compatibility, in either ourselves or our partners, we often precipitate the very separation that we fear by demanding impossible behavior from our partners.

Some problems have no solution within the relationship. Sometimes, good relationships end under no-fault conditions. That is a very fearsome prospect for a codependent person with a savior complex who wants to fix the whole world, or a love addict who needs the sexual relationship to maintain a sense of personal identity and wholeness. Codependent and obsessive, addictive people easily fall into relationships that are flawed from the beginning, in which they know the outcome is likely to be separation. Sometimes, there is no negotiable ideal resolution good enough for one or both partners. Perfectly relating, feeling the same vibrations, being on the same wavelength, even perfect holistic mutuality, can be too much of a good thing. It can eventually rupture if it becomes engulfment, stifles growth, or thwarts goals of either partner.

When the addictive honeymoon phase wanes, as it inevitably does, many of its victims awake to needs that are unmet by their partners or demands they cannot meet in the relationship. Desires for greener pastures, sexual adventure, or self fulfillment can be thwarted by their commitment. People with preferences for certain personality temperaments (primarily **SP** and **NP),** may be unable to restrain their need for openness to new possibilities outside or beyond their current relationship. Sometimes, the need for autonomy defeats the need for belonging. Sometimes, wounds from loves lost in the past intrude and reignite grief that mars the present relationship unconsciously.

Commitment often seems to compromise the euphoria of courtship to some degree. Courtship is not permanent, intimacy illuminates the mystery, and lust is the most transient component of relationships. In successful relationships, idealization evolves, changes, and ripens. But, in others it reverses. It seems almost preordained that a codependent lover who idealizes the beloved in a "love is blind" stupor, who initially ignores the burdens involved, will come to de-idealize. That new perception can bring death of the relationship if we cannot accept reality, or remove the barriers to fulfillment of our needs. The sense of perfect harmony between lovers often proves to be illusory and fragile when real world issues intervene.

Even compatible, ecstatic sexuality and childbearing can present powerful potential for disharmony later among deeply committed married couples. There are both psychological and situational factors that predispose one or both lovers to respond to disappointments either with renewed hope, stoicism, apathy, anger, or threat of abandonment. De-idealization often is motivated by hurt, disappointment, anger, or an attraction to somebody else. Career goals or other personal and family interests can intrude and pull one away from a person to whom you thought you were firmly committed. Then, you can rationalize perfectly good reasons for leaving. Personality factors can drive your decisions, as when thinking and feeling decision processes pull you in opposite directions until you decide which driver will take control, your logical thinking or your emotions and values. While you are deciding, the raging conflict about what to do can make you crazy, with the tension keeping you on the razor's edge of ambivalent confusion until you come down clearly on one side or the other. The process of deciding can take many months and, even, years.

Wounded adult children often enter harmful, abusive relationships, or relationships overloaded with burdens from the outset. Many of their intimate relationships likely will break up eventually when the burdens exceed the tolerable threshold of pain. They may pull back from making a full commitment when they realize they are repeating previous mistakes. Latent issues of narcissism (over valuing self) or borderline (under valuing self) personalities may surface after the relationship matures. Those suffering from neurotic pessimism are excellent candidates for breakup as they permit depression to darken their perception of reality in relationships. Even psychologically healthy individuals may go through several love affairs before they choose the one to provide holistic, intimate pair-bonding. Every broken relationship provides an opportunity to grow into a more holistic lover, even though it might seem quite futile at the time we are suffering relentless, excruciating, painful loss again.

Some breakups represent such a complexity of human behavior they are impossible to understand, even by professional therapists. Why do we have to kiss so many frogs? Why can't we just find our princess or knight on the white horse and live happily ever after? The answer might be found in the process an infant bird must experience in breaking out of the egg shell. If some concerned caretaker attempts to help, the young bird does not develop the strength that it needs to fly. Only by struggling to break out of the egg shell by itself will it develop the strong wings that it needs later to be a fully functioning adult bird. Similarly, nature has provided that we must do some things for ourselves to learn and to grow. Working our way through relationships toward becoming more healthy seems to be one of them.

Facing The Pain and Disappointment

Losses can occur through breakup of single couples, separation and divorce of married couples, and death of a spouse. There are no statistics on how many single couples separate annually, but we may assume that the results can be equally traumatic, if not as costly. The aftermath of breakups can, and often does, last for a lifetime.

Buddhists believe the one immutable law of the universe is that everything is impermanent and everything is changing. Anything that has a beginning must also have an ending, so endings are an inherent part of life. This situation causes them to believe that life includes suffering. When he realized that traditional Newtonian mechanical theories could no longer explain his mathematical models of sub-atomic phenomena, Albert Einstein wrote in his autobiography, "It was as if the ground had been pulled out from under one, with no firm foundation to be seen anywhere upon which one could have built." That is the way you may feel when you realize relationships also are destined to change, end, and recycle. Failure to accept this law leaves one grasping onto others for security that can cause the pain of insecurity we are trying to avoid. Sometimes, the changes between the partners cannot be contained and the relationship ruptures. Only if you are impossibly whole yourself can you freely choose commitment to your relationships or to abandon them when they no longer meet your needs without any trauma.

Many people get married imagining all their needs will be magically met for life. But, with all its advantages, marriage also brings more responsibilities, restrictions, loss of freedom, more expectations, and more disappointments, in addition to the benefits. Unresolved infantile needs that may not be troublesome in uncommitted single living often become crucial in a marital relationship. Solutions to the unconscious unresolved dilemmas of childhood often are sought in a mate, and then fought out with that mate. Marriage can start to look like a no-win situation. The drive to marry, philander, divorce, and to pair again seems to be here to stay, so you need to grieve relationships that end. You need to know how to leave a relationship that is unacceptably unhealthy or is not working, in which the burdens intolerably exceed the benefits. You need to learn to preserve your self-esteem through the guilt from inflicting pain and grief of separation upon your partner if you choose to leave.

The sands of time flow quickly, except in the hour of pain, when it seems your world has stopped completely. But, you can learn to manage the grief process and the recovery from loss, experience the pain, and walk through the dark abyss of the valley of the shadow of death it may seem you are in. If you do not insist on grasping obsessively and compulsively onto a lost love, you can get over it and become a more healthy person in the process, no matter what your stage of life. Sooner or later you just have to change the sheets and go on with your life. Although admittedly very painful to absorb and even more so to experience, that is the lesson of this chapter. You may be much happier and contented with life if you learn it.

When Enough Is Enough

If the relationship does not nurture the growth of both partners and meet enough of their changing physical, intellectual, emotional, and spiritual needs sufficiently, it can begin to deteriorate. When that happens, the partners experience a reduction of tolerance for each other and more touchy problems limit their sharing of feelings and ideas. More and more unresolved conflicts begin driving a wedge in between the couple. They begin drifting apart eventually, and avoiding each other. The relationship is terminated when one or both parties asks for a formal ending. Sometimes the breakup comes as a shock after you give up a large piece of your self to another and then find that it and him/her are gone unexpectedly.

Before the ending actually comes, and whether you choose it or your partner does, there is a predictable time of self-deception or denial and avoidance on both sides. Deciding to break up is just as fearful as deciding to commit is at the beginning. Both decisions are loaded with all the risk of the unknown potential consequences of the choice. It seems to be human nature for both partners to insist on disbelieving what would be obvious to an objective observer. Both of them distort their painful reality for a time to preserve their lost dreams. Even when a lover is clearly betrayed, he/she may willfully distort valid perceptions to preserve the illusion that the relationship is not threatened, if it is the locus of all hopes and dreams, the reason for living, the source of self-security and fills the holes in our incomplete development that we all possess.

Following the predictable stage of denial, there come anger, bargaining (i.e., negotiating alternatives), and depression, prior to acceptance, according to studies by Elizabeth Kubler-Ross on reactions to loss. The rejected lover must eventually acknowledge the fact of loss and let go of the current reality, including the sense of self-esteem and enlarged identity that came with the relationship. The alternative is to continue denying the reality and degrade or ingratiate him/herself while he/she continues to hope the dreaded termination won't happen.

Letting go of a painful relationship may be terrifyingly fearful if you cannot visualize a more happy single future without your partner. If your partner leaves, the task of giving up the need to control and letting go may be devastating for the codependent. Some people wait until they develop the potential for a new relationship to cushion the termination or to provide a safety net intentionally before they move. You may experience extreme suffering and depression if the perceived isolation of separation seems even more bleak and despairing than staying. Often, the benefits, whether physical/sexual, intellectual, emotional, or spiritual, in a relationship demand extremely high offsetting burdens of some kind before termination becomes worthwhile. The threshold of tolerance seems to vary, and some people need more pain than others to spur them to a decision. Some people won't leave until it hurts too much not to.

An important issue to resolve is how you feel about initiating a breakup, i.e., how you resolve the responsibility of splitting. You may experience painful guilt if you believe your departure represents a betrayal of sacred trust in you by your partner, creates immense jealousy, demeans the value and self esteem of your partner, or causes great suffering. There is nothing so repugnant as labeling yourself distrustful, cruel, insensitive, or lacking integrity. Leo Madow has offered several steps towards accommodating guilt. **First,** realize guilt is a normal defensive reaction to violation of your values. **Second,** review your standards of behavior to see if they generate excessive amounts of guilt from failure to reach your goal of perfectionism. **Third,** examine your conscience to see if it is overly strict and unduly rigid. **Fourth,** make such restitution or amends as you think are reasonable in the circumstances. Finally, forgive yourself for your imperfections, strive to improve them, and maintain your self worth.

If you decide to leave, choose an appropriate time and place to deliver your decision in a calm and compassionate manner. Your message can be delivered in person, if you have enough courage, or by telephone or even with a note if you fear some violent reaction or just don't want the personal confrontation. Acknowledge the response of your partner, whether it is rage, panic, hysteria, remorse, or any other deep emotion. Remember he/she is likely to feel all the fear of infantile abandonment, and be sympathetic to the impact of your message on your partner's self esteem.

Try to be as comforting as possible without breaching your boundaries, and reassure him/her that your departure reflects your decision and is not a rejection of the person or a demeaning of his/her character in any way (unless his/her behavior has been abusive or disloyal). Try to be as helpful as you can while he/she absorbs the shock. Even though your departure may have been clearly anticipated by both of you, the adjustment to reality still may be difficult and even devastating. If you are dissolving a marriage, Constance R. Ahrons shows there is such a thing as a good divorce, provided that children are given first priority, and the decisions are not all left up to lawyers to negotiate.

It may be very difficult to initiate a breakup if your belief in perfectionism causes you to label yourself as a failure and immoral user when things do not work out ideally. You may want to avoid the pain to yourself and your partner due to your own perceived mistakes and so stay in a relationship too long after you realize it is not working or that you need to move on. Staying too long often only makes the decision more difficult and the results more painful.

It does not do us any good to engage in self-torture by indulging in destructive self-talk after a termination, whether through death or separation. Adult children are likely to take full responsibility for everything that happens, no matter whose fault it really is. Uncertain self esteem can be demolished with automatic thoughts of regret or guilt. Sometimes, it is nobody's fault. Ruminating over obsessive guilt, worry, and regret can consume us and make us feel powerless to control our future relationships, and that leads to hopelessness and then to depression. Self-torturing thinking is so automatic for codependents that we might not have realized how it depletes our energy and impedes the handling of our lives. Adult children are so used to it that we might actually feel at home with worry, regret, and guilt.

If we initiate a breakup, we likely will feel some guilt. Rabbi Harlan J. Wechsler suggests there is a place for a guilty conscience in life. If we really did something that violates our standards of behavior, destroys the covenant we have made, and causes a breakup, some form of punishment likely will be demanded by our conscience, and guilt could be the result. If it is a legal matter, the courts may provide the punishment. If it is a moral matter, we will punish ourselves through grief and anger turned inward, leading to depression. One way or other, justice will be served.

Guilt can stimulate us to take action including repentance and making amends if possible. Guilt can call us to remorse, to confession, to renunciation, and finally to resolution and reconciliation, to strive toward becoming a better human being, to change our ways, to do better next time. However, once the debt is paid and the mourning completed, continuing to destroy ourselves with obsessive guilt serves no more purpose. Ultimately, guilt must be fused with self forgiveness time and again, and again. We can choose to believe that there are no mistakes, that each breakup merely is the consequence of our choice, and that we are free to choose again. There always is the nagging doubt about whether you are doing the right thing. Only with future perfect hindsight can this question be answered with confidence, and maybe not even then.

If we are the loser in a breakup, we may feel anger, want to fix blame on the other, and immediately seek revenge. We are not victims in the losses of life unless we choose to harbor resentment and goals of martyrdom and perfectionism. For the sake of mental health, we must let ourselves feel all the emotions of loss to their extreme, no matter how fearful, and permit them to flow through us so healing can take place. We can choose to feel calm and peaceful inside no matter what is happening on the outside. This is easier if we can forgive the other for being and doing what they think is best for themselves, because our own pain may be lessened and shortened.

When you decide to terminate, there are several different ways to do it, according to findings of Letty Pogrebin. She divided the process of ending a relationship into three different styles: baroque endings, classical endings, and romantic endings. **Baroque endings** are accompanied by agitation, accusations, flaming exit speeches, slammed doors, and broken pottery. **Classical endings** include more rational, lucid, dignified, and calm exit behaviors, possibly after several attempts at reconciliation or negotiation of differences have failed. **Romantic endings** are slower fade outs, usually because the cause of the ending may be less specific, too mystical to grasp, or too distressing to confront. One or other partner gradually just drifts away. So, endings can either be abrupt or much more gentle, absorbing time to adjust to the feelings of loss, failure, and abandonment that may be involved.

If you decide to deliver a message of termination after all attempts to sustain your love or get what you want have failed, or you decide other priorities have intervened, or the burdens are too high, I recommend that you deliver it compassionately, with empathy for the feelings of your partner. Be considerate of your partner and avoid complaining or demeaning his/her character or behavior. If he/she is primarily verbal, I recommend that you do it in person, face to face. If he/she is more visual, then you may feel more comfortable putting it into writing. Just say, "We have enjoyed a very important time together that was extremely good for me. I appreciate all you have contributed to my life. Nevertheless, I have concluded that the benefit/burden ratio of this relationship *(is no longer healthy for me) (no longer works for me) (no longer meets my needs) (no longer permits me to do what I must do on my own) (is too threatening to me) (demands more than I can give).* Since you do not choose to *(or cannot)* meet my needs, *(or I have found someone who meets my needs) (or I must be free to do what I am called to do on my own)* I have decided to end it." You don't have to provide lots of details unless you are asked. Be brief, but completely honest. Then end it, with love and appreciation for the lessons you learned from each other. Take responsibility for your own part in creating and terminating the relationship and do not try to reinstate it after you have made that decision.

I think continuing contact or attempting to be platonic friends with ex-lovers is cruel sado-masochism myself, although some people seem to do it successfully. Sometimes periodic contact is necessary for legal or financial reasons, as in the case of divorce. Although this may sound cold hearted to Feeling type readers, I believe all such contacts should be at arms length and as brief as possible. Avoid taking responsibility for the grief and recovery of your ex-partner. If either partner threatens the other or self destruction, I recommend you seek professional help immediately. Remove all the linking objects that linger from the relationship in your place as soon as possible. Keep some transitional objects around for a time if they are comforting, but these too should go as soon as possible. Keep only the few things that will be keepsakes, forever a part of your memories.

If your partner terminates, try to avoid condemning yourself for somehow failing, and give yourself permission to experience the process of grief. Picking yourself up and starting over again can be a growth experience if you let it teach you lessons you need to learn. Most counselors recommend that you learn to reconstruct a life alone before you attempt to make any new connections. If you leave, try to avoid beating yourself up for making that choice and review the reasons you did it to confirm that it was best. Painful as it is to do so, it is possible to learn some lessons from the experience. You may be comforted with these words from *A Course in Miracles,*

> *"Trials are but lessons that you failed to learn presented once again, so where you made a faulty choice before you now can make a better one, and thus escape all pain that what you chose before has brought to you."* *(Text, page 620.)*

Caution: *If you feel compelled to stalk a partner who has left you, or to make continual attempts to get back together, it could indicate a serious mental disorder that needs professional treatment. Particularly, if you feel compelled to threaten or otherwise obsess about your loss, I urge you to get professional treatment immediately.*

We Must Grieve and Go On

Breakups usually are followed by predictable reactions through grieving to recovery. The reactions often include a state of numbness and shock, disorientation, denial, anger, bargaining, mourning, setting blame, guilt, unforgiven regrets, resignation, depression, rebuilding, and resolution. Therapists affirm that almost everyone goes through some or all of these predictable grief reactions when they experience a loss. Therefore, they are considered to be normal, although they admittedly often are extremely painful and disabling for far longer than you think you can tolerate.

Since love provides an awareness of self and a boost to self-esteem, its loss through separation, divorce, or death often is felt as a significant contraction or reduction of self. We also experience the painful loss of all the behavior our lover provided that filled up the holes in our incomplete makeup, whether they are physical/sexual, intellectual, emotional, or spiritual. A. H. Almaas explained it this way, "If the person dies or the relationship ends, I don't feel I am losing that person, I feel that I am losing whatever was filling my holes. The loss of the person is experienced as a loss of your self because you saw that person as filling a part of you. You experience the loss of a part of yourself, that is why it is so painful, like something has been taken out of you (or has been amputated.) Sometimes you feel as if you lost your heart, your sexuality, sometimes your security, your strength, your will, whatever the person fulfilled for you. Whenever you lose a person close to you, you feel whatever hole you had that the person filled."

Susan Forward explained that if the loss is through rejection or infidelity, it can make you think you are unloved and unlovable. If your childhood fears, shame, embarrassment, and unworthiness are unleashed, rejection can make you feel permanently and fatally flawed - not pretty enough, not smart enough, not rich enough, not sexy enough, not witty enough, not manly/womanly enough, not talented enough, not successful enough, etc. Perhaps there is some truth to all of the above since no one is perfect in every way. If so, you may have to work on accepting yourself as you are, possibly with the help of a therapist. The power of such negative thoughts may have roots deep in your childhood experience that must be exposed and confronted, mourned and released. The actual childhood you experienced is not so important as the perception of it you may have had that drives your current thinking unconsciously. Since it is your thinking that controls your feelings, your sense of confidence and desirability, changing your thinking can change your feelings.

Ethel Person described the effects of love loss this way, "The "we" that encompassed the world is reduced to the "I" that is but an atom. The uniqueness that the lover felt as a consequence of being in love vanishes and leaves him feeling depleted, worthless, his life void of meaning. When one is rejected in love, the sense of loss can afflict the very core of the self, fracturing that self, rendering one an emotional amputee. One experiences overwhelming sorrow not only for the loss of love, but for the loss of the faith, hope, and innocence that go with it. It is not just this love that has ended, but also the belief that (commitment) can last a lifetime."

While it may not be clear to us as we suffer through the externally-imposed pain of losses, we can choose to believe the universe is unfolding precisely as it should. We can choose to believe that our tiny role in it also is right on schedule. Sometimes we must travel through white water to get to the calm ride on the other side. It seems that we must repeat painful patterns until we get our lessons right. We need not assume personal responsibility for the ad hoc relationship that ends. Ask yourself why you chose to get deeply involved in the first place. What holes in your makeup were being filled that you now have the opportunity of filling up for yourself. I believe our task is to learn the lessons we are given as efficiently as possible so that we can reach our highest good in this life.

Coping with a crisis requires that we encounter five major groups of tasks, i.e., 1) establishing some meaning and understanding the personal significance of the situation, 2) confronting the reality and responding to the requirements of the external situation we face, 3) sustaining or creating conversations with family members, friends, or professionals who can be helpful in resolving the crisis, 4) preserving some reasonable emotional balance by managing the upsetting feelings aroused by the situation and, 5) preserving a satisfactory self-image and maintaining a sense of competence and control.

To these tasks, we must apply certain skills to the extent we possess them. These include using logical analysis and mental discipline, redefining our thinking patterns, seeking information and support, taking problem solving actions, identifying rewards to motivate new behavior, regulating our emotional affects within reasonable limits, discharging our emotions and letting go of our past attachments and investments, and coming to some resignation and acceptance. Each person is unique in these coping resources due to personality preferences, stresses related to the event, and various social and environmental factors. Many of us need some help in resolving the life changing events that accompany breakup of a relationship in which we have invested a good deal physically, emotionally, intellectually, and spiritually. So it is no disgrace to ask for help from those closest to you.

The research of Emmy Gut indicates that the engrossing inner work of grief, including depression, serves an important process in our adaptive function when the task of reorientation is too complex to be handled successfully by rational efforts. So does crying. Joyce Brothers learned that crying actually triggers the brain to release pain relieving chemicals. "Crying," she learned, "does not just feel good, it appears to be an evolutionary device for adapting to emotional stress. When a woman is sad or angry, crying removes the chemicals that build up during stress and makes her feel better. Tears contain one of the brain's natural pain relievers. They also contain prolactin, a hormone that encourages secretion of tears. Women have half again as much prolactin as men, which explains in part why women cry more than men do. The value of tears has been known since time immemorial, even though no one understood their physiological function until recently."

In *Recovery From Loss* (Health Communications 1990), Gary Harbaugh and I described a powerful new model of the tasks of grief. It reflects our great sensitivity and empathy for all those who suffer this monumental reaction to severe loss. In our model, the tasks of grief are: acknowledging the loss, experiencing the feelings, substituting for what was lost, detaching from the investment in the past, and reconstruction of a new life in the NOW. To these tasks, we applied the resources of personal wholeness: physical, intellectual, emotional, and spiritual. Onto this model, we overlaid the unique coping resources of the individual, according to the ranking of dominant and inferior personality functions based on the MBTI that were assessed by Allan Hammer. He compared personality types with coping resources and found that people bring differing strengths and weaknesses to grief, as might be supposed. He showed that people must use their extraversion to maintain sufficient social support, their physical resources to assure rest, exercise, and nutrition, their intellectual resources to assure cognitive, logical, rational thinking, their emotional resources to feel the pain and facilitate healing, and their spiritual resources to connect with God, a Higher Power, or universal energy. Since these resources are related to the preferred hierarchy of personality functions, they will be ranked differently according to personality types, and they will manifest in different reactions to bereavement.

Working through the grieving process after a breakup can take much longer than you expected. A loved one never really leaves us in a spiritual sense and remains forever in our memory and heart. Sigmund Freud observed that remembering was the best way to forget. Repetitious recall is the only way of coming to terms with your loss, realizing it is gone forever, and that you must go on and live in the now. Timing of your grief process, and the amount of suffering depend on your degree of attachment and emotional investment, the amount and quality of social support available, how dependent or ambivalent you were in the relationship, the quantity and depth of regrets, and how highly you value the loss.

The sense of social isolation you experience can add considerably to the suffering. Unfortunately, the expressed feelings of grief often are too emotional for your friends, family, and associates to witness. Despair and depression seem to be contagious and, therefore, to be avoided. There is a lot of truth to the adage, "Laugh and the world laughs with you; cry, and you cry alone." Our culture does not handle emotional outbursts well. Expressing the feelings of grief in public is a social taboo in this country. There are no prescribed rituals to mark the ending of a relationship, so it may be helpful to find a support group or therapist to help you express the feelings of grief in a sympathetic environment. If friends and relatives cannot be effective witnesses to your grief, sometimes a professional therapist is a good investment.

Once an ad hoc romance is dead, usually it is impossible to resurrect the relationship, unless the partners are so dysfunctional that they perceive no alternative or are hopelessly addicted to each other. If you are involved in a breakup, try to part as friends, with nonjudgmental, unconditional love and good wishes for the future happiness of your departed partner. Although it is easier said than done, do not despair, and try to not take it personally. You may be justified to feel self- righteous and vindictive for a time, but hanging onto such feelings only keeps you attached to the past and prevents you from detaching so you can move on. It is never all your fault, and sometimes it is no one's fault. It just may be time for the partners to continue on their path of life in separate ways. Try to consider it as a transitional, learning experience. Try to identify what went wrong, and seek to avoid in the future any mistakes you may have made. Forgive yourself for not being perfect, accept your share of responsibility, experience the pain of separation, pick yourself up, and start again after the season of healing. Use the time alone to reconstruct your self image, purge the toxins, and redevelop your sense of self-worth, or reconcile yourself to being alone.

Going It Alone

Some people may think that getting involved in a new relationship immediately will help to put a serious loss behind you. Mexicans have a saying: "One nail drives out another." However, counselors recommend that you avoid making any new romantic and sexual commitments during this time of healing, so the necessary withdrawal of investment and detachment can be completed first. Letting go of the compulsive-obsessive bondage to the departed lover is absolutely necessary for healing.

Picking up a new romance on the rebound is not fair to the person you select for the transition, or healthy for yourself if the detachment is not well along. The necessity to confront a crisis of loss can remind you of the idealized relationship with any lovers that you lost previously. Opening old memories can retrigger simmering, unresolved grief all over again. When old, undischarged grief is piled onto the current ending, the combined stress can be overwhelming. Therefore, it is important to finish the grieving process for every loss. Obviously, this is much easier and simpler to say than it is to do. It is a difficult transition, but most people find they can make their way through it.

Ernest Hemingway wrote in *A Farewell to Arms*, "The world breaks everyone, then some become strong at the broken pieces." Ultimately, however, Hemingway chose not to continue his personal struggle and ended his own life. So, the consequences of isolation should not be minimized and must be treated very seriously. About 15 percent of seriously depressed people ultimately take their own lives. Living alone after enjoying holistic intimacy with a significant other may require massive adjustments to lifestyle changes and overcoming extreme feelings of abandonment, isolation, worthlessness, and hopelessness. If you believe there will be no more intimate relationships for you, the outlook can seem grim and despairing.

Symptoms of depression can include a wide range of physical, intellectual, emotional, and spiritual affects including sleeplessness, loss of appetite, mental disorganization, fear, intellectual exhaustion, spiritual alienation, and illness. Anger and outrage at the way life has treated you can deplete your energy and distort life for years if forgiveness is not forthcoming. Letting go of sex, self-esteem, acceptance, or whatever you got from your partner that filled up your holes can cause panic and require lifelong readjustment to the loss.

When we are alone, not by choice but by circumstance, it may be that life is trying to teach us something spiritually very profound through these symptoms. The metaphysician might say that we unconsciously choose all of life's experiences for the lessons we want to learn. The psychologist may say we create our own reality by making our own choices. In any event, the test of our psychological maturity is the ability to tolerate, if not enjoy, being alone at times and to channel loneliness into positive growth. As scary as it seems, you may learn to discover who you really are when alone and to break the tendency to be physically, intellectually, emotionally, and spiritually dependent upon others. The person whose relationships are not obsessive, compulsive, or addictive is one who likes and values her/his own company because he/she likes and values her/him self.

Loneliness can be a despairing, draining, painful experience, especially if it appears to be a permanent condition. When we are utterly alone, the unfulfilled need to belong to someone can make us feel unwanted, bypassed, rejected, or abandoned. We can feel infantile panic when we confront the holes in our makeup. Our instinct is to reach out to others, to want to get in touch with someone, to see a friendly face, to hear a sympathetic voice, to share a hug, to be acknowledged. We want, somehow, to belong to somebody again, to get our holes filled. Since it may be very difficult to replace all that loss of the intimate partner represents, we may have to develop substitutes in other ways. Social isolation is something we do to ourselves because we can always make 4 or 5 friends to help fill our holes if we really want to after our season of healing is complete. People who have conquered the experience of single living report their greatest sorrows and highest joys must be experienced alone because our deepest experiences cannot be shared with anyone.

Of loneliness, Thomas Wolfe wrote in *The Hills Beyond*,

> *"The whole conviction of my life now rests upon the belief that loneliness, far from being a rare and curious phenomenon, peculiar to myself and to a few other solitary men, is the central and inevitable fact of human existence....All this hideous doubt, despair, and dark confusion a lonely man must know, for he is united to no image save that which he can gather for himself with the vision of his own eyes and brain. (When alone) He is sustained and cheered and aided by no party, he is given comfort by no creed, he has no faith in him except his own. And often that faith deserts him, leaving him shaken and filled with impotence. And then it seems to him that his life has come to nothing, that he is ruined, lost, and broken past redemption, and that morning – bright shining morning, with its promise of new beginnings – will never come upon the earth again as it did once."*

Being alone, by itself, is neither painful nor joyous. It may be our thoughts about it that create our feelings about it. Shakespeare wrote in "Hamlet," Act II, Scene 2, "There is nothing either good or bad, but thinking makes it so." And, the ancient Proverb put it, "As he thinks in his heart, so is he." (Proverbs 23:7) Modern psychologists (Peck, Seligman, Beck, Burns, et al) are beginning to reaffirm this basic truth; they are using positive thinking or cognitive therapy to treat successfully the negativity that leads to helplessness, paralysis, and depression. David G. Myers interviewed happy people who were wealthy and poor, healthy and sick, young and old, married and single. He found that they have in common a supportive group of friends, they keep busy in work and play that they enjoy, they are filled with hope, they choose their own destiny, they have a loving relationship that includes good sex and intimacy, they have a lot of self-esteem, and they possess a faith in some God or Higher Power. In other words, happy people seem to have come to some accommodation with life in all four quadrants of wholeness, physical, intellectual, emotional, and spiritual.

When we are alone, our new, expanded self can see things differently through the eyes of intuition. We can abandon the fear of isolation and seek loneliness for communion with our higher self. It is a time to tap into our spiritual resources through affirmations, meditation, and prayer. We need no longer fear desertion by a loved one – because we can learn to appreciate our selves with an unconditional lover's eyes. When we are alone, our suffering can turn into compassion for others. We can become wounded healers. When the panic eases and the pain of aloneness moderates, an unalloyed spiritual contentment can come. We no longer need to be tied to any kind of hurt, to barrenness, or filled by other human beings. Give yourself permission to experience the growth that only comes during painful alonement. Give yourself the opportunity of filling your own holes from within.

In solitude, many highly creative people coped with stress of loss, learned self-reliance, and the self-discovery of their creative wholeness. The healing value of a time of solitude during periods of mourning and stress, the creative solitude of sleep, and the strong relationship between solitude and creativity are well established. Being alone to meditate and pray has been proven to reduce stress, and lower the physical reactions to devastating trauma.

Read the following quote from the diary of Admiral Richard E. Byrd as he lived alone at an isolated weather station at the South Pole during the winter of 1934:

> *"Here are imponderable processes and forces of the cosmos, harmonious and soundless. Harmony, that is it. A gentle rhythm, the strain of a perfect chord, the music of the spheres. It is enough to catch that rhythm, momentarily to be myself a part of it. In that instant I felt no doubt of man's oneness with the universe. The conviction came that the rhythm is too orderly, too harmonious, too perfect a product of blind chance — that, therefore, there must be purpose in the whole and that man is part of that whole and not an accidental off-shoot. It is a feeling that transcends reason, that goes to the heart of a man's despair and finds it groundless. The universe is a cosmos, not a chaos, and man is rightfully a part of that cosmos as is the day and night."*

Charles Lindbergh also described such a transcending experience during his first solo trans-Atlantic non-stop flight in 1927.

> *"Over and over again on the second day of my flight, I would return to mental alertness sufficiently to realize I had been flying while I was neither asleep nor awake. My eyes had been open. I had responded to my instruments' indications and held generally to my compass course, but I had lost sense of circumstance and time. During immeasurable periods, I seemed to extend outside my plane and my body, independent of worldly values, appreciative of beauty, form, and color without depending upon my eyes. As a child, I had lain in the cornfields of my father's farm and felt a similar sense of being beyond mortality while I gazed at the sky. It was an experience in which both the intellect and senses were replaced by what might be termed a matterless awareness and I recognized that vision and reality interchange, like energy and matter."*

Perhaps the way Jesus used aloneness for his empowerment can serve as a lesson or model for us, also. He began his ministry alone wandering and fasting for 40 days and nights in the wilderness. He often left his disciples and went off alone to pray and commune with God. When he returned to them, his ministry was in a new place each time. As I write this, it is Easter time again. I am reminded of his anguish during his last week on earth. As he contemplated his pending ordeal the night of his indictment, Jesus walked off alone into the Garden of Gesthemane, leaving his disciples to dose. Concluding his prayer of supplication to God, he was empowered to say, "Nevertheless, not my will, but yours be done." (Matthew 26:36-39) For those who believe, you may find comfort in this story told of Jesus who said, "I am with you always, even unto the end of the earth." (Matthew 28: 20)

As humans with dominant egos demanding self fulfillment, we may not be able to reach the level of cosmic consciousness that St. Paul, Admiral Byrd, Charles Lindbergh, Jesus, and many other stalwart spiritual leaders did, but it is a goal worth striving for. The following words of the hymn, "In The Garden," composed by C. Austin Miles in 1912, may help illustrate the feeling of peace and empowerment that solitude can bring when you use it to get in touch with God or universal energy as you conceive it to be:

"I come to the garden alone, while the dew is still on the roses. And the voice I hear, falling on my ear, the Son of God discloses. He speaks and the sound of his voice is so sweet, the birds hush their singing. And the melody that he gave to me within my heart is singing. I'd stay in the garden with him, though the night around me be falling. But, he bids me go; through the voice of woe, his voice to me is calling. And, he walks with me and he talks with me, and he tells me I am his own. And the joy we share as we tarry there, none other has ever known."

Your loneliness may help you to find something to live for with passion, something great enough, possibly, to die for. The late President, John F. Kennedy, reportedly said, "I believe there is a God. I see the storm coming and I believe He has a hand in it. If He has a part and a place for me, I believe that I am ready." Another time he said, "We choose to go to the moon in this decade and to do these other things, not because they are easy, but because they are hard." Anthony Storr suggested embracing solitude is necessary for such intuitive revelation as this. An ideally balanced person finds meaning in his life by combining interpersonal relationships with his inner personal interests, i.e., balancing his introversion with his extraversion. When no intimate relationships are available, other interests can take over some of the functions usually performed by close partners, such as writing this book has for me. People who avoid such opportunities may deny themselves the chance to find out who they really are, to become truly whole as they were at birth.

Lewis Smedes suggested it is even possible, and healthy, to be grateful for solitude and the experience of anxiety that it brings. "Most people have undercurrents of anxiety in their lives. Our culture is a syndicate of escapes from the anxieties our culture causes. But there is a catch: We cannot overcome anxiety by escaping it. Could it be better to take our anxieties into our consciousness? To be alone with them? To surrender ourselves and the things we are anxious about to God? And then, when relief comes, to give it time to sink in and stir about in our minds until gratitude takes over. We can permit ourselves to feel the deepest anxieties of life so that we can also feel the joy of release from them. It may take time for gratitude to overcome us. And it may come only through excruciating suffering. We cannot control it. But we can give it space (to happen). We can keep the windows (of our soul) open. We can be ready for gratitude when it comes."

Here is a composite set of practical suggestions to help you manage (if it is impossible to conquer) your loneliness:

HOW TO WORK ON LONELINESS

1. Compile a list of everyone you know including friends, acquaintances, relatives, etc. Put it on a set of 3 x 5 cards or enter it into a personal computer database. Try to include some things you know each person is interested in. If this list is too short for comfort, work on getting more new people into your life.

2. Contact at least one or more friends each day to discuss what you are doing and what interests them. Review and practice the suggestions in Chapter 8 by Dale Carnegie on "How to Make Friends and Influence People."

3. Identify your interests and get involved in activities that act on them. You never meet anybody new if you stay at home. (If you are a socially isolating person, work on becoming more extraverted, although this can be an energy consuming task for introverts.)

4. Try to find substitutes for the missing contribution that was made to your life by your lost lover. Pinpoint what you are missing the most, (physical/sexual, intellectual, emotional, and spiritual) based on your personality preferences, (review Chapter 3) and make the effort to fill that void by asking people for what you want, without guilt or apology.

5. Try to balance the lonely time of your life by adjusting your schedule to make room for visiting or phoning people who can make you feel better.

6. Separate friends from acquaintances and companions and concentrate on building platonic friendships, even if only with 2 or 3 good friends with whom you have the most in common.

7. Acknowledge loneliness as a temporary part of your life and indulge yourself in solitary treats or gifts that contribute to your self-esteem and as a reward for tolerating your condition.

8. Get a pet, because it can give you unqualified love and companionship when human presence is absent.

9. Learn what your needs really are and avoid people and situations that do not contribute to them, but compound your loneliness. Look for activities that make you feel good about yourself. Ask friends for what you want from them. Accept both the yes with appreciation and the no you might get in response without taking rejection personally.

10. Care for your body with proper rest, exercise, and diet to minimize risk of health problems. You don't need any such complications on top of your emotional situation.

11. Do something personally nice for yourself - pamper yourself - purchase a special gift you have been wanting, visit some friends or relatives you haven't seen for a while, join a health club, get some regular treatments from a same-sex massage therapist, find a group of people who can meet regularly together, share hugs, and discuss your feelings.

Rebuild From Spiritual Strength

When we feel overwhelmed by change, with too many options, too much stimuli, and no reliable social guidelines, there may be more confusion than joy. When you have experienced that there are no guarantees and no permanence in life, disillusionment may result. I don't think you can ever assume you are home safe. Either resignation or panic may seem the only alternatives, but neither is necessary. We can learn to live happily without all the answers; indeed, we must learn to live with the questions.

When all of our assumptions about life fail to work for us, we naturally are in a crisis, but you can develop a new strategy for life that will provide the flexibility to deal with the changes in your future in a positive way. In a crisis, there may appear to be no adequate, functional answer as we realize that we cannot retreat to what used to be and cannot see a way out. Yet, Helen Keller, born blind and deaf, said, "The best way out is always through." We sense the separation from our comfortable past set of assumptions, and we experience shock. We may withdraw into ourselves and isolate from others for a time to conserve our emotional energy. If it appears that we have been living according to a myth all our lives, it can be shattering to realize that we no longer can rely on our assumptions about what we thought was real or true. We may experience a change in mood and mental process as we question our perception about reality. We can become open to change, risk vulnerability, and experiment with new behavioral options and new relationships in a period of transition.

Through the transition of recovery, we can integrate a new set of assumptions with the old. We can reorganize our behavior on a new level as we assume a new life script. Although we may have to force ourselves through the steps of change, it is through the new behavior that we grow. Although it is painful, such growth integrates the past with the present and leads us into the future. In this process, we can have a new feeling of owning and directing our own lives if we get reacquainted with our inner self, our Higher Power, or God, as you conceive him to be. If we try to manage the crises of life by following old rules set down by others under the external values of society, stagnation and a sense of loss of self can result. Change may bring chronic anxiety if we get stuck in the uncertain phase of transition without moving on. If you keep doing what you're doing, you will keep getting what you're getting. However, if we can learn to lead our lives by our own internal psychic needs, we can achieve ever higher growth and continuing rediscovery of self. That makes it possible to develop ourselves continually as we accept the challenges of change throughout the rest of our lives.

Every person must experience this continuous process of spiritual change alone, although committed couples may be able to reinforce each other during this process. When we are alone, we must filter out all the options for ourselves as we await new intimate relationships. We must assume the risk of decision making by ourselves as we move into an unfamiliar pattern of new life, one that often involves disposable ad hoc relationships in our mobile culture. We must learn to manage our own lives without asking permission, without getting the approval of others, without apologizing for our mistakes, without punishing ourselves for missed opportunities, without saying I should or I shouldn't, without being afraid to say no or yes. We must not give up our power to any other person. Through the transitions of life, we can seek increasing, spiritual maturity that will help us become more:

- **Self-aware,** able to be in touch with our feelings;
- **Centered,** knowing our values and priorities;
- **Focused,** being selective and able to make decisions;
- **Committed,** involved with others and responsible for our actions;
- **Creative,** innovative, flexible, and open;
- **Autonomous,** able to think for ourselves;
- **Concerned,** caring, and understanding of others;
- **Competent,** drawing upon all our inner physical, intellectual, emotional, and spiritual resources;
- **Confident** that we can shift with the demands of change and crisis; and
- **Secure** in the acceptance of the challenge of growth through change.
- **Ruthless** in deciding to protect our own boundaries, but compassionate in delivering our decisions to intimate others.
- **Compassionate** with others who do not share our new level of spiritual discernment.

During times alone, we have the potential of contacting our inner core, our Higher Power, or God, as you conceive him to be. Ancient seers of India discovered the spiritual benefits of meditation centuries before Christ. Modern practitioners of Yogi and Buddhist traditions still demonstrate its power to heal and energize human beings. Unfortunately, Western Christianity has lost touch with the profound spiritual benefits that it provides. Meditation has proven for me to be a very effective way to achieve a "fourth state", neither awake, asleep, or dreaming. Extensive medical studies prove that meditation reduces tension and stress, promotes relaxation, mitigates disease, and actually extends life. Meditation enables you to become conscious of the self. Awareness of your place in the universe becomes more obvious. Energy, peace, and contentment are imparted to your soul. Even the cells of your body feel pampered and serene when you are meditating. So, I recommend that you practice a simple meditation procedure for 15 to 20 minutes twice each day, whether you are in a relationship or not. Just sit comfortably with eyes closed and count silently backward from 50 to zero, 49, 48, 47, upon exhaling, and repeat several times while you sit comfortably and concentrate on your breathing. After a few weeks you may begin to feel more energy, less stressful, and more peaceful internally.

Now, you must reorient your concept of time to just being in the moment, without guilt or remorse for the past or anticipation of the future. Few of us know what we really want, and none of us consciously knows what is best for us. We must trust our Higher Power, Holy Spirit, God, Creator, Self, Universe, or whatever you choose to call your spiritual core of infinite energy, for helping us make the best choices. We can choose to trust in faith that each choice is the right choice for us at this time and place. We can choose to believe that each relationship that ends was a transitional, healing, and learning experience, intended by our Creator for our good, even though growth always is accompanied by pain as well as joy.

So, try to live happily in the present time and place, wherever it may be. Live one day at a time, maybe even one hour at a time, and let go and let God look out for the future. Plan your affairs as though you are going to live forever, but live as though you might die tomorrow. You are a child of the universe, and you have a right to be here.

William Ernest Henley expressed his enlightenment in the poem "Invictus." Read and absorb these words of his healing poem in your time of need - read it many times to reinforce in your subconscious mind that you have a healthy self within that will provide all that you need.

"Out of the night that covers me,
Black as the pit from pole to pole,
I thank whatever gods that be
for my unconquerable soul.
In the fell clutch of circumstance
I have not winced or cried aloud,
Under the bludgenings of chance
My head is bloody but unbowed.
Beyond this place of wrath and tears
Looms but the horror of the shade,
And yet the menace of the years
Finds, and shall find me unafraid.
It matters not how straight the gate,
How charged with punishments the scroll,
I am the master of my fate,
I am the captain of my soul."

Healing and Looking Again

After we know the fear and terror of losing an intimate ad hoc relationship and have made some adjustment to the loss, contemplating a new commitment and the potential for future loss can make us wary of entering into such an intimate relationship again. Or, the needs of infantile nurturing, attachment hunger, and love addiction, i.e., getting our holes filled, can propel us toward it again.

It is OK to admit we are incomplete and need the benefits of an ad hoc relationship to feel whole. No one is a perfectly completed human, so we can choose to give ourselves permission to seek a new love. Marion Solomon makes the case for the power of positive dependency in intimate relationships. As you know by now, relationships can be a battleground for unresolved needs, or a safe place in which to mend each other's wounds. In her experience, Solomon says once people understand the infantile preverbal sources of their needs, they can work out their growth together and strengthen each other in the process. She believes we choose someone to help us work out our unfinished business, whether it is healing a wounded inner child, or perfecting the less developed functions of personality.

However, managing new relationships as you emerge from a loss is a very sensitive and fragile process because your feelings probably still are very close to the surface and are stimulated easily. Take time to reconstruct your self esteem, reconcile your ambiguity, and reconnect with your native self worth. This process may take several months, or even years to accomplish, depending on the level of your need and your resistance to change. When you are ready to search again, perhaps you can set as a goal the mastering of these rules for positive dependency as proposed by Solomon:

1. Remember that your partner needs love also. Give signs of love generously with praise, compliments, hugs, gifts, passion or whatever your partner values as a love gift.
2. Remember that every adult has unfilled dependency needs from preverbal childhood. Listen for the imprinted messages from your own and your partner's childhood to help you understand the real meaning of your partner's words, without shame or guilt.
3. Battles around money, work, family, and sex often mask deeper needs for bonding. These battles may be substitutes for emotions beyond words. Be aware of possible unconscious issues requiring unconditional love, understanding, and acceptance.
4. There is no rule of relationships that demands the truth, the whole truth, and nothing but the truth. Do not say things that will cause pain or shame.
5. Choose your battles carefully, after you own responsibility for your own feelings. Evaluate carefully which issues are so important to you that they are not negotiable. Keep everything else open for discussion and compromise.
6. Do not depend on a partner to fill all your needs. Develop interests together, but also develop separate interests. Share your excitement of life with others outside the relationship and it will come back to you in many ways. Remember that giving and receiving are the same.
7. Be generous with your body, not only in sex, but through gentle strokes, massage, a back rub, or gentle holding depending upon your partner's response. Touch is a basic means of bonding, sharing, and connecting.
8. Validate your partner's feelings and needs and magnify his or her positive qualities through effective mirroring. Comment on your observations and be attentive to mood swings without attempting to fix every situation.
9. Be generous with forgiveness when you inevitably fail each other, hurt each other, or do things that seem unforgivable. Be sure to remove the beam from your own eye before you criticize the speck in your partner's eye.
10. Seek intimacy on all four levels of being, physical, intellectual, emotional, and spiritual.

The recovering bereaved person desperately needs patience, understanding, and unlimited tolerance in the process of new pair-bonding. It is always a matter of reciprocal matching under conditions of high risk and uncertainty. The decision to be an interdependent unit with another person again creates many issues. Many people are driven by their holes to try again because they can be emotionally and mentally damaged in just a few weeks of enforced social isolation.

Intimacy fulfills adult needs such as the benefits of sharing experiences and responsibilities and the deep satisfactions in mutual caring, affection, and support. It also arouses many infantile longings hidden in the dysfunctional child within us in varying degrees for unending nurturing, for utter symbiotic security to maintain our existence, our identity, our self-esteem, and our happiness. In a crisis we want to replace the lost symbiotic connection with mother. Living together in an intimate and continuous mode becomes a part of the central definition of who we are. In such a relationship, we can play out all the tapes that make up our being: the child, the parent, the adult. It is wonderful to be in a relationship where you are accepted just as you are, and painful to be in one where you are not. It is not healthy if we lose ourselves and become dependent on the relationship for symbiosis.

We need meaningful work and close relationships for the maintenance of self-esteem. We need friends in whom we can confide and share the experiences of life. I believe people need something to do, something to hope for, and someone to love. So pamper yourself a little. Feed your senses in moderation with the smells, sights, sounds, tastes, and touches that are pleasant to you. And practice healthy, positive, optimistic thinking. Realize that your present unhappiness is not your fault, it is a temporary phase of your life that will pass, and the future definitely will be better.

Although healthy people live in balance between their needs for autonomy and belonging, the icing on the cake of happiness and contentment seems to be that special intimate relationship with a significant other person. People recovering from distress of lost loved ones first have to develop some schema or system of thought to make sense out of the distress. Then they also can choose to make a new relationship of a fruitful kind with another person, while learning from the mistakes of the past. Pamper yourself a little. Treat all your senses with moderation in terms of sight, sound, taste, and touch. Practice optimistic, positive thinking and find someone who needs what you have to give and give unconditionally.

Ironically, it seems that you are more likely to find a new love partner when you least feel the need for one. Survivors who seem to have the best chance of achieving success in new intimate relationships are whole people — they have worked out their deepest emotional problems and have conquered the demons of fear, anxiety, rage, rejection, guilt, ambivalence, codependence, and unfinished business. They have found their new place in the world. They recognized that it takes a lifetime of work to maintain honest, intimate relationships. They can give the new relationship the care it needs to survive because they have mastered their own survival and because they no longer are hoping that romantic love or erotic attraction will save them.

This achievement requires that we be free of dependency on other people, free of neurotic involvements, free of historical hangovers from childhood, free of narcissistic hunger for self-esteem, free of the baggage of lost loves, but also free of obligations, duties, fears, and irrational hopes. When we are free of addiction to other people we become much more ourselves, our real selves, our authentic selves, and we find our real identity. There is balance, completeness, totality, harmony, fullness, contentment when we grow past the need for any type of external support from others, be it physical/sexual, emotional, intellectual, or spiritual. All inner compulsion will be gone for the person is realized based on fullness, richness, and innate value. Such an individual is then a mature human being, a complete person. He/she has reached the station of being, "I AM." Then we can be a healthy partner once again. Because few of us reach this station of life, most of us are merely filling our holes temporarily with other people. Thus, a sense of recurring loss is inevitable.

Many people who have come through periods of loss have found new avenues for reconstruction. They found companionship in work, community projects, family, or even pets, after they developed good platonic friendships. All of these pursuits merely are appeasements to our controlling ego. Healthy people made strong commitments to their own self development. They found new intimacy only when they were able to love, not out of fear of being alone, or out of need to addictively lose themselves in connection with another, but out of the strength of their own new identity. They have been through the valley of the shadow of death of their own ego, and emerged whole and complete for all their suffering. They can send out a signal of healthy "want" for intimacy that is not an addictive "need." The latter can drive prospects away with fear of engulfment. Healthy people do not want to provide the fix for a love relationship addict.

When in a healthy condition, you can set as a goal a synergistic form of love. Recall from Chapter 4, that is one in which both people become greater than either one could become alone. In contrast is a parasitic, symbiotic form of love in which one person takes far more than he/she gives to the relationship until the person who does more of the giving is all used up, except for what it takes to leave the relationship. Often, you must give more than your partner in a healthy, intimate relationship, temporarily. Mature people are able to do that without keeping score. The roles of adult, parent, and child can be exchanged as needed without threatening the power or equality of either partner when both are healthy.

Both partners feed each other in a synergistic relationship in a balanced way. Although neither one of them may be totally secure in their own identity, they can enjoy a passionate love that endures for life if they can grow independently, together. As long as lovers share a mutual fascination with each other they can sustain a passionate love in which autonomy and merger alternate, experiencing periodic "love attacks." Such lovers make a passionate commitment to each other, physically, intellectually, emotionally, and spiritually, if not legally. They learn how to perpetuate mystery, uncertainty, and novelty while integrating them into a dependable relationship. Excitement can be sustained by periodic short separations that provide new inner insights, sharing mutually satisfying projects together, living unconventionally, and by achieving access to and sharing the primitive reaches of each other's souls. They become true soul mates as they realign their behavior and values toward common goals of life.

The great American humorist, Will Rogers, said, "Even if you are on the right track you will get run over if you just sit there." So, it is time to begin living the life that is before you. An appropriate story is told of world-famous cellist Pablo Casals. When people asked him why he continued to practice 5 hours per day after age ninety, he replied, "Because I think I am making some progress." Although the past is never completely dead nor even completely past, there is nothing left to do but to put the past behind you and go on with your life. To make progress.

In the next, and final chapter, I will explain the role of professional therapy in helping people work through ad hoc relationship difficulties. Although professional help is expensive, it may be appropriate for you to consider. Perhaps developing a support group based on this book also would be an effective form of personal development. In any case, the value of sharing your life with others verbally has been proved to be a healthy thing to do.

Eleven:

The Power of Confiding

Only mature people can create mature relationships. Normal living with our families and "common sense" often does not prepare people for this complex culture. It is much like the blind leading the blind. When a relationship crisis strikes, people sometimes find their coping resources are not sufficient for the task. A part of being human is suffering from time to time in solitude, but it is not healthy to remain isolated for too long. Sometimes both friends and families fail to bring comfort, and your resources seem to be overtaxed. When that happens, it can be helpful and healing to find a professional listener with whom to talk.

Shakespeare had Macbeth verbalize human misery in this plaintive request to his physician about the depression of his wife: "Canst thou not minister to a mind diseased, Pluck from the memory a rooted sorrow, Raze out of the written troubles of the brain, And with some sweet oblivious antidote Cleanse the stuffed bosom of that perilous stuff which weighs upon the heart?" The physician replied, "Therein the patient must minister to himself." (Act V, Scene 3) Today, one sees a therapist.

However, those who can afford it may enter counseling only to be disappointed because they don't know what to expect or how to manage this new form of intimate ad hoc relationship. So, I have added this chapter to provide some guidelines to help you get more from what Sigmund Freud called "the talking cure" and M. Scott Peck called, "The Road Less Traveled," from a line by poet Robert Frost.

We do not think ill of anyone seeking medical attention for a physical disability, but let people know you are seeing a counselor for a mental illness and the red flags sometimes still come out, unfortunately. Misguided people who feel threatened when they confront the prospect of psychological dis-ease in a friend, partner, or associate have ended careers and relationships. So, many sufferers are reluctant to see a professional therapist. We are talking about the benefits of professional support and encouragement when friends, relations, and intimate others cannot meet your needs. We are not talking about pathological mental illness that threatens human health because that would be far beyond my ability and the scope of this chapter.

I don't think there should be any social stigma attached to seeking professional help to put some freedom and control back into your life. We do not judge a person negatively who seeks medical help for a physical problem. The fact that a person seeks emotional or mental therapy means that person actually is becoming more whole and integrated, with a more balanced physical, intellectual, emotional, and spiritual response to the struggles of life. When you think about it, you may agree that the most mentally healthy people are those who have benefitted from profession-al therapy. Those who have not had this experience may actually be the worse.

The Value of Professional Therapy

Most experts point out the value of having friends people can share their troubles and triumphs with. James W. Pennebaker showed that without knowing how, friends often play the role of therapist for us. His research showed that having nonjudgmental friends to share your troubles with, as well as your joys, reduces medical illness and is a proven aid to good health.

Deborah Tannen, John Gray, Suzette Elgin, and others pointed out that women are more likely to get together just to talk, while men usually only get together to share some activity, without much self disclosure. This situation is unfortunate for men because a very powerful connection between people occurs when sharing each other's psychic pain. The benefits of talking about our troubles and stresses was known to Shakespeare, who wrote these lines for Macbeth, "Give Sorrow words; the grief that does not speak knits up the o'erwrought heart and bids it break." The same goes for anger, fear, and guilt also.

People need to have a sense of control over their lives and when uncontrollable events happen, we are put at risk of illness. Perceived helplessness and hopelessness can have a devastating physical and emotional impact. Holding back our thoughts and feelings, even about positive events such as falling in love, getting a new job, or win-ning the lottery, can be hard work. Suppression of feelings gradually undermines the body's immune defenses against disease, according to a generation of studies reported by Pennebaker. He found that people who are most at risk for disease are those who experience a trauma, continue to think about it, but who do not put it into words. Visually oriented people may prefer to write and auditory people may prefer to talk. Either way, getting our negativity out where we can deal with it is definitely good for our physical health.

Growing use of health maintenance organizations also has limited the authorized funding for long term therapies. In response, several forms of short term therapies are being introduced. Habib Davanloo reported that new practitioners of brief therapy claim that it can provide a much quicker and more lasting way of freeing people from the painful trauma of dysfunctional history. Several short term forms of therapy are available, and they can be very effective in addressing specific problems if properly tailored to the individual. One of the most revolutionary forms is called Thought Field Therapy. Developed during the 1980s in California by Dr. Roger J. Callahan, it promises practically instantaneous relief from several forms of mental disorders, as well as relief from grief and loss of love. This method seems to make use of several metaphysical theories about human energy fields and the relationship between mind and body. TFT is promoted by Callahan Techniques, Ltd. of Indian Wells, CA. Details can be obtained on the Internet at *http:/www.tftrx.com.*

The lessons to learn in all forms of therapy are that life is difficult, that this too shall change, and if you don't learn to take responsibility for your self, the price is always psychologically very high. I think the potential benefits of as much therapy as you can afford are well worth the investment, provided it is with a good therapist that you can trust and believe in, one who can provide solace and enable personal growth through empathic communications.

Choosing Therapy

You may be wondering how you can tell if professional counseling or therapy is warranted for you. If your sense of identity and positive self esteem are below normal limits, the stress can be one indication. Stress can be measured by several diagnostic instruments. A self diagnostic measure is assessment of your "self abilities", a term defined by Lisa McCann and Laurie Pearlman in terms of these four criteria:

First is the ability to tolerate and regulate strong emotions without self-fragmenting or acting out in unhealthy ways. This means that you can experience deep feelings, whether pain or joy, without a major or permanent disruption in your sense of psychological stability. The **second criterion** is self capacity or the ability to be alone without being lonely. This means you can enjoy time alone without feeling emptiness or abandonment. The **third criterion** is the ability to calm yourself through processes of self soothing or nurturing when ambiguity, uncertainty, and loss of control prevail. This means you can usually recover from emotional distress without relying on other people for external support. The **fourth self capacity** is the ability to control self loathing and shame in the face of criticism or guilt. This means you can accept and integrate criticism or rejection without major or permanent damage to your sense of self worth.

If your capacity in any of these four areas is below comfortable limits it may be a valid indication for you to consider entering professional therapy. James F. Masterson posed the following ten-point checklist for a mature real self in action while meeting the challenges of normal living. The lack or significant incapacity on several of them also may be some criteria for entering therapy:

1. The capacity to experience a wide range of feelings deeply with liveliness, joy, vigor, excitement, and spontaneity.
2. The capacity to expect appropriate entitlement – healthy individuals build up a sense of deserving mastery and pleasure, and the resources necessary to achieve these objectives. They take care of themselves and do not expect others to fix them.
3. The capacity for self-activation and assertion – to identify one's own unique individuality, wishes, dreams, and goals and to be assertive in expressing them autonomously. This capacity also includes taking the necessary steps to make these dreams a reality and supporting and defending them when they are under attack.
4. Acknowledgment of self esteem – confidence that one can cope with a problem or crisis in a creative way with affirmation that they are worthwhile and have effective skills and abilities, not always relying on others to fuel their self worth.

5. The ability to soothe our own painful feelings without wallowing in personal misery, even to experiencing depression and working through it without avoidance and denial.

6. The ability to make and stick to commitments, both to relationships and to one's own professional, personal, social, and private goals.

7. Creativity - the ability to find unique solutions for life's problems as they are presented to us for solution, and to endure the anxiety of uncertainty that comes with the potential of failure and criticism, even rejection.

8. Intimacy - the ability to experience and express the real self fully and honestly in a close relationship with another person without feeling anxiety, engulfment, or abandonment.

9. The ability to be alone without feeling abandonment depression, to manage one's behavior and feelings through periods when there is no special person to lean on, without despair or pathological need to fill life with meaningless activity or relationships.

10. Continuity of self - the capacity to know and recognize that we have a core of spiritual being that persists through time and space, i.e., the awareness of and acknowledgment of the "I AM" that lives on at the end of physical life.

11. (My addition) Experiencing the peace and contentment that come with intuitive awareness of the spiritual essence of self regardless what is happening on the outside. In Buddhist philosophy, this state is called "enlightenment" and Carl G. Jung called it "individuation."

If you believe adequate competence in very many of these areas is lacking in your makeup, it may be a signal that professional therapy would be helpful in finding and building the real self. The goal of all therapy is to help the patient learn to make decisions and choose behavior that will enhance personal development and improve his/her self image, i.e., overcoming the trauma caused by a faulty childhood experience. Your self esteem is enhanced with the confidence that you can manage your life successfully. Since people won't change unless it hurts too much not to, a significant personal crisis, sometimes even motivating thoughts of suicide, often is needed to induce one to seek this form of help. Its goals are to replace defensive mechanisms with adaptation and new capacity to direct your own life, to perceive situations realistically, to cope constructively with challenges in life, and to create building blocks that will sustain your new self. A mature self that is neither deflated (borderline syndrome) or inflated (narcissism) from what is normal and healthy is the goal.

What a Therapist Can Do for You

First, please recognize that therapy cannot remove all your anxiety, depression, helplessness, anger, indecisiveness, or obsessions. Also, therapy probably cannot help you feel better and more confident without some stress because all growth is painful. Neither can therapy replace faulty parenting and magically give you another family history. And, therapy cannot remove problems from your life. But, it can help you to build a more healthy life. When he was asked what the purpose of psychoanalysis was, Frank J. Bruno said the founder of modern psychotherapy, Sigmund Freud replied, "To replace neurotic suffering with ordinary human misery", i.e. to navigate the waves between imagined ideal imagery and the pain upon discovering the hard facts of life.

Martha Stark described the process of working through therapy in three phases. The **first phase** is one of confronting the infantile distortion, illusion, and entitlement that is painfully depressing unresolved grief from loss of an imperfect childhood. The **second phase** involves helping the patient recognize dysfunction was not his fault in childhood, but it is his responsibility as an adult to get on with the business of life. The **third and terminal phase** is one that transitions from looking to the therapist for advice as a perfect surrogate parent, to looking to ones own resources for growth and security. All of us can benefit from grieving and letting go of an our dysfunctional families. Good therapy helps us re-parent ourselves and go on to assume responsibility for our choices, accepting a world that is flawed, imperfect, and largely impersonal. This transition from infantile dependence to adult independence can be painful, expensive, and long, as the patient must confront and defeat his tendency to avoid change that is full of risk and unpredictable results. If therapy is terminated prematurely, the patient can be left more troubled than he was at the beginning.

Recovering From Loss

This book is about ad hoc relationships that often end prematurely, so some discussion of recovery from loss is appropriate. Western culture no longer condones grieving in public. Consequently, when a close loved one dies or a marriage is dissolved, most people are not prepared for the impact of grief because they have little or no experience with it. The late anthropologist, Margaret Mead wrote, "When people are born we rejoice, and when they are married, we jubilate, but when they die we try to pretend nothing happened." So it is with divorce.

T.H. Holmes and R.H. Rahe ranked spousal bereavement at the top of human stressors, giving it a score of 100, from which all other losses are compared. The stress from divorce was rated second, and loss of a child and loss of a parent follow closely. Although grief generally is considered to be a normal reaction to loss, its impact can be very severe, and it can disrupt the lives of survivors and their families for many years after the loss. It is manifested by changes in emotions and thought processes, behavioral changes, interpersonal and social changes, physical complaints, pathological outcomes, and sometimes death. No wonder our society avoids grief like the plague.

Only a very few books have chronicled the experiences of widowers, presumably because men are not expected to grieve at all. I mentioned my previously published book, *Recovery From Loss*, in the last chapter. Yet, Scott and Silverman report chances of widowers being killed in a car accident increase by 300 percent, our chances of committing suicide increase by 400 percent, our chances of dying from heart disease increase by 600 percent, and our chance of dying from a stroke increase by 1000 percent. After they interviewed 20 widowers of all ages, they described the consequences of losing a wife this way, " — you may feel cut adrift not just from your friend and companion and lover, and from your social circuit, but from the whole human community, from the entire metaphysical cosmos. The loss of a mate can create an inexplicably potent sense of aloneness. It can even create in you a sense that somehow you have died... You are in a life-threatening situation, you have lost the one single person who more than anyone helped you sustain your life, (and) you may be, to a large extent, without the skills you need to survive." Then they go on to say, "This book will not release you from the problems you are facing, nor will it pre-scribe a cure."

John Bowlby wrote, "The loss of a loved one is one of the most intensely painful experiences any human being can suffer, and not only is it painful to experience, but also painful to witness, if only because we're so impotent to help." Colin M. Parkes echoes this sentiment when he says, "Pain is inevitable (for both survivor and care giver) in such a case and cannot be avoided. It stems from the awareness of both par-ties that neither can give the other what he wants. The helper cannot bring back the person who's gone, and the bereaved person cannot gratify the helper by seeming (to be) helped."

It is not unusual for a volunteer care giver who has not completed his/her process to say, "You never get over it, you just learn to live with it." When a survivor realizes the frustration of volunteers as well as professional care givers, situational depression and a feeling of hopelessness can set in. This feeling can help explain the phenome-non of getting "stuck" in a particular phase of grief. If survivors cannot sense progress, feelings of frustration and futility can add to their devastating discomfort. Therapy can help move the process along.

Other Benefits of Therapy

A therapist who is appropriately trained and experienced may provide a secure relationship in which a person can safely regress to infancy, and relive the pain and anger related to faulty parenting. Through temporary dependence upon the therapist, a "wounded child" can rebuild a real self after the false self is abandoned. However, this process can be lengthy, and is full of suffering as the lifelong self is painfully grieved and a new self is constructed. If the therapist serves as a surrogate parent, the "inner child" is encouraged to rebuild a new self that may not be compatible with existing friends and significant others. In the process of experimenting with changes through trial and error, existing relationships may be stressed to the point of breakup. When the person is married, such growth may motivate a divorce if a spouse cannot adjust to the likely changes that will result, although the person may feel better in his/her new lifestyle.

Lomas wrote, "It would appear that there is no easy solution to the ills of mankind. Our governments do not bestow peace, our laws do not prevent crime, our science does not bring plenty for all and our doctors do not heal us. In view of this unhappy state of affairs, we should not expect to find a method of psychotherapy that would make a decisive and overwhelming improvement in our condition." In fact, there are as many methods of psychotherapy as there are therapists because the process is based on a relationship that is unique between two people. Both the client and the therapist bring unresolved, unconscious, and highly subjective opinions to the relationship. Both of them are struggling to help one of them live with troubling situations and, maybe, learn and grow in the process.

Therapists may have in common the ability to help free you of what Robert L. McKinley calls your infantile interpersonal habit. That is the way you learned to operate with mother before you could talk. It is usually based on sadding, whimpering, helplessing, discontenting, and suffering, and throwing away your personal peace to get what you needed to survive. Therapy works by confronting these habits and imparting new ways of getting your needs met through healthier ad hoc relationships. Treatments can be grouped into four general forms of intervention.

Stan J. Katz and Michael Franz Basch described them as follows: **psychodynamic,** which deals with often- hidden or unconscious influence of childhood development on character and motivation - this method relies on lengthy self analysis of memories from childhood experiences to help rationalize adult dysfunctions; **behavioral,** which focuses on one's capacity for change in actions - it emphasizes the power to overcome unhealthy habits and replace them with normal behavior, **cognitive,** which seeks to reduce a person's pain by altering the manner of reasoning about the situation and learning to rely on the inner strength and logic to counter unrealistic illusions which we all carry as excess baggage, and the **humanist approach,** that explores your basic outlook on life, your values, and your self-image, i.e., your wholeness, through intuitive discoveries of universal principles.

There also are **medical forms** of treatment, including prescription drugs, in-hospital care, and electro-shock methods, but these may only be administered by a medically qualified psychiatrist and should be based upon a diagnosis of electro-chemical malfunctions in the brain. Professionals are divided on the use of drug treatments for certain mental disorders, including depression. You can find those who say depression is caused by biochemical malfunctions in the brain that can only be corrected with drugs, and you can find others who say depression is caused by learned faulty thinking that can and should only be treated with cognitive therapy. Others claim that clinical depression is treated most effectively with a combination of drugs and cognitive therapy. Finding a professional you can trust and feel comfortable with may be the best solution to this controversy.

A trained, professional therapist may help you by acknowledging your dilemma in a safe, nonjudgmental environment, and showing human concern and empathy through means known as transference and counter transference. By playing out unpleasant roles from the past with your therapist, and receiving the professional interpretation of those roles, they are unlocked from the unconscious forgotten memories and made available for reinterpretation. Also, recall from chapter 3 that buried in the unconscious is your least developed or inferior aspect of personality. When you are stressed, it can take over your more dominant, or developed functions and cause emotional havoc and cast you into your shadow, or primitive mode, as explained by Naomi Quenk. A good therapist who knows Jungian methods can help you live through the despair and feelings of hopelessness by invoking your auxiliary function, while the inferior function is strengthened and integrated into your personality in a more balanced way. It is like sending in the second string quarterback to run a football team when the lead quarterback is disabled for a while. If certified by Consulting Psychologists Press, they can administer the Myers-Briggs Type Indicator and help you to validate your personality preferences. Then, you can handle stress better.

A therapist also can help you to dig into your memories and pull up thoughts and emotions that might be deeply buried, so they do not continue driving you into unhealthy behavior. Theories about counseling include the idea that faulty perceptions about the past distorts the present, and past difficulties and mistakes are repeated until we learn our lessons. Therapy should help a person become aware of how he/she distorts current events and situations to recreate old, unresolved conflicted situations. Recovery is based on uncovering old conflicts and resolving them so their distorting influence is abolished. By just encouraging you to talk without judgment, with complete attention and compassion, a therapist can help you access your spiritual depths, even when you may think you do not have any religious beliefs. You will learn to help yourself by discovering your own spiritual truth, a truth of sweetness and richness you may never suspected lies deeply within you. Through his/her strength, peace, and deep compassionate attention, the therapist will help you awaken your own soul.

An effective therapist can supply what Anthony Storr called a corrective psychological experience, and Emmy Gut calls productive information processing. A human trait is wishing to maintain the status quo learned in childhood, no matter how dysfunctional or painful it is. We resist all forms of change, even for the better, because of fear of the unknown and anticipation of the pain of growth. McKinley said we attempt to get our needs met by displaying discontent, suffering, and anger learned from prelanguage infancy. Gut observed that disturbed clients who come to her for therapy often are burdened by psychological disabilities such as: cognitive bias, which produces (among other difficulties) a distorted image of self and others; unrealistic aspirations and expectations; inhibitions and repressions, particularly of emotional or sexual responses, but very frequently also of thinking, at least about certain subjects or in certain situations; a variety of pathological defenses; and excessive anxiety, guilt, shame, or anger.

If the therapist can understand and empathize with your infantile thoughts and feelings, he/she can reinforce you and begin to help repair your damaged adult self, even if you are seriously depressed or even addicted to unhealthy substances or behavior. A therapist can help you get out of your own way and remove the unconscious personal barriers, i.e., your negative self or shadow image, you may set up against your own healing. A Jungian therapist can help you identify and work out of the grip of your fourth, undeveloped function by identifying and implementing your more developed and, thus, reliable functions. Only in that state of mind can we live comfortably with the normal burdens of life, its uncertainty, boredom, routine, frustration, and disappointment.

A therapist also can moderate relations between loving but conflicted partners who are deadlocked, or when one partner is in seemingly hopeless conflict between two choices. Before you end an ad hoc relationship of long standing, perhaps engaging a family therapist can help you both work out your reactions to inevitable differences without a breakup. Even healthy couples can benefit from the objective mediation of a third party when conflicts threaten their peace. Understanding and applying the distinctions that arise from personality and behavioral differences can be a powerful aid to therapy with confused couples.

If you are stuck in an abusive or addictive relationship and cannot get out, a therapist may help you look at the issues more honestly and without distortion. Professional counseling may help you decide whether to work on improving the situation with your partner, to accept it and yourself as is, or to leave based upon your personal benefit/burden ratio. If you are staying for the wrong reasons, a therapist may help you dig into the causes, such as infantile attachment hunger or interpersonal addiction, and help to remove the paralyzing effects that keep you stuck in a painful relationship. If you are uncertain about leaving, therapy may help to clarify the benefit/burden ratio and set you free without guilt while working through fear of being alone. Therapy can help you find the sense of security, wholeness, identity, and self worth needed to keep yourself from repeating the destructive patterns of the past.

Selecting A Therapist

Therapy and counseling possess different legal definitions. States may have definite laws regulating counselors and require specific credentials. They can be trained in a variety of fields including social work, psychology, psychiatry and pastoral counseling. In many states therapy is not that regulated, and literally anyone can call themselves a therapist. In these situations, clients must be specific about their needs and goals if therapy is to be effective. For therapy to be effective, Lewis M. Andrews posed these three criteria that must be met: The therapist must genuinely like the client. The therapist must understand the codependent problem well enough to treat the client. And, the therapist must be able to separate from the client when it is time. Therapists are human too. They can get too fond of, or dependent upon the client, so that the relationship becomes a replay of the relationship between codependent client and dysfunctional parent.

As with medical treatment, confidence in your care giver is a primary criteria for psychic healing. To begin your search, you can obtain names of qualified persons from the various professional associations, e.g., the American Psychological Association, the American Psychiatric Association, the National Association of Social Workers, and the American Association of Pastoral Counselors. Members of each of these disciplines offer different combinations of training, skills, and methods. Each of these associations has regional or state offices from which you can request referral resources. Many local governments have agencies related to mental health that can recommend or provide resources that might be helpful. If you have friends in therapy, perhaps they might recommend their professional to you.

Exploring the options for therapy available to you in your area may require selecting several available therapists and having a consultation with each to find the person with whom you prefer to work. Don't be reluctant to do a little shopping before you make a commitment. Your personal feeling about the relationship from the first few encounters will be important to your decision. Hans H. Strupp offers this advice when selecting a therapist; "Avoid therapists who fail to show common courtesy in human interactions, who are overly zealous, who make extravagant claims, and who in general lack human qualities of warmth, concern, respect, understanding, and kindness. Beware of pompousness, hostility, harshness, lack of seriousness, seductiveness, inappropriate familiarity, and phoniness of all kinds. Above all, make sure the therapist impresses you as a decent human being whom you can trust with your inner most secrets."

Therapists can practice in both group sessions or in private counseling. Group sessions are less expensive and they encourage interactions with average people who have problems similar to yours. Moderated groups provide a safe environment to work out your behavior in a clinical setting. The key to effectiveness of all therapy is being comfortable about intimate sharing, with complete confidence in protection of your privacy. Unfortunately, the form of therapy that is best for you may not be easily or quickly determined because this form of treatment is still much more art than science. Therapy requires your complete and honest participation. For all their training, therapists cannot read your mind to discover your deepest thoughts.

The process of therapy is essentially one of listening to, thinking about, and speaking to a person seeking help in a way that changes his/her behavior and increases confidence in meeting the challenges of life. It may require some trial and error experimentation with several different therapists before the one that suits your situation unfolds. Whatever it is, therapy is not a science that can be replicated from one situation to another. Both the client and the therapist are unique people and the two working together comprise a relationship more of communication than medicine. Thus, as in art, the benefits are in the "eye" of the beholder.

Andrews suggested the most effective form of therapy occurs (1) when the patient can employ his/her own inner voice of intuition, instinct, hunch, or gut feel about what is best, and (2) when working with a therapist whose character and empathy are tuned into the needs of the patient rather than themselves. Without these two essential ingredients, many studies constructed to prove the benefits of therapy could not verify that any form of therapy was better than just letting time take its natural course. Most normal, troubled people eventually worked out their problems in their own way, especially if they had empathic friends who could share their strength and provide a supportive, attentive ear without attempting to offer plaintive solutions or judgmental advice.

McKinley says that both therapist and client work on each other from their own learned interpersonal habit. Some therapists have not outgrown their own infantile behavior. Some therapists are only too eager and willing to validate and reinforce the values, behavior, and attitudes of their paying clients to reinforce their own agendas. At considerable risk of criticism by radical feminists, I must insert that Ilene J. Philipson thinks the feminist movement has created a growing demand for women therapists who agree with and reinforce the objectives of the Women's Movement. She notes the percentage of therapists who are female has steadily increased since the early 1970s as more liberal women seek counseling from therapists who validate and reinforce their gender bias against men, and the trend continues.

McKinley suggests the best therapist is one who has mastered the skill of seeing his/her own and the client's interpersonal negotiating styles. Jung thought it was necessary for a therapist to be a "wounded healer." He said doctors can only hope to help their patients with that which they have put right in themselves first. In the best situations, both therapist and client feed on each other's experience. They sit and learn together while the client gains release from dependence on discontenting, angering, suffering, sadding, whimpering, inferiorating, afraiding, and performing, according to McKinley. Clients learn their own interpersonal habit and they learn to abandon discontenting as the preferred way of negotiating. They learn to remove the barriers to peace and contentment, which is our natural birthright.

If you and your therapist are meant to experience the spiritual exaltation and to acquire the learning that can take place from the interaction with each other, you may realize the transformation that comes with enlightenment, i.e., the knowledge of non-material existence in the realm of the super conscious. When therapists learn to probe the depths of what Jung called the collective unconscious, we may be given a new form of treatment for our human pain and suffering that is not dependent upon drugs that merely mask the symptoms without curing the underlying psychic disorder. You may also become conscious of the lessons you need to learn in this life and aware of the plan you have chosen to carry out your mission. When you reach that level of understanding, the trials and joys of life will be seen in their new perspective as lessons to be learned, and your tolerance and acceptance of all aspects of your life will be enhanced beyond human understanding.

Some Notes of Caution

Therapy is a very powerful and intimate relationship between two people. Joseph M. Natterson and Raymond J. Friedman describe and illustrate the inevitable enmeshment that occurs unconsciously between therapist and client. Thus, both individuals bring to the relationship all their training and experience through self disclosure that goes far beyond most human relationships. Some therapists are well qualified for the work they do. But a therapist also is human and brings to the counseling session all the issues of his/her learning and experience. Natterson and Friedman prove that the profession tends to attract people who have significant pathology of their own to work through. Psychiatrists and psychologists do not all complete their own work in therapy before they are authorized to practice professionally. If therapists fail to clear their own issues, they can bring a very sick personality into the counseling room and cause severe damage to a vulnerable client.

Ilza Veith reported that medical writers knew back in the 12th century about this problem. She said they wrote, "Healthy and serene persons impart pleasure to others, whereas those of the opposite constitution can even bring disease." Such transfer did not require physical contact, it was rather a spiritual interaction. In this manner a physician can affect a patient favorably or adversely, depending on whether the spiritual conditions of the two are healthy.

Therapists of all disciplines are divided about the manner in which people recall events of their past and the role of memory in adult development. Some therapists have become advocates of recovering so-called repressed memories. Supposedly, these memories contain events of childhood that were so traumatic they were pushed into unconsciousness so they could do no further harm. Such "childhood trauma" therapists advocate recreating these alleged events intentionally through guided imagination in order to confront the abuser and heal the psychic wound of the victim through abreaction. Some therapists believe that most, if not all, troubling adult behavior is the result of such repressed memories. In their zeal, many of them have created a mad-hatter chamber of fantasies in which the therapist can seemingly discern events in the past that the client has no conscious knowledge of. The troubled client who has come to the therapist for help is not likely to contradict the therapist who is assumed to have superior knowledge about the cause of such problems. They may assume that, like medical doctors, therapists have specific diagnosis methods for their difficulties when that is not true.

Elizabeth Loftus speaks for memory experts who do not agree with the repressed memory theory. She contends that the very shock of traumatic events tends to keep them in conscious memory. In fact, people who experience major shocks often relive the events over and over in their minds as a method of accommodating to them. Wartime experiences of soldiers often are cited as examples. When they repress such memories they usually are conscious of doing so to avoid the pain. Her experiments also have shown that many people tend to fabricate and imagine details of memorable events, thus making them very unreliable witnesses. Further, there is absolutely no scientific evidence that adult unhappiness is always attributed to experiences in pre-verbal infancy. Many people survive unbelievably harmful childhoods and become happy, productive adults.

In any event, it is now apparent that some therapists can use their position of authority and superior knowledge to incite troubled clients to break family relations and accuse siblings and parents of unprovable childhood abuse, even satanic cult worship and kidnapping by space aliens in UFOs, countering evidence notwithstanding. The extreme views of some therapists were aired by the Public Broadcasting System for its 1995 documentary, "Divided Memories." Douglas R. Sawin stated on camera, "We all live in a delusion. Do any of us know the truth? All childhood memories are somewhat different than they actually occurred. I don't care if it is true or not. What is important to me is that I hear the patient's truth. What actually happened is irrelevant to me. It does not matter. The therapy has nothing to do with reality."

In stark contrast to that view is that of psychiatrist, Robert Langs: "Too many analysts utilize as a defense the notion that reality doesn't matter; so long as the material is present, they argue, it can be analyzed. This in no way is true; reality is crucial, just as the patient's unconscious fantasies and introjects are crucial, and reality takes precedence as well. It must be determined in order to understand the degree to which a segment of material is not reality, but distorted fantasy. — It is clearly crucial to have a means of developing conditions under which unconscious fantasies may be communicated by the patient, and their presence and functions detected and identified, so that the therapist may be in a position to interpret them and thus provide the patient with insights through which the effects of these pathological fantasy formations can be sufficiently modified to provide lasting symptomatic relief."

How this controversy among therapists will ultimately work out is still uncertain. Some of them have been sued for the problems they caused to innocent families and vulnerable clients who were turned into mentally ill monsters, according to Pulitzer Prize winning author, Richard Ofshe. The PBS special graphically depicted the damage that incompetent therapy can inflict upon vulnerable clients and their trusting families. The balance between validating suspected illusions of unstable clients and helping them cope with reality is a very delicate matter. If the prospect of long term therapy with its assured income is tempting enough, an unethical therapist may look forward to encouraging pathology to keep the client dependent and attached. As reported by Ofshe, some psychiatric hospitals have diagnosed and scheduled therapy to correspond to the available insurance coverage, terminating treatment as soon as the money runs out.

Warning: In extreme cases, some vulnerable people have been attracted to harmful cult leaders masking as professional therapists and religious leaders. The Cult Awareness Network estimates that possibly as many as 20 million needy, confused people are involved in some form of unhealthy cult. A cult leader may be identified from the following marks of a destructive personality:

- *Mind Control - manipulation by use of coercive persuasion or behavior modification techniques without your informed consent.*
- *Charismatic Leadership - claiming divinity or special knowledge and demanding unquestioning obedience with power and privilege.*
- *Deception - recruiting and fund raising with hidden objectives and without full disclosure of the use of mind controlling techniques, including use of front groups.*
- *Exclusivity - secretiveness or vagueness by followers regarding their activities and beliefs.*
- *Alienation - separation from family, friends, and society, with a change in values that makes the cult a new family evidenced by abrupt or subtle personality and behavior changes.*
- *Exploitation - financial, physical, or psychological pressure to give money, to spend a great deal on specialized courses or give excessively to special humanitarian projects and to engage in inappropriate sexual activities, even child abuse.*
- *Totalitarian View - promoting dependency and extolling goals of the group over individual freedom and encouraging unethical or illegal behavior while claiming goodness and divine rights.*

Periodically, news sources report another mass suicide as cult leaders drive their followers into the pit of their destiny. Possibly the worst recorded outcome of cultism was the voluntary suicide by 911 adults and children in the infamous Jonestown cult on November 18, 1978 in Guyana. Another such event occurred in March of 1997 when 39 members of a group called "Heaven's Gate" followed their leader in suicide in southern California. He convinced them they were transitioning to a higher plane of existence in order to meet up with a spaceship hiding behind the Hale-Boggs comet then visible in the sky.

A vulnerable client may be misled and even grossly harmed by an unprofessional therapist who projects his/her own unhealed experiences onto the client. Such an incompetent therapist may be granted unlimited authority by a vulnerable client, and relationships can be harmed instead of helped.

How can an untrained layperson tell if the therapist is sick? It may be difficult until after the damage has been done, unfortunately. So it is healthy to be a bit skepti-cal about any therapist who does some or all of the following things in counseling sessions:

1. Attempts to seduce you.
2. Recommends a specific course of action without offering options.
3. Repeatedly uses his/her own situation and experience as an example to justify an opinion or recommendation.
4. Projects his/her own values upon you.
5. Injects unsolicited and highly judgmental opinions about your behavior or that of your relationship partner.
6. Leads you away from thinking for yourself while inducing you to become dependent upon the therapist.
7. Induces you to fabricate memories of childhood abuse when no such events eas-ily come to mind, thereby transferring blame for adult behavior onto unsuspect-ing family members.
8. Employs hypnosis or other mind altering techniques to encourage you into harmful mental and associative disorders.
9. Recommends hospital treatment without supporting a second opinion.
10. Habitually breaks appointments or is unavailable for help in crisis situations.
11. Relates private and confidential information about other clients, friends, or his/her own personal life.

As you interview therapists, ask about their credentials and what professional soci-eties they belong to. Ask if that society provides a code of ethics to which your thera-pist subscribes. Good therapists may not have professional credentials, and some untrained lay people offer legitimate services. But, if your therapist consistently acts to create a pattern such as the above, I recommend that you contact the society and voice your concerns. If the behavior persists, I strongly suggest that you make a few appointments with another therapist of your liking and get a second opinion about your needs. Do not be reluctant to leave a therapist without notice if you think his/her behavior is less than the professional quality you deserve and for which you are pay-ing. There are too many good, ethical therapists to be harmed by an unethical, sick one.

Managing The Relationship With Your Therapist

The first rule in therapy is that you are in charge. You are the customer and you have every right to be satisfied, happy, and even delighted. However, ethical therapists are people too, and they deserve to be treated fairly and respectfully. If your clinical performance, behavior, or appearance are beyond reasonable limits, the therapist has the option of declining to serve, or to refer you to another therapist more likely to meet your needs. Ideally, therapy can shorten the time you need to work through the stressful issues being faced. It should help you come to some comfortable accommodation of your situation with less stress, anxiety, or depression than you would encounter on your own. However, some clients find little help, even after trying several different therapists for several years. Such people may subconsciously prefer the state they are in for the benefits it provides them, even though the burdens are severe. If a person projects sickness, they are relieved of many responsibilities of normal living that they may wish to avoid. If a person persists in an abusive relationship, they may be unconsciously living out a victim role for its benefits. Sensing such a futile situation may be cause enough for the therapist to resign or refer you to another.

It may be that becoming somewhat dependent upon your therapist for a while is warranted to provide a means of restoring your selfhood that is lacking. Therapy may properly include temporary regression to childhood in order to work up a new healthy adult within. But, you must guard against merely changing one form of addiction or codependence for another. There definitely is the danger that you and the therapist can foster shifting your attachment hunger from an undesirable partner to the therapist. Classical therapists may rely on regression to dependency in order to help their clients reconstruct a mature adult character. However, the aim of a competent professional includes ending of such dependency and the fostering of your own self-reliance. The proper aim of all professionals is to enable the person who comes to them to become strong enough and free enough to leave them as soon as possible.

Unfortunately, some therapists are tempted to hold onto a client for financial gain. Even the most ethical professionals may find it difficult to sense the appropriate time for departure. Professional therapy can be very expensive. You are the only person who can decide if the investment is worth the results and when it is time to leave. If you listen to your feelings you will know when that time comes. One indication will be when you no longer feel the need to talk about your situation and prefer to do other things with your time and money. Jung described his patients who reached this point in therapy, achieving peace of mind after long, but fruitful, struggles this way:

> *"If you sum up what people tell you about their (distressing) experiences, you can formulate it this way: They came to themselves, they could accept themselves, they were able to become reconciled to themselves, and thus were reconciled to adverse circumstances and events. This is almost like what used to be expressed by saying, He has made his peace with God, he has sacrificed his own will, he has submitted himself to the will of God."*

Usually, reaching such a resolution requires much courage, strength, and flexibility to face unexpected and, often, unpleasant personal insights. Recall that Freud said the proper aim of therapy is to replace neurosis with normal human suffering. As with the uncontrollable forces in nature, it seems we must experience uncontrollable psychic storms to experience calm, we must know uncontrollable sickness to discern health, and we must fear uncontrollable death to enjoy life. In Chinese philosophy, the Yin of life includes the Yang also.

Unfortunately, some people with a compulsive need for control and power may find therapy to be just an extension of their dysfunctional personal lives. The therapist becomes a surrogate for dysfunctional partners. In these situations, the therapist actually becomes the victim of super controlling clients. They may include the therapist, who does not do their bidding or reinforce their narcissism, with all their other dysfunctional relationships, and leave treatment before they achieve any real growth. Such people may gain little from therapy although they may repeat the process with several therapists.

Opening up, dealing with, and releasing self defeating beliefs can cause bitter suffering that you may wish to avoid by quitting. You are likely to feel worse for a time before you start feeling better as previously denied issues are confronted. It is important to keep your therapy moving along through these rough times. Discuss your progress openly with your therapist and set some goals or criteria for deciding when to end therapy. This separation will take some planning because the loss of this close relationship may, itself, set up a reaction to loss again.

Be cautioned against relying too much on a counselor or therapist for too long because he/she may also become a source of addictive dependency. The client can become dependent upon the therapist and the therapist can become dependent upon the client. Although transference and counter transference between patient and therapist can be, and some believe they must be, an integral part of the relationship, they can become distorted and actually contribute to further dysfunction. Freud taught that transference was some previous relationship from childhood manifesting to avoid confronting a painful aspect of therapy. Some therapists now believe that transference is productive in the counseling relationship if it is recognized for what it is.

Your progress with a particular therapist likely will taper off sometime. Then, you must decide when to end further treatment or to seek another approach with a different therapist. If your therapist is dedicated to your growth, he/she will be eager to help you ease your way out and on when you are ready. Some therapists who have not completely worked out their own codependence may have problems letting go of a dependent client. With them, it can be harder getting out than it was getting in. It may take months or years before you think you are ready to go on alone but, eventually, the time will come to assume responsibility for your own life and to leave therapy.

Saying goodbye is painful for both therapist and client, and there will likely be some grief for both you and your therapist to experience. Therefore, most professionals suggest that termination be done gradually, first reducing the frequency of sessions before actually scheduling the last one. You should tell your therapist of your plans in advance so people on the waiting list may be scheduled into your time slot. Giving forewarning also will cushion the shock of your decision. The joy of learning how to face the challenges of life should be sufficient graduation gift for both of you. Of course, you can always return for a tune up session from time to time to boost your confidence and maintain your progress.

Evaluating Results of Therapy

Psychotherapy is under more consumer advocacy scrutiny than ever before. With third party insurance and managed health care, and reports of negative results, therapists from all disciplines are under pressure to account for their treatment and complete it in short order. Sometimes the results may actually be harmful to the client/patient and to related people including family members, friends, and coworkers. In the past, therapists acknowledged very little responsibility for the social results that changes in their clients evoked. Thus, if a client decided to divorce a spouse or leave a job or insult some friends, therapists assumed no responsibility for the people who might be harmed by such a decision. More recently innocent third parties, who have allegedly suffered harm from actions of a therapist, have been successful at bringing lawsuits for damages. In particular, there have been increasing lawsuits against therapists to recover damages for false accusations by adult children of alleged childhood sexual abuse by a parent. Therapists are beginning to realize their risk when patients/clients actually become worse with extended therapy.

Ethical therapists will have worked through most of the issues faced by clients and will not permit their personal unfinished business to intrude in your private counseling sessions. Those who haven't can make things worse rather than better for their clients. If you have any doubts about the professional integrity of your therapist, do not hesitate to end your relationship and seek another professional immediately.

The comprehensive discussion of the potentially negative effects of psychotherapy by Hans H. Strupp attests to its growing significance to the practice. He notes that whether or not therapy is successful is a subjective decision, depending upon the criteria used for evaluation. There is no doubt that many clients and therapists both experience situations that end in perceived failure. Both Jung and Peck said they estimated therapy helped cure about one third of their clients, possibly helped another third, and was no help to another third.

Strupp recommends that the outcome should be evaluated based upon three criteria, i.e., the assessment of society, the assessment of the therapist, and the assessment of the subject client. The ideal situation would be for all three opinions to converge toward a common agreement on improvement over a long term after therapy is concluded. The modern tendency is for insurance companies, society, and interested third parties to hold therapists accountable for the outcome, even to the point of filing malpractice lawsuits against therapists when the outcome causes harm to society or to the individual. Until such lawsuits, therapists felt little or no obligation for any antisocial behavior of their clients.

However, Strupp observes the three criteria for success are not always in agreement. For example, therapy may encourage someone to leave a traditional marriage and seek a lesbian or homosexual lifestyle, causing losses for family and friends. Society may frown on this outcome and the individual may lose his/her job, but both the individual and the therapist may concur in the opinion that it was a desirable outcome of therapy. Or, a therapist may induce a client to behave adequately by his /her own values and the standards of society, but leave the client with continuing feelings of isolation or disorientation and, thus, concluding therapy was a failure. A third optional outcome may be where the client chooses to leave both his social norms and the therapy, and then live happily and contentedly in some unorthodox lifestyle at the disdain of both society and therapist.

With the three different criteria each going up or down after therapy, up to eight different variations on outcome are possible. Researchers may collect data about such outcomes, but they cannot place a value on them. As Strupp says, "Whether a particular therapy outcome is judged as positive or negative clearly depends on who is making the judgment, and the nature of the judge's perspective and values." The final evaluation comes down to the subjective assessment of the client concerning his/her feelings about self and relationships. He notes that whether or not therapy is successful is a subjective decision. If you think it was successful, then it was, and if you don't think so, then it was not.

You might also consider this transformation as one who is peering through binoculars and has adjusted them so that the blurred images seen separately through two eyes are merged into the one single sharply focused view. When you have this experience, life will never be the same again. It may take some time for your unique insight to develop after the course of therapy is finished. Jean Shinoda Bolen has observed that therapy is like feeding the roots of a plant. Personal growth may proceed mostly underground for some time before it becomes obvious above ground. Thus, an outcome that seems to be failure today may be perceived as success some time in the future.

Sharing in Self-help Support Groups

If professional therapy is not available to you for cost or any other reason, a support group might be just as beneficial. Support is having a relationship with someone you can talk to who is actually listening and, as such, is a lifelong need. Note that what therapy provides is a safe place to talk with a knowledgeable, caring, witness you can trust. Pennebaker showed that these benefits can be obtained from caring laymen as well as professionals. After you end therapy, you may feel the need to continue in a similar intimate relationship with close associates. As Margaret Mead said, "Never doubt that a small group of thoughtful, committed citizens can change the world. Indeed, that is the only thing that ever has." And Carl Jung wrote, "Since the self stands for the essence of individuation, and individuation is impossible without a relationship to ones social environment, it is found among those of like mind with whom individual relations can be established."

There is plenty of research, reported by Bill Moyers, now showing that people who think of themselves as being socially isolated get sicker from heart disease, strokes, cancer and all other fatal illnesses than those who believe they are part of a larger community with some common interests. His researchers showed that seriously ill people fare better and often live longer if they are members of a support group of similar sufferers. Support groups are springing up all over to offset the sense of isolation many people feel as they trod back and forth to work from their lonely apartments and single family houses with multiple TV sets and personal computers keeping them separated from each other. There seems to be something healthy prompting people to get together just to share their energies. As noted at the beginning of this chapter, that function can be provided sometimes by family and friends, but often it is not.

Support groups are quite popular now all over the country. They are convened by average people to deal with a wide variety of issues. If you cannot find one that exists for ad hoc relationships, perhaps you can start one, using this book as a guide. All you need to do is identify a group of people who want to work on common issues in coupling together.

Consider at the beginning whether the group should be coed or separate gender. Coed groups may be effective if all the people are single or married. Sometimes married people meeting in separate groups can enable men and women to be more open and receive more effective opinions about their issues. Either way, they can share what happened during the week and gain strength, courage, and valuable ideas from each other. Such a group may review and discuss this book as a guide during the process of discovery. Once the book is completely reviewed, the subsequent time can be devoted to discuss specific issues of members.

The facilitator does not need to be a professional for a support group to be effective. Merely having a mutual interest in helping each other can produce effective results. It is an idea worth trying. Perhaps you are called to get such a group started in your neighborhood. Support groups led by concerned lay people can be especially healthy aids to recovery from loss. A few basic ground rules of operations can make them very effective healing experiences.

These operating rules offered by William H. Friedman will help all support groups run more smoothly:

1. Choose a quiet meeting place without distractions. Sometimes churches or other public facility managers will make such a place available for weekly meetings at a convenient time for the participants. Homes are suitable meeting places provided a quiet, isolated room big enough is available.

2. Open each meeting with a short restatement of its purpose, e.g., healing the wounds within through communal sharing. Cite the research of Dr. James W. Pennebaker showing that opening up and confiding in others is good for your mental, spiritual, and physical health. Keep the sessions to two hours or less.

3. Start and end each meeting precisely at the agreed upon times. Give each newcomer a few minutes to share his/her background and objective for joining the group. Then have those in the group who volunteer to do so, give a short summary of their backgrounds to the newcomer.

4. Use first names only, following with the first letter of the last name - unless participants specifically decide to share their full names. Exchange telephone numbers and encourage members to call each other between meetings to share further. Often, close friendships are developed this way.

5. During the meeting, members may cite a section of this book that is speaking to them then. Other members may then comment on the way the same material has affected their lives. However, avoid cross talk between members and specific responses directed to one who has just spoken. Such cross talk can be harmful to the healing process and create a codependent environment, especially if it involves judging or advising by unqualified speakers. Avoid discussion of private therapy, religion, politics, or other sensitive issues that may cause cross talk or debate. You want to create a safe place where people can be free to express their feelings without being judged, rejected, or ill advised. Each member should share only his/her own experience, feelings, strength, and despair or hope. Cross talk can occur after the formal meeting, but only if someone asks specifically for feedback.

6. If it is part of the agreement, take a collection at each meeting to compensate the space provider, and compile a central account for occasional group socials.

7. Encourage expressions of negative and positive feelings alike, complete with profanity and tears or laughing and hugging if a person wants to make such a disclosure. Let all expressions of emotions be OK without judging them. Do not deny or prevent expression of any strong emotions or belittle tears and rages. Have some soft tissues handy.

8. Alternate leadership of the group regularly so no one person becomes a teacher or takes on responsibility for fixing broken members of the class. Each person must be free to work out his/her own healing.

9. Encourage everyone to continue attending while they feel healing results, but encourage everyone to leave the group when their work is well along, and possibly slightly before complete healing, so they can transition to self love on their own, and make room for others. Support groups should not be permitted to become a lifetime crutch or substitute for self-reliance.

10. If the group grows beyond ten to twelve members, consider starting a second group. Healing may be attenuated if too many people prevent adequate time for sharing.

    Caution: If any member of the group seems uncontrollably disruptive or misbehaves to the point of alarming or threatening other members, that person should be carefully, but seriously invited to leave and encouraged to get professional help.

When To Leave

Although I have emphasized the health benefits of having a safe and totally confidential place to share your feelings with intimate listeners throughout life, that is not to say that we should become fixated in a broken, dysfunctional state for ever. It is possible to label oneself as permanently ill or psychologically diseased. Then, you may find those who would like to keep you in a state of "recovery" all your life. Therapy and support groups should not become a permanent substitute for a normal social life and community participation. Therapy can be a comfortable safe place in which to avoid the pain, risk, and anxiety of continual growth. While it is desirable to have a safe place of self disclosure for maintenance touch ups periodically, you may wonder, as I did, how you can know when you are healthy enough to forego professional therapy and support groups. Here is a list of criteria prepared by Stan J. Katz that may help you answer that question. These are his signs of completed recovery:

1. You no longer engage in the type of behavior that caused your problems. You have quit falling in love with people who betray you and have established an equal, honest, and loving relationship with someone who makes you genuinely happy.
2. You no longer crave the type of problematic behavior that fed your addictive needs. You have replaced your unhealthy values with healthy ones.
3. Your thoughts and conversation are no longer dominated by recounting the same recurrent problems and issues. You may have actually forgotten what you are recovered from.
4. You are not hooked on any substitute relationships or replacement addictions. You understand the difference between legitimate needs and artificial crutches.
5. You no longer blame your past problems, partners and parents for any current mistakes, frustrations, and disappointments. You have the strength and power to face each new situation as it comes.
6. You no longer need the thrill of problems and conflicts to make you feel special and unique. You have found a way to connect and to care about others and to make a useful contribution to the world.
7. Your social life no longer revolves around support groups and friends who share your problems. Your new relationships are based on free exchange of ideas, ambitions, and activities, and they involve a wide range of interests.
8. You have confidence that you can prevent new problems from overtaking and controlling your life. You can identify potential problems, confront them honestly, assess the situations and match them with appropriate responses, and recognize when you cannot handle them alone.
9. Your life is in balance, with honest acceptance of your strengths and weaknesses and a program of development in all four quadrants of wholeness, physical, intellectual, emotional, and spiritual.
10. You no longer view your life exclusively in terms of one day at a time, and take things as they come. You embrace the longer term view of the future, while assuming full responsibility for your present.

Mature, healthy adults live through such a transition continually as they age, giving up the past and learning new coping skills as appropriate. Kenneth Levin writes that healthy people have "a predisposing inclination to approach the world anticipating gratification and an inclination to interpret experiences in a positive, promising light." That may be more or less difficult for you to do. The secret is in expecting that benefits of your new life will far exceed the burdens of giving up your old life. Some people seem to accept the benefits more easily, while others resist giving up the burdens, i.e., they hang onto childish behavior and beliefs. It may be that extraverts, who respond to events, people and things outside themselves will be less able to give up their externally driven stimulants, while introverts, who respond more to ideas, concepts, and information from inside themselves, are less prone to being controlled by events outside themselves.

For all the knowledge about human behavior gained during this century, it is still uncertain how much people can change. Some people seem to be more elastic than others. Desire seems to have a lot to do with it and, of course, valuing the benefits of change more than the burdens also helps. All growth is painful and scary as we must let go of familiar discomfort to move into uncertain futures. It does seem that having a significant other person in your life can be a powerful motivation for change in order to create a more loving, happy relationship. It seems that only by having the experience of forming such a bond and growing together and yet separately can we reach our full human potential. It is a continuous process of discovery that can always benefit from renewal through therapy. One who learned this lesson said, "It is like spring cleaning. You get to dust off of everything and sort through stuff. You get to throw a lot of junk away." Another said it is like weeding your garden. Once is never enough.

Transition

Now, we have completed Part III. I believe I have been chosen as a channel to bring this information to you, after I learned it for myself. Nowhere has that mission been more clear to me than in choosing the words for the closing paragraphs. Many times I have had to boot up my computer to insert another golden nugget from another expert in human relations that added another piece to the puzzle, or to delete passages that did not belong. I can see the whole picture on the box now and I believe the work is finished. My role as teacher and yours as student now is completed.

To the question about what he wanted his book to accomplish for its readers, Buddhist Master Sogyal Rinpoche answered, "I want every human being not to be afraid of life, and to find the ultimate happiness that can only come from an understanding of the nature of mind and of reality. May whoever reads this book derive rich and unending benefit from it, and may these teachings transform their hearts and minds." He quoted the Buddha, "I have shown you the way to liberation, now you must take it for yourself." I feel much the same way about this book.

My own search for wisdom has led me to silent contemplation. There is a saying in Taoism, "One who speaks does not know, and one who knows does not speak." And so it was with Lao-tzu who observed that a mark of wisdom was to stop asking for explanations, give up all control, and stop trying to change the world because it is already perfect.

As I close this work now, I wish you life, love, liberty, and the pursuit of happiness, the inalienable rights of every human being. Helen Keller, born deaf and blind, said, "Life is either a daring adventure or it is nothing." If this is not the time for you to learn these lessons, then please pass the book along to another person you know. In any case, cultivate joy, passion, humor, and curiosity. My best wishes for enjoying the ad hoc life without divorce go with you.

Appendix I:

Study Guide

This concluding section contains some exercises recommended to be worked through in order to help you internalize the main concepts of each chapter. You can complete these exercises at your own pace, in private, or with a study group. In any case, completing this section will help you to make the words of each chapter more effective in actual behavioral applications for your life. Although they may appear burdensome at first glance, persistence in completing these exercises will help you reinforce their many benefits to your personal growth, and help you make happy, healthy ad hoc relationships.

Study Guide for Chapter 1: Outgrowing Imperfect Role Models.

1. Write a short one or two page autobiography.

2. Describe why it is important to review your family of origin.

3. Define "codependency" in your own words.

4. Describe the role of self esteem in human relations.

5. Prepare a plan for improving your personal self esteem.

6. Make a list of all the things your parents did that require your forgiveness.

7. Describe how you will forgive them.

8. Prepare a plan for implementing the A.C.T. resources in your life.

9. Describe your personal version of an ideal family of origin.

10. Make a list of family of origin topics you would like to review with significant others.

Study Guide for Chapter 2: Overcoming Social Factors.

1. Describe four general roles of children in families.

2. Relate the several types of dysfunctional parents to your own parents.

3. Review the social situation of your teenage years in terms of music, religion, politics, and social lifestyles.

4. Describe how the social expectations of men and women changed in the last half of the 20th century.

5. Describe what social expectations of men and women did not change in the last half of the 20th century.

6. Describe social forces that tend to drive short term ad hoc relationships.

7. Discuss the implications of healthy dependency on moving beyond the past.

8. Discuss the meaning of this phrase, "We are drowning in information and starved for knowledge."

9. Write a short prediction of your forecast for relations between men and women in the next decade.

10. Support or criticize this phrase, "The more things change, the more they stay the same."

Study Guide for Chapter 3: Blending Different Personalities.

1. List some of the advantages of the Myers-Briggs Type Indicator (MBTI).

2. Prepare a brief description of your present life and future goals in terms of Figure 3.1.

3. Describe briefly the four scales of the MBTI and try to self select your personal four letter preference.

4. Relate how the two scales depicting functions of personality are most likely to affect intimate relationships.

5. Discuss the implications of gender differences on the T-F scale.

6. Describe the differences between extraversion and introversion and their influence over the functions of perception and decision making.

7. Describe the differences between a J preference and a P preference.

8. Use the MBTI in describing how people may be affected by stressful relationships.

9. Relate the RATS formula to intimate relationships.

10. Discuss what is still confusing you about the MBTI application to intimate relationships.

Study Guide to Chapter 4: Searching, Searching, Searching.

1. Describe and defend or criticize the genetic roles of men and women.

2. Compare and contrast the basic sexual and psychological drives.

3. Relate the phases in dating and contrast the benefits of aquaintances, companions, friends, and lovers to your life experience.

4. Relate the types of talking styles to some of your personal experiences.

5. Prepare a plan for searching and for dealing with shyness and rejection.

6. Compile a compatibility check list for your ideal significant other person.

7. Describe the benefits of having several platonic friendly relationships.

8. Construct a plan for small talk, search talk, and straight talk.

9. Prepare a benefit/burden ratio for your last or present intimate relationship.

10. Discuss the political and social implications of feminism.

Study Guide for Chapter 5: The Sexual Question.

1. Defend or criticize the opinion of Lore Chesterfield about sexual intercourse.

2. Describe your own situational ethics concerning sex between consenting adults.

3. Describe some of the changes in attitudes about sex since World War II.

4. Discuss the addictive potential of sex.

5. Compare and contrast the two opposing moral beliefs about sex.

6. Choose the moral code most like your own and write a brief defense of it.

7. Write a plan for meeting your sexual needs in an ethical and moral manner.

8. Describe the gender aspects of sexuality that are most important to you.

9. Write a brief novel-like description of your most pleasurable sexual fantasy.

10. Make a benefit/burden ratio for sex on the rebound.

Study Guide for Chapter 6: Holistic Love and Self Esteem.

1. Discuss your personal aim for romantic love.

2. Describe the role of four primary Greek styles of love in your personal life.

3. Relate the four-stage model of love attributed to the Washington Ethical Society to your own life.

4. Compare and contrast love addiction with sexual addiction.

5. Describe some evidence of love addiction in your personal life.

6. Describe the concept of "limerance" in terms of its attributes.

7. List several positive attributes of addictive love.

8. Contrast holistic love with addictive love.

9. Create a personal plan for moving toward holistic love.

10. Describe some appropriate and inappropriate applications for jealousy.

Study Guide for Chapter 7: Intimate Communications.

1. Define the meaning of "dialogue."

2. Relate the four communicating styles defined by Ned Herrmann to the MBTI types of personality.

3. Describe why the receiver is the true master of communications.

4. Discuss why John Gray said, "Men are From Mars and Women are From Venus" and relate it to the gender roles of men and women.

5. Describe and rank your personal preferences for visual, auditory, and kinesthetic communications.

6. Discuss this phrase, "There is a difference between a therapeutic hug and a romantic embrace."

7. Describe appropriate and inappropriate ways of communicating feelings.

8. Select a specific personal need and prepare a seven step dialogue for seeking its fulfillment from your closest friend.

9. Write out the seven Verderber suggestions for practicing active listening.

10. Select a recent interpersonal conflict and describe how the five negotiating styles might be applied to it.

Study Guide for Chapter 8: Holistic Intimacy and Commitment.

1. Describe the AME manliness code and discuss how it affects intimacy between men and women.

2. Describe the differences in how men and women value intimacy that are most useful to you.

3. Describe some factors that make commitment a unilateral decision.

4. Describe the needs for dependency and autonomy in your own personal make up.

5. Discuss the Covenant with your significant other and revise it or confirm it as is.

6. Describe the differing outlooks on marriage attributed to men and women.

7. Consider your own or a known marriage, and relate it to the considerations for a happy marriage.

8. Review the adult spousal, parental, and sibling family units of your family of origin and relate it to the professional ideal.

9. Discuss the barriers and time table for achieving a successful second marriage that includes step families and connect them to the criteria for a healthy family by Delores Curran.

10. Construct your own personal style of negotiating to get your needs met.

Study Guide for Chapter 9: Loving Through Conflicts.

1. Describe some of the benefits of conflicts in intimate relationships.

2. Relate the four unproductive faulty strategies people use to avoid getting hurt in conflicts (by John Gray) to your own personal behavior.

3. Describe several situations most likely to cause conflicts among intimate couples.

4. Describe the concepts of "boundaries" and "life scripts."

5. Discuss the Jungian concepts of Anima and Animus that may underlay many conflicts between intimate couples.

6. Describe the MBTI implications that apply to stressful conflict situations, including some personal examples of encoded communications.

7. Discuss the limitations of forgiveness in conflict resolution.

8. Practice applying the cognitive distortions by using the process of Figure 9-1 in a typical conflict situation.

9. Apply the Awareness Wheel to a specific conflict situation.

10. Recall the benefit/burden ratio that resulted in a previous relationship break up.

Study Guide for Chapter 10: Healing Inevitable Losses.

1. Explain why losses are inevitable.

2. Relate the predictable stages in response to loss by Elizabeth Kubler-Ross to several loss events of your life.

3. Discuss the role of guilt in breaking up.

4. Describe some typical reactions to loss of a loved one.

5. Describe why it is important to learn how to live alone.

6. Relate the physical, intellectual, emotional, and spiritual aspects of grief to the MBTI.

7. Relate your personal concept of a Higher Power to grief management and recovery from loss.

8. Practice the technique of conscious breathing and meditation and teach it to someone else.

9. Compare the benefits of a rebound love affair with the burdens.

10. Resolve to be a better lover next time, and master the rules for positive dependency.

Study Guide for Chapter 11: The Power of Confiding.

1. Explain how to know when therapy may be helpful.

2. Discuss some benefits of therapy.

3. Prepare some criteria for selecting a therapist.

4. Discuss the contrasting views about reality and truth in therapy.

5. Write some criteria for knowing when to leave therapy.

6. Discuss some of the subjective aspects of evaluating the results of therapy.

7. Describe your personal motivation for joining or forming a self-help support group.

8. Discuss how this book might be used by a support group.

9. Evaluate your personal degree of mental health according to the criteria provided by Stan J. Katz.

10. Prepare a brief list of people you know who could benefit from this book, and tell them about it.

Appendix II:

Bibliography

Following is a list of books that I read in the research for this model of healthy relationships. **The material from these authors has been so integrated into the text it was impossible to footnote the sources on each page.** Therefore, this work is primarily a synthesis of all their work rather than a unique creation of my own. Wherever a specific source was used, the author was noted in the text. **Any omission or misquotation of a source used in the text is purely unintentional.** Other sources included interviews with support groups, instructions received from my professional counselors, and the lectures and interactions occurring at seminars conducted by the Washington Ethical Society and the Institute for Attitudinal Studies in Alexandria, VA. Undoubtedly, many other books will be published on this subject regularly, so I suggest that you visit the psychology section of your favorite local book store periodically for possible additions.

A Course In Miracles. The Foundation For Inner Peace, Tiburon, CA 1985
Ahrons, Constance R., **The Good Divorce.** HarperCollins Publishing, NY 1994.
Akhtar, Salman, **Quest for Answers - A Primer of Understanding and Treating Severe Personality Disorders.** Jason Aronson, Northvale, NJ 1995
Almaas, A. H., **Diamond Heart, Book One, Elements of the Real in Man.** Diamond Books, Almaas Publications, Berkeley, CA 1987
Andrews, Lewis M., **To Thine Own Self Be True.** Doubleday/Dell Publishing Group, NY 1987
The Augustine Fellowship, **Sex and Love Addicts Anonymous.** The Augustine Fellowship, Sex and Love Addicts Anonymous, Fellowship-Wide Services, Inc. Boston. 1986
Atwood, George A., and Stolorow, Robert D., **Faces In A Crowd - Intersubjectivity in Personality Theory.** Jason Aronson, Northvale, NJ 1993
Bach, George and Torbet, Laura, **The Inner Enemy: How to Fight Fair With Yourself.** William Morrow & Company, NY 1983
Bach, Sheldon, **The Language of Perversion and The Language of Love.** Jason Aronson, Northvale, NJ 1994
Backus, William, **Finding the Freedom of Self Control.** Bethany House Publishers, Minneapolis, MN 55438
Badal, Daniel W., **Treatment of Depression and Related Moods.** Jason Aronson Northvale, NJ 1988
Barlow, David H. and Cerny, Jerome A., **Psychological Treatment of Panic.** The Guilford Press, NY 1988

Bass, Ellen and Davis, Laura, **The Courage To Heal.** HarperCollins Publishers, Inc. NY 1992

Bassoff, Evelyn S., **Mothering Ourselves - Help and Healing for Adult Daughters.** Penguin Books, NY 1991

Bassoff, Evelyn S., **Between Mothers and Sons - The Making of Vital and Loving Men.** Penguin Books, NY 1994

Beattie, Melody, **Codependent No More.** Harper & Row NYC 1987

Beattie, Melody, **Beyond Codependency.** Harper & Row, NY 1989

Beck, Aaron T., **Love Is Never Enough.** Harper & Row, NY 1988

Becker, Carol, **The Invisible Drama**. Macmillan, New York, 1987

Bennet, E.A., **What Jung Really Said.** Shocken Books, NY 1983

Benson, Herbert, **The Relaxation Response.** 1975

Berne, Eric, **Games People Play.** Grove Press, NY 1964

Bernstein, Doris, **Female Identify Conflict In Clinical Practice.** Jason Aronson, Inc. Northvale, NJ 1993

Berry, Carmen Renee, **When Helping You Is Hurting Me.** Harper & Row, 1988

Blanck, Gertrude, **The Subtle Seductions,** Jason Aronson, Inc. Northvale, NJ 1987

Blinder, Martin, **Choosing Lovers.** Glenbridge Publishing Ltd. Macomb, IL 1989

Bolen, Jean Shinoda, **The Tao Of Psychology - Synchronicity and the Self.** Harper and Row, 1982.

Bowlby, John, **Attachment and Loss: Loss, Sadness, and Depression (vol III)** Basic Books, NY 1980

Bowers, Margaretta K. et.al., **Counseling The Dying.** Jason Aronson, Inc., Northvale, NJ 1994

Bozarth - Campbell, Alla, **Life is Goodbye, Life is Hello.** Compcare Publications, Minn., MN 1985

Bradshaw, John, **The Family. Health Communications, Inc.** Deerfield Beach, FL 1988

Bradshaw, John, **Homecoming.** Bantam Books, NY 1990

Brasch, Michael Franz, **Understanding Psychotherapy, The Science Behind the Art.** Basic Books, Inc. NY 1988.

Brazier, David, Zen Therapy, **Transcending the Sorrows of the Human Mind.** John Wiley & Sons, Inc., NY 1995

Brennan, Barbara Ann, **Hands Of Light, A Guide To Healing Through The Human Energy Field.** Bantam Books, NY 1988

Broder, Michael, **The Art of Living Single.** Macmillan Publishing Company, NY 1988

Brooks, Michael, **Instant Rapport.** Warner Books, Inc. NY 1989

Brothers, Joyce, **Widowed.** Ballantine Books, NY 1990

Brownsword, Alan W., **It Takes All Types.** Baytree Publishing Company, San Anselmo, CA 1987

Bruno, Frank J. **Psychological Symptoms.** John Wiley & Sons, NY 1993

Burgess, Jane K., **The Single Again Man.** D. C. Heath and Company, Lexington, MA 1988

Burns, David D., **Feeling Good.** NAL Penguin Inc. New York 1980

Burns, David D., **Intimate Connections.** NAL Penguin Inc. New York 1985

Buscaglia, Leo, **Loving Each Other.** Fawcett Books/Random House NY 1984

Buss, David M., **The Evolution of Desire.** Basic Books, NY 1994.

Cabot, Tracy, **Man Power.** St. Martin's Press, NY 1988

Campbell, Joseph, ed. **The Portable Jung.** Penguin Books, NY 1985

Carlson, Dwight L., **Overcoming Hurts and Anger.** Harvest House, Eugene, OR 1981

Carnegie, Dale, **How To Win Friends And Influence People.** Simon & Shuster, NY 1936

Capra, Fritjof, **The Tao of Physics.** Shambhala Publications, Inc. Boston 1991

Cermak, Timmen L., **A Time To Heal.** Avon Books, NYC 1988

Cermak, Timmen L., **Diagnosing and Treating Co-Dependence.**

Cheek, Jonathan M., **Conquering Shyness.** G.P. Putnam's Sons, NY 1989

Childs, James M., **Christian Anthropology and Ethics.** Fortress Press, Philadelphia 1978

Chopra, Deepak, **Quantum Healing, Exploring The Frontiers of Mind/Body Medicine.** Bantam Books, NY 1990

Colton, Helen, **Touch Therapy.** Kensington Publishing Corp. NY 1983

Cooper, Judy and Maxwell, Nilda, **Narcissistic Wounds.** Jason Aronson, Inc., Northvale, NJ 1995

Cranston, Sylvia and Williams, Carey, **Reincarnation - A New Horizon in Science, Religion, and Society.** Crown Publishers Inc. , NY 1984.

Crawford, Verlaine, **Ending the Battle Within.** High Castle Publishing, Ilyllwild, CA 92509

Curran, Dolores, **Traits of a Healthy Family.** Ballantine Books, NY 1984

Davanloo, Habib, **Short Term Dynamic Psychotherapy.** Jason Aronson, Inc. Northvale, NJ 1992

Davis, Martha, Eshelman, Elizabeth, McKay, Matthew, **The Relaxation & Stress Reduction Workbook.** New Harbinger Publications, Inc. Oakland, CA 1995

DeAngelis, Barbara, **How To Make Love All The Time.** Dell Publishing Company, NY 1988

DeAngelis, Barbara, **Are You The One For Me.** Delacorte Press, NY 1992

Dennis, Wendy, **Hot and Bothered.** Viking, Harmondsworth Middlesex, England 1992

Dewald, Paul, **The Supportive and Active Psychotherapies**. Jason Aronson, Northvale, NY 1994

Diamond, Jed, **Looking For Love In All The Wrong Places.** G. P. Putnam's Sons, NY 1988

Dienstfrey, Harris, **Where The Mind Meets The Body.** HarperCollins, NY 1991

Dixon, Jeane, **Yesterday, Today, and Forever.** Andrews, McMeel & Parker. Kansas City, MO 1987

Dorpat, Theodore L., **Denial and Defense In The Therapeutic Situation.** Aronson, Northvale, NJ 1994

Dyer, Wayne W., **Pulling Your Own Strings.** Avon Books, NY 1978

Dyer, Wayne W., **You'll See It When You Believe It.** Avon Books, NY 1989

Eaker Weil, Bonnie, **Adultery, the Forgiveable Sin.** Carol Communications, Inc. NY 1993

Elgin, Suzette Haden, **Genderspeak: Men, Women, and the Gentle Art of Verbal Self-Defense.** John Wiley & Sons, Inc. NY 1993.

Embelton, Gary et.al., **Freeing Ourselves From Our Family of Origin.** Jason Aronson, Inc. Northvale, NJ 1996

Emery, Gary, **Own Your Own Life.** Signet NAL Books, NY 1982

Engel, Beverly, **The Emotionally Abused Woman.** Lowell House, RGA Publishing Group. Los Angeles 1990

Ehrenberg, Otto and Ehrenberg, Miriam, **The Psychotherapy Maze: Getting In and Out of Therapy.** Jason Aronson, Inc. NY 1994

Farber, Barry, **Making People Talk.** William Morrow and Company, NY 1987

Farrell, Warren, **The Myth of Male Power.** Simon & Schuster, NY 1993

Faucett, Robert & Carol Ann, **Personality and Spiritual Freedom.** Image Books, Doubleday. NY 1987

Felton-Collins, Victoria, **Couples And Money.** Bantam Books, NY 1990

Fensterheim, Herbert and Baer, Jean, **Making Life Right When It Feels All Wrong.** Macmillan Publishing Company, NY 1988

Fine, Sara F. and Glasser, Paul H., **The First Helping Interview.** Sage Publications. Thousand Oaks, CA 1996

Fisher, Helen E., Anatomy of Love, **The Natural History of Monogamy, Adultery, and Divorce.** W.W. Norton & Company, Inc. NY 1992

Fishman, Barbara Miller, **Resonance, The New Chemistry of Love.** Harper Collins, San Francisco, CA 1994.

Forward, Susan and Craig Buck, **Obsessive Love.** Bantam Books, Dell Publishing Group Inc., NY 1991

Frazier, Shervert H., **Psychotrends: What Kind of People Are We Becoming.** Simon & Schuster, NY 1994.

Freeman, Lucy, **Listening to the Inner Self.** Jason Aronson, Inc. Northvale, NJ 1984

Freeman, Lucy and Strean, Herbert, **Understanding and Letting Go of Guilt.** Jason Aronson, Inc. Northvale, NJ 1995

Friedman, William H., **How to Do Groups.** Jason Aronson, Inc., Northvale, NJ 1994

Friel John, and Friel, **Linda, An Adult Child's Guide To What's Normal.** Health Communications, Inc. Deerfield Beach, FL 1990.

Fromm, Eric, **The Art of Loving.** Harper and Row, NY 1956

Gardner, Richard A., **Sex Abuse Hysteria.** Creative Therapeutics, Cresskill, NH 1991

Garner, Alan, **Conversationally Speaking.** McGraw-Hill, NY 1981

Gaylin, Willard, **The Male Ego.** Viking Penguin, NY 1992

Gerber, Richard, **Vibrational Medicine.** Bear & Company, Santa Fe, NM 1988

Goldberg, Herb, **The Hazards of Being Male.** NAL Penguin Signet, NY 1987

Goldberg, Jane G. **The Dark Side of Love.** Tarcher/Putman, NY 1993

Goldman Carl, **On Being a Psychotherapist.** Jason Aronson, Northvale, NJ 1993

Goldstein, William, **An Introduction To The Borderline Conditions.** Jason Aronson, Inc. Northvale, NJ 1991.

Goleman, Daniel, **Emotional Intelligence,** Bantam Books, NY 1995

Gorski, Terry, **Relationships** (Audio Tape) 1989

Goulter, Barbara, and Minninger, Joan, **The Father-Daughter Dance.** G. P. Putnam's Sons, NY 1993

Grant, Harold W., et al, **From Image To Likeness.** Paulist Press, Ramsey , NJ 1983

Gray, John., **Men Are From Mars and Women Are From Venus.** HarperCollins Booka, NY 1992

Griest, John H. and Jefferson, James W., **Depression and Its Treatment.** Warner, NY 1984

Gullo, Stephen and Church, Connie, **Loveshock.** Simon and Shuster, NY 1988

Gurman, Alan S. and Rice, David G., **Couples in Conflict.** Jason Aaronson,, NY 1975

Hajcak, Frank, and Garwood, Patricia, **Hidden Bedroom Partners.** Libra Publishers, Inc., San Diego, CA. 1987

Halpern, Howard M., **How to Break Your Addiction to a Person.** Bantom, NY 1982

Harbaugh, Gary L., **The Faith-Hardy Christian.** Augsburg Publishing House, Minneapolis, MN 1988

Harbaugh, Gary L., **God's Gifted People.** Augsburg Publishing House, Minneapolis, MN 1990

Harbaugh, Gary L. **Personality and the Perception of Loss.** Library of Congress, Washington, DC, 1986

Hartzler, Margaret, and Hartzler Gary, **Using Type with Couples.** Type Resources, Gaithersburg, MD 1988

Hayes, E. Kent, **Why Good Parents Have Bad Kids.** Doubleday, NY 1989

Hayes, Jody, **Smart Love.** Jeremy P. Tarcher Inc. Los Angeles, CA 1985

Hedges, Lawrence, **Remembering, Repeating, and Working Through Childhood Trauma.** Jason Aronson, Northvale, NJ 1994

Hemfelt, Robert, Minirth, Frank, and Meier, Paul, **Love Is A Choice.** Thomas Nelson, Inc. Nashville, TN 1989.

Hendricks, Gay, and Hendricks, Kathlyn, **Conscious Loving, The Journey to Co-Committment.** Bantam Books, NY 1990

Herrmann, Ned, **The Creative Brain.** Brain Books, Lake Lure, NC 1988

Hite, Shere, **Women and Love, A Cultural Revolution in Progress.** Alfred A. Knopf, NY 1987

Hirsh, Sandra, and Kummerow, Jean, **Life Types.** Warner Books, NY 1989

Hobe, Phyllis, **Never Alone.** Macmillan Publishing Company, NY 1986

Hoffman, Bob, **No One Is To Blame.** Recycling Books, Oakland, CA 1988

Hollis, Judi, **Fat and Furious - Women and Food Obsession.** Ballantine Books, NY 1994

Horner, Althea, **Being & Loving.** Jason Aronson, Inc. Northvale, NJ 1990.

Hritzuk, John, **The Silent Company: How to Deal With Loneliness.**

Jackins, Harvey, **Fundamentals of Co-Counseling Manual.** Rational Island Publishers, Seattle, WA 1982

Jackins, Harvey, **The Reclaiming of Power.** Rational Island Publishers, Seattle, WA 1983

James, John W. and Cherry, Frank, **The Grief Recovery Handbook.** Harper and Row, New York 1988

Jampolsky, Gerald, **Love Is Letting Go of Fear.** Celestial Arts, Millbrae, CA 1979

Jeffers, Susan, **Feel the Fear And Do It Anyway.** Harcourt Brace Javonovich, San Diego, New York, London, 1987

Jeffers, Susan, **Opening Our Hearts To Men.** Ballantine Books, NY 1989

Jordan, Paul and Jordan, Margaret, **Do I Have To Give Up Me To Be Loved By You?** Compcare Publishers, Minneapolis, MN 1983

Jung, Carl G., **Psychological Types**. Princeton University Press. 1971

Jung, Carl G., **Modern Man In Search of a Soul.** Harcourt Brace Jovanovich, NY 1933

Jung, Carl G., **Memories, Dreams, Reflections.** Vintage Books, Random House, NY 1989

Katz, Stan J. and Liu, Aimee E., **The Codependency Conspiracy.** Warner Books, NY 1991

Kerr, John, **A Most Dangerous Method, the Story of Jung, Freud, and Sabina Spielrein.** Alfred A. Knopf, NY 1993

Kiersey, David and Bates, Marilyn, **Please Understand Me.** Promotheus Nemesis Book Co. 1984

King, Norman, **The First Five Minutes.** Prentice-Hall, NY 1987

Kipnis, Aaron R., **Knights Without Armor, A Practical Guide for Men In Quest of Masculine Soul.** Jeremy Tarcher, Inc. Los Angeles 1991.

Kliman, Ann S., **Crisis: Psychological First Aid.** Jason Aronson, Northvale, NJ 1994

Kottler, Jeffrey, **Private Moments, Secret Selves.** Jeremy P. Tarcher, Inc. Los Angeles 1990

Kroeger, Otto and Thuesen, Janet M. **Type Talk.** Delacorte Press, NY 1988

Kroeger, Otto and Thuesen, Janet M. **16 Ways To Love Your Lover.** Delacorte Press, NY 1994

LaBruzza, Anthony L., **Using DSM-IV A Clinician's Guide to Psychiatric Diagnosis.** Jason Aronson, Inc. Northvale NJ 1994

Langs, Robert, **Psychotherapy, A Basic Text.** Jason Aronson, Northvale, NJ 1992

Langs, Robert, **Unconscious Communication in Everyday Life.** Jason Aronson, Inc., Northvale, NJ 1993

Langs, Robert, **The Listening Process.** Jason Aronson, Inc., Northvale, NJ 1992

Lansky, Philip S., "The Mind And The Masters, A Doctor's Assessment of Qigong", **New Age Journal,** Jan. - Feb. 1990 Rising Sun Publications, Brighton, MA

Lanyon, Richard I., and Goodstein, Leonard D., **Personality Assessment, Third Edition.**

John Wiley & Sons, Inc. NY 1997

Lasch, Christopher, **The Culture of Narcissism. American Life in An Age of Diminishing Expectations.** W.W. Norton & Co., NY 1979

Lao-tzu, **Tao te Ching** (translated by Stephen Mitchell,) Harper Collins Publishers, NY 1988

Lauer, Robert H. and Jeannette C., **Mastering Life's Unpredictable Crises.** Little, Brown & Company, NY 1988

L'Engle, Madeleine, **Two-Part Invention, The Story of a Marriage.** HarperCollings, NY 1989

Leman, Kevin, **The Pleasers.** Dell Publishing, New York, 1987

LeVay, Simon, **The Sexual Brain.** The MIT Press, Cambridge MA, 1993.

Levin, Kenneth, **Unconscious Fantasy in Psychotherapy.** Jason Aronson, Northvale, NJ, 1993

Levine, Linda and Barback, Lonnie, **The Intimate Male.** New American Library, NY 1983

Levy, Steven T. **Principles of Interpretation.** Jason Aronson, Northvale NJ, 1990

Lieberman, Morton and Tobin, Sheldon, **Experience of Old Age: Stress, Coping and Survival.** Basic Books, NY 1983.

Lindemann, Carol, **Handbook of the Treatment of the Anxiety Disorders.** Jason Aronson, Inc. Northvale, NJ 1996

Locke, Steven and Colligan, Douglas, **The Healer Within.** E.P. Dutton, NY 1986

Loftus, Elizabeth, and Ketchum, Katherine, **The Myth Of Repressed Memory.** St. Martens Press, NY 1994

Lomas, Peter, **Cultivating Intuition: An Introduction to Psychotherapy.** Jason Aronson Inc., Northvale, NJ 1993

Love, Patricia, **The Emotional Incest Syndrome.** Bantam Books, NY 1990

Lubetkin, Barry and Oumano, Elena, **Bailing Out - The Healthy Way to Get Out of a Bad Relationship and Survive.** Prentice Hall Press, NY 1991

Madow, Leo, **Guilt - How to Recognize and Cope With It.** Jason Aronson Inc. Northvale, NJ 1988

Malone, Patrick. T., and Malone, Thomas P., **The Art of Intimacy.** Prentice Hall, New York, 1987

Mann, James and Goldman, Robert, **A Casebook In Time-Limited Psychotherapy.** Jason Aronson, Northvale, NJ 1994

Marlin, Emily, **Relationships in Recovery.** Harper & Row, NY 1990

Maslow, Abraham, **Motivation and Personality.** 2nd Edition Harper & Row, NY 1970

Mason, M., **Facing Shame: Families in Recovery.** W. W. Norton, NY 1987

Masterson, James F., **The Search For The Real Self.** The Free Press, Macmillan, Inc. NY 1988

May, Gerald G., **Addiction and Grace.** Harper and Row. NY 1987

May, Rollo, **The Meaning of Anxiety.** Simon and Schuster, New York, 1979

May, Rollo, **Love and Will.** Dell, New York, 1969

McAllister, Linda, **I Wish I'd Said That.** John Wiley & Sons, NY 1992

McArthur, Dorothea S., **Birth Of A Self In Adulthood.** Jason Aronson, Inc., Northvale, NJ 1988

McCann, I. Lisa, and Laurie Anne Pearlman, **Psychological Trauma And The Adult Survivor.** Brunner/Mazel, New York, 1990

McConnell Adeline, and Anderson, Beverly, **Single After Fifty.** McGraw-Hill, NY 1978

McGill, Michael E., **The McGill Report on Male Intimacy.** Harper and Row, NY 1985

McKay, Matthew, and Patrick Fanning, **Self-Esteem.** New Harbinger Publications, Oakland, CA 1987

McKinley, Robert L., **Personal Peace, Transcending Your Interpersonal Limits.** New Harbinger Publications, Inc. Oakland, CA 1989

McMartin, Jim, **Personality Psychology, A Student Centered Approach.** Sage Publications, Inc., Thousand Oaks, CA 1995

Mellody, Pia, **Facing Codependence.** Harper & Row, San Francisco, 1989

Mendelsohm, Ray, **How Can Talking Help.** Jason Aronson, NJ 1992

Michael, Robert T. et al, **Sex In America, A Definitive Survey.** Little, Brown and Company, NY 1994

Millon, Theodore, **Disorders of Personality, DSM-IV and Beyond.** John Wiley & Sons, Inc. NY 1996

Miller, Sherod, Wackman, Daniel, Nunnally, Elam, and Saline, Carol, **Straight Talk.** New American Library. NY 1982

Mitchell, Steven, **Tao de Ching.** Harper Collins Publishers, NY 1988

Money, John, **Love and Love Sickness.** The Johns Hopkins University Press, 1980

Montagna, Donald, **Paper titled, "When Love Fails"** Unpublished, Washington Ethical Society 1983

Montagna, Donald and Nancy, **Various Workshop Handouts.** Unpublished, Washington Ethical Society 1989

Montgomery, Ruth, **Here and Hereafter.** Fawcett World Library, NY 1968

Moore, Burness E. and Fine, Bernard D., **Psychoanalytic Terms & Concepts.** American Psychoanalytic Association 1990

Moore, Linda L., **Release From Powerlessness, A Guide for Taking Charge of Your Life.** Kendall/Hunt Publishing Company, Dubuque, IA 1991

Moyers, Bill, **Healing and The Mind.** Doubleday division of Bantam Doubleday Dell Publishing Group, Inc. NY 1993

Mueller, William J. and Aniskiewicz, Albert S., **Psychotherpeutic Intervention in Hysterical Disorders.** Jason Aronsom, Northvale, NJ 1986

Myers-Briggs, Isabel B., **Gifts Differing.** Consulting Psychologists Press, 1980

Myers-Briggs, Isabel B., **Introduction to Type.** Consulting Psychologists Press, Palo Alto rev. 1987

Myers, Isabel Briggs and McCaulley, Mary H., **Manual: A Guide To the Development and Use of the Myers-Briggs Type Indicator.** Consulting Psychologists Press, Palo Alto, CA 1985

Myers, David G., **The Pursuit of Happiness.** William Morrow and Company, NY 1992

Naisbitt, John, **Megatrends 2000.** William Morrow and Company, NY 1990

Natterson, Joseph M. and Friedman, Raymond J., **A Primer of Clinical Inter-Subjectivity.** Jason Aronson, Northvale, NJ 1995

Neubauer, Peter B. and Neubauer, Alexander, **Nature's Thumbprint. The New Genetics Of Personality.** Psychotherapy Book Club, Northvale, NJ 1990

Novak, William, **The Great American Man Shortage And What You Can Do About It.** Bantam Books, NY 1983

Ofshe, Richard, and Ethan Watters, **Making Monsters; False Memories, Psychotherapy and Sexual Hysteria.** Charles Scribner's Sons, NY 1994

Ogden, Thomas H., **Projective Identification & Psychotherapeutic Technique.** Jason Aronson, Inc., Northvale, NJ 1991

O'Neill, Nena and George, **Shifting Gears.** M. Evans, NY 1974

Ornstein, Robert and Swencionis, Charles, **The Healing Brain.** The Guilford Press, NY 1990

Ornstein, Robert, **The Roots of the Self.** HarperCollins Publishers, NY 1993

Osherson, Samuel, **Wrestling With Love, How Men Struggle With Intimacy.** Ballantine

Books, NY 1992

Papernow, Patricia L., **Becoming a Stepfamily.** Hossey-Bass Publishers, San Francisco, CA 1993

Parkes, Colin M., **Recovery From Bereavement.** Basic Books, NY 1983

Parkes, Colin M., **Bereavement: Studies of Grief in Adult Life.** International Universities Press, NY 1986

Peck, M. Scott, **The Road Less Traveled.** A Touchstone Book 1978

Peele, Stanton, **Love and Addiction.** Signet NAL Books, New York 1975

Pennebaker, James W., **Opening Up - The Healing Power of Confiding In Others.** William Morrow and Company, Inc. NY 1990

Person, Ethel S., **Dreams of Love and Fateful Encounters.** Penguin Books, New York, 1988

Phillips, D., **How to Fall Out of Love.** Houghton Mifflin, Boston 1978

Philipson, Ilene J., **On the Shoulders of Women - The Feminization of Psychotherapy.** Guilford Press, NY 1993

Pieczenik, Steve, **My Life Is Great. Why Do I Feel So Awful?** Warner Books, NY 1990

Pillari, Vimala, **Scapegoating In Families.** Brunner/Mazel, Inc. NY 1991

Pines, Ayala M., **Keeping the Spark Alive.** St. Marten's Press, NY 1988

Pines, Ayala M., **Romantic Jealousy, Understanding and Conquering the Shadow of Love.** St. Martins Press, NY 1992

Pipher, Mary, **Saving The Selves of Adolescent Girls.** Ballantine Books, NY 1994

Pittman, Frank S., **Man Enough, Fathers, Sons, and The Search for Masculinity.** G. P. Putnams Sons, NY 1993

Pogrebin, Letty Cottin, **Among Friends.** McGraw-Hill Book Company, NY 1987

Pollard, John K., **Self Parenting.** Generic Human Studies Publishing, Malibu, CA 1987

Potash, Marlin S., **Hidden Agendas.** Delacorte Press, NY 1990

Quenk, Naomi L., **Beside Ourselves - Our Hidden Personality in Everyday Life.** CPP Books, Palo Alto, CA 1993

Rhodes, Sonya and Potash, Marlin S., **Cold Feet - Why Men Don't Commit.** E.P. Dutton/NAL Books, NY 1988

Ring, Kenneth, **Life At Death.** William Morrow and Company, NY 1980

Riso, Don Richard, **Discovering Your Personality.** Houghton Mifflin Company, NY 1995

Rinpoche, Sogyal, **The Tibetan Book of Living and Dying.** HarperSanFrancisco, NY 1992

Robbins, Anthony, **Unlimited Power.** Ballantine Books, Random House, NY 1987.

Roiphe, Katie, **The Morning After.** Little, Brown and Company. NY 1993

Rubin, Lillian B., **Erotic Wars - What Happened To the Sexual Revolution.** Farrar. Straus, & Giroux, NY 1990.

Sager, Clifford J., **Marriage Contracts and Couple Therapy.** Brunner/Mazel Publishers, NY 1976

Scarf, Maggie, **Intimate Partners.** Random House, NY 1987

Schaeffer, Brenda, **Is It Love Or Is It Addiction?** Hazelden Educational Materials 1987

Schimmel, Solomon, **Seven Deady Sins.** MacMillan Free Press, NY 1992

Schuyler, Dean, **A Practical Guide to Cognitive Therapy.** W. W. Norton and Company, NY 1991

Scolastico, Ron, **Healing the Heart, Healing the Body.** Hay House, Inc. Carson, CA 1992

Secunda, Victoria, **Women and Their Fathers.** Delacorte Press, NY 1992

Seeburger, Francis F., **Addiction and Responsibility.** Crossroad Publishing Company, NY 1993.

Segaller, Stephen and Berger, Merrill, **The Wisdom Of The Dream, The World of C. G. Jung.** Shamghala Publications, Inc. Boston, MA 1989

Seligman, Martin E. P., **Learned Optimism.** Alfred A. Knopf, Inc. New York, 1990

Shahan, Lynn, **Living Alone and Liking It.** Warner, Beverly Hills, CA 1981

Siegel, Bernie S., **Love, Medicine, & Miracles.** Harper and Row, NY 1986

Sills, Judith, **A Fine Romance.** Jeremy P. Tarcher, Inc. Los Angeles, 1987

Sills, Judith, **How to Stop Looking for Someone Perfect and Find Someone To Love.** Ballantine Books, 1984.

Singer, June, **Boundaries of the Soul: The Practice of Jung's Psychology.** Jason Aronson, Northvale, NJ 1994

Shain, Merle, **When Lovers Are Friends.** Bantam Books. NY 1978

Smalley, Gary and Trent, John, **The Blessing.** Thomas Nelson Publishers, 1986

Smedes, Lewis B., **Forgive and Forget.** Simon and Schuster, Inc. New York 1986

Smedes, Lewis B., **Caring & Commitment: Learning to Live the Love We Promise.** Harper & Row, NY 1988

Smedes, Lewis B., **A Pretty Good Person.** Harper & Row, NY 1990

Smoot, George, and Davidson, Keay, **Wrinkles in Time.** William Morrow and Company. NY 1993

Solomon, Marion, **Lean On Me - The Power of Positive Dependency.** Simon & Schuster, NY 1994

Stark, Martha, **Working With Resistance.** Jason Aronson, NJ 1994

Stein, Murray, **In Mid-Life: A Jungian Perspective.** Center for Application of Psychological Type, Gainesville, FL 1983

Stearns, Ann K., **Living Through Personal Crisis.** Ballantine Books. NY 1984

Storr, Anthony, Solitude, **A Return to the Self.** Free Press, NY 1988

Strupp, Hans H., **When Things Get Worse, The Problem of Negative Effects in Psychotherapy.** Jason Aronson, Northvale, NJ 1977.

Stuart, Richard B. and Jacobson, Barbara, **Second Marriage. Make It Happy. Make It Last.** Penguin Books, Canada 1985

Sussman, Michael B., **A Curious Calling - Unconscious Motives for Practicing Psychotherapy.** Jason Aronson, Northvale, NY 1992.

Tagliaferre, Lewis and Harbaugh, Gary L., **Recovery From Loss.** Health Communications, Inc. Deerfield Beach, FL. 1990

Tannen, Deborah, **You Just Don't Understand: Women and Men in Conversation.** William Morrow and Company, New York. 1990

Tatelbaum, Judy, **You Don't Have To Torture Yourself.** Harper and Row. NY 1989

Tennov, Dorothy, **Love and Limerance.** Scarborough House, Chelsea, MI 1986

Timmons, Tim and Hedges, Charlie, **Call It Love Or Call It Quits.** Word Publishing. Dallas, TX 1988

Toffler, Alvin, **Future Shock.** Random House, NY 1970

Trout, Susan S., **To See Differently.** Three Roses Press, Washington, DC 1990

Van Sweden, Robert C., **Regression to Dependence.** Jason Aronson, Northvale, NJ 1995

Veith, Ilza. Hysteria, **The History Of A Disease.** Jason Aronson, Northvale, NJ 1993

Verderber, Rudolph F., **Communicate! 4th Edition.** Wadsworth Publishing Company, Belmont, CA 1984

Viney, Linda L., **Life Stories: Personal Construct Therapy with the Elderly.** John Wiley & Sons. NY 1993

Viscott, David, **I Love You, Let's Work It Out.** Simon & Schuster, NY 1987

Von Franz, Marie-Louise, and Hillman, James, **Jung's Typology.** Spring Publications, Dallas 1982

Wallerstein, Judith S. and Blakeslee, Sandra, **The Good Marriage - How and Why Love**

Lasts. Houghton Mifflin Co., NY 1995

Walters, Richard, **Sexual Friendship.** Libra Publishers, Inc. San Diego, CA 1988

Wapnick, Kenneth, **The Fifty Miracle Principles of "A Course In Miracles."** Foundation for "A Course In Miracles", Crompound, NY 1985

Warme, Gordon, **Reluctant Treasures - The Practice of Analytic Psychotherapy.** Jason Aronson, Northvale, NJ 1994

Wechsler, Harlan J., **What's So Bad About Guilt?** Simon & Schuster, NY 1990

Wegscheider-Cruse, Sharon, **Learning to Love Yourself.** Health Communications, Inc. Deerfield Beach, FL 1987

Weinhold, Barry K. and Janae B., **Breaking Free of the Co-Dependency Trap.** Stillpoint Publishing Co. Wallpole, NH 1989.

W. Claire, **God, Where is Love.** Books West, Rancho Bernardo, CA 1989

Weiss, Brian L., **Many Lives, Many Masters.** Simon & Shuster, Ny 1988]

Welwood, John, **Journey Of The Heart.** Harper Collins Publishers, NY 1990

Westheimer, Ruth and Lieberman, Louis, **Sex and Morality.** Harcourt, Brace Jovanovich, Orlando, FL 1988

White, George L. and Mullen, Paul E., **Jealousy, Theory, Research, and Clinical Strategies.**

Whitfield, Charles L., **Healing The Child Within.** Health Communications, Deerfield Beach, FL 1987.

Wilde, Stuart, **Affirmations.** White Dove International, Inc. Taos, NM 1987

Williamson, Marianne, **A Return To Love, Reflections On the Principles of A Course in Miracles.** HarperCollins, NY 1992

Wolfe, Thomas, **The Hills Beyond.** Harper and Brothers, NY 1941

Woititz, Janet G., **Struggle For Intimacy.** Health Communications, Inc. Deerfield Beach, FL 1985

Woititz, Janet G., **Healthy Parenting.** Simon & Schuster, NY 1992

Wrightsman, Lawrence S., **Adult Personality Development, Theory and Concepts.** Sage Publications, Thousand Oaks, CA 1994

Yapko, Michael D., **When Living Hurts.** Brunzel/Mazel, Inc. NY 1988

Yapko, Michael D., **Suggestions of Abuse: True and False Memories of Childhood Sexual Abuse.** Jason Aronson, Northvale, NJ 1994

Young-Eisendrath, Polly, **You're Not What I Expected.** William Morrow and Company, Inc. NY 1993

Zilbergeld, Bernie, **The New Male Sexuality.** Bantam Books, NY 1992

Zukav, Gary, **The Dancing Wu Li Masters - An Overview of the New Physics.** Bantam Books, NY 1980